School and Society

The Open University
Faculty of Educational Studies
The School and Society Course Team

B. R. Cosin
I. R. Dale
G. M. Esland
D. F. Swift

School and Society
A sociological reader

Prepared by the
School and Society Course Team
at The Open University

London   Routledge & Kegan Paul
in association with The Open University Press

... is first published by ...
... Routledge & Kegan Paul ...

Set in ... and printed in ... by ... The Open University ...

No part of this book may be reproduced in any form without permission from the publisher, except for the quotation of brief passages in criticism.

ISBN 0 710 071 884
(pbk 0 710 071 ...)

First published 1971
by Routledge & Kegan Paul Ltd
Broadway House, 68–74 Carter Lane,
London EC4V 5EL
Reprinted 1973, 1974
Printed in Great Britain by
Cox & Wyman Ltd, London, Reading and
Fakenham
ISBN   0 7100   7187 6 (c)
ISBN   0 7100   7188 4 (p)

Contents

Acknowledgments

The Open University and the publishers would like to thank the following for permission to reproduce copyright material. All possible care has been taken to trace ownership of the selections included and to make full acknowledgment for their use.

Reading 1   *International Encyclopedia of the Social Sciences*, David L. Sills (ed.), vol. 15, 550–5. Copyright © 1968 by Crowell Collier and Macmillan, Inc.

2   National Foundation for Educational Research in England and Wales.

3   *American Journal of Sociology* and the University of Chicago Press.

4   Conseil international de la philosophie et des sciences humaines: Unesco, Paris.

5   Martinus Nijhoff, The Hague.

6   *Berkeley Journal of Sociology*, 1963, 8(1), 39–60.

7   Howard S. Becker and Blanche Geer, 'Student Culture in Medical School', *Harvard Educational Review*, 28, Winter 1958, 70–80, Copyright © 1958 by President and Fellows of Harvard College.

8   Howard S. Becker and Blanche Geer, 'Latent Culture: A Note on the Theory of Latent Social Roles', *Administrative Science Quarterly*, 1960, 5, 304–13.

9   Basil Bernstein and *New Society*, 26 February 1970, 344–7.

10   Julienne Ford, Douglas Young and Steven Box and the *British Journal of Sociology*, 1967, vol. 18, no. 4, 370–81.

11   The American Anthropological Association, *American Anthropologist*, vol. 66, no. 6 (2), 1964, 133–6.

12   The Society for Applied Anthropology, *Human Organization*, 1969, vol. 28, no. 3, 217–26.

13   *Social Psychology through Symbolic Interaction*, Gregory Stone and Harvey Farberman (eds). Copyright 1970 by Ginn and Company, a Xerox Company, through Xerox College Publishing, Waltham, Mass. 02154.

14   E. Durkheim, *Education and Sociology*, New York, 114–16, 123–34. Copyright © 1956 by Crowell Collier and Macmillan, Inc.

15   Anthony Platt and The American Academy of Political and Social Science, Philadelphia.

16   *European Journal of Sociology*, 1966, VII, 105–15.

17   The American Sociological Association, *American Sociological Review*, 1940, no. 5, 439–52.

18   The American Sociological Association, *Journal of Educational Sociology*, 1952, no. 25, 451–65.

19   *Sociometry*, 1964, 27(1), 40–53.

20   Julius A. Roth, *Timetables*. Copyright © 1963, by The Bobbs-Merrill Company, Inc., by permission of the publisher.

21   Howard S. Becker and The University of Chicago Press.

22   D. A. Young, W. Brandis and the University of London Institute of Education.

23   Earl Rubington, and Martin Weinberg (eds), *Deviance: The International Perspective*, New York, Macmillan.

Copyright © 1968 by Crowell Collier and Macmillan, Inc.

24 Basil Bernstein, H. L. Elvin and R. S. Peters, and The Royal Society.

25 Basil Bernstein and *New Society*, 14 September 1967, 351–3.

26 Routledge Kegan Paul Ltd, London, and Harcourt Brace Jovanovich, Inc., New York.

27 Lawrence and Wishart Ltd, London, and International Publishers Co. Inc., New York.

29 The author.

30 Faber and Faber Ltd, London, and Harcourt Brace Jovanovich, Inc., New York.

31 F. R. Leavis and Chatto and Windus Ltd, London.

32 The author.

33 Longmans, London, and the Association Montessori Internationale.

34 & 35 The author and Cambridge University Press, London.

36 E. Durkheim, *Elementary Forms of the Religious Life*, New York. Copyright © 1961 by Crowell Collier and Macmillan, Inc.

37 *Higher Education Review*, 1969, 1(3), 70–85. Copyright L. A. Jackson.

38 *Higher Education Review*, 1969, 1(2) 45–54. Copyright F. R. Jevons.

39 *Universities Quarterly*, 1970, 24(4), 402–21.

40 James S. Coleman, 'The Concept of Equality of Educational Opportunity', *Harvard Educational Review*, 38, Winter 1968, 7–22. Copyright © 1968 by President and Fellows of Harvard College.

Introduction

This selection of readings is intended to accompany the teaching material for the course 'School and Society'.* We hope that it will also provide a convenient and useful source of material for the large number of people who have developed an interest in the sociology of education.

The main theoretical focus of the course—and the one which lies behind the selection of readings in this volume—is the reciprocal relationship between social structure and knowledge. We believe that, in its recent developments, this perspective is capable of providing valuable and fruitful insights for the study of educational processes. We recognize, however, that it represents something of a development from the theoretical perspectives which have recently been employed in the sociology of education. Because of this, we have chosen a high proportion of papers devoted to *ways of thinking* about social phenomena rather than to descriptions of behaviour in educational settings.

Our justification for including these papers is that they effectively clarify, and make explicit, a theoretical framework through which we can construct explanations of the social reality of the school. Wherever possible we do include writings on education, but the need to present appropriate conceptual analysis was always the prime factor in our decisions.

Discussions of the applicability of the readings to the study of education are offered in the books which have been specially written for the course. At this stage, it may be helpful if we indicate in more general terms the kinds of insight which this perspective can provide.

The development of the sociology of education in Britain and America has been devoted to two main kinds of enquiry—analysis of educational achievement in terms of the stratification patterns which prevail in a society, and an approach to educational

* 'School and Society' is a second-level course produced by the Faculty of Educational Studies of the Open University.

organizations as social systems. By focusing on the relationship between educational success and failure and the membership of particular social classes, these studies have demonstrated that middle-class children have a much greater likelihood of entering university than working-class children.[1] In order to explain these differences in achievement, the concept of educability was developed. This refers to an individual's capacity to achieve through the education system. It is thought to be compounded of such qualities as his cognitive style, his language forms, and his intrinsic motivation to achieve. What has been lacking, however, is a framework for analysing how these different qualities are made relevant in the classroom and how they come to function as criteria of success and failure. The relationship between social class and educational achievement, therefore, needs further investigation. We need to know how particular educational *identities* (e.g. the 'good' pupil, and the 'difficult' pupil) are *constructed* and *taken for granted* through the rules and procedures of the classrooms and through the definitions which teachers apply to their pupils.

The social system studies have viewed the school as an organization—or a sub-system—within a larger social system. From this perspective, the school is seen as a unit in a network of interrelated organizations each of which influences and is influenced by the others. It has been customary for sociologists who use this approach to explain the activity of an organization in terms of its structure and its functional relationships with other organizations. Thus, the school might be analysed in terms of its official and unofficial structures and the patterns of decision-making which arise within them. Its relationship to various political and economic organizations may then be analysed through, for example, the supply of skilled manpower.

Some sociologists have expressed considerable unease about explanatory schemes such as those we have outlined. It is said that in these perspectives social structure and organization are *reified*—that is, they are considered as if they were 'things' capable of sustaining themselves without human activity.[2] Berger and Pullberg have criticized such sociological schemes as 'dehumanizing' and have suggested that they 'mark the point at which sociology has lost its own subject'. As they would put it, they ignore the problematic nature of the human world. In studying the objective world, there is a danger that the subjective will be forgotten. Man is not simply a passive agent on whom the forces of society and history operate. He is an active being who comes to terms with the uncertainty of human life through his power to interpret and adjust. In other words, he does not simply receive his reality, he *constructs* it also.

In terms of the sociology of education neither the educability studies nor the social systems model have taken the everyday activity of school life seriously as phenomena to be explained. Neither has endeavoured to focus on the *intersubjectivity* of this everyday life; on the processes through which individuals negotiate and attach meanings to their worlds.

To be fair to them, of course, they have not tried to do so. Both have been successful in their own way (especially the social stratification approach, which has contributed significantly to the establishment of a new pattern of secondary education).

The next stage of development for both approaches could well be in the direction which this course is taking. The social stratification studies have established that there are class-based differences in educational achievement and the obvious next step is to try to find out the reasons for these differences. Similarly, the social systems approach has produced a model of the school as a formal organization and now needs to consider the substantive content of school life.

Clearly, it is a fruitful question to ask how and with what consequences teachers and pupils differently experience school. One of the themes which runs through the bulk of these readings is that individuals construct their reality through *negotiations* with each other. Both teachers and pupils 'know' certain things of one another, and of their joint activities during the school day. This knowledge rests on sets of *typifications*—the categories and descriptions which are commonly used by actors in a situation. Some of these are localized and limited to only one or two schools, but many have become embedded in the entire fabric of the education system. In order, then, to try to understand the processes by which pupils come to be defined and classified, and the taken-for-granted rules and assumptions which under-pin teaching and learning, we chose as our guiding perspective the sociology of knowledge.

Recently, there has been a resurgence of interest in this field and a notable feature of its development has been the fusion which has occurred of hitherto discrete intellectual traditions—particularly between some ideas of Marx, the phenomenology of Alfred Schutz and the social psychology of George Herbert Mead.[3]

A synthesis of these intellectual traditions is the basis for the selection of readings in this volume.

References

1 The educability studies are too numerous to list here, but see particularly J. W. B. Douglas, *The Home and the School*, Penguin Books, and the summary of research by A. Little and J. Westergaard, 'The trend of class differentials in educational opportunity in England and Wales', *British Journal of Sociology* (1964), **15** (4), 301–16.

2 cf. P. L. Berger and S. Pullberg, 'Reification and the sociological critique of consciousness', *History and Theory* (1964), xx and *New Left Review* (1966), **35**. See also D. Silverman, *The Theory of Organizations*, Heinemann 1970, ch. 6.

3 The rationale and implications of the synthesis of the ideas of Marx, Mead and Schutz is provided by P. L. Berger and T. Luckmann, *The Social Construction of Reality*, Allen Lane, the Penguin Press 1967, and P. L. Berger, 'Identity as a problem in the sociology of Knowledge', which is included in the present volume. See also the Introduction to *The Sociology of Knowledge: A Reader*, by J. E. Curtis and J. W. Petras, Duckworth 1970; A. Schutz, 'The Problem of Social Reality', *Collected Papers*, vol. 1, The Hague, Martinus Nijhoff, 1962; A. Schutz, Reflections on the problem of relevance, *The Problem of Relevance*, ed. R. M. Zaner, Yale University Press 1970.

Section I   Teaching and learning as the construction of reality

The readings in this section provide ways of understanding teaching and learning as social processes. Although both sets of activities are concerned with the development of certain 'inner' qualities, such as new forms of understanding and experience, this usually has to be accomplished in particular institutional settings and through socially acceptable forms of relationship. These have an important bearing on the pupil's experience of the reality of the classroom and, therefore, on the quality of his learning.

We can conceptualize the relationship between teachers and pupils as a process of negotiation. From their different experiences, they each bring to the classroom their own definitions of reality and their own understandings of the world. These differences between their social worlds have to be negotiated through the institutional rules and procedures which regulate the interaction in the classroom.

A central idea in these readings is that individuals construct their reality by defining and interpreting the situations in which they find themselves, and that the meanings which they attach to objects and experiences are generated and exchanged in social interaction. These and several related issues are considered by Blumer in his discussion of the ideas of George Herbert Mead. His article has been included because it contains many insights which can be developed in an analysis of the activity of the classroom. Teachers and pupils can be seen as continually participating in the definition and interpretation of each other's actions. How these arise and what their consequences are have important implications for the pupil's career in the school.

The article by Blanche Geer focuses specifically on the interaction between the processes of teaching and those involved in learning. She suggests that the relationship between pupils and teachers is essentially one of conflict, and outlines two aspects of the relationship where this is apparent.

In the first place, teaching and learning involves an *exchange of knowledge*. The teacher's institutional position is based on his expertise in a particular field of knowledge, of which the pupil's own experience is, by definition, inferior. According to this view, teaching is 'an attempt to change the pupil by introducing him to new ideas'. It is 'an assault on the self, and resistance to it can be explained as unwillingness to upset one's inner *status quo*.' Clearly the ways in which a teacher defines and handles a pupil's 'common sense' knowledge in relation to the knowledge embodied in the subjects of the curriculum will be an important factor in his management of conflict.

Teacher–pupil relationships are also likely to be characterized by a *bargaining for control*. Although the teacher, by virtue of his institutional power, is likely to dominate the classroom interaction, he himself is constrained by the limitations which pupils seek to impose on his behaviour.

The article by Berger and Kellner was included because of the parallel which can be drawn between the on-going conversation of marriage partners and the verbal interaction between teachers and pupils. They are particularly concerned to show how the meanings which are conveyed through the marital conversation gradually transform the identities of the partners. This article underlines the important relationship which exists between language and reality. Marriage partners come together as strangers. They have unshared pasts and have inhabited more or less different social worlds. Through the marital conversation their different definitions of reality are re-interpreted and a shared view of reality becomes established. The marriage conversation, therefore, upholds and validates for its participants a world which is real.

Schutz's essay, 'The stranger', makes many similar points. Schutz was concerned here with the problems which individuals have in discovering order and coherence when they find themselves in new situations. His example of the alien in a strange community points up the difficulties which arise for an individual when what was taken for granted has to be rethought and reinterpreted. In terms of the school, this essay suggests how we might consider the interpretive problems facing a child who is continually presented with new knowledge. Cognitively the school child is always a stranger, and his school life is a continual process of accommodation to strangeness.

One final aspect of teaching and learning as negotiation with which this section is concerned is the teacher's professional knowledge. In their day-to-day interaction with their pupils, teachers are repeatedly evaluating and classifying particular characteristics of their work, their ability and, in some cases, their appearance. The labels and categories—the 'images'—which are applied have become embedded in the teacher's professional knowledge and his professional responsibility. They are, however, important in defining the parameters within which pupils obtain their school experience and the criteria by which they are organized and assessed.

The extract from Elizabeth Goodacre's book, *Teachers and their Pupils' Home Background*, provides an example of this. She suggests from her research that a knowledge of their pupils' social class background influences some teachers' conceptions of their

ability and might lower their expectations of what the pupil can achieve. The assumptions which teachers hold of their pupils and the labels which they apply to them go some way to actually *producing* school success and failure.

This point is taken considerably further by Werthman, who looks specifically at the processes by which certain pupils come to be defined as 'delinquent'. He suggests that 'delinquency' is a label applied by some teachers to particular pupils who refuse to accept the legitimacy of their authority. It arises in the 'bargaining for control' which is a feature of teacher–pupil interaction. 'Since teachers exercise authority in a variety of ways, becoming a "delinquent" depends in large measure on whether these various claims are accepted. This is why gang members are frequently "delinquent" in one class and ordinary students in the adjoining room.' Clearly, Werthman's suggestion that the category 'delinquent' is socially constructed in the interaction between particular teachers and pupils leads us to raise questions about the generation of other labels and their consequences for the teacher's and pupil's school experience. The significance of these definitions for the teacher's classroom management and their organization in his pedagogy are discussed in the introduction to Section II.

1 Teaching

Blanche Geer

A conventional view of teaching holds that it requires no more than Mark Hopkins, a boy, and a log. Common sense tells us we may dispense with the log but that two people, not necessarily man and boy, are essential. Further, there must be an understanding between the two that one knows more about something than the other and should impart it. According to this view, the act of teaching is a simple process: it is to give or impart knowledge.

The conventional view provides us with a plausible model. It suggests popular notions of what may go wrong: poor teaching occurs when teachers have too little knowledge or too little skill to impart the knowledge they have. Yet the model is not satisfying. In referring only to the teacher, it neglects the interaction of teacher and pupil, and it fails to explain the universal, if intermittent, resistance of pupils, the hostility, sometimes alternating with admiration and love, so often directed at teachers.

For there is conflict in teaching; it is a tension-filled, chancy process. Resistance to teaching occurs among pupils who are able and anxious to learn; it occurs when teachers teach well. It is not confined to schools but frequently occurs in the informal teaching situations of everyday life, as everyone knows who has tried to teach a friend to drive a car.

We can approach understanding of one source of the conflict between teacher and pupil if we think of teaching as an attempt to change the pupil by introducing him to new ideas. In this model, teaching is an assault on the self, and resistance to it can be explained as unwillingness to upset one's inner *status quo*. Plausible as it may seem, the model is nevertheless limited in application. It illuminates the rare case: the pupil sufficiently aware of the power of ideas to fear and combat them, the pupil with an eager and persuasive teacher of a subject full of ideas of the kind that open new worlds of understanding of self. It

Source: *International Encyclopedia of the Social Sciences*, ed. D. L. Sills, New York: Free Press (1968) (15), 560–5.

does not explain the much more common case of the forgetful, indifferent pupil who has a dull teacher of a dry subject. But it is probable that there is as much, if not more, conflict between teacher and pupil in the latter case than in the former. We need a model of teaching that fits all types of pupils, teachers, and subjects.

A conflict model of teaching

In every teaching situation, the teacher is, at least temporarily, the superior and his pupil the subordinate, a relationship we may express in propositional form as follows: A (the superior) originates interaction for B (the subordinate), and B responds according to A's wishes; more simply, A gives orders that B obeys (Homans 1951, 244). From the superior's standpoint, this statement describes a situation in which his ability to control B's response is unquestioned—an ideal not always attained. When control is uncertain, the ideal takes on the force of obligation: if A does not control B's response, he should; as superior, it is his responsibility.

We can apply this conditional form of Homans' proposition to teaching. As teacher, A originates interaction for B by imparting knowledge or directing him to it. At the same time, A accepts the obligation to see to it that B responds as he (A) wishes. In fulfilling his responsibility, A evaluates the correctness of B's response and controls B's behavior during the interaction sufficiently to make correct response possible. Essentially A's role is that of command and B's of submission.

While not inevitable, conflict between teacher and pupil is predictable in this model (Waller (1932) 1965, 195). The absence, rather than the presence, of resistance requires explanation when one person seeks so much control over another. Teaching, in this model, is *making* the pupil learn; and a teacher's task is one of so managing the conflict his efforts may provoke that submission is temporary and the pupil's spirit unbroken.

Reduction of conflict. Our difficulties with teaching in everyday life suggest that subordination is indeed central to teaching. We feel most at ease when A's status outside the teaching dyad is superior to B's. If not always gladly, young people accept teaching from their elders, and neophytes take it from old hands. Subordination becomes an issue, however, when A is equal or inferior in status to B. In these circumstances, we use a variety of devices to mitigate conflict. Between friends, what is essentially a nonreciprocal relationship can be phrased, 'I'll teach you to swim, if you teach me to . . .' Each takes responsibility for the other in this interaction, but not simultaneously. We depend on the promised reversal of role to sweeten subordination.

In more structured relationships, reciprocity may be impossible. Situations arise in which one of two persons equal in rank knows something the other must know to carry on his work. When this happens, the latter may be induced to ask for help, so that the teacher seems less like a teacher because he does not originate the interaction. The word 'teaching' is not used. Instead, one colleague 'helps out' another or 'lends a hand'. The helper may go out of his way to make clear that he considers himself superior in knowledge to his colleague solely on the matter at hand.

Teaching is inappropriate when B has very high status. Captains of ships are not teachable during command, or company presidents on matters of business. In fact, it is folk wisdom not to try to teach anyone his business, whatever his rank. When instruction is needed, high-ranking people employ a consultant on specific problems for which he is asked to furnish solutions to be tried out only after he has gone. Deprived of control over his pupil's learning and of opportunity to evaluate it, the consultant is less threatening to the man who hires him, but he leaves the scene with an uncomfortable sense of unfulfilled responsibility.

Not using the word 'teaching' when teaching is being done, inducing the pupil to ask for it, reciprocity of role, and strict limitation of the area of expertise are devices commonly used to avoid the conflict inherent in teaching. Yet uneasiness, if not hostility, remains. Friend, consultant, and helper still feel responsible for their pupil's response and may try to control it. Learners must hide from themselves the knowledge that even in such a truncated relationship they may have revealed themselves incapable of correct response. One can send away the teacher but not before he has taken one's measure.

School and classroom

The devices that mitigate conflict between teacher and pupil in everyday life are seldom used (although they may be play-acted) in the schoolroom. The teacher's status as an adult makes reciprocity of role unthinkable, since he cannot be put in the position of child-pupil. In so-called democratic teaching methods, interaction may seem to originate with the pupil, but all except the youngest sense the teacher's guiding hand and frequently resent the pretence (Seeley *et al.* 1956, 271).

A pupil may take the initiative by asking for help with a problem, so that the teacher becomes a tutor–consultant who acts as if both he and the pupil had to satisfy outside examiners. But this form of interaction is necessarily infrequent; no matter what efforts school and teachers make to teach individuals, much of the day continues in the lockstep the school's economy of time and space requires. The teacher talks to all his pupils as a unit; he assigns lessons and gives examinations to the group. If there are outside examiners, he does his own testing and grading first. It is only at the end of a schooling sequence, when pupils move on to another system, that teacher and class join efforts to pass examinations.

Authority of the teacher

In everyday teaching situations, we minimize potential conflict by limiting the teacher's power or pretending it does not exist. Schools do the opposite. They support and legitimate his authority in a number of ways. The teacher has the advantage of his own ground —the self-contained unit of the classroom and the enclosing walls of the school building, which cut the pupil off from the rest of his world. The teacher has dependable allies in other teachers, the school administration, and the state. His methods of control and evaluation (discipline and grading) receive institutional support in the record keeping of the administration. While there may be misunderstandings among these allies of the teacher and vulnerability to outside pressures, they have the advantage of being adults dealing with children. They maintain a continuing order in which the pupil is always subject to the authority of a teacher, in a school the law requires him to attend.

The school also bolsters the teacher's authority by legitimating his claims to knowledge. It assures the community that its teachers have academic degrees and experience. Furthermore, the school-teacher deals with knowledge systems that have an objective character intrinsically separate from the person of both the teacher and the pupil (Simmel 1950, 132). Teacher and pupil do not simply agree, as in informal teaching, that the teacher has superior knowledge; it is a matter of public consensus that he does.

With so many allies and so much support of his authority, the teacher's position seems unassailable. If there is to be some form of conflict between him and his pupils, he must surely win. Pupils are not defenseless, however. Their parents may intercede, and the law usually forbids corporal punishment. In the classroom they have the great advantage of being many to the teacher's one. Like any group, pupils can better their condition by acting together to solve common problems, and a united class provides a teacher with a formidable opponent.

In strictly run schools, however, where grades are of primary importance, the teacher often avoids conflict between himself and his pupils by encouraging conflict among the pupils themselves. He prevents pupils from joining in collective action against him by inducing them to compete with each other in classwork. He has each pupil recite to him rather than to the class and upholds the fiction that learning takes place legitimately only within the dyad of teacher and pupil. When a teacher structures interaction in the classroom in this way, pupils are very aware that they offer the same product to a teacher whose chief role is that of evaluator of products. But, as Marshall ((1963) 1965, 181–3) notes, similarity need not divide: competitors often become partners. When they do, a new form of conflict develops, in which pupils unite to bargain with the teacher about the terms of their co-operation with him. In modern egalitarian societies, where teachers often feel uncomfortable in an authoritarian role and deplore competition for grades, bargaining is probably the most frequent form of conflict between teacher and pupils.

Bargaining between teacher and pupils

The fact that the school's economy requires the teacher to treat his class as a unit in many, if not all, respects undoubtedly facilitates the development of consensus and collective action on the part of pupils or, as it has elsewhere been called, 'student culture' (Becker *et al.* 1961, 435–7). The term designates a subtle use of the businessman's device of limiting the area of the teacher's expertise. This student action is a drive for a modicum of autonomy expressed in bargaining with the teacher about matters he does not conventionally define as teaching but for which he nevertheless feels responsible: control of the pupil's behavior during learning.

By listening carefully to what a teacher says he wants in class and comparing among themselves what grades or comments he gives for what kinds of work, and by 'trying things on' (mass shoelace tying, for instance) in the early days of a school term, a class may reach a consensus about its teacher's standards, both academic and disciplinary. It then transforms what the teacher says and does into rules for him to follow. He must not change these rules the class makes for him, and he must apply them to all pupils.

It does not matter much how high a teacher sets standards of quiet, neatness of work, or promptness, although there will be protests if his standards are out of line with those of other teachers. What does matter is consistency of application. In the eyes of his pupils, this is the teacher's part of the bargain. If it is not kept, he can expect trouble. Teachers who fail

to understand the basic premise—'We will behave properly, if you behave properly'—find themselves continually engaged in disciplining pupils rather than imparting knowledge.

Some of the rules of the bargain pupils make with a teacher are in that gray area continually subject to negotiation—degrees of neatness or quietness, for example. Other rules are clear cut: a teacher may not give a test on things not in the text or on matters not covered in class. Rules vary from classroom to classroom and from one school to another, of course, and with the age and sophistication of pupils. But everywhere the largely unspoken bargain his pupils make with him constrains the teacher's behavior whether he knows it or not.

Pupils have effective sanctions which they use to reward and punish teachers who fail to live up to the bargain, sanctions few teachers can withstand. On one day, when a visitor comes, they delight the teacher with exemplary behavior; on the next, they generate an uproar in the classroom that is loud enough to echo in the ears of the principal, the parents, and the entire community. Dependent on his pupils' good will and co-operation, the teacher soon accedes to the bargaining practices of the class, often entering the game on his own behalf. He says, in effect, 'If you will be quiet, you may have more time for the test'; by this action he not only recognizes and thus strengthens the collectivity but also tolerates illicit academic practice in order to secure discipline (Blau (1955) 1963, 215–17).

The bargain also defines the teacher's jurisdiction. Pupils agree that in his classroom the teacher may legitimately control the academic (lessons and tests), attempt to control the quasi-academic (note passing and pencil sharpening), and justly refer the nonacademic (dress and morals) to the more encompassing authority of the principal. In pupils' eyes, however, it is always the academic that legitimizes a teacher's control. Hallways, washrooms, and yards are spatially removed from books and study; the teacher controls them as he can.

The teacher is not likely to see the logic of these distinctions. He knows that if he is to control one pupil's academic response in the classroom, control of the whole class is a prerequisite, and that control of the class depends upon the discipline of adjacent rooms and hallways. The school administration, pursuing its bureaucratic course, also finds behavior unrelated to the academic threatening to the smooth functioning of the school and to its reputation. As a consequence, the dress, manners, and morals (sometimes the families of pupils in the case of less privileged groups) become areas of expertise and attempted control. In some schools, teachers and administration rationalize the extension by asserting responsibility, difficult to realize, over the 'whole child'. It often is in such apparently unimportant matters as proper dress that bargaining between teacher and pupils breaks down, opening the way to various forms of a thir form of conflict—revolt

Whatever its form—competition among pupils that the teacher must carefully perpetuate, bargaining in which he must share, or revolts he must put down—conflict is difficult for the teacher who clings to the conventional idea that his sole function is one of imparting knowledge. If he thinks of himself as a superior controlling the behavior of many unruly subordinates, he may eventually come to enjoy the battle.

Training institutions for teachers

Teachers' colleges and university schools of education supply the school system with employees and share with it the long-range goal of educating the young. In view of this close relationship, we might expect training institutions to prepare teachers for conflict with pupils, but they do not. Instead, they follow the conventional model with which we began: to teach is to impart or offer knowledge. Would-be teachers learn subject matter and techniques of teaching. They take courses in test construction and interpretation, but testing is not recognized as a device for controlling pupils, and discipline (control of a collectivity) is seldom considered a proper subject of instruction. Off-hand, such disjunction between the everyday work of an occupation and the training one receives for it seems extraordinary. Yet wherever training is separated from practice (which is to say, wherever there are schools), we find a similar situation. Most schools teach much that is never used and fail to teach what is.

We may explain the disjunction by referring to the situational perspectives (sets of beliefs and actions) of the various groups in the training institution that together make up its culture. People in both the schools and the training institutions for teachers develop ways of acting, goals, and interests in response to the particular problems posed by their situation (Becker *et al.* 1961, 34–7). Schools and teachers' colleges are both part of the larger hierarchy of educational institutions devoted to a common goal, but their immediate situations differ.

While school people must deal with local politics, neighborhoods (good and bad), parents, and other interest groups, teachers' colleges exist in an academic setting different in situational imperatives and constraints. Theirs is the world of colleges and universities so apt to grant prestige, with all its privileges, largely to the scholarly disciplines. Since the conventional model of teaching emphasizes knowledge, it fits the academic world better than the conflict model with its insistence on social skills. Faculties of education may be 'school-bred'—many institutions require professors to have taught in the public schools (Hughes 1963a, 152)—but the trend in such faculties over the years is toward a looser tie with the schools. Set apart on his campus with his higher pay and status, the teacher of teachers loses touch with teachers of children. His institution may formally reflect the organization of the school system by its division into special, elementary, and high school programs, and state licensing regulations may set the sequence of students' courses; but these articulating devices tend more to restrict innovation by both training school and student than to bring future teachers closer to the conflict central to teaching.

Recruiting

The disjunction of training and work, which prevents the transmission of usefully exact knowledge of what to expect in an actual teaching situation, undoubtedly helps the school system to recruit young teachers. It is possible to fill teaching jobs even under conditions of shortage, but the schools want to do more than fill them. Like other service institutions and businesses, they want recruits of high ability committed to a life-time career. In a word, they want professionals.

Unfortunately, students of the highest ability seldom enter training institutions for teachers (Vertein 1961), and not all graduates teach (Osborn & Maul 1961). There are excellent reasons for this. Of the proud old callings, teaching requires the least formal education and consequently the least investment of time, money, and energy. The school of education provides a relatively unspecific college program that can do no harm. To enter training is in no sense a commitment to a career. For would-be athletes, musicians, and artists uncertain of success as performers and for women whose first choice of career is marriage, a degree in education is a form of occupational insurance.

Although teaching is highly visible to children early in their lives, the exposure is not likely to attract them to the occupation. The teacher is too much of a daily antagonist to generate, for example, the charisma of the physician who comes to help the family in time of trouble. For children of manual workers, teaching may carry prestige; but for those of higher social origins, it is more likely to seem a hard life for the reward. As a woman's occupation, it also bears the stigma (for both sexes) of woman's low status in comparison with men; yet it is not feminine enough, except at the nursery level, to attract women strongly.

People who do enter teaching discover that in comparison with other occupations it is startlingly lacking in the auxiliary rewards that facilitate commitment (Becker 1960). Industry and business offer promotion to more responsible positions, while school teaching offers only increases in pay and trivial seniority privileges. Teachers leave the classroom, of course, to become specialists or administrators; but as long as they continue to teach, there is little opportunity for the more-than-local influence possible in other professions through publication, lecturing, and consultation.

Although teachers deal with people rather than with things (an ancient status distinction), the people they deal with are minors. They miss the rewards, psychological and political, of serving people of high status and power. Their daily work is often programmed by state departments of education; nonteachers supervise and direct them in ways which make the autonomy prized by traditional professionals and entrepreneurs impossible. Under such conditions, we should not be surprised that the recruiting of committed professionals is difficult.

Career and profession

Once started on a teaching career, the disjunction between their preparation and actuality in the schools often hits teachers hard. Faced as they are each day with hostile children interminably bargaining for greater autonomy, we may wonder why any of them continue. In the absence of research we can only speculate, but it is probable that many people find themselves committed to teaching because a first-choice career fails them. The desired marriage or acceptance in some world of athletics, literature, or art never materializes. Teachers may also commit themselves unwittingly because the occupation permits other involvements. For a married man, low pay may necessitate moonlighting, and this second job, fitted to a teaching schedule, may become so rewarding that he continues to teach. Married women who find that teaching fits well with household and child-rearing duties may also continue in teaching.

There is, in addition, the security of tenure and, frequently, happiness in inertia. School tasks repeat and repeat; year after year the round is the same. One may become so marked by immersion in the world of a slum school that one feels unfitted for any other (Becker 1952, 474). Responsibility to individuals is lessened by the constant turnover of pupils who sit in one's class for a year and are gone. In time, bargaining for control of a class may become enjoyable. Some of the very things about teaching that discourage neophytes may keep veterans at it (Geer 1966).

Teachers as professionals

More positively, people may commit themselves to teaching because it is, in many respects, a profession. Teachers cannot claim the separate identity given by control of an esoteric body of knowledge (Hughes 1963*b*, 657), but they do have the esoteric skills of the classroom. They do not have professional societies strong enough to protect them from the incursions of the community, parents, and experts on education

outside the school system, but it is usually in the interest of the principal to protect them (Becker 1953, 133–9). They are supervised, but there is still something left of the lonely eminence of the classroom. Visibility of performance is low; and few people believe we have learned as yet how to measure teaching ability (Brim 1958).

In the community, teaching seems to retain some of the more unpleasant aspects of a profession. There are remnants of the expectation that teachers should be models of propriety for the young: even adults are sometimes embarrassed in their exacting presence. The public objects to demands for higher pay because teachers live on taxpayer's money. They ought to serve the community gladly.

Teachers themselves display ambiguity about their status by having unions as well as professional societies. The latter have little control (although they increasingly attempt it) over ethics, recruiting, training, or legislation affecting teachers. They have not yet decided whether school administrators and specialists should be included in their associations as 'teachers' or kept out as bosses and rivals. Unions help teachers to fight for higher pay and against the encroachments of duties in schoolyards, lunchrooms, and toilets. But they are more apt to lower that prestige so important to a marginal profession than to heighten it.

Teachers feel they have a poor public image and inadequate public appreciation, but for many teaching is a step up in social class and therefore in respect. Large city systems help teachers to get the additional education required for specialization and raises in pay. Opportunity to transfer to the pleasanter working conditions in middle-class schools comes with seniority (Becker 1953). For men, schoolteaching may be a stopgap, if no longer a stepping-stone on the way to more prestigious careers. For women, it can be a satisfying and even creative occupation that intrudes less than others upon a husband and children.

Teachers are not professionals in the usual sense. They do not have clients who choose them, terminate the relationship, or bring to it the immediate need of help that tempers the client's subordination to the physician or lawyer. In a broader sense, they are professionals with the society for client. We cannot do without their transmission, however imperfect, of its heritage. It is even probable that society would be quite different had children no opportunity to engage in conflict with their superior, the teacher, and hence no opportunity to learn early something of the strength that collective action brings to subordinates.

References

Baron, George, and Tropp, Asher (1961). Teachers in England and America. pp. 545–57 in A. H. Halsey, Jean Floud and C. Arnold Anderson (eds), *Education, Economy and Society*. Collier-Macmillan.

Becker, Howard S. (1952). The career of the Chicago public schoolteacher. *American Journal of Sociology* 57, 470–7.

Becker, Howard S. (1953). The teacher in the authority system of the public school. *Journal of Educational Sociology*, **27**, 128–41.

Becker, Howard S. (1960). Notes on the concept of commitment. *American Journal of Sociology* 66, 32–40.

Becker, Howard S. (1962). The nature of a profession. Vol. 62, pp. 27–46 in National Society for the Study of Education, *Yearbook*. Part 1: Education for the Professions. Univ. of Chicago Press.

Becker, Howard S. *et al.* (1961). *Boys in White: Student Culture in Medical School*. Univ. of Chicago Press.

Blau, Peter ((1955) 1963). *The Dynamics of Bureaucracy: A Study of Interpersonal Relations in Two Government Agencies*. Rev. ed. Univ. of Chicago Press.

Brim, Orville G. (1958). *Sociology and the Field of Education*. New York: Russell Sage Foundation.

Floud, Jean, and Scott, W. (1961). Recruitment to teaching in England and Wales. pp. 527–44 in A. H. Halsey, Jean Floud and C. Arnold Anderson (eds), *Education, Economy and Society*.

Friedenberg, Edgar Z. (1965). *Coming of Age in America*. New York: Random House.

Geer, Blanche (1966). Notes on occupational commitment. *School Review* 74 (1), 31–47.

Homans, George C. (1951). *The Human Group*. Routledge & Kegan Paul.

Hughes, Everett C. (1963a). Is education a discipline? pp. 147–58 in John Walton and James L. Kuethe (eds), *The Discipline of Education*. Madison: Univ. of Wisconsin Press.

Hughes, Everett C. (1963b). Professions. *Daedalus* 92, 655–68.

Kob, Janpeter ((1958) 1961). Definition of the teacher's role. pp. 558–76 in A. H. Halsey, Jean Floud and C. Arnold Anderson (eds), *Education, Economy and Society*. This article is abridged and translated from Janpeter Kob's *Das soziale Berufsbewusstsein des Lehrers der höheren Schule*.

Marshall, Thomas H. ((1963) 1964). *Class, Citizenship and Social Development: Essays*. Garden City, N.Y.: Doubleday. Essays first published in book form as *Sociology at the Crossroads and Other Essays*. An edition was published in 1963 by Heinemann.

Mason, Ward S. (1961). *The Beginning Teacher; Status and Career Orientations: Final Report on the Survey of New Teachers in the Public Schools 1956–57*. U.S. Office of Education, Circular no. 664. Washington: U.S. Office of Education.

Osborn, W. W., and Maul, R. C. (1961). New emphasis needed in teacher recruitment. *Midland Schools* 75, 20–1.

Parsons, Talcott ((1959) 1961). The school class as a social system: Some of its functions in American society. pp. 434–55 in A. H. Halsey, Jean Floud and C. Arnold Anderson (eds), *Education, Economy and Society*. First published in *Harvard Educational Review*.

Seeley, John R. *et al.* (1956). *Crestwood Heights: A Study of the Culture of Suburban Life*. New York: Basic Books.

Simmel, Georg (1950). *The Sociology of Georg Simmel*. Edited and translated by Kurt H. Wolff. Collier-Macmillan. See especially pp. 118–44 on 'The isolated individual and the Dyad'.

Snider, G. R., and Long, D. (1961). Are teacher education programs attracting academically able students? *Journal of Teacher Education* 12, 407–11.

Stinchcombe, Arthur L. (1965). *Rebellion in a High School*. Chicago: Quadrangle Books.

Vertein, Lester D. (1961). A study of the personal–social and intellectual characteristics of a group of State College students preparing to teach. *Journal of Experimental Education* 30, 159–92.

Waller, Willard W. ((1932) 1965). *The Sociology of Teaching*. Wiley.

2 Teachers and their pupils' home background

E. J. Goodacre

This study of teachers' attitudes towards their pupils' home background and their expectations and assessments of individual pupils was designed as part of a larger, three-stage project concerned with the teaching of reading in infant schools. The project was initiated by the National Foundation for Educational Research in September 1958, and was carried out with the assistance of the London County Council Education Committee and Officers, the Ministry of Education Inspectorate and the Child Development Department of the University of London Institute of Education.

The main aims of the three-year inquiry were (1) to investigate the nature and extent of the task of teaching infants to read, particularly in schools in areas where little assistance could be expected from children's homes, and (2) to study the reading readiness, attainment and progress of the children in relation to their individual attributes, home circumstances and school conditions.

The results of the first stage of the investigation—a survey of methods, materials, conditions and pupils' achievements in 100 schools and departments—were published early in 1967.[1] One of the most interesting aspects of the findings given in the first report was the difference between the teachers' evaluations of the children's reading ability and the children's tested performance. The teachers' assessments (based on their records of book level reached) indicated that children in middle- and upper-working-class areas showed markedly superior reading ability in comparison with children in lower-working-class areas, with the middle-class pupils showing superior attainment. However, the superiority of middle-class pupils was not found when pupils' reading attainments were tested by means of standardized reading comprehension group tests. The working-class pupils appeared to do better than might have been expected,

especially in relation to tested attainment, but the lower-working-class pupils were markedly inferior in comparison with the other two groups, whichever criteria was used—estimated or tested reading attainment.

The fact that the upper-working-class pupils did better than might have been anticipated, particularly in relation to the more objective criteria (scores on a standardized test), suggested that factors other than teaching methods and school conditions might affect the level of pupils' reading attainment. One such factor might be the teachers' expectations of their pupils' abilities and attainment. These expectations might also serve to explain the difference between pupils' tested and assessed attainments; and it is possible that, in fact, teachers' assessments reflect the standards they apply to pupils from particular social environments.

It is, of course, obvious that teachers do formulate opinions about their pupils' home background, and that their attitudes towards pupils—either as groups or as individuals—will affect in some way their teaching methods and their expectations as to the pupils' attainments. Since this project was initiated, there have been signs of an increasing awareness of the effects of home background and parental attitudes upon children's educational attainments. The evidence collected for the first report in this series indicated the possibility that the teachers' assessments of pupils' attainments might be affected by these attitudes, and there is also evidence from other sources . . . that teachers' attitudes, as well as the pupils' self-evaluation, influence the behaviour of their pupils in the classroom.

Additional evidence of the influence of pupils' home background on pupils' attainment has been included in the Plowden Report,[2] together with a number of recommendations aimed at securing better co-operation between the teacher and the parent. As yet, however, there has been very little study of the

Source: E. J. Goodacre, *Teachers and their Pupils' Home Background*, Slough: National Foundation for Education Research (1968), xi–xiv, 14–25.

process by which teachers become aware of differences in parental attitudes and formulate their opinions about home influences.

It is, therefore, important to discover not only how teachers' attitudes affect their actions, but how they come to formulate them and in what circumstances. This raises a multiplicity of questions. What, for instance, are the standards the teachers apply to different types of pupils? What are they really referring to when they talk about 'good' and 'poor' homes? This report attempts to examine the following questions in relation to infants in a cross-section of schools in an urban setting:

1 What importance do infant teachers attach to pupils' home background in the teaching of reading?

2 How do teachers categorize pupils in relation to their home background?

3 What is the extent of teachers' personal contacts with pupils and their homes and what clues do they use as a basis for their impressions of pupils' home conditions?

4 If paternal occupation is used as a criterion for assessing pupils' home background, how reliable are teachers as judges?

5 What inferences do teachers make about pupils whose parents follow different types of occupation?

6 To what extent do such inferences affect teachers' ratings of individual pupils?

7 Do teachers of infants have certain social and psychological characteristics, distinguishing them from teachers of older children in the educational system, which would be of importance in considering teachers' attitudes to pupils and their homes?

8 How far are differences in teachers' attitudes to pupils' home backgrounds related to psychological rather than sociological factors?

9 Do the personality and attitudes of the head have any direct bearing on the level of pupils' reading attainment?

10 In considering the process by which teachers formulate opinions about pupils' home background, how important are factors such as (a) the type of organization of the school in which the teacher works, (b) the teacher's position in the school, or (c) the teacher's own social class origin?

Plan of the report

Chapter I outlines the previous research which provides a background to the study, and Chapter II describes the procedure adopted in carrying it out and the type of material used. A note explaining statistical and educational significance precedes Chapter III, which summarizes the main findings. Chapters IV, V and VI deal with these findings in more detail, differences in relation to the school and teacher variables (school organization and social area; teacher position and social class origin) being reported where applicable. The report concludes with a note on future research.

It is hoped that the subject of the report will be of interest to those concerned with the practical difficulties involved in teaching young children to read, if only to encourage them to reconsider the generally accepted ideas about the influence of the home and to be more conscious of the implicit assumptions behind many of their teaching decisions.

Perhaps the report's most important contribution may be in relation to the research into the role of the teacher in remediation of learning disabilities among those pupils termed 'disadvantaged'. Certainly the teacher plays an important role in the life of pupils, but *what* it is and *how* it compensates for the disadvantages experienced by such pupils, is not clear. Further research on this aspect of education is clearly needed.

The main findings

This chapter summarizes the main findings of the second stage of the inquiry, in terms of the questions listed on page xiii of the Introduction. The findings are discussed more fully in the following chapters, and statistical evidence and analysis are given in the Appendices.

1 *What importance do infant teachers attach to pupils' home background in the teaching of reading?*

Generally the teachers considered that the pupils' home background was an important factor in learning to read; they described those aspects of the home which they believed could actively assist that process, and the abilities pupils used in learning to read which they most readily associated with differences in home conditions. They most valued the provision of suitable reading material in pupils' homes on which pupils could practise their newly acquired skill, and the type of atmosphere in which it was taken for granted by parents and child that reading was a desirable skill to be acquired. Differences in home background were most readily connected with a child's desire to learn to read and his rate of learning.

2 *How do teachers categorize their pupils in relation to home background?*

The teachers in this study appeared to be familiar with the terms 'good' and 'poor' homes as a means of categorizing pupils. When asked to describe them in their own words, they used more motivational and cultural characteristics in decribing the 'good' home. The 'good' home tended to be described as one which facilitated the teacher's task of instruction by preparing the child for participation in the formal learning situation and also for acceptance of the teacher's role in it. If a child showed no eagerness to learn to read, teachers believed that the difficulty of imparting the techniques of the skill was increased, because not only did they have to provide the appropriate systematic instruction (difficult enough if teacher and pupil used different types of language systems, dialect, etc.) but they had also to demonstrate to pupils that reading was a desirable and necessary skill.

When teachers rated the different characteristics of a 'good' home, the school's social area assumed importance. For instance, there was little difference between the ratings of teachers in middle- and upper-working-class areas, but particular motivational and cultural items assumed importance as distinguishing characteristics between the two working-class groups. These items were the ability of the parents to answer their children's questions, to provide stimulating experiences in the home and to help with school work; parents' own levels of education and intelligence, and the presence of 'good' conversation and manners in the home. Comparing the extreme social area groups, the items regarded as most important were a religious faith, parental help with school work, stable emotional home life, and a mother who did not go out to work.

Each teacher's ratings for the various items were added up to give a total score for this question, and if high scores can be interpreted as indicative of an interest in the contribution of the 'good' home, it seems likely that such an interest is related to the individual teacher's age and general personality type. The findings suggest that it is more likely to be the older or more authoritarian type of teacher, with unfavourable attitudes to pupils and their homes, who is most likely to categorize pupils in terms of 'good' or 'poor' homes.

3 *What is the extent of teachers' personal contacts with pupils and their homes, and what clues do they use as a basis for their impressions of pupils' home conditions?*

It was found that amongst these urban infant teachers, contacts with parents seldom extended beyond meetings on school premises. Few school heads had established parent-teacher organizations, and few teachers ever visited pupils' homes. Two out of three parents[3] were said to visit the school, usually for reasons connected with the child's physical well-being, and since these questions were asked of teachers of young children, parental interest at this stage was largely an expression of maternal concern.

Pupils' records of attendance and lateness were not indicative of social class differences in attitudes towards the value of education, but pupils' reasons for being away or their excuses for lateness provided teachers, to some extent, with information about the pupils' home circumstances. There was, however, some evidence to suggest that certain types of schools might find particular reasons more 'acceptable' than others.

Teachers seemed to have little difficulty in finding evidence of a child's economic circumstances. Conversations, class 'news', or actual observations of personal belongings, etc. brought to school were considered to be indications of a family's pattern of conspicuous consumption. The type and quality of a child's clothing, even in today's welfare state, still seems to be a major 'clue' for most teachers. Obvious signs such as the bare feet of the nineteen-thirties have disappeared, but indications such as the suitability of clothing from the point of view of climate and weather conditions, and the care and quality of underclothing provide a basis for comparison to the practised eye of the observer.

The teachers suggested a variety of ways in which the actions of parents could be construed as constituting parental interest in the child's reading progress. However, analysis of their answers indicated areas of difference which could well be the basis of misunderstandings between teachers and parents. There were, for instance, the different responses to the practical suggestion that parents should provide pupils with a copy of the reader in the school reading scheme, so that the child could practise at home. First, provision of the reader and parents 'hearing' their children read at home was more often suggested as a sign of parental interest by the heads than by the class teachers. Second, the head's views as to whether the parent was expected to borrow or to buy the book appeared to be related to his own social class origin. A head of working-class origin would be likely to consider a request from a parent to borrow a school reader as a sign of interest, but the same request to a head of middle-class origin might be considered as a 'trivial' reason for a visit to the school.[4]

There was evidence to suggest that the type of school organization has a bearing on the role expected of parents. For instance, more heads of the smaller, combined department schools expected parents to take an active interest in the work of the school to the extent of visiting the school to ask about the methods in use, whereas more class teachers in the infant only schools emphasized the parents' supportive role, expecting them to encourage and sustain their children in their efforts but not, at this early stage in their children's education, to want to help with school work.

4 *If paternal occupation is used as a criterion for assessing pupils' home background, how reliable are teachers as 'judges'?*

The findings were that teachers' estimates were least reliable in the lowest social areas, probably because they were unfamiliar with the degrees of responsibility or training involved in manual occupations, and were less likely to be informed about the educational requirements or intellectual concomitants and responsibilities of the newer professions and the more recently developed occupations in technology. Also, these teachers appeared to have certain predetermined notions about the type of occupations associated with particular regions, and these assumptions had considerable influence—even to the extent of being sometimes more effective than the actual recorded occupations of pupils' fathers. The evidence was not conclusive, but it seemed likely that where records of paternal occupations were not kept, teachers' inferences about the incidence of particular occupations in certain regions were less in evidence. However, in these circumstances the head's own social class background appeared to assume more importance— he tended to see the social composition of his school more in terms of his own social class origin.

5   *What inferences do teachers make about pupils whose parents follow different types of occupation?*

The teachers' lack of knowledge regarding the gradients of status in the manual classes was reflected in the tendency for teachers in lower working-class areas to see their classes as homogeneous groups, and pupils as predominantly children of fathers with manual occupations. Their tendency to stress the power and responsibility of occupations which, in the past, were related to educational mobility and hence intellectual capacity, also led them to think of pupils from the lower working-class areas not only as *socially* homogeneous groups, but also as being *intellectually* homogeneous; more teachers in the lower working-class areas tended to accept that they had no pupils of above average intellectual ability. Further, it appeared from the teachers' comments that their own language system and academically biased education might make it extremely difficult for many of them to recognize unfamiliar forms of intellectual functioning.

6   *To what extent do such inferences affect teachers' ratings of individual pupils?*

In reply to the request to complete estimates, records and predictions of individual pupils' abilities, attributes, reading attainment and progress, it was found that the teachers in the extreme social areas were less reluctant to supply information about pupils' home conditions than the teachers in the upper working-class areas. This suggested that the teachers in the extreme social areas tended to have well-structured stereotypes of the type of pupil and home they could expect. It seemed likely that these expectations were related to their ideas concerning the relationship of occupational level, social conditions and intellectual ability.

Nevertheless, when the teachers were asked to rate pupils' personal attributes, school organization rather than social area appeared to be the effective factor. The teachers in the infant only schools tended to describe pupils in more positive terms and generally seemed to favour slightly different personality characteristics from those favoured by teachers in the combined department schools.

Again, it was noticeable that the teachers in the upper working-class areas had greater difficulty in completing the assessments of environmental conditions affecting progress in reading. Teachers in infant only schools also seemed more reluctant to assess pupils in relation to the quality of their homes and the amount of parental interest, possibly because the teachers in these schools generally seemed to expect less overt signs of parental interest than did those working in the smaller combined department schools. The infant only teachers, therefore, had less concrete evidence on which to base their judgments.

The fact that more lower working-class area pupils were rated as being fond of school and, in regard to intellectual ability, were not estimated significantly differently from pupils in other areas (although on the basis of the teacher's general estimates of pupils' intellectual ability, these pupils had shown as markedly inferior), suggested that the teachers of these pupils may have lowered their standards of assessment; that is, normalized a lower level of ability in relation to their inferences about pupils from these social areas.

Evidence from the teachers' reading-readiness estimates of pupils, suggested that the teachers in the upper working-class areas, in comparison with those in the lower working-class areas, tended to provide more opportunities for assessing pupils' perceptual development and were less likely to wait for pupils' 'readiness'. Their pupils' initial enthusiasm appeared to be steadily maintained and by their second year of schooling, they were well established in the basic pre-reading skills and receiving systematic reading instruction (letter sounds and names) and so were able to attempt unknown words for themselves and to proceed at their own pace. By the second year the lower working-class pupils were undoubtedly showing enthusiasm for acquiring the skill, and possibly within a year the difference between the two groups would have been less marked. However, by the second year the approach of transfer to the junior stage of schooling appeared to affect the judgments of the teachers of the lower group, so that they were beginning to use more uniform criteria, e.g. estimates of pupils' progress and chances of success. We do not know to what extent teachers in junior schools in different areas make inferences about the different social classes and adopt diverging standards, but it seems clear that the teachers of the top infant classes react as if they believe that junior teachers will not diverge in their standards, but will rather apply uniform 'junior school standards'.[5]

7   *Do teachers of infants have certain distinctive social and psychological characteristics, distinguishing them from teachers of older children in the educational system, which would be of importance in considering teachers' attitudes to pupils and their homes?*

This study provided further evidence of the previously reported high level of professional satisfaction shown by infant teachers. Previous research indicated that, as a group, infant teachers had outstandingly good personal relationships *in school*. The present study suggested that the class teachers found their greatest satisfaction in their relationships with the children rather than with adults (colleagues or parents), whilst the major dissatisfactions were the low status accorded to infant teachers by the community[6] and the lack of opportunities for intellectual development.

These infant teachers saw themselves as cheerful, conscientious, sensible and adaptable. They believed their principal deficiencies were lack of ambition, originality, confidence and foresight. Their social background was mainly that of the intermediate and skilled occupational levels, and they tended to be predominantly 'first generation' professionals. It was not surprising, therefore, to find that they did not read widely in a vocational sense; but perhaps the most important implication of their social background lies in the fact that as a group within the education system they are likely to be verbally less fluent and articulate, less capable of putting ideas into words and arguing convincingly, which may be important considerations when they need to act as spokesmen for their pupils' educational needs. There was evidence to suggest that it was the heads who were more likely to be aware that such social and psychological characteristics acted as limitations on the scope of their role.

8 *How far are differences in teachers' attitudes to pupils' home background related to psychological rather than sociological factors?*

Whilst the infant teachers appeared generally to attach considerable importance to environmental factors, the way in which they reacted to these professional or group generalizations and the extent to which they used them—imposing preconceived and stereotyped categories upon their experiences with pupils and parents—were more likely to be related to their own basic personality. It was the more authoritarian type of teacher who tended to have an unfavourable attitude towards pupils' home backgrounds,[7] particularly in relation to pupils' parents. They were also more likely to feel pessimistic about the school's ability to change pupils' values.

Generally, heads had more favourable attitudes to pupils than had the class teachers, and the attitudes of women heads were more favourable than those of men heads. Teachers who preferred teaching pupils individually rather than in groups, tended to be more favourably disposed towards their pupils and their types of background.

9 *Do the personality and attitudes of the head have any direct bearing on the level of pupils' reading attainment?*

A head's personality did not appear to be related to his school's standards or to the staff records of pupils'

progress or reading achievement; but there may perhaps be an indirect relationship, through the medium of the head's attitudes to pupils and their homes, which could affect the staff's morale and consequently their expectations of pupils' future achievements. It seemed likely that a head's attitudes to pupils and their home backgrounds assumed most importance in relation to schools in the lower working-class areas. The head's personality and attitudes may well be a crucial factor in determining the extent to which his staff are able to 'break through the barrier of IQ depression'[8] which tends to operate so strongly in these areas.

10 *To what extent are these findings affected by (a) the type of organization of the school in which the teacher works; (b) the teacher's position in the school; (c) the teacher's own social class origin?*

(a) Some of the differences reported in relation to school organization were undoubtedly related to the distinguishing organizational characteristics of school size and pupil range. The infant only schools tend to have more pupils on roll, and their teachers have only a short period in which to become acquainted with pupils, so it is not surprising to find that the teachers in these schools experienced more difficulties in completing assessments about pupils' home conditions. However, there may be a further reason. The infant school philosophy of education may be more pervasive in the single department school, and since one of its basic tenets is the importance of the needs of the individual child, this may mean that less emphasis is being placed upon group relationships—pupils, parents, teachers. Certainly there was evidence that the teachers in the infant only schools were less concerned about overt signs of parental interest, of parents being interested in the *school's* methods and activities. They may, of course, be more prepared to approach parents and to provide them with information. They seemed to take up a more positive approach towards both pupils and parents. They were probably less interested in achieving parental approval of their approach and methods than in ensuring that parents appreciated and encouraged their children's efforts, thus strengthening pupils' motivation to learn.

The findings of the present study suggest that the combined department school may more nearly resemble the traditional school system developed in the past in which the role of socialization tends to be of primary importance, whereas the infant only schools seem to develop an autonomous role, thereby cutting across local traditional reactions and possibly facilitating social change. How much these basic differences can be related to the organizational factors of school size and age range of pupils and how much to the generally ignored fact that infant only schools are staffed solely by women under a woman head, would seem to require further research. It can be stated, however, that there were no significant differences between the attitudes of the teachers working in the two types of schools. Again, further research would be necessary to evaluate the importance of the finding in relation to heads, which indicated that they had more favourable attitudes towards pupils, and that women heads had more favourable attitudes than men.

(b) Where differences existed in relation to the teacher's position, they appeared to be mainly the result of differences in the degree of contact with parents and pupils respectively. For instance, more heads described the 'good' home in emotional and moral terms, since they were often more aware than the class teacher of the parents' personal problems and were therefore in a better position to realize the importance of an emotionally stable home for both personality development and scholastic progress of pupils. More heads mentioned parents' attendance at Open Days as a sign of parental interest, since, for them, this offered clear evidence of an additional visit made out of interest and not simply because of admission requirements. Too much weight should not be given to this point, but the reception of class teachers' answers gave the impression that many of them felt that parents only came to school to see *them* about lost property!

As has been previously noted, the existence of footwear and a pupil's general physical appearance were formerly considered to be the most reliable 'clues' to the economic circumstances of the home, whereas today the quality and condition of pupils' clothing, particularly underclothing, may assume more importance. The latter is more likely to be seen by the class teacher when supervising pupils' changing for physical training. Heads, however, appear to be more likely to rely upon their observations of parents for their 'clues'. In these circumstances the attitudes of the heads towards parents may have a more profound effect than those of their staff. One thinks, for instance, of the head who makes rules and tries rigidly to control the conditions of parents' visiting the school—an action which, in itself, may be a factor which contributes to the formation of parental and neighbourhood opinion. Since parental esteem is the head's main 'feedback' for awareness of his authority and prestige in the area, it is his action in relation to parents in particular which will directly affect his status and satisfaction with his role. That this can be a vicious circle is probably exemplified by the case of the authoritarian head whose characteristic attitudes tend to antagonize parents, thereby bringing about the very social isolation which this type of personality fears.

(c) In comparison with the other three variables, the factor of social class origin appeared to have much less effect. It seemed that generally these teachers had adopted the middle-class values associated with their profession. When differences occurred, they related to attitudes concerning the use of money. Although teachers with a working-class background appeared to have adopted the cultural values of the social class to which they aspired, they retained their original attitudes towards money. Probably their upbringing was characterized by financial difficulties, and entry to a higher social class involved for most a fight against economic odds.[9]

Differences in attitude towards the use of money may explain some differences in practice between teachers. One example brought to light in this study concerns the provision of the school reader for practice at home; teachers of working-class origin probably assume that parents would borrow a copy if they wanted one, whereas the middle-class teacher would expect the copy to be bought. There are probably other instances of differences and misunderstandings between school and home, which in fact involve differences in 'values' in the monetary sense rather than in the sense of moral principles.

Notes

1 Goodacre, E. J. (1967). *Reading in Infant Classes*. Slough: NFER.

2 Department of Education and Science: Central Advisory Council for Education (England) (1967). *Children and their Primary Schools* (Plowden Report). London: H.M. Stationery Office.

3 Since one in three parents are not seen by the teachers at school (even from the beginning of the child's schooling), one wonders to what extent lack of face-to-face relationships influences the teachers' assessments of parental interest – it may well be that the unknown, unmet parent soon comes to be regarded as the parent who 'takes little interest'. Douglas (1964) assessed parental encouragement by using the class teachers' comments at the end of the first and fourth years in the primary school and their records of the number of times parents visited the school to discuss their children's progress. It was found that on the basis of this assessment of parental interest, when parents took little interest, their children lost ground in tests and gained rather fewer places in the selection examinations than would have been expected from their measured ability.

4 Department of Education and Science (1967). 'National Survey of Parental Attitudes and Circumstances Related to School and Pupil Characteristics', Appendix 3, *Children and their Primary Schools* (Plowden Report) reported that just over a third of the parents had *bought* copies, to have at home, of some of the textbooks their children were using at school. Considerably higher proportions of parents from the non-manual than manual worker families had bought textbooks.

5 The continuing influence of the 1931 Report of the Consultative Committee on the Primary School, reprinted as recently as 1962, may have encouraged the use of uniform criteria of assessment by teachers in the junior school, since it gave the impression that the main task of the junior school teacher was to develop

pupils' reading comprehension. It suggested that few children, except for a few backward ones, would require systematic instruction after the age of seven, and therefore the implication was that top infants would achieve a specific standard irrespective of length of infant schooling or social background.

6 Bacchus (1967) reported that the male teachers in secondary modern schools with unfavourable views of their pupils tended to be 'more dissatisfied with what they got out of the job in terms of status, salary, opportunities for promotion, etc.'. It should be noted that in the present study with *infant* teachers, the association between teachers' attitudes to pupils and homes and their satisfaction with their status in the community, did not reach a statistically significant relationship. Generally, these infant teachers seemed to be relatively uninterested in opportunities for promotion. Only in regard to the *heads* was it found that those dissatisfied with their status appeared to be less optimistic about the school's power to change pupils' values (5 per cent level of significance).

7 These findings, that infant teachers' attitudes to pupils' home background are significantly associated with the personality dimension of authoritarianism, agree with those of Bacchus (1967) in relation to male teachers in the secondary modern schools.

8 Professor Kenneth B. Clark used this phrase in *Education in Depressed Areas* (1963) when describing the crucial role of the school in determining the level of scholastic achievement. He argues that standards and quality of education need not be lowered by the limitations set by home conditions; far more significant were the *general attitudes of teachers toward their pupils and the manner in which these were communicated*. Too many teachers, Clark suggested, maintain 'the pervasive and archaic belief that children from culturally deprived backgrounds are by virtue of their deprivation or *lower status position* inherently ineducable'. He proposes that schools 'break through the barrier of IQ depression', since many ideas about the absolute nature of intelligence are more relevant to assumptions about class than about education.

9 Josephine Klein (1967) has outlined some of the differences which distinguish the traditional 'roughs' in the working class from the 'respectable' working-class family. Presumably most teachers with a working-class origin would tend to come from the latter type of home. In this connection, Klein makes an interesting point when she describes how the 'respectable' family takes pains to achieve standards of domestic behaviour and social interaction which will distinguish them from the 'roughs' amongst whom they live. However, the children in these families are brought up with the knowledge that the 'roughs' are 'different' from them in only style of life – but not in economic circumstances – and that a period of illness or unemployment or some other misfortune may be sufficient to push a whole family below the poverty line.

References

Bacchus, M. K. (1967). Some factors influencing the views of secondary modern school teachers on their pupils' interests and abilities, *Educ. Res.* 9 (2), 147–50.

Clark, K. B. (1963). Educational stimulation of racially disadvantaged children. In A. H. Passow (ed.), *Education in Depressed Areas*. New York: Bureau of Publications, Teachers College, Columbia University.

Department of Education and Science: Central Advisory Council for Education (England) (1967). The 1964 National Survey: survey among parents of primary school children by Roma Morton-William, The Government Social Survey, Appendix 3 in *Children and their Primary Schools*. London: H.M. Stationery Office.

Douglas, J. W. B. (1964). *The Home and the School*. London: MacGibbon & Kee.

Klein, J. (1967). The parents of school children. In M. Croft *et al.* (eds), *Linking Home and School*. London: Longmans.

3 Sociological implications of the thought of George Herbert Mead

Herbert Blumer

My purpose is to depict the nature of human society when seen from the point of view of George Herbert Mead. While Mead gave human society a position of paramount importance in his scheme of thought he did little to outline its character. His central concern was with cardinal problems of philosophy. The development of his ideas of human society was largely limited to handling these problems. His treatment took the form of showing that human group life was the essential condition for the emergence of consciousness, the mind, a world of objects, human beings as organisms possessing selves, and human conduct in the form of constructed acts. He reversed the traditional assumptions underlying philosophical, psychological, and sociological thought to the effect that human beings possess minds and consciousness as original 'givens', that they live in worlds of pre-existing and self-constituted objects, that their behavior consists of responses to such objects, and that group life consists of the association of such reacting human organisms. In making his brilliant contributions along this line he did not map out a theoretical scheme of human society. However, such a scheme is implicit in his work. It has to be constructed by tracing the implications of the central matters which he analysed. This is what I propose to do. The central matters I shall consider, are (1) the self, (2) the act, (3) social interaction, (4) objects, and (5) joint action.

The self

Mead's picture of the human being as an actor differs radically from the conception of man that dominates current psychological and social science. He saw the human being as an organism having a self. The possession of a self converts the human being into a special kind of actor, transforms his relation to the world, and gives his action a unique character.

Source: *American Journal of Sociology* (1965–6), **71**, 535–44.

In asserting that the human being has a self, Mead simply meant that the human being is an object to himself. The human being may perceive himself, have conceptions of himself, communicate with himself, and act toward himself. As these types of behavior imply, the human being may become the object of his own action. This gives him the means of interacting with himself—addressing himself, responding to the address, and addressing himself anew. Such self-interaction takes the form of making indications to himself and meeting these indications by making further indications. The human being can designate things to himself—his wants, his pains, his goals, objects around him, the presence of others, their actions, their expected actions, or whatnot. Through further interaction with himself, he may judge, analyse, and evaluate the things he has designated to himself. And by continuing to interact with himself he may plan and organize his action with regard to what he has designated and evaluated. In short, the possession of a self provides the human being with a mechanism of self-interaction with which to meet the world—a mechanism that is used in forming and guiding his conduct.

I wish to stress that Mead saw the self as a process and not as a structure. Here Mead clearly parts company with the great bulk of students who seek to bring a self into the human being by identifying it with some kind of organization or structure. All of us are familiar with this practice because it is all around us in the literature. Thus, we see scholars who identify the self with the 'ego', or who regard the self as an organized body of needs or motives, or who think of it as an organization of attitudes, or who treat it as a structure of internalized norms and values. Such schemes which seek to lodge the self in a structure make no sense since they miss the reflexive process which alone can yield and constitute a self. For any posited structure to be a self, it would have to act upon and respond to itself—otherwise, it is merely an organization awaiting activation and release without exercising any effect on itself or on its operation. This marks the crucial weakness or inadequacy of the many schemes such as referred to above, which misguidingly associate the self with some kind of psychological or personality structure. For example, the ego, as such, is not a self; it would be a self only by becoming reflexive, that is to say, acting toward or on itself. And the same thing is true of any other posited psychological structure. Yet, such reflexive action changes both the status and the character of the structure and elevates the process of self-interaction to the position of major importance.

We can see this in the case of the reflexive process that Mead has isolated in the human being. As mentioned, this reflexive process takes the form of the person making indications to himself, that is to say, noting things and determining their significance for his line of action. To indicate something is to stand over against it and to put oneself in the position of acting toward it instead of automatically responding to it. In the face of something which one indicates, one can withhold action toward it, inspect it, judge it, ascertain its meaning, determine its possibilities, and direct one's action with regard to it. With the mechanism of self-interaction the human being ceases to be a responding organism whose behavior is a product of what plays upon him from the outside, the inside, or both. Instead, he acts toward his world, interpreting what confronts him and organizing his action on the basis of the interpretation. To illustrate: a pain one identifies and interprets is very different from a mere organic feeling and lays the basis for doing something about it instead of merely responding organically to it; to note and interpret the activity of another person is very different from having a response released by that activity; to be aware that one is hungry is very different from merely being hungry; to perceive one's 'ego' puts one in the position of doing something with regard to it instead of merely giving expression to the ego. As the illustrations show, the process of self-interaction puts the human being over against his world instead of merely in it, requires him to meet and handle his world through a defining process instead of merely responding to it, and forces him to construct his action instead of merely releasing it. This is the kind of acting organism that Mead sees man to be as a result of having a self.[1]

The act

Human action acquires a radically different character as a result of being formed through a process of self-interaction. Action is built up in coping with the world instead of merely being released from a pre-existing psychological structure by factors playing on that structure. By making indications to himself and by interpreting what he indicates, the human being has to forge or piece together a line of action. In order to act the individual has to identify what he wants, establish

an objective or goal, map out a prospective line of behavior, note and interpret the actions of others, size up his situation, check himself at this or that point, figure out what to do at other points, and frequently spur himself on in the face of dragging dispositions or discouraging settings. The fact that the human act is self-directed or built up means in no sense that the actor necessarily exercises excellence in its construction. Indeed, he may do a very poor job in constructing his act. He may fail to note things of which he should be aware, he may misinterpret things that he notes, he may exercise poor judgment, he may be faulty in mapping out prospective lines of conduct, and he may be half-hearted in contending with recalcitrant dispositions. Such deficiencies in the construction of his acts do not belie the fact that his acts are still constructed by him out of what he takes into account. What he takes into account are the things that he indicates to himself. They cover such matters as his wants, his feelings, his goals, the actions of others, the expectations and demands of others, the rules of his group, his situation, his conceptions of himself, his recollections, and his images of prospective lines of conduct. He is not in the mere recipient position of responding to such matters; he stands over against them and has to handle them. He has to organize or cut out his lines of conduct on the basis of how he does handle them.

This way of viewing human action is directly opposite to that which dominates psychological and social sciences. In these sciences human action is seen as a product of factors that play upon or through the human actor. Depending on the preference of the scholar, such determining factors may be physiological stimulations, organic drives, needs, feelings, unconscious motives, conscious motives, sentiments, ideas, attitudes, norms, values, role requirements, status demands, cultural prescriptions, institutional pressures, or social-system requirements. Regardless of which factors are chosen, either singly or in combination, action is regarded as their product and hence is explained in their terms. The formula is simple: Given factors play on the human being to produce given types of behavior. The formula is frequently amplified so as to read: Under specified conditions, given factors playing on a given organization of the human being will produce a given type of behavior. The formula, in either its simple or amplified form, represents the way in which human action is seen in theory and research. Under the formula the human being becomes a mere medium or forum for the operation of the factors that produce the behavior. Mead's scheme is fundamentally different from this formula. In place of being a mere medium for operation of determining factors that play upon him, the human being is seen as an active organism in his own right, facing, dealing with, and acting toward the objects he indicates. Action is seen as conduct which is constructed by the actor instead of response elicited from some kind of preformed organization in him. We can say that the traditional formula of human action fails to recognize that the human being is a self. Mead's scheme, in contrast, is based on this recognition.

Social interaction

I can give here only a very brief sketch of Mead's highly illuminating analysis of social interaction. He identified two forms or levels—non-symbolic interaction and symbolic interaction. In non-symbolic interaction human beings respond directly to one another's gestures or actions; in symbolic interaction they interpret each other's gestures and act on the basis of the meaning yielded by the interpretation. An unwitting response to the tone of another's voice illustrates non-symbolic interaction. Interpreting the shaking of a fist as signifying that a person is preparing to attack illustrates symbolic interaction. Mead's concern was predominantly with symbolic interaction. Symbolic interaction involves *interpretation*, or ascertaining the meaning of the actions or remarks of the other person, and *definition*, or conveying indications to another person as to how he is to act. Human association consists of a process of such interpretation and definition. Through this process the participants fit their own acts to the ongoing acts of one another and guide others in doing so.

Several important matters need to be noted in the case of symbolic interaction. First, it is a formative process in its own right. The prevailing practice of psychology and sociology is to treat social interaction as a neutral medium, as a mere forum for the operation of outside factors. Thus psychologists are led to account for the behavior of people in interaction by resorting to elements of the psychological equipment of the participants—such elements as motives, feelings, attitudes, or personality organization. Sociologists do the same sort of thing by resorting to societal factors, such as cultural prescriptions, values, social roles, or structural pressures. Both miss the central point that human interaction is a positive shaping process in its own right. The participants in it have to build up their respective lines of conduct by constant interpretation of each other's ongoing lines of action. As participants take account of each other's ongoing acts, they have to arrest, reorganize, or adjust their own intentions, wishes, feelings, and attitudes; similarly, they have to judge the fitness of norms, values, and group prescriptions for the situation being formed by the acts of others. Factors of psychological equipment and social organization are not substitutes for the interpretative process; they are admissible only in terms of how they are handled in the interpretative process. Symbolic interaction has to be seen and studied in its own right.

Symbolic interaction is noteworthy in a second way. Because of it human group life takes on the character of an ongoing process—a continuing matter of fitting developing lines of conduct to one another. The fitting together of the lines of conduct is done through the dual process of definition and interpretation. This dual process operates both to sustain established patterns of joint conduct and to open them to transformation. Established patterns of group life exist and persist only through the continued use of the same schemes of interpretation; and such schemes of interpretation are maintained only through their continued confirmation by the defining acts of others. It is highly important to recognize that the established patterns of group life just do not carry on by themselves but are dependent for their continuity on recurrent affirmative definition. Let the interpretations that sustain them be undermined or disrupted by changed definitions from others and the patterns can quickly collapse. This dependency of interpretations on the defining acts of others also explains why symbolic interaction conduces so markedly to the transformation of the forms of joint activity that make up group life. In the flow of group life there are innumerable points at which the participants are *re*defining each other's acts. Such redefinition is very common in adversary relations, it is frequent in group discussion, and it is essentially intrinsic to dealing with problems. (And I may remark here that no human group is free of problems.) Redefinition imparts a formative character to human interaction, giving rise at this or that point to new objects, new conceptions, new relations, and new types of behavior. In short, the reliance on symbolic interaction makes human group life a developing process instead of a mere issue or product of psychological or social structure.

There is a third aspect of symbolic interaction which is important to note. In making the process ȷo interpretation and definition of one another's acts central in human interaction, symbolic interaction is able to cover the full range of the generic forms ȷo human association. It embraces equally well such relationships as co-operation, conflict, domination, exploitation, consensus, disagreement, closely knit identification, and indifferent concern for one another. The participants in each of such relations have the same common task of constructing their acts by interpreting and defining the acts of each other. The significance of this simple observation becomes evident in contrasting symbolic interaction with the various schemes of human interaction that are to be found in the literature. Almost always such schemes construct a general model of human interaction or society on the basis of a particular type of human relationship. An outstanding contemporary instance is Talcott Parsons's scheme which presumes and asserts that the primordial and generic form of human interaction is the 'complementarity of expectations'. Other schemes depict the basic and generic model of human interaction as being 'conflict', others assert it to be 'identity through common sentiments', and still others that it is agreement in the form of 'consensus'. Such schemes are parochial. Their great danger lies in imposing on the breadth of human interaction an image derived from the study of only one form of interaction. Thus, in different hands, human society is said to be fundamentally a sharing of common values; or, conversely, a struggle for power; or, still differently, the exercise of consensus; and so on. The simple point implicit in Mead's analysis of symbolic interaction is that human beings, in interpreting and defining one another's acts, can and do meet each other in the full range of human relations. Proposed schemes of human society should respect this simple point.

Objects

The concept of object is another fundamental pillar in Mead's scheme of analysis. Human beings live in a world or environment of objects, and their activities are formed around objects. This bland statement becomes very significant when it is realized that for Mead objects are human constructs and not self-existing entities with intrinsic natures. Their nature is dependent on the orientation and action of people toward them. Let me spell this out. For Mead, an object is anything that can be designated or referred to. It may be physical as a chair or imaginary as a ghost, natural as a cloud in the sky or man-made as an automobile, material as the Empire State Building or abstract as the concept of liberty, animate as an elephant or inanimate as a vein of coal, inclusive of a class of people as politicians or restricted to a specific person as President de Gaulle, definite as a multiplication table or vague as a philosophical doctrine. In short, objects consist of whatever people indicate or refer to.

There are several important points in this analysis of objects. First, the nature of an object is constituted by the meaning it has for the person or persons for whom it is an object. Second, this meaning is not intrinsic to the object but arises from how the person is initially prepared to act toward it. Readiness to use a chair as something in which to sit gives it the meaning of a chair; to one with no experience with the use of chairs the object would appear with a different meaning, such as a strange weapon. It follows that objects vary in their meaning. A tree is not the same object to a lumberman, a botanist, or a poet; a star is a different object to a modern astronomer than it was to a sheepherder of antiquity; communism is a different object to a Soviet patriot than it is to a Wall Street broker. Third, objects—all objects—are social products in that they are formed and transformed by the defining process that takes place in social interaction. The meaning of the objects —chairs, trees, stars, prostitutes, saints, communism, public education, or whatnot—is formed from the ways in which others refer to such objects or act toward them. Fourth, people are prepared or set to act toward objects on the basis of the meaning of the objects for them. In a genuine sense the organization

of a human being consists of his objects, that is, his tendencies to act on the basis of their meanings. Fifth, just because an object is something that is designated, one can organize one's action toward it instead of responding immediately to it; one can inspect the object, think about it, work out a plan of action toward it, or decide whether or not to act toward it. In standing over against the object in both a logical and psychological sense, one is freed from coercive response to it. In this profound sense an object is different from a stimulus as ordinarily conceived.

This analysis of objects puts human group life into a new and interesting perspective. Human beings are seen as living in a world of meaningful objects—not in an environment of stimuli or self-constituted entities. This world is socially produced in that the meanings are fabricated through the process of social interaction. Thus, different groups come to develop different worlds—and these worlds change as the objects that compose them change in meaning. Since people are set to act in terms of the meanings of their objects, the world of objects of a group represents in a genuine sense its action organization. To identify and understand the life of a group it is necessary to identify its world of objects: this identification has to be in terms of the meanings objects have for the members of the group. Finally, people are not locked to their objects; they may check action toward objects and indeed work out new lines of conduct toward them. This condition introduces into human group life an indigenous source of transformation.

Joint action

I use the term 'joint action' in place of Mead's term 'social act'. It refers to the larger collective form of action that is constituted by the fitting together of the lines of behavior of the separate participants. Illustrations of joint action are a trading transaction, a family dinner, a marriage ceremony, a shopping expedition, a game, a convivial party, a debate, a court trial, or a war. We note in each instance an identifiable and distinctive form of joint action, comprised by an articulation of the acts of the participants. Joint actions range from a simple collaboration of two individuals to a complex alignment of the acts of huge organizations or institutions. Everywhere we look in a human society we see people engaging in forms of joint action. Indeed, the totality of such instances—in all of their multitudinous variety, their variable connections, and their complex networks—constitutes the life of a society. It is easy to understand from these remarks why Mead saw joint action, or the social act, as the distinguishing characteristic of society. For him, the social act was the fundamental unit of society. Its analysis, accordingly, lays bare the generic nature of society.

To begin with, a joint action cannot be resolved into

a common or same type of behavior on the part of the participants. Each participant necessarily occupies a different position, acts from that position, and engages in a separate and distinctive act. It is the fitting together of these acts and not their commonality that constitutes joint action. How do these separate acts come to fit together in the case of human society? Their alignment does not occur through sheer mechanical juggling, as in the shaking of walnuts in a jar or through unwitting adaptation, as in an ecological arrangement in a plant community. Instead, the participants fit their acts together, first, by identifying the social act in which they are about to engage and, second, by interpreting and defining each other's acts in forming the joint act. By identifying the social act or joint action the participant is able to orient himself; he has a key to interpreting the acts of others and a guide for directing his action with regard to them. Thus, to act appropriately, the participant has to identify a marriage ceremony as a marriage ceremony, a holdup as a holdup, a debate as a debate, a war as a war, and so forth. But, even though this identification be made, the participants in the joint action that is being formed still find it necessary to interpret and define one another's ongoing acts. They have to ascertain what the others are doing and plan to do and make indications to one another of what to do.

This brief analysis of joint action enables us to note several matters of distinct importance. It calls attention, first, to the fact that the essence of society lies in an ongoing process of action—not in a posited structure of relations. Without action, any structure of relations between people is meaningless. To be understood, a society must be seen and grasped in terms of the action that comprises it. Next, such action has to be seen and treated not by tracing the separate lines of action of the participants—whether the participants be single individuals, collectivities, or organizations—but in terms of the joint action into which the separate lines of action fit and merge. Few students of human society have fully grasped this point or its implications. Third, just because it is built up over time by the fitting together of acts, each joint action must be seen as having a career or a history. In having a career, its course and fate are contingent on what happens during its formation. Fourth, this career is generally orderly, fixed and repetitive by virtue of a common identification or definition of the joint action that is made by its participants. The common definition supplies each participant with decisive guidance in directing his own act so as to fit into the acts of the others. Such common definitions serve, above everything else, to account for the regularity, stability, and repetitiveness of joint action in vast areas of group life; they are the source of the established and regulated social behavior that is envisioned in the concept of culture. Fifth, however, the career of joint actions also must be seen as open to many possibilities of uncertainty. Let me specify the more

important of these possibilities. One, joint actions have to be initiated—and they may not be. Two, once started a joint action may be interrupted, abandoned, or transformed. Three, the participants may not make a common definition of the joint action into which they are thrown and hence may orient their acts on different premises. Four, a common definition of a joint action may still allow wide differences in the direction of the separate lines of action and hence in the course taken by the joint action; a war is a good example. Five, new situations may arise calling for hitherto unexisting types of joint action, leading to confused exploratory efforts to work out a fitting together of acts. And, six, even in the context of a commonly defined joint action, participants may be led to rely on other considerations in interpreting and defining each other's lines of action. Time does not allow me to spell out and illustrate the importance of these possibilities. To mention them should be sufficient, however, to show that uncertainty, contingency, and transformation are part and parcel of the process of joint action. To assume that the diversified joint actions which comprise a human society are set to follow fixed and established channels is a sheer gratuitous assumption.

From the foregoing discussion of the self, the act, social interaction, objects, and joint action we can sketch a picture of human society. The picture is composed in terms of action. A society is seen as people meeting the varieties of situations that are thrust on them by their conditions of life. These situations are met by working out joint actions in which participants have to align their acts to one another. Each participant does so by interpreting the acts of others and, in turn, by making indications to others as to how they should act. By virtue of this process of interpretation and definition joint actions are built up; they have careers. Usually, the course of a joint action is outlined in advance by the fact that the participants make a common identification of it; this makes for regularity, stability, and repetitiveness in the joint action. However, there are many joint actions that encounter obstructions, that have no pre-established pathways, and that have to be constructed along new lines. Mead saw human society in this way—as a diversified social process in which people were engaged in forming joint actions to deal with situations confronting them.

This picture of society stands in significant contrast to the dominant views of society in the social and psychological sciences—even to those that pretend to view society as action. To point out the major differences in the contrast is the best way of specifying the sociological implications of Mead's scheme of thought.

The chief difference is that the dominant views in sociology and psychology fail, alike, to see human beings as organisms having selves. Instead, they regard human beings as merely responding organisms and, accordingly, treat action as mere response to factors playing on human beings. This is exemplified in the efforts to account for human behavior by such factors as motives, ego demands, attitudes, role requirements, values, status expectations, and structural stresses. In such approaches the human being becomes a mere medium through which such initiating factors operate to produce given actions. From Mead's point of view such a conception grossly misrepresents the nature of human beings and human action. Mead's scheme interposes a process of self-interaction between initiating factors and the action that may follow in their wake. By virtue of self-interaction the human being becomes an acting organism coping with situations in place of being an organism merely responding to the play of factors. And his action becomes something he constructs and directs to meet the situations in place of an unrolling of reactions evoked from him. In introducing the self, Mead's position focuses on how human beings handle and fashion their world, not on disparate responses to imputed factors.

If human beings are, indeed, organisms with selves, and if their action is, indeed, an outcome of a process of self-interaction, schemes that purport to study and explain social action should respect and accommodate these features. To do so, current schemes in sociology and psychology would have to undergo radical revision. They would have to shift from a preoccupation with initiating factor and terminal result to a preoccupation with a process of formation. They would have to view action as something constructed by the actor instead of something evoked from him. They would have to depict the milieu of action in terms of how the milieu appears to the actor in place of how it appears to the outside student. They would have to incorporate the interpretive process which at present they scarcely deign to touch. They would have to recognize that any given act has a career in which it is constructed but in which it may be interrupted, held in abeyance, abandoned, or recast.

On the methodological or research side the study of action would have to be made from the position of the actor. Since action is forged by the actor out of what he perceives, interprets, and judges, one would have to see the operating situation as the actor sees it, perceive objects as the actor perceives them, ascertain their meaning in terms of the meaning they have for the actor, and follow the actor's line of conduct as the actor organizes it—in short, one would have to take the role of the actor and see his world from his standpoint. This methodological approach stands in contrast to the so-called objective approach so dominant today, namely, that of viewing the actor and his action from the perspective of an outside, detached observer. The 'objective' approach holds the danger of the observer substituting his view of the field of action for the view held by the actor. It is unnecessary to add that the actor acts toward his world on the basis of how he sees it and not on the basis of how that world appears to the outside observer.

In continuing the discussion of this matter, I wish to consider especially what we might term the struc-

tural conception of human society. This conception views society as established organization, familiar to us in the use of such terms as social structure, social system, status position, social role, social stratification, institutional structure, cultural pattern, social codes, social norms, and social values. The conception presumes that a human society is structured with regard to (*a*) the social positions occupied by the people in it and with regard to (*b*) the patterns of behavior in which they engage. It is presumed further that this interlinked structure of social positions and behavior patterns is the over-all determinant of social action; this is evidenced, of course, in the practice of explaining conduct by such structural concepts as role requirements, status demands, strata differences, cultural prescriptions, values, and norms. Social action falls into two general categories: conformity, marked by adherence to the structure, and deviance, marked by departure from it. Because of the central and determinative position into which it is elevated, structure becomes necessarily the encompassing object of sociological study and analysis—epitomized by the well-nigh universal assertion that a human group or society is a 'social system'. It is perhaps unnecessary to observe that the conception of human society as structure or organization is ingrained in the very marrow of contemporary sociology.

Mead's scheme definitely challenges this conception. It sees human society not as an established structure but as people meeting their conditions of life; it sees social action not as an emanation of societal structure but as a formation made by human actors; it sees this formation of action not as societal factors coming to expression through the medium of human organisms but as constructions made by actors out of what they take into account; it sees group life not as a release or expression of established structure but as a process of building up joint actions; it sees social actions as having variable careers and not as confined to the alternatives of conformity to or deviation from the dictates of established structure; it sees the so-called interaction between parts of a society not as a direct exercising of influence by one part on another but as mediated throughout by interpretations made by people; accordingly, it sees society not as a system, whether in the form of a static, moving or whatever kind of equilibrium, but as a vast number of occurring joint actions, many closely linked, many not linked at all, many prefigured and repetitious, others being carved out in new directions, and all being pursued to serve the purposes of the participants and not the requirements of a system. I have said enough, I think, to point out the drastic differences between the Meadian conception of society and the widespread sociological conceptions of it as structure.

The differences do not mean, incidentally, that Mead's view rejects the existence of structure in human society. Such a position would be ridiculous. There are such matters as social roles, status positions, rank orders, bureaucratic organizations, relations between institutions, differential authority arrangements, social codes, norms, values, and the like. And they are very important. But their importance does not lie in an alleged determination of action nor in an alleged existence as parts of a self-operating societal system. Instead, they are important only as they enter into the process of interpretation and definition out of which joint actions are formed. The manner and extent to which they enter may vary greatly from situation to situation, depending on what people take into account and how they assess what they take account of. Let me give one brief illustration. It is ridiculous, for instance, to assert, as a number of eminent sociologists have done, that social interaction is an interaction between social roles. Social interaction is obviously an interaction between *people* and not between roles; the needs of the participants are to interpret and handle what confronts them—such as a topic of conversation or a problem—and not to give expression to their roles. It is only in highly ritualistic relations that the direction and content of conduct can be explained by roles. Usually, the direction and content are fashioned out of what people in interaction have to deal with. That roles affect in varying degree phases of the direction and content of action is true but is a matter of determination in given cases. This is a far cry from asserting action to be a product of roles. The observation I have made in this brief discussion of social roles applies with equal validity to all other structural matters.

Another significant implication of Mead's scheme of thought refers to the question of what holds a human society together. As we know, this question is converted by sociologists into a problem of unity, stability, and orderliness. And, as we know further, the typical answer given by sociologists is that unity, stability, and orderliness come from a sharing in common of certain basic matters, such as codes, sentiments, and, above all, values. Thus, the disposition is to regard common values as the glue that holds a society together, as the controlling regulator that brings and keeps the activities in a society in orderly relationship, and as the force that preserves stability in a society. Conversely, it is held that conflict between values or the disintegration of values creates disunity, disorder, and instability. This conception of human society becomes subject to great modification if we think of society as consisting of the fitting together of acts to form joint action. Such alignment

may take place for any number of reasons, depending on the situations calling for joint action, and need not involve, or spring from, the sharing of common values. The participants may fit their acts to one another in orderly joint actions on the basis of compromise, out of duress, because they may use one another in achieving their respective ends, because it is the sensible thing to do, or out of sheer necessity. This is particularly likely to be true in our modern complex societies with their great diversity in composition, in lines of interest, and in their respective worlds of concern. In very large measure, society becomes the formation of workable relations. To seek to encompass, analyse, and understand the life of a society on the assumption that the existence of a society necessarily depends on the sharing of values can lead to strained treatment, gross misrepresentation, and faulty lines of interpretation. I believe that the Meadian perspective, in posing the question of how people are led to align their acts in different situations in place of presuming that this necessarily requires and stems from a sharing of common values, is a more salutary and realistic approach.

There are many other significant sociological implications in Mead's scheme of thought which, under the limit of space, I can do no more than mention. Socialization shifts its character from being an effective internalization of norms and values to a cultivated capacity to take the roles of others effectively. Social control becomes fundamentally and necessarily a matter of self-control. Social change becomes a continuous indigenous process in human group life instead of an episodic result of extraneous factors playing on established structure. Human group life is seen as always incomplete and undergoing development instead of jumping from one completed state to another. Social disorganization is seen not as a breakdown of existing structure but as an inability to mobilize action effectively in the face of a given situation. Social action, since it has a career, is recognized as having a historical dimension which has to be taken into account in order to be adequately understood.

In closing I wish to say that my presentation has necessarily skipped much in Mead's scheme that is of great significance. Further, I have not sought to demonstrate the validity of his analyses. However, I have tried to suggest the freshness, the fecundity, and the revolutionary implications of his point of view.

Note

1 The self, or indeed human being, is not brought into the picture merely by introducing psychological elements, such as motives and interests, alongside of societal elements. Such additions merely compound the error of the omission. This is the flaw in George Homan's presidential address, 'Bringing Man Back in' (*American Journal of Sociology* (1966), **29** (6), 809–18).

4   Marriage and the construction of reality: an exercise in the microsociology of knowledge

Peter L. Berger and Hansfried Kellner

Ever since Durkheim it has been a commonplace of family sociology that marriage serves as a protection against anomie for the individual. Interesting and pragmatically useful though this insight is, it is but the negative side of a phenomenon of much broader significance. If one speaks of *anomic* states, then one ought properly to investigate also the *nomic* processes that, by their absence, lead to the afore-mentioned states. If, consequently, one finds a negative correlation between marriage and anomie, then one should be led to inquire into the character of marriage as a *nomos*-building instrumentality, that is, of marriage as a social arrangement that creates for the individual the sort of order in which he can experience his life as making sense. It is our intention here to discuss marriage in these terms. While this could evidently be done in a macrosociological per-spective, dealing with marriage as a major social institution related to other broad structures of society, our focus will be microsociological, dealing primarily with the social processes affecting the individuals in any specific marriage, although, of course, the larger framework of these processes will have to be under-stood. In what sense this discussion can be described as microsociology of knowledge will hopefully become clearer in the course of it.[1]

Marriage is obviously only *one* social relationship in which this process of *nomos*-building takes place. It is, therefore, necessary to first look in more general terms at the character of this process. In doing so, we are influenced by three theoretical perspectives—the Weberian perspective on society as a network of meanings, the Meadian perspective on indentity as a social phenomenon, and the phenomenological analysis of the social structuring of reality especially as given in the work of Schutz and Merleau-Ponty.[2] Not being convinced, however, that theoretical lucidity is necessarily enhanced by terminological ponderosity, we shall avoid as much as possible the use of the sort

Source: *Diogenes* (1964), **46** (1), 1–23.

of jargon for which both sociologists and phenomen-ologists have acquired dubious notoriety.

The process that interests us here is the one that constructs, maintains and modifies a consistent reality that can be meaningfully experienced by individuals. In its essential forms this process is determined by the society in which it occurs. Every society has its specific way of defining and perceiving reality—its world, its universe, its overarching organization of symbols. This is already given in the language that forms the symbolic base of the society. Erected over this base, and by means of it, is a system of ready-made typifications, through which the innumerable experiences of reality come to be ordered.[3] These typifications and their order are held in common by the members of society, thus acquiring not only the character of objectivity, but being taken for granted as *the* world *tout court*, the only world that normal men can conceive of.[4] The seemingly objective and taken-for-granted character of the social definitions of reality can be seen most clearly in the case of language itself, but it is important to keep in mind that the latter forms the base and instrumentality of a much larger world-erecting process.

The socially constructed world must be continually mediated to and actualized by the individual, so that it can become and remain indeed *his* world as well. The individual is given by his society certain decisive cornerstones for his everyday experience and conduct. Most importantly, the individual is supplied with specific sets of typifications and criteria of relevance, predefined for him by the society and made available to him for the ordering of his everyday life. This ordering or (in line with our opening considerations) nomic apparatus is biographically cumulative. It begins to be formed in the individual from the earliest stages of socialization on, then keeps on being en-larged and modified by himself throughout his bio-graphy.[5] While there are individual biographical differences making for differences in the constitution of this apparatus in specific individuals, there exists in the society an overall consensus on the range of differences deemed to be tolerable. Without such consensus, indeed, society would be impossible as a going concern, since it would then lack the ordering principles by which alone experience can be shared and conduct can be mutually intelligible. This order, by which the individual comes to perceive and define his world, is thus not chosen by him, except perhaps for very small modifications. Rather, it is discovered by him as an external datum, a ready-made world that simply is *there* for him to go ahead and live in, though he modifies it continually in the process of living in it. Nevertheless, this world is in need of validation, perhaps precisely because of an ever-present glimmer of suspicion as to its social manufacture and relativity. This validation, while it must be undertaken by the individual himself, requires ongoing interaction with others who co-inhabit this same socially constructed world. In a broad sense, *all* the other co-inhabitants of this world serve a validating function. Every morning the newspaper boy validates the widest co-ordinates of my world and the mailman bears tangible validation of my own location within these co-ordinates. However, some validations are more significant than others. Every individual requires the ongoing validation of his world, including crucially the validation of his identity and place in this world, by those few who are his truly significant others.[6] Just as the individual's deprivation of relationship with his significant others will plunge him into anomie, so their continued presence will sustain for him that *nomos* by which he can feel at home in the world at least most of the time. Again in a broad sense, all the actions of the significant others and even their simple presence serve this sustaining function. In everyday life, however, the principal method employed is speech. In this sense, it is proper to view the individual's relationship with his significant others as an ongoing conversation. As the latter occurs, it validates over and over again the fundamental definitions of reality once entered into, not, of course, so much by explicit articulation, but precisely by taking the definitions silently for granted and conversing about all conceivable matters on this taken-for-granted basis. Through the same conversation the individual is also made capable of adjusting to changing and new social contexts in his biography. In a very fundamental sense it can be said that one converses one's way through life.

If one concedes these points, one can now state a general sociological proposition: the plausibility and stability of the world, as socially defined, is dependent upon the strength and continuity of significant relationships in which conversation about this world can be continually carried on. Or, to put it a little differently: the reality of the world is sustained through conversation with significant others. This reality, of course, includes not only the imagery by which fellowmen are viewed, but also includes the way in which one views oneself. The reality-bestowing force of social relationships depends on the degree of their nearness,[7] that is, on the degree to which social relationships occur in face-to-face situations and to which they are credited with primary significance by the individual. In any empirical situation, there now emerge obvious sociological questions out of these considerations, namely, questions about the patterns of the world-building relationships, the social forms taken by the conversation with significant others. Sociologically, one must ask how these relationships are *objectively* structured and distributed, and one will also want to understand how they are *subjectively* perceived and experienced.

With these preliminary assumptions stated we can now arrive at our main thesis here. Namely, we would contend that marriage occupies a privileged status among the significant validating relationships for adults in our society. Put slightly differently: marriage is a crucial nomic instrumentality in our society. We would further argue that the essential social functionality of this institution cannot be fully understood if this fact is not perceived.

We can now proceed with an ideal-typical analysis of marriage, that is, seek to abstract the essential features involved. Marriage in our society is a *dramatic* act in which two strangers come together and redefine themselves. The drama of the act is internally anticipated and socially legitimated long before it takes place in the individual's biography, and amplified by means of a pervasive ideology, the dominant themes of which (romantic love, sexual fulfilment, self-discovery and self-realization through love and sexuality, the nuclear family as the social site for these processes) can be found distributed through all strata of the society. The actualization of these ideologically pre-defined expectations in the life of the individual occurs to the accompaniment of one of the few traditional rites of passage that are still meaningful to almost all members of the society. It should be added that, in using the term 'strangers', we do not mean, of course, that the candidates for the marriage come from widely discrepant social backgrounds—indeed, the data indicate that the contrary is the case. The strangeness rather lies in the fact that, unlike marriage candidates in many previous societies, those in ours typically come from different face-to-face contexts—in the terms used above, they come from different areas of conversation. They do not have a shared past, although their pasts have a similar structure. In other words, quite apart from prevailing patterns of ethnic, religious and class endogamy, our society is typically exogamous in terms of nomic relationships. Put concretely, in our mobile society the significant conversation of the two partners previous to the marriage took place in social circles that did not overlap. With the dramatic re-definition of the situation brought about by the marriage, however, all significant conversation for the two new partners is now centered in their relationship with each other—

and, in fact, it was precisely with this intention that they entered upon their relationship.

It goes without saying that this character of marriage has its root in much broader structural configurations of our society. The most important of these, for our purposes, is the crystallization of a so-called private sphere of existence, more and more segregated from the immediate controls of the public institutions (especially the economic and political ones), and yet defined and utilized as the main social area for the individual's self-realization.[8] It cannot be our purpose here to inquire into the historical forces that brought forth this phenomenon, beyond making the observation that these are closely connected with the industrial revolution and its institutional consequences. The public institutions now confront the individual as an immensely powerful and alien world, incomprehensible in its inner workings, anonymous in its human character. If only through his work in some nook of the economic machinery, the individual must find a way of living in this alien world, come to terms with its power over him, be satisfied with a few conceptual rules of thumb to guide him through a vast reality that otherwise remains opaque to his understanding, and modify its anonymity by whatever *human relations* he can work out in his involvement with it. It ought to be emphasized, against some critics of 'mass society', that this does not inevitably leave the individual with a sense of profound unhappiness and lostness. It would rather seem that large numbers of people in our society are quite content with a situation in which their public involvements have little subjective importance, regarding work as a not too bad necessity and politics as at best a spectator sport. It is usually only intellectuals with ethical and political commitments who assume that such people must be terribly desperate. The point, however, is that the individual in this situation, no matter whether he is happy or not, will turn elsewhere for the experiences of self-realization that do have importance for him. The private sphere, this interstitial area created (we would think) more or less haphazardly as a by-product of the social metamorphosis of industrialism, is mainly where he will turn. It is here that the individual will seek power, intelligibility and, quite literally, a name—the apparent power to fashion a world, however Lilliputian, that will reflect his own being: a world that, seemingly having been shaped by himself and thus unlike those other worlds that insist on shaping him, is translucently intelligible to him (or so he thinks); a world in which, consequently, he is *somebody*—perhaps even, within its charmed circle, a lord and master. What is more, to a considerable extent these expectations are not unrealistic. The public institutions have no need to control the individual's adventures in the private sphere, as long as they really stay within the latter's circumscribed limits. The private sphere is perceived, not without justification, as an area of individual choice and even autonomy. This fact has important consequences for the shaping of identity in modern society that cannot be pursued here. All that ought to be clear here is the peculiar location of the private sphere within and between the other social structures. In sum, it is above all and, as a rule, only in the private sphere that the individual can take a slice of reality and fashion it into his world. If one is aware of the decisive significance of this capacity and even necessity of men to externalize themselves in reality and to produce for themselves a world in which they can feel at home, then one will hardly be surprised at the great importance which the private sphere has come to have in modern society.[9]

The private sphere includes a variety of social relationships. Among these, however, the relationships of the family occupy a central position and, in fact, serve as a focus for most of the other relationships (such as those with friends, neighbors, fellow-members of religious and other voluntary associations). Since, as the ethnologists keep reminding us, the family in our society is of the conjugal type, the central relationship in this whole area is the marital one. It is on the basis of marriage that, for most adults in our society, existence in the private sphere is built up. It will be clear that this is not at all a universal or even cross culturally wide function of marriage. Rather has marriage in our society taken on a very peculiar character and functionality. It has been pointed out that marriage in contemporary society has lost some of its older functions and taken on new ones instead.[10] This is certainly correct, but we would prefer to state the matter a little differently. Marriage and the family used to be firmly embedded in a matrix of wider community relationships, serving as extensions and particularizations of the latter's social controls. There were few separating barriers between the world of the individual family and the wider community, a fact even to be seen in the physical conditions under which the family lived before the industrial revolution.[11] The same social life pulsated through the house, the street and the community. In our terms, the family and within it the marital relationship were part and parcel of a considerably larger area of conversation. In our contemporary society, by contrast, each family constitutes its own segregated sub-world, with its own controls and its own closed conversation.

This fact requires a much greater effort on the part of the marriage partners. Unlike an earlier situation in which the establishment of the new marriage simply added to the differentiation and complexity of an already existing social world, the marriage partners now are embarked on the often difficult task of constructing for themselves the little world in which they will live. To be sure, the larger society provides them with certain standard instructions as to how they should go about this task, but this does not change the fact that considerable effort of their own is required for its realization. The monogamous character of marriage enforces both the dramatic and the precarious nature of this undertaking. Success or failure hinges on the present idiosyncrasies and the fairly unpredictable future development of these idiosyncrasies of only two individuals (who, moreover, do not have a shared past)—as Simmel has shown, the most unstable of all possible social relationships.[12] Not surprisingly, the decision to embark on this undertaking has a critical, even cataclysmic connotation in the popular imagination, which is underlined as well as psychologically assuaged by the ceremonialism that surrounds the event.

Every social relationship requires objectivation, that is, requires a process by which subjectively experienced meanings become objective to the individual and, in interaction with others, become common property and thereby massively objective.[13] The degree of objectivation will depend on the number and the intensity of the social relationships that are its carriers. A relationship that consists of only two individuals called upon to sustain, by their own efforts, an ongoing social world will have to make up in intensity for the numerical poverty of the arrangement. This, in turn, accentuates the drama and the precariousness. The later addition of children will add to the, as it were, density of objectivation taking place within the nuclear family, thus rendering the latter a good deal less precarious. It remains true that the establishment and maintenance of such a social world make extremely high demands on the principal participants.

The attempt can now be made to outline the ideal-typical process that takes place as marriage functions as an instrumentality for the social construction of reality. The chief protagonists of the drama are two individuals, each with a biographically accumulated and available stock of experience.[14] As members of a highly mobile society, these individuals have already internalized a degree of readiness to re-define themselves and to modify their stock of experience, thus bringing with them considerable psychological capacity for entering new relationships with others.[15] Also, coming from broadly similar sectors of the larger society (in terms of region, class, ethnic and religious affiliations), the two individuals will have organized their stock of experience in similar fashion. In other words, the two individuals have internalized the same overall world, including the general definitions and expectations of the marriage relationship itself. Their society has provided them with a taken-for-granted image of marriage and has socialized them into an anticipation of stepping into the taken-for-granted roles of marriage. All the same, these relatively empty projections now have to be actualized, lived through and filled with experiential content by the protagonists. This will require a dramatic change in their definitions of reality and of themselves.

As of the marriage, most of each partner's actions must now be projected in conjunction with those of the other. Each partner's definitions of reality must be continually correlated with the definitions of the other. The other is present in nearly all horizons of everyday conduct. Furthermore, the identity of each now takes on a new character, having to be constantly matched with that of the other, indeed being typically perceived by people at large as being symbiotically conjoined with the identity of the other. In each partner's psychological economy of significant others, the marriage partner becomes the other *par excellence*, the nearest and most decisive co-inhabitant of the world. Indeed, all other significant relationships have to be almost automatically re-perceived and re-grouped in accordance with this drastic shift.

In other words, from the beginning of the marriage each partner has new modes in his meaningful experience of the world in general, of other people and of himself. By definition, then, marriage constitutes a nomic rupture. In terms of each partner's biography, the event of marriage initiates a new nomic process. Now, the full implications of this fact are rarely apprehended by the protagonists with any degree of clarity. There rather is to be found the notion that one's world, one's other-relationships and, above all, oneself have remained what they were before—only, of course, that world, others and self will now be shared with the marriage partner. It should be clear by now that this notion is a grave misapprehension. Just because of this fact, marriage now propels the individual into an unintended and unarticulated development, in the course of which the nomic transformation takes place. What typically *is* apprehended are certain objective and concrete problems arising out of the marriage—such as tensions with in-laws, or with former friends, or religious differences between the partners, as well as immediate tensions between them. These are apprehended as external, situational and practical difficulties. What is *not* apprehended is the subjective side of these difficulties, namely, the transformation of *nomos* and identity that has occurred and that continues to go on, so that all problems and relationships are experienced in a quite new way, that is, experienced within a new and ever-changing reality.

Take a simple and frequent illustration—the male partner's relationships with male friends before and after the marriage. It is a common observation that such relationships, especially if the extra-marital partners are single, rarely survive the marriage, or, if they do, are drastically re-defined after it. This is typically the result of neither a deliberate decision by the husband nor deliberate sabotage by the wife. What rather happens, very simply, is a slow process in which the husband's image of his friend is transformed as he keeps talking about this friend with his wife. Even if no actual talking goes on, the mere presence of the wife forces him to see his friend differently. This need not mean that he adopts a negative image held by the wife. Regardless of what image she holds or is believed by him to hold, it will be different from that held by the husband. This difference will enter into the joint image that now must needs be fabricated in the course of the ongoing conversation between the marriage partners—and, in due course, must act powerfully on the image previously held by the husband. Again, typically, this process is rarely apprehended with any degree of lucidity. The old friend is more likely to fade out of the picture by slow degrees, as new kinds of friends take his place. The process, if commented upon at all within the marital conversation, can always be explained by socially available formulas about 'people changing', 'friends disappearing' or oneself 'having become more mature'. This process of conversational liquidation is especially powerful because it is onesided—the husband typically talks with his wife about his friend, but *not* with his friend about his wife. Thus the friend is deprived of the defense of, as it were, counter-defining the relationship. This dominance of the marital conversation over all others, is one of its most important characteristics. It may be mitigated by a certain amount of protective segregation of some non-marital relationships (say, 'Tuesday night out with the boys', or 'Saturday lunch with mother'), but even then there are powerful emotional barriers against the sort of conversation (conversation *about* the marital relationship, that is) that would serve by way of counter-definition.

Marriage thus posits a new reality. The individual's relationship with this new reality, however, is a dialectical one—he acts upon it, in collusion with the marriage partner, and it acts back upon both him and the partner, welding together their reality. Since, as we have argued before, the objectivation that constitutes this reality is precarious, the groups with which the couple associates are called upon to assist in co-defining the new reality. The couple is pushed towards groups that strengthen their new definition of themselves and the world, avoids those that weaken this definition. This in turn releases the commonly known pressures of group association, again acting upon the marriage partners to change their definitions of the world and of themselves. Thus the new reality is not posited once and for all, but goes on being re-defined not only in the marital interaction itself but also in the various maritally based group relationships into which the couple enters.

In the individual's biography marriage, then, brings about a decisive phase of socialization that can be compared with the phases of childhood and adolescence. This phase has a rather different structure from the earlier ones. There the individual was in the main socialized into already existing patterns. Here he actively collaborates rather than passively accommodates himself. Also, in the previous phases of socialization, there was an apprehension of entering into a new world and being changed in the course of this. In marriage there is little apprehension of such a process, but rather the notion that the world has remained the same, with only its emotional and pragmatic connotations having changed. This notion, as we have tried to show, is illusionary.

The re-construction of the world in marriage occurs principally in the course of conversation, as we have suggested. The implicit problem of this conversation is how to match two individual definitions of reality. By the very logic of the relationship, a common overall definition must be arrived at—otherwise the conversation will become impossible and, *ipso facto*, the relationship will be endangered. Now, this conversation may be understood as the working away of an ordering and typifying apparatus—if one prefers, an objectivating apparatus. Each partner ongoingly contributes his conceptions of reality, which are then 'talked through', usually not once but many times, and in the process become objectivated by the conversational apparatus. The longer this conversation goes on, the more massively real do the objectivations become to the partners. In the marital conversation a world is not only built, but it is also kept in a state of repair and ongoingly refurnished. The subjective reality of this world for the two partners is sustained by the same conversation. The nomic instrumentality of marriage is concretized over and over again, from bed to breakfast table, as the partners carry on the endless conversation that feeds on nearly all they individually or jointly experience. Indeed, it may happen eventually that no experience is fully real unless and until it has been thus 'talked through'.

This process has a very important result—namely, a hardening or stabilization of the common objectivated reality. It should be easy to see now how this comes about. The objectivations ongoingly performed and internalized by the marriage partners become ever more massively real, as they are confirmed and reconfirmed in the marital conversation. The world that is made up of these objectivations at the same time gains in stability. For example, the images of other people, which before or in the earlier stages of the marital conversation may have been rather ambiguous and shifting in the minds of the two partners, now become hardened into definite and stable characterizations. A casual acquaintance, say, may sometimes have appeared as lots of fun and sometimes as quite a bore to the wife before her marriage. Under the influence of the marital conversation, in which this other person is frequently 'discussed', she will now come down more firmly on one *or* the other of the two characterizations, or on a reasonable compromise between the two. In any of these three options, though, she will have concocted with her husband a much more stable image of the person in question than she is likely to have had before her marriage, when there may have been no conversational pressure to make a definite option at all. The same process of stabilization may be observed with regard to self-definitions as well. In this way, the wife in our example will not only be pressured to assign stable characterizations to others but also to herself. Previously uninterested politically, she now identifies herself as a liberal. Previously alternating between dimly articulated religious positions, she now declares herself an agnostic. Previously confused and uncertain about her sexual emotions, she now understands herself as an unabashed hedonist in this area. And so on and so forth, with the same reality—and identity—stabilizing process at work on the husband. Both world and self thus take on a firmer, more reliable character for both partners.

Furthermore, it is not only the ongoing experience of the two partners that is constantly shared and passed through the conversational apparatus. The same sharing extends into the past. The two distinct biographies, as subjectively apprehended by the two individuals who have lived through them, are over-ruled and re-interpreted in the course of their conver-sation. Sooner or later, they will 'tell all'—or, more correctly, they will tell it in such a way that it fits into the self-definitions objectivated in the marital relation-ship. The couple thus construct not only present reality but reconstruct past reality as well, fabricating a common memory that integrates the recollections of the two individual pasts.[16] The comic fulfilment of this process may be seen in those cases when one partner 'remembers' more clearly what happened in the other's past than the other does—and corrects him accordingly. Similarly, there occurs a sharing of future horizons, which leads not only to stabiliz-ation, but inevitably to a narrowing of the future projections of each partner. Before marriage the individual typically plays with quite discrepant day-dreams in which his future self is projected.[17] Having now considerably stabilized his self-image, the married individual will have to project the future in accordance with this maritally defined identity. This narrowing of future horizons begins with the obvious external limitations that marriage entails, as, for example, with regard to vocational and career plans. However, it extends also to the more general possibilities of the individual's biography. To return to a previous illustration, the wife, having 'found herself' as a liberal, an agnostic and a 'sexually healthy' person, *ipso facto* liquidates the possibilities of becoming an anarchist, a Catholic or a Lesbian. At least until further notice she has decided upon who she is—and, by the same token, upon who she will be. The stabiliz-ation brought about by marriage thus affects the total reality in which the partners exist. In the most far-reaching sense of the word, the married individual 'settles down'—and *must* do so, if the marriage is to be viable, in accordance with its contemporary in-stitutional definition.

It cannot be sufficiently strongly emphasized that this process is typically unapprehended, almost auto-matic in character. The protagonists of the marriage drama do *not* set out deliberately to re-create their world. Each continues to live in a world that is taken for granted—and keeps its taken-for-granted character even as it is metamorphosed. The new world that the married partners, Prometheus-like, have called into being is perceived by them as the normal world in which they have lived before. Re-constructed present and re-interpreted past are perceived as a continuum, extending forwards into a commonly projected future. The dramatic change that has occurred remains, in bulk, unapprehended and unarticulated. And where it

forces itself upon the individual's attention, it is retrojected into the past, explained as having always been there, though perhaps in a hidden way. Typically, the reality that has been 'invented' within the marital conversation is subjectively perceived as a 'discovery'. Thus the partners 'discover' themselves and the world, 'who they really are', 'what they really believe', 'how they really feel, and always have felt, about so-and-so'. This retrojection of the world being produced all the time by themselves serves to enhance the stability of this world and at the same time to assuage the 'ex-istential anxiety' that, probably inevitably, ac-companies the perception that nothing but one's own narrow shoulders supports the universe in which one has chosen to live. If one may put it like this, it is psychologically more tolerable to be Columbus than to be Prometheus.

The use of the term 'stabilization' should not detract from the insight into the difficulty and precariousness of this world-building enterprise. Often enough, the new universe collapses *in statu nascendi*. Many more times it continues over a period, swaying perilously back and forth as the two partners try to hold it up, finally to be abandoned as an impossible undertaking. If one conceives of the marital conversation as the principal drama and the two partners as the principal protagonists of the drama, then one can look upon the other individuals involved as the supporting chorus for the central dramatic action. Children, friends, relatives and casual acquaintances all have their part in reinforcing the tenuous structure of the new reality. It goes without saying that the children form the most important part of this supporting chorus. Their very existence is predicated on the maritally established world. The marital partners themselves are in charge of their socialization *into* this world, which to them has a pre-existent and self-evident character. They are taught from the beginning to speak precisely those lines that lend themselves to a supporting chorus, from their first invocations of 'Daddy' and 'Mummy' on to their adoption of the parents' ordering and typifying apparatus that now defines *their* world as well. The marital conversation is now in the process of becoming a family symposium, with the necessary consequence that its objectivations rapidly gain in density, plausi-bility and durability.

In sum: the process that we have been inquiring into is, ideal-typically, one in which reality is crystal-lized, narrowed and stabilized. Ambivalences are converted into certainties. Typifications of self and of others become settled. Most generally, possibilities become facticities. What is more, this process of transformation remains, most of the time, unappre-hended by those who are both its authors and its objects.[18]

We have analyzed in some detail the process that, we contend, entitles us to describe marriage as a nomic instrumentality. It may now be well to turn back once more to the macrosocial context in which this process takes place—a process that, to repeat, is peculiar to our society as far as the institution of marriage is concerned, although it obviously expresses much more general human facts. The narrowing and stabilization of identity is functional in a society that, in its major public institutions, must insist on rigid controls over the individual's conduct. At the same time, the narrow enclave of the nuclear family serves as a macrosocially innocuous 'play area', in which the individual can safely exercise his world-building proclivities without upsetting any of the important social, economic and political applecarts. Barred from expanding himself into the area occupied by these major institutions, he is given plenty of leeway to 'discover himself' in his marriage and his family, and, in view of the difficulty of this under-taking, is provided with a number of auxiliary agencies that stand ready to assist him (such as counseling, psychotherapeutic and religious agencies). The marital adventure can be relied upon to absorb a large amount of energy that might otherwise be expended more dangerously. The ideological themes of familism, romantic love, sexual expression, maturity and social adjustment, with the pervasive psychologistic anthro-pology that underlies them all, function to legitimate this enterprise. Also, the narrowing and stabilization of the individual's principal area of conversation within the nuclear family is functional in a society that requires high degrees of both geographical and social mobility. The segregated little world of the family can be easily detached from one milieu and transposed into another without appreciably interfering with the central processes going on in it. Needless to say, we are not suggesting that these functions are deliberately planned or even apprehended by some mythical ruling directorate of the society. Like most social phenomena, whether they be macro- or microscopic, these functions are typically unintended and unarticu-lated. What is more, the functionality would be im-paired if it were too widely apprehended.

We believe that the above theoretical considerations serve to give a new perspective on various empirical facts studied by family sociologists. As we have em-phasized a number of times, our considerations are ideal-typical in intention. We have been interested in marriage at a normal age in urban, middle-class, western societies. We cannot discuss here such special problems as marriages or remarriages at a more advanced age, marriage in the remaining rural sub-cultures, or in ethnic or lower-class minority groups. We feel quite justified in this limitation of scope, however, by the empirical findings that tend towards the view that a global marriage type is emerging in the central strata of modern industrial societies.[19] This type, commonly referred to as the nuclear family, has been analyzed in terms of a shift from the so-called family of orientation to the so-called family of procreation as the most important reference for the individual.[20] In addition to the well-known socio-economic reasons for this shift, most of them rooted

in the development of industrialism, we would argue that important macrosocial functions pertain to the nomic process within the nuclear family, as we have analyzed it. This functionality of the nuclear family must, furthermore, be seen in conjunction with the familistic ideology that both reflects and reinforces it. A few specific empirical points may suffice to indicate the applicability of our theoretical perspective. To make these we shall use selected American data.

The trend towards marriage at an earlier age has been noted.[21] This has been correctly related to such factors as urban freedom, sexual emancipation and equalitarian values. We would add the important fact that a child raised in the circumscribed world of the nuclear family is stamped by it in terms of his psychological needs and social expectations. Having to live in the larger society from which the nuclear family is segregated, the adolescent soon feels the need for a 'little world' of his own, having been social-ized in such a way that only by having such a world to withdraw into can he successfully cope with the anony-mous 'big world' that confronts him as soon as he steps outside his parental home. In other words, to be 'at home' in society entails, *per definitionem*, the construction of a maritally based sub-world. The parental home itself facilitates such an early jump into marriage precisely because its controls are very narrow in scope and leave the adolescent to his own nomic devices at an early age. As has been studied in con-siderable detail, the adolescent peer group functions as a transitional *nomos* between the two family worlds in the individual's biography.[22]

The equalization in the age of the marriage partners has also been noted.[23] This is certainly also to be related to equalitarian values and, concomitantly, to the decline in the 'double standard' of sexual morality. Also, however, this fact is very conducive to the common reality-constructing enterprise that we have analyzed. One of the features of the latter, as we have pointed out, is the re-construction of the two biographies in terms of a cohesive and mutually correlated common memory. This task is evidently facilitated if the two partners are of roughly equal age. Another empirical finding to which our consider-ations are relevant is the choice of marriage partners within similar socio-economic backgrounds.[24] Apart from the obvious practical pressures towards such limitations of choice, the latter also ensure sufficient similarity in the biographically accumulated stocks of experience to facilitate the described reality-constructing process. This would also offer additional explanation to the observed tendency to narrow the limitations of marital choice even further, for example in terms of religious background.[25]

There now exists a considerable body of data on the adoption and mutual adjustment of marital roles.[26] Nothing in our considerations detracts from the analyses made of these data by sociologists interested primarily in the processes of group interaction. We would only argue that something more fundamental is involved in this role-taking—namely, the individual's relationship to reality as such. Each role in the marital situation carries with it a universe of discourse, broadly given by cultural definition, but continually re-actualized in the ongoing conversation between the marriage partners. Put simply: marriage involves not only stepping into new roles, but, beyond this, stepping into a new world. The *mutuality* of adjustment may again be related to the rise of marital equalitarianism, in which comparable effort is demanded of both partners.

Most directly related to our considerations are data that pertain to the greater stability of married as against unmarried individuals.[27] Though frequently presented in misleading psychological terms (such as 'greater emotional stability', 'greater maturity', and so on), these data are sufficiently validated to be used not only by marriage counselors but in the risk calculations of insurance companies. We would contend that our theoretical perspective places these data into a much more intelligible sociological frame of reference, which also happens to be free of the particular value bias with which the psychological terms are loaded. It is, of course, quite true that married people are more stable emotionally (i.e. operating within a more controlled scope of emotional expression), more mature in their views (i.e. inhabiting a firmer and narrower world in conformity with the expectations of society), and more sure of themselves (i.e. having objectivated a more stable and fixated self-definition). *Therefore* they are more liable to be psychologically balanced (i.e. having sealed off much of their 'anxiety', and reduced ambivalence as well as openness towards new possibilities of self-definition) and socially predictable (i.e. keeping their conduct well within the socially established safety rules). All of these phenomena are concomitants of the overall fact of having 'settled down'—cognitively, emotionally, in terms of self-identification. To speak of these phenomena as indicators of 'mental health', let alone of 'adjustment to reality', overlooks the decisive fact that reality is socially constructed and that psychological conditions of all sorts are grounded in a social matrix.

We would say, very simply, that the married individual comes to live in a more stable world, from which fact certain psychological consequences can be readily deduced. To bestow some sort of higher ontological status upon these psychological consequences is *ipso facto* a symptom of the mis- or non-apprehension of the social process that has produced them. Furthermore, the compulsion to legitimate the stabilized marital world, be it in psychologistic or in traditional religious terms, is another expression of the precariousness of its construction.[28] This is not the place to pursue any further the ideological processes involved in this. Suffice it to say that contemporary psychology functions to sustain this precarious world by assigning to it the status of 'normalcy', a legitimating operation that increasingly links up with the older religious assignment of the status of 'sacredness'. Both legitimating agencies have established their own rites of passage, validating myths and rituals, and individualized repair services for crisis situations. Whether one legitimates one's maritally constructed reality in terms of 'mental health' or of the 'sacrament of marriage' is today largely left to free consumer preference, but it is indicative of the crystallization of a new overall universe of discourse that it is increasingly possible to do both at the same time.

Finally, we would point here to the empirical data on divorce.[29] The prevalence and, indeed, increasing prevalence of divorce might at first appear as a counter-argument to our theoretical considerations. We would contend that the very opposite is the case, as the data themselves bear out. Typically, individuals in our society do not divorce because marriage has become unimportant to them, but because it has become so important that they have no tolerance for the less than completely successful marital arrangement they have contracted with the particular individual in question. This is more fully understood when one has grasped the crucial need for the sort of world that only marriage can produce in our society, a world without which the individual is powerfully threatened with anomie in the fullest sense of the word. Also, the frequency of divorce simply reflects the difficulty and demanding character of the whole undertaking. The empirical fact that the great majority of divorced individuals plan to remarry and a good majority of them actually do, at least in America, fully bears out this contention.[30]

The purpose of this article is not polemic, nor do we wish to advocate any particular values concerning marriage. We have sought to debunk the familistic ideology only insofar as it serves to obfuscate a sociological understanding of the phenomenon. Our purpose has rather been twofold. First, we wanted to show that it is possible to develop a sociological theory of marriage that is based on clearly sociological presuppositions, without operating with psychological or psychiatric categories that have dubious value within a sociological frame of reference. We believe that such a sociological theory of marriage is generally useful for a fully conscious awareness of existence in contemporary society, and not only for the sociologist. Secondly, we have used the case of marriage for an exercise in the sociology of knowledge, a discipline that we regard as most promising. Hitherto this discipline has been almost exclusively concerned with macrosociological questions, such as those dealing with the relationship of intellectual history to social processes. We believe that the microsociological focus is equally important for this discipline. The sociology of knowledge must not only be concerned with the great universes of meaning that history offers up for our inspection, but with the many little workshops in which living individuals keep hammering away at the construction and maintenance of these universes. In this way, the sociologist can make an important contribution to the illumination of that everyday world in which we all live and which we help fashion in the course of our biography.

Notes

1 The present article has come out of a larger project on which the authors have been engaged in collaboration with three colleagues in sociology and philosophy. The project is to produce a systematic treatise that will integrate a number of now separate theoretical strands in the sociology of knowledge.

2 Cf. especially Max Weber, *Wirtschaft und Gesellschaft* (Tuebingen: Mohr 1956), and *Gesammelte Aufsaetze zur Wissenschaftslehre* (Tuebingen: Mohr 1951); George H. Mead, *Mind, Self and Society* (University of Chicago Press 1934); Alfred Schutz, *Der sinnhafte Aufbau der sozialen Welt* (Vienna: Springer, 2nd ed. 1960) and *Collected Papers*, I (The Hague: Nijhoff 1962); Maurice Merleau-Ponty, *Phénoménologie de la perception* (Paris: Gallimard, 1945) and *La structure du comportement* (Paris: Presses universitaires de France 1953).

3 Cf. Schutz, *Aufbau*, 202–20 and *Collected Papers*, I, 3–27, 283–6.

4 Cf. Schutz, *Collected Papers*, I, 207–28.

5 Cf. especially Jean Piaget, *The Child's Construction of Reality* (Routledge & Kegan Paul, 1955).

6 Cf. Mead, op. cit., 135–226.

7 Cf. Schutz, *Aufbau*, 181–95.

8 Cf. Arnold Gehlen, *Die Seele im technischen Zeitalter* (Hamburg: Rowohlt 1957), 57–69 and *Anthropologische Forschung* (Hamburg: Rowohlt 1961), 69–77, 127–40; Helmut Schelsky, *Soziologie der Sexualitaet* (Hamburg: Rowohlt 1955), 102–33. Also cf. Thomas Luckmann, On religion in modern society, *Journal for the Scientific Study of Religion* (Spring 1963), 147–62.

9 In these considerations we have been influenced by certain presuppositions of Marxian anthropology, as well as by the anthropological work of Max Scheler, Helmuth Plessner and Arnold Gehlen. We are indebted to Thomas Luckmann for the clarification of the social-psychological significance of the private sphere.

10 Cf. Talcott Parsons and Robert Bales, *Family: Socialization and Interaction Process* (Routledge & Kegan Paul 1956), 3–34, 353–96.

11 Cf. Philippe Ariès, *Centuries of Childhood* (New York: Knopf 1962), 339–410.

12 Cf. Georg Simmel (Kurt Wolff ed.), *The Sociology of Georg Simmel* (Collier-Macmillan 1950), 118–44.

13 Cf. Schutz, *Aufbau*, 29–36, 149–53.

14 Cf. Schutz, *Aufbau*, 186–92, 202–10.

15 David Riesman's well-known concept of 'other-direction' would also be applicable here.

16 Cf. Maurice Halbwachs, *Les Cadres sociaux de la mémoire* (Paris: Presses universitaires de France 1952), especially 146–77; also cf. Peter Berger, *Invitation to Sociology – A Humanistic Perspective* (Garden City, N.Y.: Doubleday-Anchor 1963), 54–65 (available in Penguin).

17 Cf. Schutz, *Collected Papers*, I, 72–3, 79–82.

18 The phenomena here discussed could also be formulated effectively in terms of the Marxian categories of reification and false consciousness. Jean-Paul Sartre's recent work, especially *Critique de la raison dialectique*, seeks to integrate these categories within a phenomeno-logical analysis of human conduct. Also cf. Henri Lefebvre, *Critique de la vie quotidienne* (Paris: l'Arche 1958–61).

19 Cf. Renate Mayntz, *Die moderne Familie* (Stuttgart: Enke 1955); Helmut Schelsky, *Wandlungen der deutschen Familie in der Gegenwart* (Stuttgart: Enke 1955); Maximilien Sorre (ed.), *Sociologie comparée de la famille contemporaine* (Paris: Centre National de la Recherche Scientifique 1955); Ruth Anshen (ed.), *The Family – Its Function and Destiny* (New York: Harper 1959); Norman Bell and Ezra Vogel, *A Modern Introduction to the Family* (Routledge & Kegan Paul 1961).

20 Cf. Talcott Parsons, *Essays in Sociological Theory* (Collier-Macmillan 1949), 233–50.

21 In these as well as the following references to empirical studies we naturally make no attempt at comprehensiveness. References are given as representative of a much larger body of materials. Cf. Paul Glick, *American Families* (New York: Wiley 1957), 54. Also cf. his The family cycle, *American Sociological Review* (April 1947), 164–74. Also cf. Bureau of the Census, *Statistical Abstracts of the United States* 1956 and 1958; *Current Population Reports*, Series P-20, no. 96 (Nov. 1959).

22 Cf. David Riesman, *The Lonely Crowd* (New Haven: Yale University Press 1953), 29–40; Frederick Elkin, *The Child and Society* (New York: Random House 1960), *passim*.

23 Cf. references given above under note 21.

24 Cf. W. Lloyd Warner and Paul Lunt, *The Social Life of a Modern Community* (New Haven: Yale University Press 1941), 436–40; August Hollingshead, Cultural factors in the selection of marriage mates, *American Sociological Review* (October 1950), 619–27. Also cf. Ernest Burgess and Paul Wallin, Homogamy in social characteristics, *American Journal of Sociology* (September 1943), 109–24.

25 Cf. Gerhard Lenski, *The Religious Factor* (Garden City, N.Y.: Doubleday 1961), 48–50.

26 Cf. Leonard Cottrell, Roles in marital adjustment, *Publications of the American Sociological Society* (1933), 27, 107–15; Willard Waller and Reuben Hill, *The Family – A Dynamic Interpretation* (New York: Dryden 1951), 253–71; Morris Zelditch, Role differentiation in the nuclear family, in Parsons and Bales, op. cit., 307–52. For a general discussion of role interaction in small groups, cf. especially George Homans, *The Human Group* (Routledge & Kegan Paul 1951).

27 Cf. Waller and Hill, op. cit., 253–71, for an excellent summation of such data.

28 Cf. Dennison Nash and Peter Berger, The family, the child and the religious revival in suburbia, *Journal for the Scientific Study of Religion* (Fall 1962), 85–93.

29 Cf. Bureau of the Census, op. cit.

30 Cf. Talcott Parsons, Age and Sex in the Social Structure of the United States, *American Sociological Review* (December 1942), 604–16; Paul Glick, First marriages and remarriages, *American Sociological Review* (December 1949), 726–34; William Goode, *After Divorce* (Chicago: Free Press 1956), 269–85.

5   The stranger: an essay in social psychology
A. Schutz

The present paper intends to study in terms of a general theory of interpretation the typical situation in which a stranger finds himself in his attempt to interpret the cultural pattern of a social group which he approaches and to orient himself within it. For our present purposes the term 'stranger' shall mean an adult individual of our times and civilization who tries to be permanently accepted or at least tolerated by the group which he approaches. The outstanding example for the social situation under scrutiny is that of the immigrant, and the following analyses are, as a matter of convenience, worked out with this instance in view. But by no means is their validity restricted to this special case. The applicant for membership in a closed club, the prospective bridegroom who wants to be admitted to the girl's family, the farmer's son who enters college, the city-dweller who settles in a rural environment, the 'selectee' who joins the army, the family of the war worker who moves into a boom town—all are strangers according to the definition just given, although in these cases the typical 'crisis' that the immigrant undergoes may assume milder forms or even be entirely absent. Intentionally excluded, however, from the present investigation are certain cases the inclusion of which would require some qualifications in our statements: (a) the visitor or guest who intends to establish a merely transitory contact with the group; (b) children or primitives; and (c) relationships between individuals and groups of different levels of civilization, as in the case of the Huron brought to Europe—a pattern dear to some moralists of the eighteenth century. Furthermore, it is not the purpose of this paper to deal with the processes of social assimilation and social adjustment which are treated in an abundant and, for the most part, excellent literature[1] but rather with the situation of approaching which precedes every possible social adjustment and which includes its prerequisites.

Source: *Studies in Social Theory*, ed. A. Brodersen (*Collected Papers*, 11), The Hague: Martinus Nijhoff (1964), 91–105.

As a convenient starting-point we shall investigate how the cultural pattern of group life presents itself to the common sense of a man who lives his everyday life within the group among his fellow-men. Following the customary terminology, we use the term 'cultural pattern of group life' for designating all the peculiar valuations, institutions, and systems of orientation and guidance (such as the folkways, mores, laws, habits, customs, etiquette, fashions) which, in the common opinion of sociologists of our time, characterize—if not constitute—any social group at a given moment in its history. This cultural pattern, like any phenomenon of the social world, has a different aspect for the sociologist and for the man who acts and thinks within it.[2] The sociologist (as sociologist, not as a man among fellow-men which he remains in his private life) is the disinterested scientific onlooker of the social world. He is disinterested in that he intentionally refrains from participating in the network of plans, means-and-ends relations, motives and chances, hopes and fears, which the actor within the social world uses for interpreting his experiences of it; as a scientist he tries to observe, describe and classify the social world as clearly as possible in well-ordered terms in accordance with the scientific ideals of coherence, consistency, and analytical consequence. The actor within the social world, however, experiences it primarily as a field of his actual and possible acts and only secondarily as an object of his thinking. In so far as he is interested in knowledge of his social world, he organizes this knowledge not in terms of a scientific system but in terms of relevance to his actions. He groups the world around himself (as the center) as a field of domination and is therefore especially interested in that segment which is within his actual or potential reach. He singles out those of its elements which may serve as means or ends for his 'use and enjoyment',[3] for furthering his purposes, and for overcoming obstacles. His interest in these elements is of different degrees, and for this reason he does not aspire to become acquainted with all of them with equal thoroughness. What he wants is *graduated knowledge* of relevant elements, the degree of desired knowledge being correlated with their relevance. Otherwise stated, the world seems to him at any given moment as stratified in different layers of relevance, each of them requiring a different degree of knowledge. To illustrate these strata of relevance we may—borrowing the term from cartography—speak of 'isohypses' or 'hypsographical contour lines of relevance', trying to suggest by this metaphor that we could show the distribution of the interests of an individual at a given moment with respect both to their intensity and to their scope by connecting elements of equal relevance to his acts, just as the cartographer connects points of equal height by contour lines in order to reproduce adequately the shape of a mountain. The graphical representation of these 'contour lines of relevance' would not show them as a single closed field but rather as numerous areas scattered over the map, each of different size and shape. Distinguishing with William James[4] two kinds of knowledge, namely, '*knowledge of acquaintance*' and '*knowledge about*', we may say that, within the field covered by the contour lines of relevance, there are centers of explicit knowledge *of* what is aimed at; they are surrounded by a halo of knowledge *about* what seems to be sufficient; next comes a region in which it will do merely 'to put one's trust'; the adjoining foothills are the home of unwarranted hopes and assumptions; between these areas, however, lie zones of complete ignorance.

We do not want to overcharge this image. Its chief purpose has been to illustrate that the knowledge of a man who acts and thinks within the world of his daily life is not homogenous; it is (1) incoherent, (2) only partially clear, and (3) not at all free from contradictions.

1 It is incoherent because the individual's interests which determine the relevance of the objects selected for further inquiry are themselves not integrated into a coherent system. They are only partially organized under plans of any kind, such as plans of life, plans of work and leisure, plans for every social role assumed. But the hierarchy of these plans changes with the situation and with the growth of the personality; interests are shifted continually and entail an uninterrupted transformation of the shape and density of the relevance lines. Not only the selection of the objects of curiosity but also the degree of knowledge aimed at changes.

2 Man in his daily life is only partially—and we dare say exceptionally—interested in the clarity of his knowledge, i.e. in full insight into the relations between the elements of his world and the general principles ruling those relations. He is satisfied that a well-functioning telephone service is available to him and, normally, does not ask how the apparatus functions in detail and what laws of physics make this functioning possible. He buys merchandise in the store, not knowing how it is produced, and pays with money, although he has only a vague idea of what money really is. He takes it for granted that his fellow-man will understand his thought if expressed in plain language and will answer accordingly, without wondering how this miraculous performance may be explained. Furthermore, he does not search for the truth and does not quest for certainty. All he wants is information on likelihood and insight into the chances or risks which the situation at hand entails for the outcome of his actions. That the subway will run tomorrow as usual is for him almost of the same order of likelihood as that the sun will rise. If by reason of a special interest he needs more explicit knowledge on a topic, a benign modern civilization holds ready for him a chain of information desks and reference libraries.

3 His knowledge, finally, is not consistent. At the same time he may consider statements as equally valid which in fact are incompatible with one another. As a father, a citizen, an employee and a member of his church he may have the most different and the least congruent opinions on moral, political, or economic matters. This inconsistency does not necessarily orginate in a logical fallacy. Men's thinking is distributed over subject matters located within different and differently relevant levels, and they are not aware of the modifications they would have to make in passing from one level to another. This and similar problems would have to be explored by a logic of everyday thinking, postulated but not attained by all the great logicians from Leibniz to Husserl and Dewey. Up to now the science of logic has primarily dealt with the logic of science.

The system of knowledge thus acquired—incoherent, inconsistent, and only partially clear, as it is—takes on for the members of the in-group the appearance of a *sufficient* coherence, clarity, and consistency to give anybody a reasonable chance of understanding and of being understood. Any member born or reared within the group accepts the ready-made standardized scheme of the cultural pattern handed down to him by ancestors, teachers, and authorities as an unquestioned and unquestionable guide in all the situations which normally occur within the social world. The knowledge correlated to the cultural pattern carries its evidence in itself—or, rather, it is taken for granted in the absence of evidence to the contrary. It is a knowledge of trustworthy *recipes* for interpreting the social world and for handling things and men in order to obtain the best results in every situation with a minimum of effort by avoiding undesirable consequences. The recipe works, on the one hand, as a precept for actions and thus serves as a scheme of expression: whoever wants to obtain a certain result has to proceed as indicated by the recipe provided for this purpose. On the other hand, the recipe serves as a scheme of interpretation: whoever proceeds as indicated by a specific recipe is supposed to intend the correlated results. Thus it is the function of the cultural pattern to eliminate troublesome inquiries by offering ready-made directions for use, to replace truth hard to attain by comfortable truisms, and to substitute the self-explanatory for the questionable.

This 'thinking as usual', as we may call it, corresponds to Max Scheler's idea of the 'relatively natural conception of the world' (*relativ natürliche Weltanschauung*);[5] it includes the 'of-course' assumptions relevant to a particular social group which Robert S. Lynd describes in such a masterly way—together with their inherent contradictions and ambivalence—as the 'Middletown-spirit'.[6] Thinking-as-usual may be maintained as long as some basic assumptions hold true, namely: (1) that life and especially social life will continue to be the same as it has been so far; that is to say, that the same problems requiring the same solutions will recur and that, therefore, our former experiences will suffice for mastering future situations; (2) that we may rely on the knowledge handed down to us by parents, teachers, governments, traditions, habits, etc., even if we do not understand its origin and its real meaning; (3) that in the ordinary course of affairs it is sufficient to know something *about* the general type or style of events we may encounter in our life-world in order to manage or control them; and (4) that neither the systems of recipes as schemes of interpretation and expression nor the underlying basic assumptions just mentioned are our private affair, but that they are likewise accepted and applied by our fellow-men.

If only one of these assumptions ceased to stand the test, thinking-as-usual becomes unworkable. Then a 'crisis' arises which, according to W. I. Thomas's famous definition, 'interrupts the flow of habit and gives rise to changed conditions of consciousness and practice'; or, as we may say, it overthrows precipitously the actual system of relevances. The cultural pattern no longer functions as a system of tested recipes at hand; it reveals that its applicability is restricted to a specific historical situation.

Yet the stranger, by reason of his personal crisis, does not share the above-mentioned basic assumptions. He becomes essentially the man who has to place in question nearly everything that seems to be unquestionable to the members of the approached group.

To him the cultural pattern of the approached group does not have the authority of a tested system of recipes, and this, if for no other reason, because he does not partake in the vivid historical tradition by which it has been formed. To be sure, from the stranger's point of view, too, the culture of the approached group has its peculiar history, and this history is even accessible to him. But it has never become an integral part of his biography, as did the history of his home group. Only the ways in which his fathers and grandfathers lived become for everyone elements of his own way of life. Graves and reminiscences can neither be transferred nor conquered. The stranger, therefore, approaches the other group

as a newcomer in the true meaning of the term. At best he may be willing and able to share the present and the future with the approached group in vivid and immediate experience; under all circumstances, however, he remains excluded from such experiences of its past. Seen from the point of view of the approached group, he is a man without a history.

To the stranger the cultural pattern of his home group continues to be the outcome of an unbroken historical development and an element of his personal biography, which for this very reason has been and still is the unquestioned scheme of reference for his 'relatively natural conception of the world'. As a matter of course, therefore, the stranger starts to interpret his new social environment in terms of his thinking as usual. Within the scheme of reference brought from his home group, however, he finds a ready-made idea of the pattern supposedly valid within the approached group—an idea which necessarily will soon prove inadequate.[7]

First, the idea of the cultural pattern of the approached group which the stranger finds within the interpretive scheme of his home group has originated in the attitude of a disinterested observer. The approaching stranger, however, is about to transform himself from an unconcerned onlooker into a would-be member of the approached group. The cultural pattern of the approached group, then, is no longer a subject matter of his thought but a segment of the world which has to be dominated by actions. Consequently, its position within the stranger's system of relevance changes decisively, and this means, as we have seen, that another type of knowledge is required for its interpretation. Jumping from the stalls to the stage, so to speak, the former onlooker becomes a member of the cast, enters as a partner into social relations with his co-actors, and participates henceforth in the action in progress.

Second, the new cultural pattern acquires an environmental character. Its remoteness changes into proximity; its vacant frames become occupied by vivid experiences; its anonymous contents turn into definite social situations; its ready-made typologies disintegrate. In other words, the level of environmental experience of social objects is incongruous with the level of mere beliefs about unapproached objects; by-passing from the latter to the former, any concept originating in the level of departure becomes necessarily inadequate if applied to the new level without having been restated in its terms.

Third, the ready-made picture of the foreign group subsisting within the stranger's home-group proves its inadequacy for the approaching stranger for the mere reason that it has not been formed with the aim of provoking a response or a reaction from the members of the foreign group. The knowledge which it offers serves merely as a handy scheme for interpreting the foreign group and not as a guide for interaction between the two groups. Its validity is primarily based on the consensus of those members of the home group who do not intend to establish a direct social relationship with members of the foreign group. (Those who intend to do so are in a situation analogous to that of the approaching stranger.) Consequently, the scheme of interpretation refers to the members of the foreign group merely as objects of this interpretation, but not beyond it, as addressees of possible acts emanating from the outcome of the interpretive procedure and not as subjects of anticipated reactions towards those acts. Hence, this kind of knowledge is, so to speak, insulated; it can be neither verified nor falsified by responses of the members of the foreign group. The latter, therefore, consider this knowledge—by a kind of 'looking-glass' effect[8]—as both irresponsive and irresponsible and complain of its prejudices, bias, and misunderstandings. The approaching stranger, however, becomes aware of the fact that an important element of his 'thinking as usual', namely, his ideas of the foreign group, its cultural pattern, and its way of life, do not stand the test of vivid experience and social interaction.

The discovery that things in his new surroundings look quite different from what he expected them to be at home is frequently the first shock to the stranger's confidence in the validity of his habitual 'thinking as usual'. Not only the picture which the stranger has brought along of the cultural pattern of the approached group but the whole hitherto unquestioned scheme of interpretation current within the home group becomes invalidated. It cannot be used as a scheme of orientation within the new social surroundings. For the members of the approached group *their* cultural pattern fulfills the functions of such a scheme. But the approaching stranger can neither use it simply as it is nor establish a general formula of transformation between both cultural patterns permitting him, so to speak, to convert all the co-ordinates within one scheme of orientation into those valid with the other—and this for the following reasons.

First, any scheme of orientation presupposes that everyone who uses it looks at the surrounding world as grouped around himself who stands at its center. He who wants to use a map successfully has first of all to know his standpoint in two respects: its location on the ground and its representation on the map. Applied to the social world this means that only members of the in-group, having a definite status in its hierarchy and also being aware of it, can use its cultural pattern as a natural and trustworthy scheme of orientation. The stranger, however, has to face the fact that he lacks any status as a member of the social group he is about to join and is therefore unable to get a starting-point to take his bearings. He finds himself a border case outside the territory covered by the scheme of orientation current within the group. He is, therefore, no longer permitted to consider himself as the center of his social environment, and this fact causes again a dislocation of his contour lines of relevance.

Second, the cultural pattern and its recipes represent only for the members of the in-group a unit of coinciding schemes of interpretation as well as of expression. For the outsider, however, this seeming unity falls to pieces. The approaching stranger has to 'translate' its terms into terms of the cultural pattern of his home group, provided that, within the latter, interpretive equivalents exist at all. If they exist, the translated terms may be understood and remembered; they can be recognized by recurrence; they are at hand but not in hand. Yet, even then, it is obvious that the stranger cannot assume that his interpretation of the new cultural pattern coincides with that current with the members of the in-group. On the contrary, he has to reckon with fundamental discrepancies in seeing things and handling situations.

Only after having thus collected a certain knowledge of the interpretive function of the new cultural pattern may the stranger start to adopt it as the scheme of his own expression. The difference between the two stages of knowledge is familiar to any student of a foreign language and has received the full attention of psychologists dealing with the theory of learning. It is the difference between the passive understanding of a language and its active mastering as a means for realizing one's own acts and thoughts. As a matter of convenience we want to keep to this example in order to make clear some of the limits set to the stranger's attempt at conquering the foreign pattern as a scheme of expression, bearing in mind, however, that the following remarks could easily be adapted with appropriate modifications to other categories of the cultural pattern such as mores, laws, folkways, fashions, etc.

Language as a scheme of interpretation and expression does not merely consist of the linguistic symbols catalogued in the dictionary and of the syntactical rules enumerated in an ideal grammar. The former are translatable into other languages; the latter are understandable by referring them to corresponding or deviating rules of the unquestioned mother-tongue.[9] However, several other factors supervene.

1 Every word and every sentence is, to borrow again a term of William James, surrounded by 'fringes' connecting them, on the one hand, with past and future elements of the universe of discourse to which they pertain and surrounding them, on the other hand, with a halo of emotional values and irrational implications which themselves remain ineffable. The fringes are the stuff poetry is made of; they are capable of being set to music but they are not translatable.

2 There are, in any language, terms with several connotations. They, too, are noted in the dictionary. But, besides these standardized connotations, every element of speech acquires its special secondary meaning derived from the context or the social environment within which it is used and, in addition, gets a special tinge from the actual occasion in which it is employed.

3 Idioms, technical terms, jargons and dialects, whose use remains restricted to specific social groups,

exist in every language, and their significance can be learned by an outsider too. But, in addition, every social group, be it ever so small (if not every individual), has its own private code, understandable only by those who have participated in the common past experiences in which it took rise or in the tradition connected with them.

4   As Vossler has shown, the whole history of the linguistic group is mirrored in its way of saying things.[10] All the other elements of group life enter into it—above all, its literature. The erudite stranger, for example, approaching an English-speaking country is heavily handicapped if he has not read the Bible and Shakespeare in the English language, even if he grew up with translations of those books in his mother-tongue.

All the above-mentioned features are accessible only to the members of the in-group. They all pertain to the scheme of expression. They are not teachable and cannot be learned in the same way as, for example, the vocabulary. In order to command a language freely as a scheme of expression, one must have written love letters in it; one has to know how to pray and curse in it and how to say things with every shade appropriate to the addressee and to the situation. Only members of the in-group have the scheme of expression as a genuine one in hand and command it freely within their thinking as usual.

Applying the result to the total of the cultural pattern of group life, we may say that the member of the in-group looks in a single glance through the normal social situations occurring to him and that he catches immediately the ready-made recipe appropriate to its solution. In those situations his acting shows all the marks of habituality, automatism and half-consciousness. This is possible because the cultural pattern provides by its recipes typical solutions for typical problems available for typical actors. In other words, the chance of obtaining the desired standardized result by applying a standardized recipe is an objective one; that is open to everyone who conducts himself like the anonymous type required by the recipe. Therefore, the actor who follows a recipe does not have to check whether this objective chance coincides with a subjective chance, that is, a chance open to him, the individual, by reason of his personal circumstances and faculties which subsists independently of the question whether other people in similar situations could or could not act in the same way with the same likelihood. Even more, it can be stated that the objective chances for the efficiency of a recipe are the greater, the fewer deviations from the anonymous typified behavior occur, and this holds especially for recipes designed for social interaction. This kind of recipe, if it is to work, presupposes that any partner expects the other to act or to react typically, provided that the actor himself acts typically. He who wants to travel by railroad has to behave in that typical way which the type 'railroad agent' may reasonably expect as the typical conduct of the type 'passenger', and

vice versa. Neither party examines the subjective chances involved. The scheme, being designed for everyone's use, need not be tested for its fitness for the peculiar individual who employs it.

For those who have grown up within the cultural pattern, not only the recipes and their possible efficiency but also the typical and anonymous attitudes required by them are an unquestioned 'matter of course' which gives them both security and assurance. In other words, these attitudes by their very anonymity and typicality are placed not within the actor's stratum of relevance which requires explicit knowledge *of* but in the region of mere acquaintance in which it will do to put one's trust. This interrelation between objective chance, typicality, anonymity and relevance seems to be rather important.[11]

For the approaching stranger, however, the pattern of the approached group does not guarantee an objective chance for success but rather a pure subjective likelihood which has to be checked step by step, that is, he has to make sure that the solutions suggested by the new scheme will also produce the desired effect for him in his special position as an outsider and newcomer who has not brought within his grasp the whole system of the cultural pattern but who is rather puzzled by its inconsistency, incoherence, and lack of clarity. He has, first of all, to use the term of W. I. Thomas, to *define* the situation. Therefore, he cannot stop at an approximate acquaintance with the new pattern, trusting in his vague knowledge *about* its general style and structure, but needs an explicit knowledge *of* its elements, inquiring not only into their *that* but into their *why*. Consequently, the shape of his contour lines of relevance by necessity differs radically from those of a member of the in-group as to situations, recipes, means, ends, social partners, etc. Keeping in mind the above-mentioned interrelationship between relevance, on the one hand, and typicality and anonymity, on the other, it follows that he uses another yardstick for anonymity and typicality of social acts than the members of the in-group. For to the stranger the observed actors within the approached group are not—as for their co-actors—of a certain presupposed anonymity, namely, mere performers of typical functions, but individuals. On the other hand, he is inclined to take mere individual traits as typical ones. Thus he constructs a social world of pseudo-anonymity, pseudo-intimacy and pseudo-typicality. Therefore, he cannot integrate the personal types constructed by him into a coherent picture of the approached group and cannot rely on his expectation of their response. And even less can the stranger himself adopt those typical and anonymous attitudes which a member of the in-group is entitled to expect from a partner in a typical situation. Hence the stranger's lack of feeling for distance, his oscillating between remoteness and intimacy, his hesitation and uncertainty, and his distrust in every matter which seems to be so simple and uncomplicated to those who rely on the efficiency of unquestioned recipes which have just to be followed but not understood.

In other words, the cultural pattern of the approached group is to the stranger not a shelter but a field of adventure, not a matter of course but a questionable topic of investigation, not an instrument for disentangling problematic situations but a problematic situation itself and one hard to master.

These facts explain two basic traits of the stranger's attitude toward the group to which nearly all sociological writers dealing with this topic have rendered special attention, namely (1) the stranger's objectivity and (2) his doubtful loyalty.

1 The stranger's objectivity cannot be sufficiently explained by his critical attitude. To be sure, he is not bound to worship the 'idols of the tribe' and has a vivid feeling for the incoherence and inconsistency of the approached cultural pattern. But this attitude originates far less in his propensity to judge the newly approached group by the standards brought from home than in his need to acquire full knowledge *of* the elements of the approached cultural pattern and to examine for this purpose with care and precision what seems self-explanatory to the in-group. The deeper reason for his objectivity, however, lies in his own bitter experience of the limits of the 'thinking as usual', which has taught him that a man may lose his status, his rules of guidance, and even his history and that the normal way of life is always far less guaranteed than it seems. Therefore, the stranger discerns, frequently with a grievous clear-sightedness, the rising of a crisis which may menace the whole foundation of the 'relatively natural conception of the world', while all those symptoms pass unnoticed by the members of the in-group, who rely on the continuance of their customary way of life.

2 The doubtful loyalty of the stranger is unfortunately very frequently more than a prejudice on the part of the approached group. This is especially true in cases in which the stranger proves unwilling or unable to substitute the new cultural pattern entirely for that of the home group. Then the stranger remains what Park and Stonequist have aptly called a 'marginal man', a cultural hybrid on the verge of two different patterns of group life, not knowing to which of them he belongs. But very frequently the reproach of doubtful loyalty originates in the astonishment of the members of the in-group that the stranger does not accept the total of its cultural pattern as the natural and appropriate way of life and as the best of all possible solutions of any problem. The stranger is called ungrateful, since he refuses to acknowledge that the cultural pattern offered to him grants him shelter and protection. But these people do not understand that the stranger in the state of transition does not consider this pattern as a protecting shelter at all but as a labyrinth in which he has lost all sense of his bearings.

As stated before, we have intentionally restricted our topic to the specific attitude of the approaching stranger which precedes any social adjustment and refrained from investigating the process of social assimilation itself. A single remark concerning the latter may be permitted. Strangeness and familiarity are not limited to the social field but are general categories of our interpretation of the world. If we encounter in our experience something previously unknown and which therefore stands out of the ordinary order of our knowledge, we begin a process of inquiry. We first define the new fact; we try to catch its meaning; we then transform step by step our general scheme of interpretation of the world in such a way that the strange fact and its meaning become compatible and consistent with all the other facts of our experience and their meanings. If we succeed in this endeavor, then that which formerly was a strange fact and a puzzling problem to our mind is transformed into an additional element of our warranted knowledge. We have enlarged and adjusted our stock of experiences.

What is commonly called the process of social adjustment which the newcomer has to undergo is but a special case of this general principle. The adaptation of the newcomer to the in-group which at first seemed to be strange and unfamiliar to him is a continuous process of inquiry into the cultural pattern of the approached group. If this process of inquiry succeeds, then this pattern and its elements will become to the newcomer a matter of course, an unquestionable way of life, a shelter, and a protection. But then the stranger is no stranger any more, and his specific problems have been solved.

Notes

1 Instead of mentioning individual outstanding contributions by American writers, such as W. G. Summer, W. I. Thomas, Floridan Znaniecki, R. E. Park, H. A. Miller, E. V. Stonequist, E. S. Bogardus, and Kimball Young, and by German authors, especially Georg Simmel and Robert Michels, we refer to the valuable monograph by Margaret Mary Wood, *The Stranger: A Study in Social Relationship*, New York 1934, and the bibliography quoted therein.

2 This insight seems to be the most important contribution of Max Weber's methodological writings to the problems of social science. Cf. the present writer's *Der sinnhafte Aufbau der sozialen Welt*, Vienna 1932 (2nd ed. 1960).

3 John Dewey, *Logic, the Theory of Inquiry*, Allen & Unwin 1938, ch. 4.

4 For the distinction of these two kinds of knowledge cf. William James, *Principles of Psychology*, Macmillan 1890, vol. I, 221–2.

5 Max Scheler, Probleme einer Soziologie des Wissens, *Die Wissensformen und die Gesellschaft*, Leipzig 1926, 58ff.; Howard Becker and Hellmuth Otto

Dahlke, Max Scheler's sociology of knowledge, *Philosophy and Phenomenological Research*, vol. II, 1942, 310–22, esp. 315.

6 Robert S. Lynd, *Middletown in Transition*, Constable 1937, ch. 12, and *Knowledge for What?* O.U.P. 1939, 58–63.

7 As one account showing how the American cultural pattern depicts itself as an 'unquestionable' element within the scheme of interpretation of European intellectuals we refer to Martin Gumpert's humorous description in his book, *First Papers*, New York 1941, 8–9. Cf. also books like Jules Romains, *Visite chez les Américains*, Paris 1930, and Jean Prévost Usonie, *Esquisse de la civilisation américaine*, Paris 1939, 245–66.

8 In using this term, we allude to Cooley's well-known theory of the reflected or looking-glass self (Charles H. Cooley, *Human Nature and the Social Order* (rev. ed., New York 1922), 184).

9 Therefore, the learning of a foreign language reveals to the student frequently for the first time the grammar rules of his mother-tongue which he has followed so far as 'the most natural thing in the world', namely, as recipes.

10 Karl Vossler, *Geist und Kultur in der Sprache*, Heidelberg 1925, 117ff.

11 It could be referred to a general principle of the theory of relevance, but this would surpass the frame of the present paper. The only point for which there is space to contend is that all the obstacles which the stranger meets in his attempt at interpreting the approached group arise from the incongruence of the contour lines of the mutual relevance systems and, consequently, from the distortion the stranger's system undergoes within the new surrounding. But any social relationship, and especially any establishment of new social contacts, even between individuals, involves analogous phenomena, although they do not necessarily lead to a crisis.

6 Delinquents in schools: a test for the legitimacy of authority[1]

Carl Werthman

In the recent sociology on juvenile delinquents, the school is characterized as the major instrument and arena of villainy. Cloward and Ohlin suggest that lower class delinquents suffer from unequal '*access* to educational facilities',[2] Cohen points to their '*failures* in the classroom',[3] and Miller and Kvaraceus argue that a '*conflict* of culture' between school administrators and lower-class students is precipitating delinquent behavior.[4] Although there are many differences between contemporary sociological portraits of the lower-class juvenile delinquent, the same model of his educational problem is used by all authors. Regardless of whether the delinquent is ambitious and capable,[5] ambitious and incapable,[6] or unambitious and incapable,[7] the school is sketched as a monolith of middle-class personnel against which he fares badly.

Yet data collected by observation and interviews over a two-year period on the educational performances and classroom experiences of lower-class gang members suggest that pitting middle-class schools against variations in the motivation and capacity of some lower-class boys is at best too simple and at worst incorrect as a model of the problems faced by the delinquents.

First, during middle adolescence when the law requires gang members to attend school, there seems to be no relationship between academic performance and 'trouble'. Gangs contain bright boys who do well, bright boys who do less well, dull boys who pass, dull boys who fail, and illiterates. To cite a single example, the grades of thirty 'core' members of a Negro gang, the Conquerors, were equally distributed in the sophomore and junior years of high school. Four of the gang members are illiterate (they cannot read, write, or spell the names of the streets they live on); twelve consistently receive Ds and Fs on their report cards; and fourteen consistently receive Cs or better. Four are on the honor roll. Yet all thirty were suspended at least once a semester during the

Source: *Berkeley Journal of Sociology* (1963), 8(1), 39–60.

tenth and eleventh grades, and the average number of suspensions received per semester was above two. There was a general tendency for the illiterate and dull boys to get into more trouble than the better students, but none of them was immune from difficulty. Twenty-two of these thirty regular members spent some time in jail during this period. Differences in access, success, and failure thus did not seem to have a determinate effect on 'trouble' in school—at least among the Conquerors.

Second, difficulties occur only in some classes and not others. Good and bad students alike are consistently able to get through half or more of their classes without friction. It is only in particular classes with particular teachers that incidents leading to suspension flare up. This suggests that schools are not as monolithic as most contemporary sociologists have argued. Moreover, it suggests that something more specific about teachers than being 'middle class' produces problems, just as something more specific than being 'lower class' about gang members produces the response.

The problem

For events in high school classrooms to proceed smoothly, students must grant teachers some measure of authority. Although teachers are in a position to overlook a great deal of extra-curricular student activity in classrooms, they cannot ignore everything. Some modicum of order must be maintained if anything resembling a process of education is to take place. Most teachers thus find themselves in the position of having to act on definitions of improper behavior and hope that students will stop. The authority of teachers is put to a test in this act of communication.

Authority becomes a stable basis for interaction only when those to whom commands are issued voluntarily obey.[8] Students in classrooms, like all parties judging claims to authority made by others, must therefore decide whether treatments received at the hands of teachers are based on grounds that can be considered legitimate.

Most students accept the authority of teachers to pass judgment on practically all behavior that takes place in classrooms. The teacher is seen as a person who can pay legitimate official attention to everything that happens inside the physical confines of a school plant.[9] Since the authority of teachers is accepted at face value, most students can make sense of the specific actions teachers take towards them. Any specific action is interpreted as an instance in which this general rule is being applied.

This is why, for example, most students do not question the grades they receive. They accept the norm that teachers have the authority to grade them. This authority is more or less traditional. A report card signed by the teacher is accepted on much the same basis as are proclamations of war signed by kings. Neither are required by their subjects to give strict accounts of the decisions they make because the prerogative to make them has been granted in advance of the act.

Gang members understand the treatments they receive in no such way. They do not *a priori* accept the authority of any teacher. Final judgment on the conferral of legitimacy is suspended until it is discovered whether or not authority is being exercised on suitable grounds and in a suitable way. The burden of proof lies with the teacher.

Since teachers exercise authority in a variety of ways, becoming a 'delinquent' depends in large measure on whether these various claims are accepted. This is why gang members are frequently 'delinquent' in one class and ordinary students in the adjoining room. This paper analyses accounts of classroom situations in which gang members received unacceptable treatments, refused to recognize the authority of teachers, and were labelled 'delinquent'. These accounts are compared to classroom situations in which the treatments received were considered soundly based, the authority of teachers was accepted, and gang members remained ordinary students.[10]

Gang members make decisions to accept or reject the authority of teachers on the basis of four criteria. First, they evaluate the jurisdictional claims made by teachers. Some teachers not only insist on the physical presence of students but also expect a measure of intellectual and spiritual 'attention' as well. These teachers frequently take issue with behavior such as sleeping on desks, reading comic books, talking to neighbors, passing notes, gazing out of the window, turning around in chairs, chewing gum, and eating peanuts. Gang members do not *a priori* grant teachers the right to punish this behavior although good reasons for ceasing these activities are often accepted.

Second, under no conditions can race, dress, hair styles, and mental capacities receive legitimate official attention. Failures on the part of teachers to accept these rules of irrelevance often contribute to denial of authority.[11]

Third, gang members are extremely sensitive to the style in which authority is exercised. The frequent and consistent use of the imperative is perceived as an insult to the status and autonomy of those to whom this form of address is directed. Teachers who 're-quest' conformity are more likely to achieve desired results.

Ultimately, however, the decision to accept or reject the authority of teachers is made on the basis of a weightier concern. Teachers who consistently violate conceptions of proper jurisdiction, irrelevance rules, and modes of address will not find gang members particularly co-operative architects of authority. But the grounds on which teachers make their formal and semi-public evaluations of students tell a more important tale. Grades can be based on a number of criteria, not all of which gang members find legitimate. Moreover, the fact that they get a grade tells them nothing about the basis on which the judgment was made. They must discover the general rule used by particular teachers to assign grades with only a single application of the rule to go on.

Gang members thus find themselves in a rather serious bind. They *must* figure out the general basis on which teachers are assigning grades because their future behavior depends on what they discover. They cannot walk away from the claims made by teachers to possess authority.

Hypotheses

Their task, however, is not hopeless. Gang members do know *something* about the basis on which a grade might have been assigned. In fact, given what they know about their situation, they reduce the rules teachers might be using to four.

First, the grades might be given out fairly. Although as a rule gang members have no idea how much knowledge they possess relative to other students, they have a general idea of how 'smart' they are relative to others. They judge the intelligence of the boys and girls they know personally, and they estimate the intelligence of strangers from the contributions they make in class. They thus generate a set of expected frequencies on the basis of the hypothesis that bright boys will do better than dull boys.

(Is there any relationship between getting into trouble in school and getting good grades?) Naw. Take likes Charles. He in my classes. He bad outside, and he doing well in school. There ain't no difference. Let's put it like this. Friday, Saturday, Sunday, that's the nights for fucking, drinking, driving, fighting, killing, doing the shit you want to do. There's a lot of guys like Charles in my classes that gets A's on their report cards in school, but when they on the outside, the hell, they bad! They crazy! Dice, drink, shoot people.

(How about the ex-President of the Club? How does he do in your classes?) Johnny's smart. Johnny's got a good brain. He doing good. Everytime I see Johnny, he always got his books. He goes to the bathroom—smokes cigarettes and shoots dice like all of us—but you don't see that man cutting no classes. I swear to God, I think he really got a swell mental brain. (How about the rest of the club?) It just that some people lazier than others. Just like Donald. He in my classes. I ain't got no more brains than that man. I may know a little more than he do from the past things, but as far as that class is related and all, I don't know no more than him. The class is just as new to me as it is to him. Now if I can pass that class, he can pass that class. He didn't pass this time. He flunked. He got a F. He got a F in all his classes. I passes those classes with flying colors, with a C. That's average. I always get average grades. I don't look for no A's and B's. (Do you think you could get A's if you tried?) I doubt it. I don't see racking my brains to death to get no A on no paper. Cause I feel like a A ain't nothing. A C will get you just as far. I mean truthfully I think the highest grade I could ever get was a D. (How about Carson?) He's not smart. He dumb. I mean he goofy. He just ain't got it up here, period. We gonna get kicked out. (What for?) Fighting, gamblin, cutting classes, nasty attitude. (How about the guys who don't get in trouble. How do do they do?) Just like us. Some of them smart, some of them stupid. I mean there's a couple dudes in my classes that's born to be somebody, people with straight A's like Johnny, and then there's the real stupid ones. They just sit there all quiet, get to class on time, never gamble, smoke or nothing and they flunk. You might say we got smart ones and they got smart ones just like we got average ones and they got average ones and we got dumb ones and they got dumb ones. Everybody born on this earth ain't got the same brains.

Second, their response to the presumed authority of the teacher may enter into the grade they receive. They are conscious that the grade is a source of power, and they understand that it may be used as a weapon against them. When teachers use grades as sanctions in this way, gang members perceive it as discrimination. On the basis of the behavior observed in class, gang members divide their fellow students into those who *a priori* take as legitimate the claims to authority made by teachers and those who do not. (As a rule, the latter category is filled with friends.) Expected frequences are thus generated under this condition also. The distinction between scientists and sell-outs lies at the heart of what gang members consider the essential difference between their kind of person and 'squares'.

There's some teachers that treats everybody differently. He always get wise with the studs that ain't gonna take no shit, and they real nice to the people that just sit there, the people that kiss ass behind him. He give the good grades to the ass-kissers and he give us bad grades cause we ain't gonna suck up to him. (Are there many kinds in class who kiss up to teachers?) Yeah. There's enough. Like this one girl, she's kiss behind everybody, and the President of the school! He'll eat you if you ask him to! The bad teachers give the kiss-asses good grades and make us eat shit. They always looking for the ones that run errands, shit like that. (What kind of people are the ass-kissers? Do they wear any special kind of clothes?) Some of them come looking like a farmer or something. Jeans. Or maybe they wear a tie or something. They not like us. We come to have a good time in school as well as sometimes learn something. Some of those boys don't even enjoy parties and things like that. They allergic to girls. They just poopbutts.

The third dimension that may affect a grade is the amount of power possessed by particular students. The sources of this power stem from the possibilities of physical assault on teachers and an ability to keep a class in constant turmoil. Delinquents thus hypothesize that teachers may award grades on this basis. The boys define this possibility as 'bribery'.

(Are there any teachers who give you good grades because they are afraid of you?) Yeah. Like Mr F. He say, 'Aw, come on, why don't you go give us a break or something.' And all the lady teachers, I won't let them go with nothing. Like these teachers say, 'You do me a favor and I do you one. You straighten up in class and I'll make your grade better.' Shit like that. If you control that class, you gonna get a good grade. They afraid of you or they want you to stop fucking up the class. I control a lot of those classes. (What do you do when the teacher tries to make a deal with you?) I don't take shit. That way they gotta keep giving me a good grade. They try to con me, but I ain't going for it. Like that stud that kicked me out of class yesterday? He tell me, 'Come on, why don't you be a good guy? I'll give you a good grade if you be quiet. Why don't you go on and give me a break?' I said, 'I sure will, right on your neck!' When you get a good grade, sometimes you know the teacher is afraid of you. That's why he give it to you.

The final alternative is that grades are randomly distributed. This is a distinct possibility in large classes such as gym where teachers cannot possibly interact personally with all participants. Some students become visible of course, either as athletes, delinquents, or 'flunkies'. But it is quite possible for a particular boy to be graded on the basis of the way his name happens to strike the teacher when he sees it printed on the report card.

> When I think I deserve a C and I get a D?
> That's when I'm gonna bitch. I'm really gonna
> have something to say about it. Cause when I
> feel like I got a better grade? And get something
> lower? I feel like that teacher either prejudiced
> or he just, you know, he just don't give a damn.
> He just go down, read your name and everybodies'
> name, and go A, B, C,—A, B, C. He get to a
> special name. 'Well, I don't like this fellow, I'll
> give him a C. I don't like him. I'll give him a D.'
> You know, so on and so on. Shit. That's like they
> do in gym, seem like to me. Every damn time it
> seem like my report card came up to be a C.
> I don't mind a C if I have to get it, but I seen the
> gym teacher, you know, in the office. They have
> a whole stack of report cards. Now how a gym
> teacher gonna look at your name and go straight
> down the line, just put a grade on? Like he
> going A, B, C,—A, B, C,—A, B, C. And he just
> throw them away! And if he run across a name he
> know real good? Somebody that, you know, real
> tight with him? Go out for all the sports? You
> know, he flunky for him. Work around the gym.
> Shit like that. You know you gonna give him a
> B or something. Somebody that deserve a B, he
> gonna give a C or D. All kinda shit like that.

Thus before grades are handed down, gang members construct four alternative hypotheses or rules about the basis on which teachers evaluate them. Given what they know about the student population being graded, they make predictions about how fellow class members will be marked under three of the four alternative conditions. They know that the grade they receive will be a single case of one of these four classes of rules, but the single grade they receive will not tell them *which* rule the teacher is using. Their problem is to discover it.

Methods

As soon as the grade is handed down, gang members behave like good social scientists. They draw a sample, ask it questions, and compare the results with those predicted under alternative hypotheses. The unit of analysis is a *set* of relevant grades. The one received by a particular student is only a single member. No interpretation of a grade can be made before the others are looked at.

The sample is not selected randomly from the class. The class contains types of students constructed from the knowledge on which the predictions were based. Gang members thus divide the class into four basic sub-groups: bright students who recognize the authority of teachers; duller students who recognize the authority of teachers; bright students withholding judgment about teachers; and dull students withholding judgment about teachers. The latter two

types are like himself. They are his friends. If the gang member conducting the inquiry possesses power, this dimension will also be of concern.

As soon as the grades are delivered to the students in class, representatives of all types are sampled. First, gang members typically ask their friends what they received, and then others in the rest of the class are interviewed. Most of the 'poopbutts', 'sissies' or 'squares' will usually show a gang member their report card. Refusals to reveal grades are often dealt with sharply.

> (How do you know how the teacher is grading
> you?) Sometimes you don't man. You don't know
> whether the stud bribing you with a grade,
> whether he giving you a bad one cause you
> don't kiss behind him, or whether he straight. Or
> maybe he like the gym teachers that give out the
> grades any which way. (But how do you find
> out what basis the teacher is using?) Well, you
> gotta ask around the class. Find out what other
> kids got. Like when I get my report card? I
> shoot out and ask my partners what they got.
> Then I go ask the poopbutts what they got. (Do
> they always let you look at their report cards?)
> They can't do nothing but go for it. Like they
> got to go home sometime. I mean we shoot them
> with a left and a right if they don't come across.
> I mean this grade shit is important. You gotta
> know what's happening. (Why?) Well, shit, how
> you gonna know what the teacher like? I mean
> if he straight or not.

After the grades have been collected, the process of analysing data begins. Final conclusions can be reached at this point, however, only if the teacher has previously provided an account of the grounds being used to grade. Some teachers voluntarily provide these accounts and others do not. Although there is considerable variation in this behavior among teachers, the variation is not random. Teachers who believe that their authority in the classroom should be accepted *a priori* are less likely to volunteer the basis on which they judge students. In fact they are less likely to offer explanations of any action they take. Claims to authority are often demonstrated by not having to account for all decisions made.

On the other hand, some teachers are careful to make visible at all times the basis on which they grade. These teachers understand that they have certain students who will not accept authority in advance of proof that it is being legitimately exercised.

> (What made this teacher fair?) He'd give the class
> an equal chance to be graded. Like he'd say,
> 'How'd you like to be graded on this? Class
> average, individual, or what?' And you know,
> let's say half the class want to be graded on class
> average and the other half on individual. He just
> take the group out like that, you know, and he
> would grade you as such if that's the way you

want to be graded. I mean I felt that the teacher real fair. See, after the first report card, after he see the grades wasn't too good? He asked us how we would like him to grade, and what we would like him to do. (The grades from the first report weren't very good?) No, they weren't so hot. Cause, you know, he wanted to see how his approach did and how we would react to it. Anyway, the results wasn't so hot. Anyway, **he** gave us a choice. So I felt that was helping them, helping me, and that he seemed fair.

In addition, teachers who attempt to bribe certain students will also signal the basis on which they behave in advance of the grade. If a gang member receives a better grade than the one he expected relative to other students, he suspects a 'con'. He thus reviews his previous relationship with the teacher. If the teacher has offered him a good grade in return for good behavior, he has sufficient grounds to conclude that the grade he received was based on his power to control the class.

(How do you know when you get a good grade whether you deserved it or whether the teacher is trying to buy you off?) When they tell you personally. You know, we was in the class by ourself when they told me I could get a good grade if I stop being a troublemaker. Like Mrs C. Like in class she told the whole class, 'If you be quiet you get a good grade!' You know, everybody get a C or something on their report card. But she told me privately, I guess maybe cause I was such a troublemaker. When I see what everybody else got? And I see that they all fail or get something else? I know I got the grade cause I control the class.

Similarly, if the teacher has recently left him alone in class regardless of what he has done, he concludes that the teacher is afraid of him. In this case also he thinks that the teacher is trying to buy control.

(How do you know when you get a good grade because the teacher is afraid of you?) After you ask around the class, you know, you see everybody that shoulda done bad done bad and shit like that. And you got a good grade? Well, sometimes that teacher just leave you alone. I mean you be talking and everything and they won't say nothing. Then you know he afraid of you and he afraid you'll fire on him [slug him] if you get a bad grade.

If teachers provide the rules used to grade students in advance of the grading period, regardless of whether they are using fair criteria, bribing, or discriminating, gang members do not need to request information in order to find out what is going on. As soon as they receive their grade and compare it to others, they 'know what's happening'.

But if gang members need more information to discover the rule being used and it has not been provided in advance of the marking period, they will go to the teacher and ask for an account of the grade they received. This event typically takes place a day or two after report cards have been handed out.

If a gang member is given a grade he thinks he deserves relative to others, he suspects that the grades have been awarded fairly. But his suspicions are based only on the perceived relationship between grades and mental capacity. He can only confirm his suspicions by checking with the teacher. Moreover, if the gang member suspects that the grade is fair, his request to have the grade explained is uniformly polite.

The teacher's response to a request is crucial information to the gang member. If he receives an account of his grade and the account is at all reasonable, he concludes that the teacher is grading fairly. The very fact that the teacher provides a reason at all predisposes him to conclude that the criteria being used to pass and fail students are on the 'up and up'.

After we got our compositions back I went up to him you know. I asked him about my composition. I got a D over F and I ask him what I did wrong. He told me that he could tell by the way I write that I could do better than what I did. And he explained it to me, and he showed me what I need to improve. And he showed me, if I correct my paper, I would get a D, a straight D instead of that F. O.K. And I got the D for half the work. But anyway he showed me how I could get a regular D and pass his class. I mean I feel like that teacher was helping me. I mean he was showing me a way I could pass the class and how he was grading everybody. I mean the way he explained everything to me, I knew he was straight, that he was grading fairly.

Similarly, if a gang member receives a lower grade than expected, he suspects that teachers are using grades as a weapon to award those who accept their authority and punish those who reject it. Again, he can come to no final conclusions about the rule being used to give grades until he checks with the teacher.

If the gang member feels there is a possibility he is being discriminated against, he *demands* an account of the grade. He typically asks, 'What the *hell* did I get this for?' Moreover, since each gang member is in a slightly different position with respect to mental capacity and power, they all approach the teacher alone instead of in groups, even though they compare notes carefully after the encounter has passed.

See, me and that man, we always be fighting. Maybe because of my attitude. See, a lot of teachers grade you on your attitude toward them and not your work. And like sometimes you be talking, you know, and he say, 'Why don't you hush! Shut up! I told you once or

twice already not to be saying that in class!'
Everybody else be talking.
He say, 'Trying to get smart with me?'
'No, I say, 'I ain't trying to get smart with you.'
He say, 'What are you trying to do? Start an argument?'
And you know, I get tired of copping pleas.
'Hell yeah I'm trying to start an argument!'
So he say, 'If you keep fooling around I'm going to lower your grade.'
On the report card, the dude give me a D. I told that son of a bitch today, I know damn well my work better than a D! Cause all my tests have been C's, you know, and everybody else getting a C. I'm hip to shit like that, man.
Then he gonna tell me, 'Well, I grade on the notes and the homework more than I do the tests.'
I say, 'Well, what kind of a teacher are you? What bull shit you got on your mind?' I cussing at him all the time. That man don't move me! He bore me! He get on my damn nerves!
He look up at me. 'You trying to start a fight?'
I say, 'I'm gonna start the biggest fight you ever seen! I want my grade changed!'
And he say, 'Why don't you go sit down?'
'No man, I ain't gonna sit down till you straighten my grade out! You show me my grade in the book and I show you. I know I got a C!'
And he just say, 'Go on and sit down before I call the boys' dean to come up here and get you.'
I say to myself, 'I can't get suspended no more. If I gets suspended again, I fucked. I never will pass.' So I went and sit down. That nasty ass motherfucker just don't like bloods.

If a gang member receives a bad grade and finds the teacher frightened and apologetic, he concludes that grades have been awarded randomly. The gang member reasons that if the teacher is frightened during the encounter and grades had not been given randomly, he probably would have received a better one.

Like my gym teacher today. That fucking freak! F? Aw hell no! Nobody get no F in gym. And I stripped every day! My gym suit wasn't clean every Monday. That's just three points minus. All right. Six weeks times three is eighteen. Right? Eighteen points minus out of a hundred. How the hell you gonna get a F? And I stripped every day. All right then. So I went in there and told Mr C. I say, 'Now look here, the man gave me a F! I stripped every day. My gym suit wasn't clean every Monday. I took a shower after class every day. Now why I get a F?'
He looked in the book. 'Oh, I guess he made a mistake. I'm not sure cause I wasn't with you all during the six weeks so I give you a D.'
So I say, 'Look, man, I don't think a D's fair

either. I think I ought to get a B or C just like everyone else.'
'Well, I'll give you a D and you'll get a better grade next time.'
All the time I was talking to him he had his head in a book, and when he looked up it seemed like you could see in his eyes that he was almost scared. You know. Didn't want to say too much. It seem like almost everything you say, he agrees with you and make you look like a ass. 'Yeah. Yeah. That's right, that's right.' Stuff like that. And you know that some of the things you be saying you know is wrong. You'd be expecting him to say, 'No, that's wrong.' You know. And he'd be agreeing with everything you say. He just say, 'Well, do things right next time and I'll go on and give you a better grade.' Something like that. Then he say, 'I sorry.' He apologize to you. Shit like that. That's how you know a teacher is scared of you, and if he scared of you, he going to give you a better grade than you deserve, not a worse one! That gym man! They don't know what they give you. They just hand them out as they come up.
I finally say, 'O.K. Fuck it!' You know. I didn't want no F so I took the D. And I say, 'Well look here, man, I hope to hell I don't have your stupid ass for a gym teacher next term!'

If he is dealing with a teacher who believes it is not necessary and in fact demeaning to explain decisions to students, the gang member may receive no answer at all. His search is then frustrated, and he has been directly insulted. This frustration and anger is typically reflected in loud and obscene outbursts directed at the teacher. This is a 'classic' scene in the folklore of a delinquent gang. After blowing up at the teacher and storming from the classroom, he comes to the conclusion that he is being discriminated against, regardless of whether or not this is in fact true.

(How did Tyrone get kicked out of school?) Putting down the teachers. He didn't feel that he was given adequate grades for a term paper or work that he had passed in. He went up and told the teacher to get fucked. She went up to the Dean of Boys, and he tell Tyrone that he'd have to let him go. (Were you in his class?) Yeah. (Did you see him tell off the teacher?) Yeah. I was standing right behind him. (What happened?) Well, see we get these papers back and Tyrone, he start asking everybody what they got. So he go up to this one stud, Art, and he say, 'You see Mrs G., that bitch, she gave me a F. What's the story?'
Art say, 'She gave me a passing grade.'
Tyrone say, 'Shit. You don't do a damn thing. How come you pass and I dont?'
Art say, 'I don't know, man. Maybe she don't like you.'
So Tyrone goes up to her. He said, 'What the

hell's going on here? Why I get that F? I felt
the answer to this question was right! I think it's
right!'
She said, 'Well, no, it isn't. I'm sorry.'
He say, 'Why ain't it right?'
She say, 'I corrected it the way I saw fit.'
He say, 'Well shit! Why ain't it right?'
She say, 'Uh, would you stop using so much
profound [*sic*] language. I'll have to tell the Dean.'
He say, 'Tell the fucking Dean! He ain't nobody!
Aw fuck you!'
She told the Dean, and the Dean kicked him out.

It is important to point out that not all gang
members are able to learn something about the rules
teachers use to grade by using this procedure. The
illiterates or relatively dull students who expect
Fs even under the fair condition, and the bright gang
members who expect As and Bs, are in a further bind.
The F students cannot distinguish between the fair
case and the case of discrimination, and the A student
cannot distinguish between the fair case and the case
of being 'bribed'. Unlike the F student, however, the A
student will be particularly sensitive to discrimination.
Gang members who fall in these two categories use
other grounds to decide whether or not to co-operate
with teachers. The procedure being discussed here thus
works best for average students, those who can learn
something by receiving As and Fs. Most boys, including gang members, however, fall into this category
—at least while they are attending school.

Conclusions

Once gang members have either requested or demanded accounts from teachers, they have all the
materials needed to come to a conclusion. The accounts
that teachers give or fail to give furnish warranted
grounds for understanding one aspect of what goes
on in the classroom. The gang member has discovered
the class or rule being used to grade and thus can
understand the single grade he received. Once having
discovered the rule, however, he then faces the question of what to do about it. It is in the decisions he
makes about his future course of action that we
discover the essence of the delinquent.

If he concludes that he is being either discriminated
against, bribed, or treated randomly, he does not
modify his behavior. Even though he becomes aware
that 'kissing ass' will get him a better grade, he does not
avail himself of the technique. He is prevented by his
sense of morality. The tactic is considered illegitimate.
After all, he reasons, 'If I go for that shit I might as
well stick to the streets and pull some big-time action!'

(So you know your attitude toward the teacher
gets you bad grades sometimes?) Yeah, sometimes
it does. (Why don't you change your attitude?)
I wouldn't go kiss up to them motherfucking
teachers for nothing! Shit! They prejudiced or
they gonna hit you over the head with that

fucking grade so you gonna kiss up to them?
Well no! We supposed to be graded on what we
know. Right? Ain't that supposed to be how it
is? Damn teachers are something. I tell you they
ain't got shit but a racket going, man.
Motherfuckers get down there and kiss them
God damn principals' asses, the bosses' asses.
That's the last motherfucking thing I do! I
wouldn't go kiss that damn horse's ass for
nothing! I wouldn't do shit for that man. If I go
running over there, I'm gonna feel funny. Cause
I'm always getting in trouble. What if I go
running over there and ask him, 'Look man, why
don't you help me out in gym. Tell this man to
kinda lighten up on me cause he kinda fucking
my grades around. I ain't for all this shit. I
know I'm doing right.' You know. Shit like that.
He gonna say, 'Lee, you always want favors, but
you never want to do nothing in return. You're
always messing up in class.' And this and that
and the other shit. I'd rather be raped, man. If I
go for that shit I might as well stick to the streets
and pull some big time action! Shit! If I gonna
be corrupt? If I gonna get me a racket going like
that, shit, I ain't gonna waste my time sucking
up to no teachers! I gonna pull some big time
shit.

Practical applications

How do gang members act in classroom once they
decide that a teacher's claims to authority are illegitimate?

While gang members remain in school, either before
graduating or before being kicked out, they do not
comply with the grounds teachers use to treat them.
This fact explains much of their delinquency in the
classroom. If they feel that a teacher is discriminating
against them because his claims to authority are not
being granted, they are careful to avoid all behavior
that implicitly or explicitly recognizes this authority.
Raising a hand in class, for example, is a gesture used
by students to present themselves as candidates for
speaking. Implicit in the gesture is an understanding
that the student may not be called on. The gesture
implies further that the teacher has the authority to
grant speaking privileges in class. If a student raises
his hand, he thus implicitly makes the authority of
the teacher legitimate. This is why gang members
refuse to raise their hands in some classes and prefer
interjecting comments without being recognized. This
behavior would no doubt be treated by some theorists
as a rude and unruly by-product of 'lower-class
culture'. Lower-class or not, the behavior has its
reasons.

I'm not the quiet type in that class [California
history]. Like when we're having a discussion or
something? I don't go for all that raising your

hand. Cause everybody else on the other side of the room might—while the teacher asking you a question?—well the one that just went by, people probably still discussing it. And you might want to get in on that. And you just come on out and say something, and he tell you to get out of class. Well that shit ain't no good, man. So you know that kinda get on my nerves. But I don't mind getting kicked out of class. That ain't no big thing. I feel like—that class I got now?— if I try hard I can pass. My citizenship may not be worth a damn, but I can pass the class. (Do you always forget to raise you hand?) Hell no! I raise my hand in Civics and some of the other classes. That's interesting. But California history ain't shit. It's easy. It's simple. It's just that teacher. He a punk! He just ain't used to us. He just don't understand bloods [Negroes]. I don't raise my hand for that freak! I just tell the dude what's on my mind.

The time and circumstances that surround entering and leaving class also have implications for the implicit acceptance or rejection of authority. If a student consistently comes to class on time, he implicitly gives teachers grounds to assume that he accepts both their authority and the legitimacy of school rules. This is why gang members frequently make it a point to arrive five minutes late to class. It is no accident that gang members are suspended most frequently for tardiness. Not only is tardiness an affront to the authority of teachers but it also flaunts the claims to authority made by the school system as a whole.

We came in late to class today because he threatened us. He see us between fifth and sixth period when he was supposed to be going to one class and coming from another. We was on our way to his class. I was standing by my locker. My locker right next to his class. So he come up to me and say, 'Lee, you tell Wilson that if you two come late to class I'm gonna get you both kicked out of school.' So I went and told Billy, and we made it our business to be late. We walked in about five minutes late. Knocked on the door. He opened the door. Just went in and sat down. I looked him in the eye. Would have put a ring around it if he'd said too much. The door comes in through the back. We made a little bit of noise sitting down to make sure he see us. We giggled and laughed a little bit to make sure he noticed we were there. We try to remind him that he suppose to kick us out. It was almost to the end of the period before he kicked us out.

Gang members also have the choice of leaving class before the bell is rung, when the bell is ringing, or when the class is formally dismissed by the teacher. When they occasionally leave class before the bell is rung, they flaunt the authority of both the teacher and the school.

(What do you do when you discover that the teacher has been grading you unfairly?) Lots of times we just get up and walk out. Like you say, 'Oh man, I'm tired of this class.' You just jump up and walk out and shut the door. (What do the teachers do?) Mostly they just look at us and then resume with the rest of the class and don't say nothing. (Why don't they report you?) I guess they be glad for us to be out of their class.

More frequently, however, they wait until the bell rings to leave class instead of waiting for a sign of dismissal from the teacher. This act implicitly accepts the authority of the school while explicitly rejecting the authority of the teacher. When this happens teachers who feel they have authority to protect often take action.

After class, as soon as the bell rang, everybody jumped up. The teacher said, 'Everybody sit back down! You're not leaving right now!' So Alice jumped up. She starts walking out. He say, 'Alice, go sit down!' Alice say, 'Who the hell you talking to! I'm tired of school. I'm going home!' She walked to the door. He grabbed her. She looked at him. 'I'm gonna count to three, and if you don't get your hands off me . . . No, I ain't even gonna count! Take your hands off me!' He took his hands off. He say, 'We're going to the office this minute!' She say, 'You going to the office by yourself unless you get somebody else to go down there with you!' And so she walked away. So she was down talking to some other girls, and he say, 'Alice, would you please come!' She say, 'No! And stop bugging me! Now get out of here!' I didn't see all of the argument. I just went off and left. When I passed him I said, 'Man, you ain't nothing!' He looked at me. Then he say, 'One of these days you gonna get yours.'

In addition, gang members are careful never to use forms of address that suggest deference. 'Yes Sir' and 'No Sir' are thus self-consciously stricken from the vocabulary.

And you know like in some classes the teacher tell you you don't say 'Yes' and 'No'. It's 'Yes Sir' and 'No Sir'. They would have to whip my ass to make me say that. I don't go for it. Shit. They don't call me Mr Lee! Teacher once tried to tell me to say, 'Yes M'am'. I say, 'All right, you call me Mr Lee.' I don't like it. I feel if I did, I'd probably feel funny saying 'Yes Sir' and 'No

Sir' to somebody. (How would you feel?) I'd
feel like I was a little old punk or something.

But of all the techniques used by gang members to
communicate rejection of authority, by far the most
subtle and most annoying to teachers is demeanor.
Both white and Negro gang members have developed
a uniform and highly stylized complex of body movements that communicate a casual and disdainful
aloofness to anyone making normative claims on their
behavior. The complex is referred to by gang members
as 'looking cool', and it is part of a repertoire of stances
that include 'looking bad' and 'looking tore down'.
The essential ingredients of 'looking cool' are a
walking pace that is a little too slow for the occasion,
a straight back, shoulders slightly stooped, hands in
pockets, and eyes that carefully avert any party to the
interaction. There are also clothing aides which enhance the effect such as boot or shoe taps and a hat
if the scene takes place indoors.

This stance can trigger an incident if a teacher reacts
to it, but it is the teacher who must make the first
overt move. The beauty of the posture resides in its
being both concrete and diffuse. Teachers do not miss
it, but they have a great deal of difficulty finding
anything specific to attack. Even the mightiest of
educators feels embarrassed telling high school
students to 'stand up straight'. As the following episode
suggests, teachers typically find some other issue on
which to vent their disapproval.

The first day I came to school I was late to class
so this teacher got smart with me. He didn't
know me by name. See a lot of people have to
go by the office and see what class they in or
something. Like there was a lot of new people
there. So you know I was fooling around cause I
know nothing gonna happen to you if you late.
Cause all you tell them, you tell them you got the
program mixed or something.
When I came into the class you know I heard a
lot of hollering and stuff. Mr H. was in the class
too. He's a teacher, see. I guess he had a student
teacher or something, you know, because he was
getting his papers and stuff. So Mr H. went out.
Well this new teacher probably wonder if he
gonna be able to get along with me or something.
Cause when I came in the class, you know,
everybody just got quiet. Cause the class was
kinda loud. When I walked in the class got quiet
all of a sudden. Like they thought the Principal
was coming in or something.
So I walk into class and everybody look up. That's
natural, you know, when somebody walk into class.
People gonna look up at you. They gonna see
who it is coming in or something. So I stopped.
You know, like this. Looked around. See if there
was any new faces. Then a girl named Diane,
she say, 'Hey Ray!' You know, when I walk into
class they start calling me and stuff. They start
hollering at me.

I just smile and walk on. You know. I had my
hands in my pocket or something cause I didn't
have no books and I just walk into class with my
hands in my pockets a lot of times. I mean I
have to walk where I can relax. I'm not going to
walk with my back straight. I mean you know I
relax. (What were you wearing?) About what I
got on now. I had a pair of black slacks and a
shirt on but they weren't real high boots. They
came up to about here.
Then I looked over at the teacher. I see we had a
new teacher. He was standing in front of the
desks working on some papers and doing something. He looked at me. I mean you enter by
the front of the classroom so when you walk into
the classroom he's standing right there. You
gotta walk in front of him to get to the seats. So
then I went to sit down. Soon as I passed his
desk he say, 'Just go sit down.' Just like that.
So I stop. I turn around and look at him, then I
went and sat down. (What kind of look did you
give him?) You might say I gave him a hard
look. I thought you know he might say something
else. Cause that same day he came he got to
hollering at people and stuff. I don't like people
to holler at me. He was short, you know, about
medium build. He might be able to do a little
bit. So I say to myself, 'I better sit down and
meditate a little bit.'
So I went and sat down. I sat in the last row in
the last seat. Then he say, 'Come sit up closer.'
So I scoot up another chair or two. Then he tell
me to come sit up in the front. So I sat up there.
Then you know a lot of people was talking. A lot
of people begin telling me that he be getting
smart all day. You know Studdy? He a big
square but he pretty nice. He told me how the
teacher was. And Angela start telling me about
how he try to get smart with her. He say, 'This
is where you don't pick out no boy friend. You
come and get your education.' I mean just cause
you talk to a boy, that don't mean you be
scheming on them or nothing. It just that you
want to be friends with people.
Then he say something like, 'You two shut up or
I'll throw you out on your ear.' So he told me he'd
throw me out.
So I say, 'The best thing you can do is ask me to
leave and don't tell me. You'll get your damn
ass kicked off if you keep messing!'
Then he told me to move over on the other side.
See I was talking to everybody so he told me to
move away from everybody. And so I moved to
the other side. He told me to move three times!
I had to move three times! And then he got to
arguing at somebody else. I think at somebody
else that came in the class. You know, a new
person. So while he was talking to them, I left
out. I snuck out of class.
So I walked out the class. Went out in the yard

and started playing basketball. We were supposed to turn in the basketball out there so I took the ball through the hall on the way back in. I was gonna go back out there and play some more. See I had the ball and I passed by his class and I looked in. I seen him with his back turned and I didn't like him. That's when I hit him. I hit him with the ball. Got him! I didn't miss. Threw it hard too. Real hard!

It is easier for teachers to attack the demeanor of students directly if the encounter is formal and disciplinary. If a gang member is 'sent' to someone for punishment, the teacher or principal he appears before often makes demeanor an issue. In the following incident, a gang member is suspended for ten days ostensibly because he faced the music with his hands in his pockets and the touch of a smile on his face.

Miss W., she sent me to Mr M. cause I cussed at her. When I came to class he was talking to some gray boys [white boys] and he called me in. He talked at me like he gonna knock me out. Talked about fifteen minutes. He wasn't coming on nice. He got right down to the point. 'I think you know what you're in here for. I think you know what you did fourth period concerning Miss W.'
I say, 'Yeah, I know what I done.'
And so he just sat down and went on and talked. He told me to sit down. I was already sat down. I had my hands in my pockets. He told me to take my hands out of my pockets. (Why?) I guess he wanted my attention. I was looking down at the floor and he told me to look at him. I look at him and look down at the floor again. He

didn't say nothing then. And I walked out the woodship and I just smiled. And he say, 'Come on back here! I want to talk to you again.' So I went back there. 'What was that smile for? That little smile you gave.'
I say, 'Ain't nobody can tell me if I can smile.'
He said, 'You smiling as if you gave me a bad time. You didn't. I gave you a bad time!'
So he told me to go on down to the Principal. He told me the Principal was gonna suspend me for ten days. (Did he?) Yup.

Yet when gang members are convinced that the educational enterprise and its ground rules are being legitimately pursued, that a teacher is really interested in teaching them something, and that efforts to learn will be rewarded, they consistently show up on time, leave when the class is dismissed, raise their hands before speaking, and stay silent and awake.

I mean I feel like that teacher was helping me. I mean he was showing me a way I could pass his class. And then all the time he was telling me, you know, he was leaving me with confidence that I could do better if I wanted to. Like I mean he'd be up in front of the class you know, and he'd give the class an equal chance to be graded. I mean I felt that the teacher was real fair. Cause some of the people that were slow, he would help. I mean he wouldn't take off time just for that few little people but he would help you. He'd give you confidence. Tell you you can do better. That man used to have a desk full of people. Everyday after class you know there be somebody up there talking to him. Everybody passed his class too. He let you know that you wasn't in there for nothing.

Notes

1 This paper is part of a larger research project done with Irving Piliavin on delinquent street gangs in San Francisco. The project was initiated by the Survey Research Center at the University of California on a grant from the Ford Foundation and was later moved to the Center For the Study of Law and Society where funds were made available from the Delinquency Studies Program sponsored by the Department of Health, Education, and Welfare under Public Law 87–274.
2 Richard A. Cloward and Lloyd E. Ohlin, *Delinquency and Opportunity* (Routledge & Kegan Paul 1961), **102.**
3 Albert K. Cohen, *Delinquent Boys: The Culture of the Gang* (Routledge & Kegan Paul 1956), 115.
4 Walter B. Miller and William C. Kvaraceus, *Delinquent Behavior: Culture and the Individual*, National Educational Association of the United States 1959, **144.** See also Walter Miller, Lower-class culture as a generating milieu of gang delinquency, *Journal of Social Issues* (1958), vol. 14 for a more explicit statement of this position.
5 Cloward and Ohlin, op. cit.
6 Cohen, op. cit.
7 Miller, op. cit.
8 Chester I. Barnard, *The Functions of the Executive* (Cambridge, Mass.: Harvard University Press 1938), 163.
9 This assumption is widely shared by both sociologists and gang members. Hopefully we will some day put it to a test.
10 This model of events is based on the assumption that regardless of how students are behaving in class, they can only misbehave if a rule about proper conduct is invoked by teachers. It is in this sense that 'social groups create deviance by making the rules whose infraction constitutes deviance, and by applying those rules to particular people'. See Howard S. Becker, *Outsiders* (Collier-Macmillan 1963), 9.
11 For a general discussion of the problems created by contingent or purposive infraction of irrelevance rules see Ervin Goffman, *Encounters* (Indianapolis: Bobbs-Merrill 1961), 17–85.

Section II   The culture of the school and the teacher's presentation of self

Everyone who has ever been a pupil in more than one school, or been in more than one school class, is aware that every school and every classroom is unique. Some of the differences can, of course, be measured—and we can be sure that someone or other at some-time or other has set about trying to measure those differences between schools and classrooms which are measurable. But in spite of this we do not seem to know a great deal more about those differences than we did before. What we have suggested in the course units which are concerned with this area, and what has directed the choice of readings in this section, is that a possibly more fruitful way of trying to isolate the causes underlying those differences would be to look at the 'culture' of the school and of the classroom.

These school and classroom cultures might be seen as arising out of the coming together of the pupil and the teacher subcultures. The way in which a student subculture is formed and grows—based on agreed solutions to common problems facing the group—forms the core of the article by Hughes, Becker and Geer. The student culture they describe involves not only agreement on the solution of problems but also on the definition of what constitutes a problem, in the light of their goals.

The form the student (or pupil or teacher) culture takes, however, is not only determined by what the group members see as their problems and the perspectives they have on these problems. Another important element is what the individuals involved bring to the situation, and which of their many identities become relevant in any given situation. This is the theme of the paper by Becker and Geer. (It is, incidentally, an outgrowth of the same piece of research which formed the basis of 'Student culture and academic effort'.) They discuss the conditions, under which the cultures men participate in elsewhere, affect what goes on in the work groups. The authors ask under what conditions normally latent identities become relevant, for such identities do not influence behaviour merely by virtue of being held in common by many of the participants.

This leads us to ask which of the pupils' and teachers' identities are more or less latent in school situations and which of these frequently become relevant. Social class is a prime example of such an identity; its relevance is, however, often overlooked and pupil behaviour attributable to a social class subcultural identity is often wrongly attributed to an individual personality shortcoming.

The readings by Bernstein, and by Ford, Young and Box, have been selected to show the importance of recognizing both the nature and the source of these social class differences. Bernstein's work on sociolinguistics is by now very well known and we have selected for this volume a more general piece, which puts very clearly his basic thesis about the link between social class, language and education.*

The work by Ford, Young and Box extends the area covered by class differences among children and the authors indicate some ways in which these differences relate to particular subcultural milieus from which they derive. These are especially concerned with different social class notions of justice, friendship and privacy and they spell out some theoretical implications of the existence of these differences, suggesting specifically that the working-class child may be deficient in roleplaying ability.

*Although a paper by Bernstein is included here, it is only a summary of his work on sociolinguistics and education. Anyone interested in finding out in more detail about Bernstein's work on sociolinguistics could start off by looking at two particularly useful articles by Bernstein: 'A Sociolinguistic approach to social learning', in J. Gould (ed.), *Penguin Social Science Survey*, 1965, and 'Social class and linguistic development: A theory of social learning' in A. H. Halsey, J. Floud and C. A. Anderson (eds) *Education, Economy and Society*, Collier-Macmillan 1961.

A particularly neglected aspect of sociological studies concerned with organizations generally, as well as with those carried out on schools, has been that of the physical space in which the interaction takes place. The way in which the available space is used is taken as much for granted as is the fact that the actors within it are humans. The articles by Goffman, and the Bennetts, are, typically for Goffman, on the implications of interpersonal space. The Bennetts, on the other hand, concentrate more on the total physical environment, the values it secretes and the effects it has on the interaction which takes place within it.

The paper by Dumont and Wax brings our feet back to educational ground with its description and analysis of a particularly striking example of pupil culture at work in the classroom. The Cherokee pupils whose schools the authors studied appeared on the surface to be model pupils. They were quiet, polite and obedient—and yet they never learnt what the teachers were trying to teach. Refusing to accept the ready explanation of innate stupidity, Dumont and Wax found that when teachers accepted that the pupils had a different conception of what should go on in the classroom, and how it should go on, and went some way towards meeting this, the classroom interaction became very different. The value of this ethnographic study lies in the extent to which an analysis of an extreme 'clash of subcultures' throws light upon the similar, but perhaps less obvious, clashes that occur in our classrooms.

Section I suggested that the teacher's conception of classroom reality depended on his definitions of the activities which occurred there. These definitions were expressions of his professional responsibility and knowledge. Readings 14–18 enable us to explore one of the central features of the teacher's professional practice—his pedagogy. This refers to the principles and assumptions which underlie the classroom practices of a teacher. It encompasses, among other things, the ways in which he organizes and presents his subject-matter, his conceptions of the 'good' and 'difficult' pupil, his notion of what constitutes 'effective' learning and his ways of relating to his pupils. A teacher's pedagogical perspective, therefore, represents the operational philosophy which underpins his concrete actions in the classroom. For much of his working life, it remains implicit and taken for granted; but on the occasions when a teacher is held accountable for, or feels obliged to justify, an action, it provides a 'legitimate' body of theory which he can draw upon.

One important feature of pedagogy is that it is built upon a set of philosophical and psychological 'models' of the child and the learning process. It contains, for example, conceptions of ability and intellectual functioning, and ideas of how the child learns, framed in currently available educational theories and the vocabularies of professional debate about education.

The pupil's conception of classroom reality, and his opportunities for particular kinds of school experience, are partly contingent upon the teacher's pedagogical preferences and the assumptions which they indicate. The sociological study of pedagogy can, therefore, provide a fruitful perspective for the analysis of teacher–pupil interaction.

The extract from Durkheim's *Education and Sociology* underlines the social nature of pedagogy and learning. Durkheim criticizes some of the prevailing interpretations of education which rely on psychological explanations and which fail to take account of the social contexts in which it takes place. He argues that teaching and learning cannot be seen simply as expressions of the 'mental states' or 'human nature' of individual teachers and learners, but as also embodying the social principles, the assumptions and ideals which prevail in any set of educational arrangements.

The papers by Berger and Mills both provide ways in which we can examine the assumptions and principles which operate through the actions of teachers. Like most 'professionals', teachers are exponents of a fund of applied knowledge. They bring to the social worlds of pupils particular frames of reference and criteria which serve as a means of defining and evaluating their work and behaviour. The ideas which this knowledge contains are, therefore, closely bound up with the organization of the school. Berger argues that 'every society contains a repertoire of identities that is part of the "objective knowledge" of its members'. This objective knowledge is internalized and becomes the basis for the explanations and descriptions which human actors apply to themselves and to each other. When people describe motives or impute them to one another, they formulate their descriptions through socially-acceptable and relevant 'vocabularies'. Some of these will have become organized into 'theories'—for example, psychoanalytic theory—others are part of a fund of common-sense, everyday knowledge. Clearly, depending on by whom they are uttered, they have varying consequences for the individuals to whom they are applied.

The paper by Becker focuses on a range of 'images' which teachers may have of their pupils. He argues that, like the clients of other professionals, pupils are likely to be classified according to preconceived notions as to what constitutes an 'ideal' and a 'difficult' pupil and that this has an important bearing on the ways in which they experience school. Some of these notions, Becker suggests, have arisen from the dissemination of ideas about social-class differences and their manifestations in individual behaviour. The teachers' expectations of work standard will vary according to the social class of the pupil.

Platt's study is an excellent example of the ways in which we might conceptualize pedagogy. Substantively about delinquency, it provides ways of considering how 'images' such as those relating to 'intelligence' and features of classroom control emerged in various educational debates and became institutionalized in the school.

7 Student culture and academic effort

E. C. Hughes, H. S. Becker and Blanche Geer

Student culture in medical school[1]

Subcultures (of which student cultures are one example) develop best where a number of people are faced with common problems and interact both intensively and extensively in the effort to find solutions for them, where people who face the same contingencies and exigencies in everyday life have an opportunity to deal with these communally (Summer 1907; Cohen 1955). Medical school is an ideal hot-house for such a plant.

Medical students live with a number of pressing and chronic problems, the most important stemming from the fact that they are continuously presented with an enormous and, in any practical sense, unlimited amount of material to learn. Though students and faculty agree that the criterion for choosing what to learn should be relevance for medical practice, there is enough disagreement and uncertainty among the faculty as to what is relevant so that the student is never presented with a clear directive to guide him in his own studies. Students worry together over this problem, in one or another of its many transformations, during their four years of school.

Similarly, medical school provides extremely propitious conditions—intensive interaction and isolation from outside influences—for the development of common solutions to these problems. Students usually spend eight or more hours in school every weekday, working and studying together in the labs and on the wards, and are likely to spend many evenings and weekends together in similar activity as well. Much of their work is carried on in groups of four to twelve students, and these are arranged so differently from course to course that the students come to know many of their fellows with the intimacy that arises from close, continuous association at work. The students are insulated from contact with other people, both by reason of their crowded schedules and because they find it difficult to talk with people who are not suffering under the same pressures as they are. Even those students who have friends or brothers only a year or two ahead of them in school report that they get little help with their immediate problems from these people. Each class of approximately one hundred students goes through school as a unit, meeting the problems they face together.

This intensive interaction in an isolated group produces a particularly meaningful and essential array of those understandings and agreements we call student culture. One set of understandings specifies goals and values, telling the students that they are in school to learn those things relevant to their prospective professional futures. In the school we studied, students came to believe that they were in school to acquire the knowledge and clinical experience one must have before he can assume the responsibility of the physician for the lives of his patients, a responsibility they intended and expected to have once they finished school. They based their interpretations of the worth of various school activities on the criterion of how well this function was served in each. Another set of understandings suggested modes of co-operation designed to meet examinations and other crises, and such recurrent problems as sharing loads of clinical work assigned to groups.

The student's interpretation of specific events and issues tends to be made in categories that are part of the student culture, because these events and issues are new and unfamiliar and do not fit easily into categories provided by his earlier experiences. These cultural understandings coerce his behavior though not, at least in medical school, by methods as crude as punishment by fellow-participants in the subculture (characteristic of subcultures in the underworld or industrial work groups). It is not that the student must abide by these informal and hardly conscious agreements, but rather that they constrain his thinking and perspective almost without his being aware of it (though an occasional student may be conscious of a degree of tension between what he might like to do and what the group norms specify as correct).

The academic years

Perhaps the most important factor in the development of student culture during the freshman year is the formation of a group in which all or nearly all members have opportunities for interaction with each other. When the freshmen arrive in medical school, although they come with the common intention of becoming physicians, they are not a group in any but the nominal sense that all are in the first year class. They begin to get to know some of their fellow students right away, but this takes place not in the class at large but within small groups. The small groups are of two types. First to form are friendship groups consisting of students similar in social status who have opportunities for leisure interaction because they live near or with each other. Fraternity members, for example, most of whom are unmarried, make friends in their own house, married students get to know other married students who live in the same neighborhood or trailer camp, and unmarried students who do not belong to a fraternity get together at the student center to eat and relax in their spare time. The second type of group forms in the anatomy laboratory. As the faculty assigns students in groups of four to a dissection tank, members of different friendship groups get to know each other under the intimate conditions that dissection of the same cadaver imposes. The intersection of work and friendship groups makes it possible for each student to learn the attitudes current in other groups towards student problems, and, at the same time, carry back to his own friends solutions he and his lab partners have tried out in the course of their work together.[2]

The spread of common understandings among the freshmen is also promoted by their isolation. Unlike most graduate students, all members of the medical school class are taught together. They spend an eight-to-five day in one building. Each morning and afternoon, lectures lasting as long as the instructors wish are followed immediately by laboratory periods. Review and preparation is done at night, usually at home (for there is little or no library work) or once again in the laboratory. On a schedule like this there is little opportunity for interaction with groups outside the class, nor do the students turn to the faculty with problems except about details of daily work. For as they begin to draw together and get a sense of themselves as a group, they think of the faculty as a group opposed to their own. To ask faculty advice is to break student ranks. Thus, the students come to an understanding among themselves of what the study of medicine is and how it should be accomplished. Their notions are derived from what the faculty says and does (which are sometimes quite different), from the future they envision for themselves as physicians,

and from their past experience in getting through school and college.

The student concept of what medicine is develops first. They believe it is a great body of known facts, some of which will be imparted to them in the first year for eventual use when they become physicians. The idea that everything is important soon gets them into a dilemma, for there are more facts than they have time to learn. They are told this by the faculty, and prove it to themselves when, after studying four and five hours a night and on weekends as well, they have not mastered the material to their own satisfaction.

As they realize they can't learn everything, all but the most self-exacting students see that they must study only important things and let the rest go. But what is important? This question becomes the chief subject of discussion in student groups shortly before the first major examinations. Two points of view predominate. One group of students believes the most important facts are those they will use in medical practice. (Selection of these facts is a matter a student feels quite competent about even if he has only been in school a few weeks.) A second group of students, most of them fraternity members, takes into account the necessity of passing examinations to stay in school. On this basis, the important facts are those the faculty thinks important. Students who believe this develop various systems for finding out what the faculty wants them to know.

Although taking the examinations brings the issue of what to study to a head, it does not settle it. Rightly or wrongly, students consider some questions 'impractical', unrelated, that is, to the practice of medicine. These questions lead students of the group that believes in studying things important for medical practice to begin thinking more about what the faculty thinks these are. In preparation for the next examinations these students pool their knowledge, make use of files of old tests, and consult members of the class who already study in this way. But the examinations also contain questions students consider 'unfair'—points not emphasized in lectures or texts. Students who follow some system for learning what the faculty wants are unable to predict such questions. The faculty has not been 'playing the game'. As a result of their difficulties with the examinations, both groups of students begin to have doubts about the faculty. The practice-minded group wonders whether the faculty teaching first year subjects (most of whom are Ph.D.s) knows much about practice. The system-minded group wonders whether the faculty is agreed about what is important; if not, perhaps it is impossible to predict what will show up on an examination. Both groups consider briefly whether the faculty is 'out to get them'. The significance of all this for the development of student culture is that in their bewilderment, students draw closer together and finally settle their problem in a way acceptable to all but a few.

They agreed that they ought to study the 'basic

medical facts'. These are the only ones they have time for, as there is so much to learn. These are the facts important for practice, certain to be on examinations if the faculty is reasonable. To this central proposition the students add a number of other understandings which they apply to their daily activities.

1. Basic facts are most economically learned from textbooks. This means that lectures which do not follow the text are a waste of student time, and a faculty member who strays from the text is a poor lecturer who probably has some scientific axe to grind in connection with his own research which does not concern medical students. 2. Demonstrations and lab work which repeat classical experiments are a waste of time; the results are most easily learned in the text and students can't do them well enough to learn much anyway. 3. Theoretical material, concepts (except those which help to organize facts), and research findings not yet in clinical use, are not facts and are not useful to medical students.

These understandings of the student culture can be summed up in the student phrase 'give it to us straight', which has its counterpart in the derogatory faculty phrase 'spoon feeding'. A student will say that he does not want to be spoon fed, but points out that there is so much to learn he hasn't time to think or worry about 'minutiae' (details) and 'all that academic crud' (nonfactual material). Once they have decided the question of what and how to study, the students settle down to hard work. They are no longer worried about how to select the important things to read because 'you just go by the black type'. In the same way, they learn to get through their lab work by various short-cuts which are both approved by student culture and not penalized in examinations by the faculty. The following incident shows how such a short-cut became widely used in the class.

Each anatomy student is given a dissecting guide with explicit directions on what to do, in what order, and what to look for during the lab session. Reflection of skin is the first step in dissection of each part of the cadaver. The laboratory guide calls for great care in reflecting so as not to pull off the underlying layer of fat which adheres to the skin. Embedded in this subcutaneous fat are tough, threadlike fibers—the peripheral nerves. These are to be traced to their origins and identified. It is a slow, exasperating task; virtually impossible if reflecting is not cleanly done.

When the class began dissection of the lower leg, we noticed one group had taken off skin and fat together leaving the nerves undissected. A student at the tank said, 'You see, it's easier this way. I think it saves a lot of time because you really can't get those nerves anyway.' His partner agreed, saying, 'It's much better to get the nerves from the book.' Another student, speaking for himself and his tank partners, said, 'We knew we couldn't do the nerves because they are all different on every body. It doesn't make any difference if you do the nerves or a lot of other things.' By the third week of dissection, most groups observed were stripping off skin and fat together; identification of the peripheral nerves was omitted.

Collective behavior of this sort does not mean students do not work hard. They continue to work very hard on the things they think important. One reason for their neglect of peripheral nerves, for instance, is their haste to get to the next layer down which contains the larger structures, muscles and blood vessels, that every doctor must know about. It does mean that where the faculty fails to 'give it to them straight' in accordance with student concepts of why they are in school and what and how they ought to study, various short-cuts are devised in more or less open defiance of faculty instructions, and students who have deviant interests outside the student culture keep them increasingly to themselves (see Becker & Geer 1958).

The clinical years

During the last two years of medical school—the clinical years—the student's work consists largely of taking medical histories from and performing physical examinations on patients, in order that he may develop these skills and use the information so gained in learning how to diagnose and treat various diseases. Although he continues to be tested on his knowledge through formal examinations, he is told in various ways and believes that the crucial decisions about his future in school—whether he passes or fails, for example—are based largely on the faculty's evaluation of his clinical work. Furthermore, he believes that, having got this far, it is very unlikely that he will be flunked out of school; few such cases are known to have occurred.

The major problems requiring collective solution no longer lie in the realm of examinations. Rather, students focus their attention on how to deal with the continuous pressure of a heavy load of clinical work and how to get the most out of that work in terms of the future one envisions for himself in medicine. Student culture develops as a set of perspectives on and solutions for these problems.

The view that the function of medical school is, among other things, to train students to recognize and deal with diseases that are commonly run across in a general medical practice constitutes one such perspective, shared by almost all students, even those who do not contemplate becoming general practitioners themselves. This basic proposition itself derives in part from statements by the school's faculty and administration and in part from the inability of most students to visualize anything but general practice for themselves before they have had clinical contact with other medical specialties. Once formed, the proposition continues as a more or less unquestioned premise even after the students know more about specialized kinds of practices.

The students draw several more specific conclusions about their school work from this proposition, in the course of conversations and discussions of specific incidents. These specific items of student culture may be summarized as follows. 1. The patients whom it is really important to study thoroughly are those who have common diseases—whether simple or complicated—for which there are available treatments a general practitioner could utilize. 2. All those kinds of clinical work that they cannot imagine themselves doing in a general practice are regarded as a waste of time. 3. Courses in which they are not given practice in techniques they regard as important for the practitioner to know tend to be disliked. Matters of this kind are widely discussed among the students and have important consequences for the way they interpret their experience in school and distribute their effort and time among their many competing interests.

The following incident, one among many observed, provides a nice example of the way students collectively draw inferences from the basic proposition stated above and use these to guide their behavior in school.

In one of the third year courses students are required, at the end of the course, to turn in elaborate summaries of each case assigned to them during their time on the service. These summaries must include the important findings of their own examination, important laboratory findings, a discussion of all the possible causes for these findings, references to relevant literature, and a discussion of modes of possible treatment. They are long and require a great deal of time to prepare.

The students in one group we observed established an informal norm specifying the number of such summaries they would turn in, although they were definitely directed to turn in one on every patient they had been assigned. Over a period of several days preceding the date the summaries were due, the six students in this group discussed the matter at length and decided that they would all hand in no more than a certain number. Further, they agreed on the criteria for selecting those to be turned in, and on the premise that the real purpose for these summaries was to provide material for the faculty to quiz them on during oral exams, so that the actual number was unimportant (in spite of the definite order that all cases were to be so summarized).

The criteria for selection of cases discarded were those which it was agreed provided them with no knowledge they did not already have of treating common medical problems, or where the

work involved in preparing the summary would not add to such knowledge. Thus, patients with fractures or simple infections, whose treatment was more or less standard and afforded the students no chance to participate, were not summarized, and 'crocks' were not summarized. ('Crocks' are patients who have no physical pathology, but only vague and untreatable psychosomatic complaints, thus patients from whom nothing can be learned that might prove of use in general medical practice.)

The decision that these criteria were the relevant ones was reached in a discussion between the students in the group and in discussions with students who had been through the course previously who confirmed this interpretation.

A similar set of attitudes has grown up around the routine laboratory work—blood counts and urinalyses—the students must do on incoming patients assigned to them. They greatly resent this work because, among other reasons, it wastes their time since they themselves will not do these procedures, they think, when they are in practice.

This general frame of mind, as we have said, coerces the students' thinking to a striking degree. The following excerpt from an interview, which also illustrates the way courses are judged with reference to the amount of training they provide for the exigencies of general practice, indicates this clearly.

I asked a third year student to compare his training in surgery at the University Hospital with that he had during the other half of the quarter at the Veterans Administration Hospital to which students are also sent. (This student had definite and realistic plans to specialize in internal medicine, having even made arrangements as to whom he would practice with and where; as an internist he would, of course, do no surgery at all.)

He said, 'One thing about surgery over at the VA was that we really got to do quite a bit more. I mean, for example, they would let us sew up incisions over there, where you don't get to do that at the University. Another thing about surgery at the University is that they do a lot of very complicated operations. For example, they do a lot of heart surgery over there. Well, now, none of us are ever going to do any heart surgery. But every one of us will probably do some hernias and some appendectomies. And over at the VA you see a lot of these. So it is really a better experience for us in a lot of ways. We don't have the glamor of all that fancy surgery, but we do see the ordinary things that will be useful to us.'

Consequences of student culture

Student culture affects the larger social system in

which it is embedded—the medical school—in two ways. On the one hand, it provides the basis for a modus vivendi between the students and their superiors, providing a perspective from which students can build consistent patterns of response enabling them to fit into the activities of the school and hospital. In this respect student culture is an accommodation on the part of the students to the facts of life of the school. On the other hand, student culture provides the students with the social support that allows them, in individual instances and as a group, independently to assess faculty statements and demands so that they can significantly reinterpret faculty emphasis and, in a meaningful sense, make what they will of their education. In this sense, student culture is a mechanism that creates the conditions for considerable deviance from formally stated institutional rules.

When students first enter school their emphasis on medical practice—their belief that they are in school to learn to save lives (Becker & Geer 1958)—leads them to rebel against laboratory work, essentially nonmedical, and against the drudgery of studying for intensive academic examinations. Later, they must deal with the same problem of an overload of work in a clinical setting in which examinations are not so important although the possibility of being tested and found wanting is always present. The understandings and agreements that make up student culture, by solving these problems in one way or another, allow the students to fit into the system without being constantly so upset as to be unable to function. In this way, student culture is a mode of accommodation to what the students find expected of them in school.

At the same time student culture affects the level and direction of effort students expend while in school, by giving them a rationale for restricting the theoretically infinite amount of time and effort they might devote to their school work. More importantly, it provides them with sufficient collective support to allow them to direct their effort in quite different directions than those suggested by the faculty— considered as a unit or even considered with regard for the division of opinion within the faculty itself. Though members of a given department may feel that their course is really designed to put across such-and-such a brand of knowledge for this-and-that purpose, the students may remain relatively immune, drawing the strength to ignore the faculty's otherwise authoritative notions from the lore that makes up student culture. Student culture is thus the cornerstone of many faculty difficulties with students, one of the facts of life to which teachers must, in their turn, make some accommodation.

As we have said earlier, medical school represents an extreme case of the development and operation of student culture. We would not necessarily expect it to play so important a role in other educational institutions. But we do believe that it is likely to exist in such places and that it will likely be found to have at least the two functions we have discussed for the medical instance, that of providing a means of accommodation for the students to the difficulties of school life, and that of providing the basis for redirection of effort on the student's part, possibly in defiance of faculty standards and ideals.

Notes

1 This paper was originally read at the meetings of the American Sociological Society, 28 August 1957, Washington, D.C., and was later published in the *Harvard Educational Review*, vol. 28 (Winter, 1958), 70–80.
Our study of medical students was sponsored by Community Studies, Inc., of Kansas City, Missouri, and was further supported by grants from the Carnegie Corporation and the National Institutes of Health. Anselm Strauss has collaborated with us in both the field work and the preparation of the final report.
2 On intersecting groups, see Simmel (1955, 149–50).

References

Becker, H. S., and B. Geer. The fate of idealism in medical school. *American Sociological Review*, (1958), **23**, 50–6.
Cohen, A. K. (1956). *Delinquent Boys: The Culture of the Gang*. Routledge & Kegan Paul.
Daiches, D. (1957). Education in democratic society. *Commentary*, **23**, 336–43.
Simmel, G. (1955). *The Web of Group Affiliations*. Translated by Reinhard Bendix. Chicago: Free Press.
Sumner, W. G. (1907). *Folkways*. Boston: Ginn (also N.E.L. 1965).
Weber, M. (1924). Zur Psychophysik der industriellen Arbeit (1908–9) in *Gesammelte Aufsaetze zur Soziologie und Sozialpolitik*. Tuebingen, 61–255.

8   Latent culture: a note on the theory of latent social roles

Howard S. Becker and Blanche Geer

Administrators have always known that workers' behavior is affected by what they are and who they are away from the job. But we have had few conceptual tools for analyzing this relation. In this paper we discuss the conditions under which the cultures men participate in elsewhere may furnish the substance of the culture of the work group.

Gouldner's paper on latent social roles[1] makes a distinction that is both long-needed and provocative. He distinguishes those social roles related to identities which the group agrees are relevant to a particular social setting from those related to identities conventionally defined as 'being irrelevant, inappropriate to consider, or illegitimate to take into account' in the same context. The latter he terms *latent*, as distinguished from *manifest*, roles and identities. His research indicates that latent roles can be empirically distinguished and that they have important consequences for the behavior of people in organizations.

The importance of this conceptual advance leads us to raise the question of whether there may not be a useful distinction between characteristics of *organizations* that parallels Gouldner's distinction between roles of individuals. The role concept implies an organizational setting but does not itself describe it. Are there not distinct group characteristics which result from the operation of forces related to latent social identities on the one hand and manifest identities on the other?

Two concepts frequently used to describe organizations are *structure* and *culture*. The structure of an organization is an orderly arrangement of social relations, a continuing arrangement of kinds of people (named and defined), governed by a concept of proper behavior for them in their relations with one another. The culture of an organization consists of the conventional understandings shared by the participants in it.[2] Gouldner's analysis suggests that we might well

Source: *Administrative Science Quarterly* (September 1960), *5*, 304–13.

look for manifest and latent structures and cultures that would correspond to the manifest and latent roles he has described.

The distinction between 'formal' and 'informal' organization closely parallels, for structures, Gouldner's distinction between kinds of roles. We would like to suggest a similar distinction for the concept of culture and examine some of its implications. Classically, culture is conceived as arising in response to some problem faced by a group.[3] The problem is one that individual members of the group see as common to all members; it is a shared problem. In some way, a way of meeting the problem is arrived at, a mode of action that is agreed to be the best or most proper solution. The solution leads to, or implies, more general views and assumptions—the perspectives and values underlying the culture, its 'world view'. The organized whole of such problem solutions is the culture of the group.

People carry culture with them; when they leave one group setting for another they do not shed the cultural premises of the first setting. This phenomenon is in part what Gouldner describes in discussing latent roles and identities. Something is true of a person by virtue of the fact that he has some other social identity, which draws its being from some other social group. Among the things true by virtue of this fact is that he holds some ideas that are part of the culture of that group. In short, the members of a group may derive their understandings from cultures other than that of the group they are at the moment participating in. To the degree that group participants share latent social identities (related to their membership in the same 'outside' social groups) they will share these understandings, so that there will be a culture which can be called *latent*, i.e. the culture has its origin and social support in a group other than the one in which the members are now participating.

These latent identities are not necessarily based on prior group membership, for Gouldner's example of 'cosmopolitan' and 'local' identities makes clear that such identities may arise out of the internal 'politics' of organizations (although his distinction seems to imply membership in outside professional groups as one of the loci of 'cosmopolitanism'). It seems likely that they will usually be related to what are called 'background variables' (social class, or ethnic origin, for example), but, whether they are or not, what is important is that latent identities will not affect either individual behavior within the group or the collective behavior of the group unless they are in some way mobilized and brought into play in the daily inter-action of group members.

In other words, these latent identities must be taken account of; people must orient their behavior towards latent as well as manifest identities if understandings that are part of latent culture are to have any in-fluence on behavior in the group. The fact of being an 'old-timer' in the organization or of being a member of some particular ethnic group will not affect behavior unless these distinctions are made use of in daily interaction in groups that support and maintain the culture associated with these irrelevant identities. Latent culture is thus only *potential*; it needs to be developed in the new setting, in the sense that it has to be brought into play and applied to the new problems arising from group members. It does not influence group behavior simply by virtue of members having similar latent identities.

This culture stemming from latent identities can be contrasted with the culture peculiar to the group setting, the culture that has arisen in response to the problems its members share. This culture is not, in the pure case, affected by other (latent) identities of those participating in it. To the degree that group members face similar problems and contingencies, this culture is operative. It can be called the *manifest* culture. It need not be approved or formally specified by institutional rules and may even support deviation from those rules. But it is a culture that grows around the roles and identities relevant to the specific setting rather than those that are irrelevant or inappropriate.

An example from our current study of a medical school will clarify the distinction.[4] Medical students are alike in that they are all training to become physicians, but they differ in many other ways. In our study many of the students were from small towns and rural areas in Kansas, while others came from larger towns and cities in Kansas, Missouri, and else-where. Although these (latent) identities seldom be-came the basis of stable social groupings, they frequently underlay casual groupings arising in conversations about the best place to practice and the best style of practice (general practice or speciality). The student's latent culture associated with the size of his home town influenced his opinion in such conversations. (Several latent cultures of this kind operated among the students, particularly the latent culture associated with social class identities, which we discuss later.) But the students of this school shared another culture, which we have referred to as 'student culture'.[5] This culture grows around those problems shared by all students in the school, problems related to their manifest identities as students: the immediate necessity of mastering a vast amount of factual material, the more distant threat of failing, the diffi-culties of dealing with details of work in the hospital, and the peculiarities of certain teachers and depart-ments. A set of perspectives on these problems and specific solutions for them constituted a manifest culture, dealing with different problems in different ways, quite distinct from any latent cultures we discovered.

One point needs clarification here. The use of the terms 'manifest' and 'latent' connotes nothing about whether the cultural items operate with or against the openly expressed aims of the organization. It might be thought that manifest culture, for instance, would not operate at cross-purposes with stated organizational aims, but it well may. In medical school, the student culture has as one of its functions the support of organized deviance from the goals of the administration and faculty.[6] Yet we refer to this as manifest culture because it is tied to the students' identities as students and grows up around problems of the students' identity. Similarly, latent culture may support stated organizational aims.

We now consider some of the concomitants of this distinction between latent and manifest culture and suggest some propositions about them.

The strength and unity of a group's latent culture will, of course, depend on the character of the re-cruitment to the group. If recruitment is restricted to persons coming from a similar cultural background, latent culture will be strong and consistent; there will be no variant subcultural groups within the larger group and everyone will share the premises of the culture associated with the common latent identities. To the degree that group members have different latent identities, a latent culture will not be possible. Thus, one of the conditions for the existence of latent culture is some degree of exclusiveness or restriction of recruitment. Latent cultures are not likely to develop where recruitment to the group is indiscrimin-ate in that latent identities of recruits are diverse (in the pure case, where no two group members share any latent identity). They are likely to develop where recruitment is selective (in the pure case, where every member shares some particular latent identity).

This suggests the proposition that the independence of the manifest from the latent culture will vary with the diverseness of latent identities in the group. Manifest culture—the organized solutions to common problems of an immediate kind—may be dictated by latent culture when latent social identities are similar and the immediate problem is conceptualized by the group in terms that are restricted by their common culture associated with these identities. For instance, an occupational group drawn largely from one social class will have its occupational culture dictated by social class premises more than one which draws from all levels of the class system. One might expect the occupational culture of bankers to reflect upper-middle or upper-class culture and that of steel workers to reflect lower or lower-middle-class culture, while that of jazz musicians, who are recruited from all class levels, would not reflect the culture of any particular stratum. The latent culture would restrict solutions to immediate occupational problems within the framework of the given class culture; other solutions would not occur to members of the occupation or would be rejected as illegitimate or improper. Both bankers and musicians, let us say, may find their clients or customers difficult.[7] The musicians' solution to this problem—open hostility—might not be available to bankers because of the restrictions on such behavior in their social class culture.

But if latent culture can restrict the possibilities for the proliferation of the manifest culture, the opposite is also true. Manifest culture can restrict the operation of latent culture. The problems facing group members may be so pressing that, given the social context in which the group operates, the range of solutions that will be effective may be so limited as not to allow for influence of variations resulting from cultures associated with other identities. That is, solutions suggested by latent culture could be utilized only at the expense of breaking some very important group rule or threatening the unity and continued existence of the group.

The corollary of this proposition is that latent culture operates most in social contexts and with regard to problems that are not defined as critical for the group. The problems left to latent culture may not be of great moment, i.e. they may be considered trivial and not worthy of collective attention. Or they may be considered serious, but serious for the individual rather than the group. In either event, solutions can be derived from the culture associated with latent identities. For instance, medical students have difficulty carrying on their necessary interaction with patients; they do not at first know how to talk to them so as to make sociable intercourse easy. But this problem is not regarded as a serious one; it is not expected to lead to drastic consequences either for the individual student or for the students collectively. The student may be embarrassed by the faulty interaction, but he will not fail his course and his professional future will not be affected; nor will his failure affect the other students with whom he works. The solution is consequently left to the individual and appears to be derived from two sources: (1) from observation of practicing physicians, and (2) from past experiences in dealing with persons of various social types. Thus the upper-middle-class student, who has had more experience in dealing with persons of his own social class and with those of lower social classes, experiences less difficulty than the lower-middle-class student whose social awareness is more limited.

If problems have potential consequences for the group, however, they are not influenced by latent culture, although they might be thought equally the concern of the individual rather than the entire student group. Thus the problem of how to deal with oral quizzing by faculty members is settled by each student for himself, as he works out methods of making a good impression and avoiding censure; but these individual solutions are guided by understandings reached by the students about the kinds of solution to this problem which will not jeopardize the fate of other students. It is not solved by application of culture gained in interaction in other roles.

Problems that are serious, but affect only the individual, are more likely to be solved individually—the solutions stemming from a latent culture where this is operative. Thus a medical student has the problem of supporting himself. All students recognize this as a serious problem, but it is not one they face collectively. The problem presents a different set of contingencies and possible solutions to each student, at least theoretically. Social class subgroups among students may have some latent cultural agreements as to proper solutions to this problem, but it is not a problem that has any status in student (manifest) culture. It is left to individual solution, and thus, potentially, to solutions from latent culture.

We do not want to imply that behavior based on latent culture is individual behavior, as the above examples seem to suggest. It is still culturally influenced in the sense that the person is constrained in formulating his action by the premises of some subculture. But the actions we speak of as being based on latent culture will appear on the surface to be individual and not be constrained by such influences. This is so because latent culture, relating as it does to identities considered irrelevant and inappropriate in the setting, appears in the form of attitudes and cultural premises that are often unstated and undiscussed. These attitudes have not been consciously worked out in their relevance to the immediate situation through group discussion and interaction. Instead, they were formed in other settings and in this setting are taken for granted, although they may be shared and supported by other group members of similar latent identity.

So far we have considered only the case in which the participants either share a latent identity or do not. A further complication may be introduced by considering the possibility of several kinds of latent identities within a group, each person having one from among these kinds, so that there are several possible latent cultures and each person a potential participant in one of them. An example might be latent ethnic identities in a business organization; there might be people of several ethnic backgrounds in the organization, and each ethnic type would be a possible basis for the operation of a latent culture, but each person would be able to participate in only one of these.

In considering the consequences of such a situation,

we need to repeat a point made earlier, namely, that latent identities and latent cultures associated with them are likely to furnish the bases for the formation of latent social structures. What are more usually known as 'informal' groupings may tend to cluster around a latent culture, the members of these groupings sharing some particular latent identity. The interaction in such groups helps to maintain the person's sense of his latent identity and to maintain the latent culture by providing a group which gives social support for the use of that culture as a basis for behavior. This is important because it suggests the mechanism by which these latent identities are maintained operable in an environment in which they are regarded as irrelevant or improper, and in which they might be expected to die out.

In the situation in which several kinds of mutually exclusive latent identities are present, there may also be several latent structures (informal groups) present as well. We can now ask under what circumstances the latent culture of one of these groups might affect manifest culture by providing the solution to a problem in the immediate setting, which the whole group eventually adopts. One possibility is that groups with greater prestige or power will be more able to mold manifest culture in this way. It may be, however, that differentials in prestige or power between subgroups are not great enough for one of them to rule in this way, in which case we would expect the eventual solution to be arrived at by some process of compromise. This, of course, would only occur where the problem under consideration was not serious enough for the entire group that the solution would be dictated by the immediate setting (manifest culture) and not be subject to influence from the latent culture of any group.

In addition to the situation where there are many subgroups present, there may be only one subgroup that shares a common latent identity and culture while the remainder of the larger group is relatively diverse, not having such common identities and culture. The members of such a group will be more able to influence manifest culture than their unorganized counterparts: communication between them will proceed more easily because of culturally shared premises; they will have operating agreements almost before others are aware that there is any problem calling for solution; and so on. This suggests the more general proposition that the development of latent culture will depend on the relative strength of organization of people of differing latent identity. One subgroup may have such strength and others not.

It appears that this process operated with respect to certain problems of the medical students who had several kinds of (latent) social class identities. Some were upper middle class while the others came from lower strata. When the freshman class faced the problem of what facts and theories they should attempt to learn out of the bewildering variety they were faced with, the eventual solution—learning what the faculty wanted as evidenced by examinations and quizzes—was one which bore the mark of the (latent) social class culture of the upper-middle-class students. These students were members of medical school fraternities and thus more highly organized than the other members of the class who did not belong to fraternities. (Formal organization, as in a fraternity, should not be taken as an infallible index of the existence of latent culture, for such an organization may in fact recruit haphazardly and end with a membership with diverse latent identities, thus weakening its organization. One of the three medical fraternities in the school we studied had these characteristics. Furthermore, when people sort themselves out into groups in this way, as the students did when they joined fraternities, many 'mistakes' may be made so that people gain membership in the formal organizations without sharing the latent culture.)

Such situations warn us to keep other variables in mind. For instance, two groups defined by common latent identities may be present, yet the cultural background of one is such as to make it less likely that its members will combine effectively. It may be that upper-middle-class culture provides more experience in 'combining' of this sort so that where this group participates in an organization with members of a lower social class the situation would resemble that in which one group participates with a diverse aggregate. Also, even where the background culture did not provide this dividend of combining power, it might be that persons with certain kinds of latent social identities and cultures are more visible to one another than other persons sharing a different latent identity, thus making it easier for them to combine (as, for example, Jews as contrasted with Protestants, drug addicts in many settings, homosexuals, and so on).

Where there are two groups distinguished by common latent identities and a third which is an aggregate of diverse identities, the group with less power to maintain exclusiveness may find itself further weakened by the fact that it becomes, in effect, a residual group: everyone who does not belong to the more exclusive groups finds his place in the less exclusive group, which then has even less strength to achieve latent cultural consensus and so to make its contribution to the manifest culture.

In cases where one group's latent culture furnishes the material for the manifest culture, the process can be aided or hindered depending on whether this group more nearly fits the general public's cultural image of what members of the organization or group should be like. Everett Hughes has noted that auxiliary status traits are attached in the public mind to many statuses and that status contradictions can arise when a person possesses the key or master status trait but is deficient in the auxiliary status traits.[8] Thus all one needs to be a doctor is a license, yet it is typically assumed that an MD will be male, white, and upper middle class. A group which most nearly fits the auxiliary status specifications attached to the manifest identity (has the proper associated latent identities) may be seen as having more authoritative information or more legitimate right to suggest solutions for the manifest culture. (This process operates among medical students, where the upper-middle-class students have more influence by virtue of this; likewise among drug addicts, where those who most nearly fit the public stereotype of the depraved 'dope fiend' are commonly viewed as having the 'real lowdown' by other addicts.)

Although we have clearly done no more here than suggest many questions to be explored more fully, we have used some of these propositions in our work on medical students and hope that others may find those ideas suggestive enough to merit consideration in their own research.

Notes

1 Alvin W. Gouldner, Cosmopolitans and locals: Toward an analysis of latent social roles – I, *Administrative Science Quarterly*, 2 (1957), 281–306.

2 Cf. Robert Redfield, *The Folk Culture of Yucatan* (Chicago 1941), 132: 'In speaking of "culture" we have reference to the conventional understandings, manifest in act and artifact, that characterize societies. The "understandings" are the meanings attached to acts and objects. The meanings are conventional, and therefore cultural, in so far as they have become typical for the members of that society by reason of inter-communication among the members. A culture is, then, an abstraction: it is the type toward which the meanings that the same act or object has for the different members tend to conform. The meanings are expressed in action and the results of action, from which we infer them; so we may as well identify culture with the extent to which the conventionalized behavior of members of the society is for all the same.'

3 See W. G. Sumner, *Folkways* (Boston, 1907),§1–3.

4 This research, a sociological study of some problems of medical education, is sponsored by Community Studies, Inc., of Kansas City, Missouri, and is being carried out at the University of Kansas Medical School, to whose dean, staff, and students we are indebted for their co-operation. Professor Everett C. Hughes of the University of Chicago is director of the project. Some portions of the study are reported in Howard S. Becker and Blanche Geer, The fate of idealism in medical school, *American Sociological Review*, 23 (1958), 50–6; and Student culture in medical school (pp. 51–5 in the present volume). A monograph reporting the entire study is in preparation.

5 Ibid.

6 Ibid.

7 On the jazz musician, see Howard S. Becker, The professional dance musician and his audience, *American Journal of Sociology*, 62 (1951), 136–44.

8 Everett C. Hughes, Dilemmas and contradictions of status, *American Journal of Sociology* 50 (1945), 353–9.

9 Education cannot compensate for society[1]

Basil Bernstein

The context in which children learn is usually a middle-class one. Should we try to coax them to that 'standard', or seek what is valid in their own lives?

Since the late 1950s there has been a steady outpouring of papers and books in the United States which are concerned with the education of children of low social class whose *material* circumstances are inadequate, or with the education of black children of low social class whose *material* circumstances are chronically inadequate. A vast research and educational bureaucracy developed in the United States, which was financed by funds obtained from federal, state or private foundations. New educational categories were developed—'the culturally deprived', 'the linguistically deprived', 'the socially disadvantaged'; and the notion of 'compensatory education' was introduced as a means of changing the status of the children in these categories.

Compensatory education emerged in the form of massive pre-school programmes like Project Headstart (see Ruth Adam, *New Society*, 30 October 1969), large-scale research programmes such as those of Deutch in the early 1960s and a plethora of small-scale 'intervention' or 'enrichment' programmes for pre-school children or children in the first years of compulsory education. Very few sociologists were involved in these studies, because education was a low-status area. On the whole they were carried out by psychologists.

The focus of these studies was on the child in the family and on the local classroom relationship between teacher and child. In the last two years one can detect a change in this focus. As a result of the movements towards integration and the opposed movement towards segregation (the latter a response to the wishes of the various Black Power groups), more studies are being made in the United States of the *school*. Robert Rosenthal's classic study, *Pygmalion in the Classroom*, drew attention to the critical importance of the teacher's expectations of the child.

In this country we have been aware of the educa-

Source: *New Society*, 26 February 1970, 344–7.

tional problem since the writings of Sir Cyril Burt before the war. His book, *The Backward Child*, is probably still the best study we have. After the war, a series of sociological surveys and public inquiries into education brought this educational problem into the arena of national debate, and so of social policy. Now in Wales there is a large research unit, financed by the Schools Council, concerned with compensatory education. Important research of a different kind is taking place in the University of Birmingham into the problems of the education of Commonwealth children. The Social Science Research Council and the Department of Education and Science have given £175,000, in part for the development of special pre-school programmes concerned to introduce children to compensatory education. There is also the whole educational priority area programme (described by Anne Corbett in 'Are educational priority areas working?' 13 November 1969).

One university department of education offers an advanced diploma in compensatory education. Colleges of education also offer special courses under the same title. So it might be worth a few lines to consider the assumptions underlying this work and the concepts which describe it, particularly as my own writings have sometimes been used (and more often abused) to highlight aspects of the general problems and dilemmas.

To begin with, I find the term, 'compensatory education', a curious one for a number of reasons. I do not understand how we can talk about offering compensatory education to children who in the first place have not, as yet, been offered an adequate education environment. The Newsom Report on secondary schools showed that 79 per cent of all secondary modern schools in slum and problem areas were materially grossly inadequate, and that the holding power of these schools over the teachers was horrifyingly low. The same report also showed very clearly the depression in the reading scores of these children, compared with the reading scores of children who were at school in areas which were neither problem nor slum. This does not conflict with the finding that, on average, for the country as a whole, there has been an improvement in children's reading ability. The Plowden Report on the primary schools was rather more coy about all the above points, but we have little reason to believe that the situation is very much better for primary schools in similar areas.

Thus we offer a large number of children, both at the primary and secondary levels, materially inadequate schools and a higher turnover of teaching staff; and we further expect a small group of dedicated teachers to cope. The strain on these teachers inevitably produces fatigue and illness and it is not uncommon to find, in any week, teachers having to deal with doubled-up classes of 80 children. And we wonder why the children display very early in their educational life a range of learning difficulties.

At the same time, the organization of schools creates delicate overt and covert streaming arrangements which neatly lower the expectations and motivations of both teachers and taught. A vicious spiral is set up, with an all too determinate outcome. It would seem, then, that we have failed to provide, on the scale required, an *initial* satisfactory educational environment.

The concept, 'compensatory education', serves to direct attention away from the internal organization and the educational context of the school, and focus our attention on the families and children. 'Compensatory education' implies that something is lacking in the family, and so in the child. As a result, the children are unable to benefit from schools.

It follows, then, that the school has to 'compensate' for the something which is missing in the family, and the children are looked at as deficit systems. If only the parents were interested in the goodies we offer, if only they were like middle-class parents, then we could do our job. Once the problem is seen even implicitly in this way, then it becomes appropriate to coin the terms 'cultural deprivation', 'linguistic deprivation', and so on. And then these labels do their own sad work.

If children are labelled 'culturally deprived', then it follows that the parents are inadequate; the spontaneous realizations of their culture, its images and symbolic representations, are of reduced value and significance. Teachers will have lower expectations of the children, which the children will undoubtedly fulfil. All that informs the child, that gives meaning and purpose to him outside of the school, ceases to be valid or accorded significance and opportunity for enhancement within the school. He has to orient towards a different structure of meaning, whether it is in the form of reading books (*Janet and John*), in the form of language use and dialect, or in the patterns of social relationships.

Alternatively the meaning structure of the school is explained to the parents and imposed on, rather than integrated within, the form and content of their world. A wedge is progressively driven between the child as a member of a family and community, and the child as a member of a school. Either way the child is expected, and his parents as well, to drop their social identity, their way of life and its symbolic representations, at the school gate. For, by definition, their culture is deprived, and the parents are inadequate in both the moral and the skill orders they transmit.

I do not mean by this that in these circumstances no satisfactory home–school relations can take place or do take place: I mean rather that the best thing is for the parents to be brought *within* the educational experience of the schoolchild by doing what they can do, and this with confidence. There are many ways in which parents can help the child in this learning, which are within the parents' spheres of competence. If this happens, then the parents can feel adequate and confident both in relation to the child and the school. This may mean that the contents of the learning in school should be drawn much more from the child's experience in his family and community.

So far I have criticized the use of the concept of 'compensatory education' because it distracts attention from the deficiencies in the school itself and focuses upon deficiences within the community, family and child. We can add to these criticisms a third.

This concept points to the overwhelming significance of the early years of the child's life in the shaping of his later development. Clearly there is much evidence to support this view and to support its implication that we should create an extensive nursery-school system. However, it would be fool hardy indeed to write off the post-seven-years-of-age educational experience as having little influence.

Minimally, what is required *initially* is to consider the whole age period up to the conclusion of the primary stages as a unity. This would require considering our approach, at any *one* age, in the context of the whole of the primary stage. This implies a systematic, rather than a piecemeal, approach. I am arguing here for taking as the unit, not a particular period in the life of the child—for example, three to five years, or five to seven years—but taking as the unit a stage of education: the primary stage. We should see all we do in terms of the sequencing of learning, the development of sensitivities within the context of the primary stage. In order to accomplish this, the present social and educational division between infant and junior stages must be weakened, as well as the insulation between primary and secondary stages. Otherwise gains at any one age, for the child, may well be vitiated by losses at a later age.

We should stop thinking in terms of 'compensatory education' but consider, instead, most seriously and systematically the conditions and contexts of the educational environment.

The very form our research takes tends to confirm

the beliefs underlying the organization, transmission and evaluation of knowledge by the school. Research proceeds by assessing the criteria of attainment that schools hold, and then measures the competence of different social groups in reaching these criteria. We take one group of children, whom we know beforehand possess attributes favourable to school achievement; and a second group of children, whom we know beforehand lack these attributes. Then we evaluate one group in terms of what it *lacks* when compared with another. In this way research, unwittingly, underscores the notion of *deficit* and confirms the status quo of a given organization, transmission and, in particular, evaluation of knowledge. Research very rarely challenges or exposes the social assumptions underlying what counts as valid knowledge, or what counts as a valid realization of that knowledge. There are exceptions in the area of curriculum development; but, even here, the work often has no built-in attempt to evaluate the changes. This holds particularly for educational priority area 'feasibility' projects.

Finally, we do not face up to the basic question: What is the potential for change within educational institutions as they are presently constituted? A lot of activity does not necessarily mean *action*.

I have taken so much space discussing the new educational concepts and categories because, in a small way, the work I have been doing had inadvertently contributed towards their formulation. It might be, and has been said, that my research—through focusing upon the subculture and forms of family socialization—has also distracted attention from the conditions and contexts of learning in school. The focus on usage of language has sometimes led people to divorce the use of language from the substratum of cultural meanings which are initially responsible for the language use. The concept, 'restricted code', to describe working-class speech, has been equated with 'linguistic deprivation' or even with the 'non-verbal' child.

We can distinguish between uses of language which can be called 'context-bound' and uses of language which are less context-bound. Consider, for example, the two following stories which the linguist, Peter Hawkins, constructed as a result of his analysis of the speech of middle-class and working-class five-year-old children. The children were given a series of four pictures which told a story and they were invited to tell the story. The first picture shows some boys playing football; in the second the ball goes through the window of a house: the third shows a man making a threatening gesture; and in the fourth a woman looks out of a window and the children are moving away. Here are the two stories:

1 Three boys are playing football and one boy kicks the ball and it goes through the window the ball breaks the window and the boys are looking at it and a man comes out and shouts at them because they've broken the window so they run away and then that

lady looks out of her window and she tells the boys off. (No. of nouns: 13. No. of pronouns: 6.)

2 They're playing football and he kicks it and it goes through there it breaks the window and they're looking at it and he comes out and shouts at them because they've broken it so they run away and then she looks out and she tells them off. (No. of nouns: 2. No. of pronouns: 14.)

With the first story, the reader does not have to have the four pictures which were used as the basis for the story, whereas in the case of the second story the reader would require the initial pictures in order to make sense of the story. The first story is free of the context which generated it, whereas the second story is much more closely tied to its context. As a result, the meanings of the second story are implicit, whereas the meanings of the first story are explicit.

It is not that the working-class children do not have, in their passive vocabulary, the vocabulary used by the middle-class children. Nor is it the case that the children differ in their tacit understanding of the linguistic rule system. Rather, what we have here are differences in the use of language arising out of a specific context. One child makes explicit the meanings which he is realizing through language for the person he is telling the story to, whereas the second child does not to the same extent.

The first child takes very little for granted, whereas the second child takes a great deal for granted. Thus, for the first child, the task was seen as a context in which his meanings were required *to be made* explicit, whereas the task for the second child was not seen as a task which required such explication of meaning. It would not be difficult to imagine a context where the first child would produce speech rather like the second.

What we are dealing with here are differences between the children in the way they realize, in language use, what is apparently the same context. We could say that the speech of the first child generated universalistic meanings, in the sense that the meanings are freed from the context and so understandable by all; whereas the speech of the second child generated particularistic meanings, in the sense that the meanings are closely tied to the context and would be only fully understood by others if they had access to the context which originally generated the speech. Thus universalistic meanings are less bound to a given context, whereas particularistic meanings are severely context-bound.

Let us take another example. One mother, when she controls her child, places a great emphasis on language, because she wishes to make explicit, and to elaborate for the child, certain rules and reasons for the rules *and* their consequences. In this way the child has access through language to the relationships between his particular act which evoked the mother's control, and certain general principles, reasons and consequences which serve to universalize the particular act.

Another mother places less emphasis on language when she controls her child and deals with only the particular act: she does not relate it to general principles and their reasoned basis and consequences.

Both children learn that there is something they are supposed, or not supposed, to do; but the first child has learned rather more than this. The grounds of the mother's acts have been made explicit and elaborated; whereas the grounds of the second mother's acts are implicit, they are unspoken.

Our research shows just this. The social classes differ in terms of the *contexts* which evoke certain linguistic realizations. Many mothers in the middle class (and it is important to add not all), relative to the working class (and again it is important to add not all by any means), place greater emphasis on the use of language in socializing the child into the moral order, in disciplining the child, in the communication and recognition of feeling. Here again we can say that the child is oriented towards universalistic meanings which transcend a given context, whereas the second child is oriented towards particularistic meanings which are closely tied to a given context and so do not transcend it. This does not mean that working-class mothers are non-verbal, only that they differ from the middle-class mothers in the *contexts* which evoke universalistic meanings. They are *not* linguistically deprived, neither are their children.

We can generalize from these two examples and say that certain groups of children, through the forms of their socialization, are oriented towards receiving and offering universalistic meanings in certain contexts, whereas other groups of children are oriented towards particularistic meanings. The linguistic realizations of universalistic orders of meaning are very different from the linguistic realizations of particularistic orders of meaning, and so are the forms of the social relation (for example, between mother and child) which generate these. We can say, then, that what is made available for learning, how it is made available, and the patterns of social relation, are also very different.

Now, when we consider the children in school, we can see that there is likely to be difficulty. For the school is necessarily concerned with the transmission and development of universalistic orders of meaning. The school is concerned with making explicit—and elaborating through language—principles and operations as these apply to objects (the science subjects) and persons (the arts subjects). One child, through his socialization, is already sensitive to the symbolic orders of the school, whereas the second child is much less sensitive to the universalistic orders of the school. The second child is oriented towards particularistic orders of meaning which are context-bound, in which principles and operations are implicit, and towards a form of language use through which such meanings are realized.

The school is necessarily trying to develop in the child orders of relevance and relation as these apply to persons and objects, which are not initially the ones he spontaneously moves towards. The problem of educability at one level, whether it is in Europe, the United States or newly developing societies, can be understood in terms of a confrontation between (a) the school's universalistic orders of meaning and the social relationships which generate them, and (b) the particularistic orders of meanings and the social relationships which generate them, which the child brings with him to the school. Orientations towards 'meta-languages' of control and innovation are not made available to these children as part of their initial socialization.

The school is attempting to transmit un-common-sense knowledge—i.e. public knowledge realized through various 'meta-languages'. This knowledge is what I have called universalistic. However, both implicitly and explicitly, schools transmit values and an attendant morality, which affect the contents and contexts of education. They do this by establishing criteria for acceptable pupil and staff conduct. These values and morals also affect the content of educational knowledge through the selection of books, texts and films, and through the examples and analogies used to assist access to public knowledge (universalistic meanings). Thus, the working-class child may be placed at a considerable disadvantage in relation to the *total* culture of the school. It is not made for him; he may not answer to it.

The universalistic functions of language—where meanings are less context-bound—point to an 'elaborated code'. The more particularistic functions point to a 'restricted code'. Because a code is restricted it does not mean that a child is non-verbal, nor is he in the technical sense linguistically deprived, for he possesses the same tacit understanding of the linguistic rule system as any child. It does not mean that the children cannot produce, at any time, elaborated speech variants in *particular* contexts.

It is critically important to distinguish between speech variants and a restricted code. A speech variant is a pattern of linguistic choices which is specific to a particular context—for example, when talking to children, a policeman giving evidence in a court, talking to friends whom one knows well, the rituals of cocktail parties, or train encounters. Because a code is restricted it does not mean that a speaker will not in some contexts, and under specific conditions, use a range of modifiers or subordinations, or whatever. But it does mean that where such choices are made they will be highly *context-specific*.

This 'concept code' refers to the transmission of the deep-meaning structure of a culture or subculture—the 'code' meaning structure.

'Codes', on this view, make substantive the culture or subculture by controlling the linguistic realizations of contexts critical to socialization. Building on the work of Professor Michael Halliday, one can distinguish four critical contexts:

1 The regulative contexts: these are the authority relations where the child is made aware of the moral order and its various backings.

2 The instructional contexts: here the child learns about the objective nature of objects and acquires various skills.

3 The imaginative or innovating contexts: here the child is encouraged to experiment and re-create his world on his own terms and in his own way.

4 The interpersonal contexts: here the child is made aware of affective states—his own and others.

In practice these are interdependent, but the emphasis and contents will vary from one group to another. I suggest that the critical orderings of a culture or subculture are made substantive, are made palpable, through the way it realizes these four contexts linguistically—initially in the family. If these four contexts are realized through the predominant use of restricted speech variants with particularistic —i.e. relatively context-tied—meanings, then the deep structure of the communication is controlled by a restricted code. If these four contexts are realized predominantly through elaborated speech variants, with relatively context-independent—i.e. universalistic —meanings, then the deep structure of communication is controlled by an elaborated code. Because the code is restricted, it does not mean that the users *never* use elaborated speech variants. It only means that such variants will be used infrequently in the process of socializing the child in his family.

The 'concept code' makes a distinction similar to the distinction which linguists make between the 'surface' and 'deep' structure of the grammar. (See David Havano, *New Society*, 9 January 1969, and Ernest Gellner, 29 May 1969, on Noam Chomsky's work.) Sentences which look superficially different can be shown to be generated from the same rules.

The linguistic choices involved in a précis will be markedly different from the linguistic choices involved in a self-conscious poem. These in turn will be markedly different from the linguistic choices involved in an analysis of physical or moral principles: or different again from the linguistic realization of forms of control by a mother. But they may all, under certain conditions, reveal that speech codes—either restricted *or* elaborated—underlie them.

Now because the subculture or culture, through its forms of social integration, generates a restricted code, it does not mean that the resultant speech and meaning system is linguistically or culturally deprived, that the children have nothing to offer the school, that their imaginings are not significant. Nor does it mean that we have to teach the children formal grammar. Nor does it mean that we have to interfere with their dialect.

There is nothing, but nothing, in the dialect as such, which prevents a child from internalizing and learning to use universalistic meanings. But if the contexts of learning—for example, the reading of books—are not contexts which are triggers for the children's imaginings, are not triggers for the children's curiosity and

explorations in his family and community, then the child is not at home in the educational world. If the teacher has to say continuously, 'Say it again, dear; I didn't understand you', then in the end the child may say nothing. If the culture of the teacher is to become part of the consciousness of the child, then the culture of the child must first be in the consciousness of the teacher.

This may mean that the teacher must be able to understand the child's dialect, rather than deliberately attempting to change it. Much of the context of our schools is unwittingly drawn from aspects of the symbolic world of the middle class, and so when the child steps into school he is stepping into a symbolic system which does not provide for him a linkage with his life outside.

It is an accepted educational principle that we should work with what the child can offer; why don't we practise it? The introduction of the child to the universalistic meanings of public forms of thought is not 'compensatory education'; *it is education*. It is not making children middle class; how it is done, through the implicit values underlying the form and content of the educational environment, might.

We need to distinguish between the principles and operations that teachers transmit and develop in the children, and the contexts they create in order to do this. We should start knowing that the social experience the child already possesses is valid and significant, and that this social experience should be reflected back to him as being valid and significant. It can only be reflected back to him if it is part of the texture of the learning experience we create. If we spent as much time thinking through the implications of this as we do thinking about the implications of Piaget's development sequences, then it would be possible for schools to become exciting and challenging environments for parents, the children themselves and teachers.

We need to examine the social assumptions underlying the organization, distribution and evaluation of knowledge, for there is not one, and only one, answer. The power relationships created outside the school penetrate the organization, distribution and evaluation of knowledge through the social context. The definition of 'educability' is itself, at any one time, an attenuated consequence of these power relationships.

We must consider Robert Lynd's question: 'knowledge for what?' And the answer cannot be given only in terms of whether six-year-old children should be able to read, count and write. We do not know what a child is capable of, as we have as yet no theory which enables us to create sets of optimal learning environments; and even if such a theory existed, it is most unlikely that resources would be available to make it substantive on the scale required. It may well be that one of the tests of an educational system is that its outcomes are relatively unpredictable.

Note

1 This article is a more spelled-out version of one which forms a chapter in *Education for Democracy*, ed. Colin Stoneman and David Rubenstein, Penguin Education Special (1970), 110–21.

References

Bernstein, Basil (1970). A sociolinguistic approach to socialization: with some reference to educability, in J. Gumperz and Dell Hymes (eds), *Directions in Sociolinguistics*. New York: Holt, Rinehart & Winston.

Bernstein, Basil and Henderson, D. (1969). Social class differences in the relevance of language to socialization. *Sociology* 3 (1).

Fantini, M. D. and Weinstein, G. (1968). *The Disadvantaged: Challenge to Education*. Harper & Row.

Halliday, M. A. K. (1969). Relevant models of language. *Educational Review* 22 (1).

Hawkins, P. R. (1969). Social class, the national group and reference. *Language and Speech* 12(2).

10 Functional autonomy, role distance and social class[1]

Julienne Ford, Douglas Young and Steven Box

An observation commonly made about working-class[2] childhoods is that they are characterized by long periods in which parental control is virtually absent.[3] At the earliest opportunity children are allowed to go out to play in the streets, local parks, playgrounds and building-sites, or to go alone to the local cinema. One might assume from this that working-class children grow up with a highly developed sense of independence and an ability to cope with ambiguity. Yet our knowledge of the adult working class indicates the opposite. Their lives have a routinized collective quality in which notions of the traditional are standards for 'the proper'.[4] The lives of adults are governed by what we may call 'rulefulness' whereas those of children seem to be anarchic.

In this paper we intend to explain this paradox by exploring the implications of differential relationship to social structure for individual dramaturgical skill. We argue that the show of role distance[5] is a mode of role-playing normally available only to the middle class, while working-class behaviour is more typically an expression of rulefulness. Thus we consider that interpretation of society in dramaturgical terms[6] is not wholly useful to an understanding of working-class behaviour; for the latter 'receive' rather than 'interpret' social structure.[7]

Where social structure is 'received' emphasis is on the imperative natures of mores without reference to a legitimating rationale. The only possible answer to the question 'Why?' is 'Because it is right'. This 'emphasis on the binding power of the more and folkways ... on the blind adherence to custom corresponds with a society populated by people playing roles principally as sets of expectations with which they must comply.'[8] Where structure is 'interpreted', on the other hand, custom is seen as defining *ranges* of tolerable variation rather than the precise content of behaviour. The individual thus interprets concrete social events in the light of abstract principles—he has

Source: *British Journal of Sociology* (1967), *18* (4), 370–81.

a 'theory' of social structure. In this case ideas of what is situationally appropriate rather than what is 'right' provide parameters for behaviour. The discretionary element in role behaviour thus affords the options not only of playing but also of *playing at*[9] roles.

Examples of this can be found in the different meanings which persons from different social class backgrounds impute to a similar form of address. Both middle- and working-class persons may call a policeman 'Officer', but the former may do so with an awareness that to play out his citizen role in a deferential manner may be situationally advantageous to him, while the latter may do so because he sees it as the 'proper' thing to do.

Far from being at odds with differential childhood behaviours, we argue that these adult social class differences in role-playing actually derive from certain differences in childhood experience. For we hope to show that it is only in a condition of functional autonomy[10] that the option of role distance is created for the actor. We argue that working-class patterns of elementary behaviour[11] are productive of functional dependence, while those of the middle class tend to generate independence, or functional autonomy. Intervening in these processes are the distinctive concepts of *justice*, *friendship* and *privacy* which characterize the social classes.

We shall first describe these ideal types of social exchange behaviour[12] in terms of class conceptions of justice, friendship and privacy. Then we shall discuss the interrelations of the concepts of *social exchange*, *functional autonomy* and *role distance* on a higher level of abstraction. Finally we shall suggest some implications of our observations for the Interactionist conception of society.

Class notions of justice, friendship and privacy

An individual's conception of justice is centrally related to his basic notions about the difference between individuals[13] and will hence affect his approach to social exchange. If we accept the premise that the child's earliest idea of justice is based on parity of distribution[14] we can trace the way in which this notion is modified for both social classes, and draw out the implications of this for differential dramaturgical perception.

In a cultural–historical sense, the working-class family setting can be seen as one of chronic scarcity of material resources; in these circumstances distribution within the household is governed by rationing. This rationing must be effected in order both to ensure physical survival and to minimize conflict within the family. Both these imperatives favour a distribution according to the ascribed statuses of age, sex and familial function. For example where distribution of food is concerned physiological necessity dictates that the working males shall be favoured. Allocation on the bases of such highly visible criteria as age and sex also provides an overtly just rationale for distribution, and in this manner rationing is effected with minimum threat to group cohesion.

The necessity to avoid conflict within the group also explains why the sanctions maintaining these principles of distribution tend to be characterized by appeals to self-evidence. Since the mother not only lacks material resources but also the time for any complicated explanations these appeals will be backed ultimately by recourse to physical or verbal coercion. Thus the child learns a model of justice as a self-evident order, as something which is 'right and proper'; while parity remains the underlying principle he modifies this in consideration of a growing number of overt status distinctions.

Congruent with this conception of justice is the working-class concept of friendship as a dense area of reciprocal rights and duties based on parity. The child has learned from his experiences in the family to categorize people in terms of simple ascribed status distinctions. Since this is the only mode of differentiation between individuals of which he is aware, status equivalence (in terms of age and sex) becomes the sole criterion of eligibility for friendship. Friends emerge, from the undifferentiated category of individuals of similar status, as children become willing to accept a greater degree of interaction with one another on a 'share and share alike' principle. Hence interpersonal approach behaviours will be concerned with demonstrations of willingness to share; this may be in swopping, lending, or even passing the ball in a game. Thus friendship can be seen to grow out of behavioural rather than verbal demonstration, and confirmation of reciprocal social exchange.

Working-class friendships can therefore be expected to be high on both scope and pervasiveness[15] for as the demands for reciprocity intensify, both the number of friends it is possible to have and the frequency of extra-friend interaction will be restricted.[16] Thus working-class friendships are multi-functional rather than segmentary, a situation which may lead to a lack of differentiation between friends and self and a minimization of unique behaviours. For, as Simmel[17] has pointed out, the more the group becomes differentiated from non-members the less the members can be differentiated from each other: the distinct group is the homogeneous group.

The mode of friendship described here, with its age-specific and unindividuated activities, will clearly not provide the child with experience of social exchange which is cumulative and transferable. Participation in the initiation and termination of working-class friendships does not lead to the learning of generalizable interpersonal techniques. On the one hand the initial approach behaviours are geared to subculturally peculiar activities and do not engender any learning of universally valid principles of exploration. Friendship formation is therefore a one-time activity, or at least one which is seldom repeated. On the other hand the termination of such friendships is also a rare event, since the restricting elements in the procedures defend them from intrusion. For relationships based on behavioural demonstration are particularly fragile: whereas verbal expressions of withdrawal and reparation can be subject to later reinterpretation, behavioural indiscretions are undeniably disruptive and hence usually final. Fear of the certain consequence of negative behaviours on the part of any member leads to an institutionalized caution in in-group relations. So in a double sense the working-class friendship pattern precludes experimentation in role-playing techniques.

The homogeneous long enduring working-class friendship group is thus characterized by reciprocal social exchange on the basis of intrinsic rather than extrinsic reward: for the powerful affective bond becomes of primary importance.[18] The friendship is therefore in the very fullest sense unindividuated, for it is characterized by an extreme lack of segmental participation; indeed the role segmentation involved in it may be even less than that involved in the love relationship for, as Simmel has said, 'This entering of the whole undivided ego into the relationship may be more plausible in friendship than in love for the reason that friendship lacks the specific concentration on one element which love derives from its sensuousness. . . . It may therefore be more apt than love to connect a whole person with another in its entirety.'[19] Such a situation has little use for the concept of privacy and the verbal planning procedure of 'tact'[20] that go with it.

In contrast with the above the middle-class child can be seen as developing a theory of justice which takes account of individual differences. He is aware not only of status distinctions but of individual circumstances, of special local attributes; thus for example he would recognize 'being miserable' as a circumstance mitigating reciprocal duty, indeed as a special need entailing certain rights.

Congruent with his theory of justice is his approach to friendship formation. For him there is a range of characteristics to be considered in differentiating the eligible from the ineligible in the process of choosing friends. He scans others for points of similarity, for willingness to be explored. Whereas the working-class child takes interests for granted as being largely identical and confronts his peers totally, 'on the other hand, unique individuals can engage one another only at odd points or at rare intervals. Like meshed gears they can touch only at limited segments of their perimeters.'[21] Here the confrontation is activity-specific; the child may ask, 'I like fishing. How about you?' Hence the resultant friendship is itself activity-specific rather than total.[22] These friendships are based on the extrinsic benefits to be gained from reciprocal exchange. For this reason these scanning procedures may provide cumulative experience, in effect apprenticeship, in the instrumental use of expressive behaviours which is central to much adult middle-class role-playing.[23]

The distinctive nature of middle-class ideas of privacy is understandable in the light of the above. The concept which Simmel discusses under the head of 'discretion' is really only applicable to the middle-class interpersonal relationship. Discretion, which 'consists ... in staying away from knowledge of all that the other does not expressly reveal to us',[24] can only apply where social exchange is extrinsic rather than intrinsic, segmented rather than total. The notion of 'safeguard distance',[25] which applies in the working class only outside friendship boundaries, is present in all middle-class interpersonal behaviour.

Thus far we have argued that the different conceptions of justice, friendship and privacy which characterize the social classes produce differences in the degree to which children gain cumulative experience of manipulation of social exchange processes which will be relevant to adult role-playing.[26] We consider that these differences, which will be analysed below as differences in the condition of functional autonomy, derive from the differential relationship to social structure of the social classes. We have indicated that the characteristic working-class conception of justice may have derived historically from scarcity of material resources;[27] this pattern may have assumed cultural autonomy which accounts for its persistence even in the absence of such scarcity. One can less readily 'explain' the pattern of justice and the derivative conceptions of friendship and privacy for the middle class. Clearly the conditions described for working-class families are absent; there is no shortage of goods or of maternal time. It might, however, also be suggested, following Blau,[28] that their relative resources place them in an advantageous position in the processes of social exchange in which they engage.

Parallel conceptions of the way in which relationship to social structures affects social relations can be found in the work of both Simmel and Durkheim, but while they saw these conditions as linked to cultural–historic trends we argue that differences obtain syn-chronically between social classes.[29] Simmel in his discussion of the form of social differentiation[30] argues that

> modern man has too much to hide to sustain friendship in the ancient sense. ... Modern personalities are perhaps too uniquely individualized to allow full reciprocity of understanding and receptivity. ... The modern way of feeling tends more heavily towards differentiated friendships which cover only one side of the personality, without playing into other aspects of it.

For Simmel this was a consequence of the segmented nature of role-playing in modern life, and stemmed from his highly sophisticated version of the *Gemein-schaft–Gesellschaft* continuum.

Durkheim's[31] ideal types of solidarity are again related on an historical dimension. The society, characterized by mechanical solidarity, in which homogeneous individuals stand in total affective relationship to one another, is seen as historically replaced by the organic mode of solidarity, where uniquely differentiated individuals relate to one another through their instrumental requirements.[32] Yet we consider, with Merton,[33] that there is no historical tendency for one mode of solidarity and social relationship to replace the other. We argue instead that the differentiation obtains synchronically and is related to social class.

Social exchange, functional autonomy and role distance

In the above discussion we have been concerned to argue that, only where an individual's social exchange transactions place him in a position of functional autonomy, does he acquire role-playing techniques which enable him to exploit the interaction situation to his benefit. It is now time to turn our attention to consideration of the interrelations of the concepts of social exchange, functional autonomy and role distance on a more abstract level.

The notion that most social behaviour is of a reciprocal or exchange nature is by now widely accepted.[34] Ego's actions are clearly affected by his expectations of alter's reciprocal, though not necessarily complementary,[35] reactions. Of course it would be tautologous to discuss all interaction in exchange terms, for, as Gouldner cautions, the notion of reciprocity must be supplemented by that of force.[36] Yet the 'elementary' behaviour with which we are here concerned certainly falls into the category which it is useful to discuss in these terms.[37]

If we consider the individual actor as a system part, then the relevance of Gouldner's discussion of functional autonomy for the analysis of interpersonal relations becomes clear. The various system parts can be seen as offering and requiring different goods, and services; their very heterogeneity makes them interdependent. Yet, because exchange does not occur

in isolated dyadic relations, the needs of one individual structure may be 'spread' such that they are
satisfied by a large number of others. It is in this
way that functional autonomy or independence is
attained; for the individual structure is not dependent
on any one structure for all its needs.[38]

Varying degrees of functional autonomy can be
explained initially with reference to Blau's categoriz-
ation of alternatives to compliance (dependence).[39]
Where a structure A has a particular need which can
only be fulfilled by one particular other structure, B,
then A is potentially dependent on B. However, if
A can *either* supply inducements to B, *or* force B to
benefit it without reciprocation (or, of course if A
can, in some way, do without the gratification in
question), then A can avoid dependence on B.
However, as indicated above, a dyadic exchange
relation does not occur in isolation but in the context
of a complete system of exchanges. Thus it must be
emphasized that A's ability to avoid dependence on B
will be determined by A's relative independence in
respect to all its other relations of exchange. For,
clearly, not only the ability to supply inducements, but
also the ability to use force, will depend on resources
external to the particular exchange relation in question.

Blau's fourfold choice schema is thus ultimately
reducible to the single issue of the extent to which a
structure is able to 'spread its risks', derive different
benefits from different structures, and hence attain
functional autonomy.

The claim has been made above that, for the individual actor, the situation of functional autonomy
can be seen as a prerequisite for the enactment of
role distance behaviours. We shall now turn to a
closer examination of this.

Goffman sees his formulation of role distance as
providing 'a sociological means of dealing with one
type of divergence between obligation and actual
performance'.[40] Role distance behaviours, then, are
those which 'constitute a wedge between the individual
and his role, between his doing and being'.[41] What the
actor is doing when he expresses role distance is to
deny the 'virtual self', or 'ready-made me', implied by
the role; but he does not deny that he is playing the
role. Whether this is done by extreme casualness—
insinuation that the role can be played without effort
—or by deliberate 'overplaying',[42] the effect is the
same: the actor is claiming that he is not defined by
his role, it is only a segment of his whole being. Role
distance is thus a situational expression of role
segmentation, a signal to others of the existence of
exchange transactions external to the current relationship.

Now role segmentation is ultimately dependent on
audience segregation.[43] For, only when the role-
others figuring in one of an individual's role sets do
not figure in others, can the individual avoid dependence on one role relationship[44] for full definition
of his identity. On the other hand, when an individual
plays out most of his roles in front of the same au-

dience, he becomes entirely dependent on them:
because they alone can define him. It is only where
roles are played to a variety of different audiences
that the actor can say to one group of role-others, 'I
am not only what you think I am. I am also something
else.' Thus where the various roles which constitute
the whole self are played before several different
audiences, that is to say where there is functional
autonomy in social exchange, then role distance
techniques are always possible as means of retreat
from one self to another.

Now, for an actor to take advantage of the options
available to him in a situation of functional autonomy,
it is necessary for him to have a dramaturgical perspective on society. Instead of a vision of society as a
prison in which behaviour is governed by rules, he
must see it as a loosely written play, flexible enough to
withstand many variant interpretations.[45]

Summary and discussion

We have argued above that working-class culture is of
a 'received' type, and that the conditions surrounding
the transmission and reception of this culture are
likely to produce behaviour which is best described
as 'ruleful'. By contrast the middle class can be understood as 'interpreting' rather than 'receiving' a
culture. They come to learn the broad range of
behaviours which are tolerable in a given situation,
the rationales for these behaviours, and the consequences likely to follow from the various different
strategies.[46]

The theme of this paper can now be summarized
briefly. The particular notions of justice to which
working-class children are introduced can be seen as
giving rise to conceptualizations of friendship based
on 'total' affective relations. Thus early social exchange transactions take place in a situation of
functional dependence, rather than autonomy. Such
associations preclude the development of notions of
privacy outside of those involved in crude in-group/
out-group distinctions. In these circumstances they
do not gain experience of universally valid interpersonal behaviour techniques such as role distance.

As a result of these childhood experiences adult
working-class persons, when they are afforded
functional autonomy (such as that which is involved in
the physical separation of work and home life),
are unable to make up the dramaturgical option. They
are able only to *play* but not to *play at* roles.

Thus it seems to us that a serious limitation is
imposed upon the sociological view of society as
drama. The suggestion that man attempts consciously
to control his presentation of self, and to maximize
his gratification from the identity options available
to him, entails a misleading assumption of voluntarism.
Berger suggests that if men, reflecting on why they
obey institutional imperatives, say, 'I have no choice',
they are deceiving themselves.[47] Even where there is
no choice within a particular role, he argues 'neverthe-

less the individual has the choice of stepping outside the role'. Similarly Sartre maintains that to act only within the requirements of a role is to act in 'bad faith', and he sees 'bad faith' as a dishonest rejection of freedom.[48]

Yet we have attempted to show that, for those who are not in a situation of functional autonomy, and for those who have not acquired the relevant skills to exploit such a situation, the option of role distance is not available.

If the above interpretation is correct then, in addition to imposing limitations on the utility of the Interactionist perspective, it has crucial implications for certain research procedures and also for educational policy. If we have given a true description of the way in which the working-class individual is related to social structure then limits are set upon the validity of his reportage of structure. Often respondents are required to give 'reasons' for behaviour or views; where the questions used are open-ended the answers may look like rationales. However, these responses may, in fact, be merely 'received' ideas: they may represent no more than the respondents' perceptions of what is the proper answer to give.[49] In some cases, however, the working-class respondent may find a question requiring a reason for actions or attitudes so meaningless than he does not even have a 'received' notion of what answer to give. Bernstein and Young, in a study of social class differences in conceptions about the use of toys, gave a closed schedule in which mothers were required to rank six 'ideas about what toys are for' in order of importance. They found a tendency for working-class mothers to rank in a purely random manner while middle-class respondents showed a clear pattern of preference.[50] Thus the idea of 'received' structure indicates critical problems for questionnaire design and the interpretation of data.

The above discussion also suggests certain practical imperatives in the field of the sociology of education. For, if one of the major handicaps which the working-class child suffers is deficiency in role-playing ability, then the relevant remedial measures are those directed towards impregnating the child with a dramaturgical awareness. Only the individual who has this dramatic skill will be able to *create* structure: Only he can experience the freedom which can come from exploitation of a functionally autonomous situation.

Notes

1 We are very grateful to Peter M. Blau for helpful comments on an earlier draft of this paper.

2 Throughout this paper a conception of social class in terms of two simple ideal types will be employed. We are, of course, aware that the detailed picture is more complex than this. However we consider that the literature on the 'new' class structure suggests that certain core features of 'middle' and 'working' class subcultures remain distinct. There is a vast literature which could be cited to support our usage; two of the most recent overviews are: M. Kahan, D. Butler and D. Stokes, On the analytical division of social class, *Brit. J. Sociol.* **17** (2) (1966), 122–32, and D. Lockwood, Sources of variation in working class images of society, *Sociol. Rev.* **14** (1966), 249–67.

3 See for examples of this, J. Klein, *Samples from English Cultures* (Routledge & Kegan Paul 1965), vol. 1; W. B. Miller, Lower class culture as a generating milieu for gang delinquency, *J. of Social Issues* **14** (1958), 5–9; J. B. Mays, *Growing Up in the City* (Liverpool Univ. Press 1954).

4 See for one example, R. Hoggart, *The Uses of Literacy* (Penguin 1958).

5 On this see E. Goffman, Role distance, in *Encounters* (Indianapolis: Bobbs Merrill, 1961), 83–152. For a recent discussion of the concept see R. L. Coser, Role distance, ambivalance and transition status, *Amer. J. Sociol.* **72** (1966), 173–87.

6 For examples, see E. Goffman, *Presentation of Self in Everyday Life* (New York: Anchor 1959); P. Berger, *Invitation to Sociology* (Penguin), esp. ch. 6; G. J. McCall and J. L. Simmons, *Identities and Interactions* (Collier-Macmillan 1966). For summaries of the main tenets of this school of thought see A. M. Rose (ed.), *Human Behaviour and Social Processes* (Routledge & Kegan Paul), 3–19; and B. J. Biddle and B. J. Thomas, *Role Theory: Concepts and Research* (Wiley 1966), 3–4.

7 It has been suggested that man is differentiated from the animals in that the latter can only receive meanings whereas he can create them; see R. A. Schermerhorn, Man the unfinished, *Sociol. Quarterly* **4** (1963), 5–17. We believe however that the equation of the human with the voluntary is misleading, and that this differentiation also obtains *between* men.

8 R. Turner, Role taking: process versus conformity, in A. Rose, op. cit., **38**. Turner is not talking, as we are, about two distinct modes of role-taking. He sees what we call 'received' and 'interpreted' structures as alternative modes of explanation of role-taking in general.
Other students have isolated some aspects of received culture in their relationship to childhood socialization. See, for example, M. L. Kohn, Social class and parental values, *Amer. J. Sociol.* **64** (1959), 337–51, and Social class and the exercise of parental authority, *Amer. Sociol. Rev.* **24** (1959), 352–66.

9 This is Goffman's (1961) distinction, op. cit., **99**.

10 A. W. Gouldner, Reciprocity and autonomy in functional theory, in L. Gross (ed.), *Symposium on Sociological Theory* (New York: Harper, Row 1959).

11 For an explanation of the use of this term, see G. C. Homans, *Social Behaviour: its Elementary Forms* (Routledge & Kegan Paul 1961), pp. 3–7.

12 Exchange theory has enjoyed renewed interest in recent years. In addition to Homans, op. cit., see also P. M. Blau, *Exchange and Power in Social Life* (Wiley 1964), and A. Kuhn, *The Study of Society* (London: Social Science Paperbacks 1966), pt V.

13 'To act justly then, is to treat all men alike except where there are relevant differences between them.' S. I. Benn and R. S. Peters, *Social Principles and the Democratic State* (Allen & Unwin 1959), **111**.

14 J. Piaget, *The Moral Judgment of the Child* (Routledge & Kegan Paul 1968).

15 For a discussion of the use of these terms, see A. Etzioni, *Comparative Analysis of Complex Organizations* (Collier-Macmillan 1961), 160–4.

16 There is surprisingly little evidence available on social class differentials in number, intensity and duration of friendships. For findings tending to support our hypothesis see F. Dotson, Patterns of voluntary association among urban working class families, *Amer. Sociol. Rev.* **16** (1951), 687–93; W. A. Anderson, Family social participation and social status self rating, loc. cit., vol. 11 (1946), 253–58. For more direct evidence of the relationship between social class and gregariousness see E. Katz and P. F. Lazarsfeld, *Personal Influence* (Collier-Macmillan 1964).

17 G. Simmel, in *The Sociology of Georg Simmel* (Collier-Macmillan 1965), **110**. See also D. N. Levine, The structure of Simmel's social thought, in K. H. Wolff (ed.), *Essays on Sociology, Philosophy, and Aesthetics* (New York: Harper 1959), **15**.

18 Blau, op. cit., ch. 12. He divides reciprocal social exchange into that centred upon intrinsic reward and that deriving rewards in a manner extrinsic to the relationship itself. The former he calls 'mutual attraction' and it is characterized by a high affective content.

19 Simmel, op. cit., 325.

20 M. Lipman, Some aspects of Simmel's conception of the individual, in Wolff, op. cit. (1959), 134.

21 Ibid., p. 315.

22 The activity-specific nature of the typical middle-class friendship is illuminated by Elizabeth Bott, *Family and Social Network* (London: Tavistock 1964), 77.

23 See for example, Coser, op. cit.

24 Simmel, op. cit., 321.

25 W. G. Head, Adaptive sociology, *Brit. J. Sociol.* **12** (1961), 23–40. The concept of social distance as used since Bogardus is somewhat similar to the idea of discretion, see E. Bogardus, Social distance and its practical implications, *Sociol. and Soc. Res.* **17** (1933), 265–71. However this concept has generally been limited to the analysis of inter-group distance; see, for examples, L. I. Pearlin and M. Rosenberg, Nurse-patient social distance, and the structural context of the mental hospital, *Amer. Sociol. Rev.* **27** (1962), 56–62; C. Kadushin, Social distance between client and professional, *Amer. J. Sociol.* **67** (1962), 517–31; J. R. Landis, D. Datwyler and D. S. Dorn, Race and social class as determinants of social distance, *Sociol. Soc. Res.* **51** (1966), 78–86. For one study not entailing this limitation, see J. M. Beshers *et al.*, Social distance strategies and status symbols: An approach to the study of social structure, *Sociol. Quarterly* **4** (1963), 311–24.

26 The related idea that role-playing ability increases with role-playing experience is fairly well documented. See, for examples, J. H. Mann and C. H. Mann, The effect of role-playing experience on role-playing ability, *Sociometry* **22** (1959), 64–74; and H. G. Gough and D. R. Peterson, The identification and measurement of predispositional factors in crime and delinquency, *J. Consulting Psychol.* **16** (1952), 207–12.

27 In addition to the pattern of allocation *within* the family described above there is a further reason why one might expect scarcity of resources to affect ideas of justice. For it follows from the assumptions of exchange theory that those in structural positions of relative disadvantage will tend to have a more overtly equalitarian approach to distributive justice. Those, on the other hand, who are favoured by the system of stratification, must justify their own advantage in terms of more complicated notions of just distribution.

28 Blau, op. cit., ch. 4.

29 In addition to the traditional dichotomies cited above certain recent variations on the *Gemeinschaft–Gesellschaft* theme entail conceptions similar to those employed here. See, for examples, A. Southall, An operational theory of role, *Hum. Relat.* **12** (1959), 17–34; R. Frankenberg, *Communities in Britain* (Penguin 1966); and, for the essence of the dichotomy divorced from the more naïve association with a rural-urban continuum. R. E. Pahl, The rural-urban continuum, *Sociologia Ruralis* **6** (3–4) (1966), 299–326.

30 Simmel, op. cit., 326.

31 E. Durkheim, *The Division of Labour in Society* (Collier-MacMillan 1964).

32 For a useful summary-description of these ideal types, see P. A. Sorokin, *Contemporary Sociological Theories* (New York: Harper 1928).

33 R. K. Merton, Durkheim's 'division of labour in society', *Amer. J. Sociol.* **40** (1934), 319–28.

34 For a summary of most of the major usages, see Blau, op. cit.

35 A. W. Gouldner, The norm of reciprocity, *Amer. Sociol. Rev.* **27** (1962), 31–41. An 'equal' exhange of goods or services is described by the term complementarity. Reciprocity can entail either equal or unequal exchange.

36 Ibid.

37 Indeed it fulfils the two criteria advanced by Blau for the definition of exchange behaviour: (i) it is oriented towards ends that can only be achieved through interaction with others; (ii) it seeks to adapt means to achieve those ends. Blau, op. cit., Introduction.

38 Gouldner (1959), op. cit.

39 Blau, op. cit., ch. 5. The four fold choice schema is adapted from R. M. Emerson, Power dependence relations, *Amer. Sociol. Rev.* **27** (1962), 31–41.

40 Goffman (1961), op. cit., 115.

41 Ibid., 108.

42 For one example of application of the technique of 'underplaying' and 'overplaying', see T. Burns and G. M. Stalker, *The Management of Innovation* (London: Tavistock 1959), 215–16.

43 Goffman (1961), op. cit., 91.

44 Southall, op. cit. He distinguishes between role and role relationship. A teacher has one role and as many role relationships as pupils; a father who has his son as partner in his business has one role relationship and two roles.

45 These opposing perspectives are discussed by Berger, op. cit., chs 4 and 6.

46 For reasons of brevity we have not developed a further elaboration of this distinction by including in our discussion the obviously related concepts of 'sociological ambivalence', 'cognitive dissonance' and 'intolerance of ambiguity'. See, on these respectively, R. K. Merton and E. Barber, Sociological ambivalence, in E. A. Tiryakian (ed.), *Sociological Theory, Values and Sociocultural Chance* (Collier-Macmillan 1963), 91–120; L. Festinger, *A Theory of Cognitive Dissonance* (Evanston: Row, Peterson 1957); E. Frenkel-Brunswick, Intolerance of ambiguity as an emotional

and perceptual personality variable, *J. Personality* **18** (1949–50), 109–43.

47 Berger, op. cit., 142.

48 J. P. Sartre, *L'Etre et le néant* (Paris: Gallimard 1943).

49 They appeal, in other words, to an acceptable 'vocabulary of motives'. See H. Gerth and C. W. Mills, *Charac-ter and Social Structure* (Routledge & Kegan Paul 1953), ch. 5.

50 B. Bernstein and D. Young, Social class differences in conceptions of the uses of toys, *Sociology* **1** (1967), 131–40.

11 The neglected situation

Erving Goffman

It hardly seems possible to name a social variable that doesn't show up and have its little systematic effect upon speech behavior: age, sex, class, caste, country of origin, generation, region, schooling; cultural cognitive assumptions; bilingualism, and so forth. Each year new social determinants of speech behavior are reported. (It should be said that each year new psychological variables are also tied in with speech.)

Alongside this correlational drive to bring in ever new social attributes as determinants of speech behavior, there has been another drive, just as active, to add to the range of properties discoverable in speech behavior itself, these additions having varied relations to the now classic phonetic, phonemic, morphemic and syntactical structuring of language. It is thus that new semantic, expressive, paralinguistic and kinesic features of behavior involving speech have been isolated, providing us with a new bagful of indicators to do something correlational with.

I'm sure these two currents of analysis—the correlational and the indicative—could churn on for ever (and probably will), a case of scholarly coexistence. However, a possible source of trouble might be pointed out. At certain points these two modes of analysis seem to get unpleasantly close together, forcing us to examine the land that separates them— and this in turn may lead us to feel that something important has been neglected.

Take the second-mentioned current of analysis first—the uncovering of new properties or indicators in speech behavior. That aspect of a discourse that can be clearly transferred through writing to paper has been long dealt with; it is the greasy parts of speech that are now increasingly considered. A wagging tongue (at certain levels of analysis) proves to be only one part of a complex human act whose meaning must also be sought in the movement of the eyebrows

and hand. However, once we are willing to consider these gestural, nonwritable behaviors associated with speaking, two grave embarrassments face us. First, while the substratum of a gesture derives from the maker's body, the form of the gesture can be intimately determined by the microecological orbit in which the speaker finds himself. To describe the gesture, let alone uncover its meaning, we might then have to introduce the human and material setting in which the gesture is made. For example, there must be a sense in which the loudness of a statement can only be assessed by knowing first how distant the speaker is from his recipient. The individual gestures with the immediate environment, not only with his body, and so we must introduce this environment in some systematic way. Secondly, the gestures the individual employs as part of speaking are much like the ones he employs when he wants to make it perfectly clear that he certainly isn't going to be drawn into a conversation at this juncture. At certain levels of analysis, then, the study of behavior while speaking and the study of behavior of those who are present to each other but not engaged in talk cannot be analytically separated. The study of one teasingly draws us into the study of the other. Persons like Ray Birdwhistell and Edward Hall have built a bridge from speaking to social conduct, and once you cross the bridge, you become too busy to turn back.

Turn now from the study of newly uncovered properties or indicators in speech to the first-mentioned study of newly uncovered social correlates of speech. Here we will find even greater embarrassment. For increasingly there is work on a particularly subversive type of social correlate of speech that is called 'situational'. Is the speaker talking to same or opposite sex, subordinate or superordinate, one listener or many, someone right there or on the phone; is he reading a script or talking spontaneously; is the occasion formal or informal, routine or emergency? Note that it is not the attributes of social structure

Source: *The Ethnography of Communication*, ed. John J. Gumperz and Dell Hymes (*American Anthropologist* special publication), *66* (6), part 2 (1964), 133–6.

that are here considered, such as age and sex, but rather the value placed on these attributes as they are acknowledged in the situation current and at hand.

And so we have the following problem: a student interested in the properties of speech may find himself having to look at the physical setting in which the speaker performs his gestures, simply because you cannot describe a gesture fully without reference to the extra-bodily environment in which it occurs. And someone interested in the linguistic correlates of social structure may find that he must attend to the social occasion when someone of given social attributes makes his appearance before others. Both kinds of student must therefore look at what we vaguely call the social situation. And that is what has been neglected.

At present the idea of the social situation is handled in the most happy-go-lucky way. For example, if one is dealing with the language of respect, then social situations become occasions when persons of relevant status relationships are present before each other, and a typology of social situations is drawn directly and simply from chi-squaredom: high-low, low-high and equals. And the same could be said for other attributes of the social structure. An implication is that social situations do not have properties and a structure of their own, but merely mark, as it were, the geometric intersection of actors making talk and actors bearing particular social attributes.

I do not think this opportunistic approach to social situations is always valid. Your social situation is not your country cousin. It can be argued that social situations, at least in our society, constitute a reality *sui generis* as He used to say, and therefore need and warrant analysis in their own right, much like that accorded other basic forms of social organization. And it can be further argued that this sphere of activity is of special importance for those interested in the ethnography of speaking, for where but in social situations does speaking go on?

So let us face what we have been offhand about: social situations. I would define a social situation as an environment of mutual monitoring possibilities, anywhere within which an individual will find himself accessible to the naked senses of all others who are 'present', and similarly find them accessible to him. According to this definition, a social situation arises whenever two or more individuals find themselves in one another's immediate presence, and it lasts until the next-to-last person leaves. Those in a given situation may be referred to aggregatively as a *gathering*, however divided, or mute and distant, or only momentarily present, the participants in the gathering appear to be. Cultural rules establish how individuals are to conduct themselves by virtue of being in a gathering, and these rules for commingling, when adhered to, socially organize the behavior of those in the situation.[1]

Although participation in a gathering always entails constraint and organization, there are special social arrangements of all or some of those present which entail additional and greater structuring of conduct. For it is possible for two or more persons in a social situation to jointly ratify one another as authorized co-sustainers of a single, albeit moving, focus of visual and cognitive attention. These ventures in joint orientation might be called *encounters* or face engagements. A preferential mutual openness to all manner of communication is involved. A physical coming together is typically also involved, an ecological huddle wherein participants orient to one another and away from those who are present in the situation but not officially in the encounter. There are clear rules for the initiation and termination of encounters, the entrance and departure of particular participants, the demands that an encounter can make upon its sustainers, and the decorum of space and sound it must observe relative to excluded participants in the situation. A given social gathering of course may contain no encounter, merely unengaged participants bound by unfocused interaction; it may contain one encounter which itself contains all the persons in the situation—a favored arrangement for sexual interaction; it may contain an accessible encounter, one that must proceed in the presence of unengaged participants or other encounters.

Card games, ball-room couplings, surgical teams in operation, and fist fights provide examples of encounters; all illustrate the social organization of shared current orientation, and all involve an organized interplay of acts of some kind. I want to suggest that when speaking occurs it does so within this kind of social arrangement; of course what is organized therein is not plays or steps or procedures or blows, but turns at talking. Note then that the natural home of speech is one in which speech is not always present.

I am suggesting that the act of speaking must always be referred to the state of talk that is sustained through the particular turn at talking, and that this state of talk involves a circle of others ratified as co-participants. (Such a phenomenon as talking to oneself, or talking to unratified recipients as in the case of collusive communication, or telephone talk, must first be seen as a departure from the norm, else its structure and significance will be lost.) Talk is socially organized, not merely in terms of who speaks to whom in what language, but as a little system of mutually ratified and ritually governed face-to-face action, a social encounter. Once a state of talk has been ratified, cues must be available for requesting the floor and giving it up, for informing the speaker as to the stability of the focus of attention he is receiving. Intimate collaboration must be sustained to ensure that one turn at talking neither overlaps the previous one too much, nor wants for inoffensive conversational supply, for someone's turn must always and exclusively be in progress. If persons are present in the social situation but not ratified as participants in the encounter, then sound level and physical spacing will have to be managed to show respect for these accessible others while not showing suspicion of them.

Utterances do of course submit to linguistic constraints (as do meanings), but at each moment they must do a further job, and it is this job that keeps talk participants busy. Utterances must be presented with an overlay of functional gestures—gestures which prop up states of talk, police them, and keep these little systems of activity going. Sounds are used in this gestural work because sounds, in spoken encounters, happen to be handy; but everything else at hand is systematically used too. Thus many of the properties of talk will have to be seen as alternatives to, or functional equivalents of, extra-linguistic acts, as

when, for example, a participant signals his imminent departure from a conversational encounter by changing his posture, or redirecting his perceivable attention, or altering the intonation contour of his last statement.

At one level of analysis, then, the study of writable statements and the study of speaking are different things. At one level of analysis the study of turns at talking and things said during one's turn are part of the study of face-to-face interaction. Face-to-face interaction has its own regulations; it has its own processes and its own structure, and these don't seem to be intrinsically linguistic in character, however often expressed through a linguistic medium.

Note

1 I have attempted to present this argument in detail in *Behavior in Public Places* (Collier-Macmillan 1963).

12 Cherokee school society and the intercultural classroom

Robert V. Dumont, Jr, and Murray L. Wax

Indian education is one of those phrases whose meaning is not the sum of its component words. Notoriously, 'education' is an ambiguous word used to justify, idealize, or to criticize a variety of relationships. In the context where the pupils are members of a lower caste or ethnically subordinated group, education has come to denominate a unidirectional process by which missionaries—or others impelled by motives of duty, reform, charity, and self-sacrifice—attempt to uplift and civilize the disadvantaged and barbarian. Education then is a process imposed upon a target population in order to shape and stamp them into becoming dutiful citizens, responsible employees, or good Christians.[1]

In the modern federal and public school systems serving Indian children, there is less of the specifically religious quality; but the active presence of the missionizing tradition, however secularized, is still felt. To appreciate this fully, we must remind ourselves that the purpose of education presented to, and often enforced upon, the American Indians has been nothing less than the transformation of their traditional cultures and the total reorganization of their societies.[2] By denominating this as *unidirectional*, we mean to emphasize that the far-reaching transformations which have been occurring spontaneously among Indian peoples are neglected in the judgments of the reforming educators.[3] As a major contemporary instance, we need but turn to the first few pages of a recent book, representing the work of a committee of high repute. The initial paragraph states that the goal of public policy should be 'making the Indian a self-respecting and useful American citizen' and that this requires 'restoring his pride of origin and faith in himself', while on the following page we find that very origin being derogated and distorted with the left-handed remark: 'It would be unwise to dismiss all that is in the traditional Indian culture as being necessarily a barrier to change.'[4] The mythic image of

Source: *Human Organization* (Fall 1969), *28* (3), 217–26.

an unchanging traditional Indian culture does not bear discussion here. Rather, we direct attention to the fact that such a remark could be advanced as the theme of a contemporary book about Indians, and that this book then received favorable reviews both from liberals involved in Indian affairs and from the national Indian interest organization. Clearly, such reviewers take it for granted that Indian education should be unidirectional—e.g. none seemed to think it noteworthy that the last chapter of the book is on 'Policies Which Impede Indian Assimilation', the implication of that title being that the necessary goal is total ethnic and cultural dissolution.

An alternate way of perceiving the unidirectionality which characterizes 'Indian education' is to note the curious division of labor bifurcating the process of cultural exchange with Indian peoples. That is, missionaries and educators have devoted themselves to instructing the Indians but not to learning from or being influenced by them; whereas ethnographers have devoted themselves to learning from the Indians but not to teaching or influencing them. Thus, the ethnographers valued the learning of the native languages, while the schoolmasters and missionaries only seldom bothered to learn them, even when the native language was the primary tongue of their Indian pupils and the primary domestic and ceremonial medium of the community in which they were laboring.[5]

Because Indian educational programs have been unidirectionally organized, deliberately ignoring native languages and traditions, they have had to proceed more via duress than suasion. Today the duress is in the laws of compulsory attendance, as enforced by an appropriate officer; but the climax of traditional 'Indian education' was the forcible seizing or kidnapping of Indian children by agents of the U.S. government. These children were then incarcerated in boarding establishments whose programs were designed to shape them within the molds of the conquering society. Yet the irony of this crude and brutal effort was that, while the mass of children underwent profound changes, their very aggregation provided them with the need and opportunity to cohere and resist. Like the inmates of any total institution, Indian pupils developed their own norms and values, which were neither those of their Indian elders nor those of their non-Indian instructors. This process of autonomous development has continued to distinguish much of Indian conduct in relation to modern programs and schools, including the classroom we will be reviewing.[6]

Tribal Cherokee communities

The consequence of the various reformative and educational programs aimed at the Indian peoples has been not to eliminate the target societies but, paradoxically, to encourage an evolution which has sheltered an ethnic and distinct identity, so that today there remain a relatively large number of persons, identified as Indians, and dwelling together in enclaved, ethnically and culturally distinctive communities. The Tribal Cherokee of contemporary northeastern Oklahoma are not untypical.[7] Like other Indian communities, they have lost to federal, state , and local agencies the greater measure of their political autonomy. Many contemporary Indian peoples do have 'Tribal Governments', but these do not correspond to traditional modes of social organization or proceed by traditional modes of deliberation and action. In the specific case of the Oklahoma Cherokee, for instance, the Tribal Government is a nonelected, non-representative, and self-perpetuating clique, headed by individuals of great wealth and political power, while the Tribal Cherokee are among the poorest denizens of a depressed region, whose indigenous associations are denied recognition by the Bureau of Indian Affairs.

The Cherokee of Oklahoma once practiced an intensive and skilled subsistence agriculture, which has all but disappeared as the Indians have lost their lands and been denied the opportunity to practice traditional forms of land tenure. The rural lands are now used principally for cattle ranching (often practiced on a very large scale) and for tourism and a few local industries (e.g. plant nurseries, chicken processing), or crops such as strawberries, which require a cheap and docile labor supply. Until the recent building of dams and paved highways and the concomitant attempt to develop the region as a vacationland, the Tribal Cherokee were able to supplement their diet with occasional game or fish, but they now find themselves harassed by state game and fish regulations, and subjected to the competition of weekend and vacation sportsmen.

Like the other Indian societies of North America, the Cherokee have been goaded along a continuum that led from being autonomous societies to being a 'domestic dependent nation' and thence to being an ethnically subordinated people in a caste-like status.

In Oklahoma there is a distinctive noncaste peculiarity, since a vast majority of the population proudly claim to be of 'Indian descent' as this signifies a lineage deriving from the earliest settlers. To be 'of Cherokee descent' is, therefore, a mark of distinction, particularly in the northeast of Oklahoma, where this connotes such historic events as 'Civilized Tribes' and the 'Trail of Tears'.[8] Yet, paradoxically, there exist others whose claim to Indianness is undeniable, but whose mode of life is offensive to the middle class. The term 'Indian' tends to be used to denote those who are considered idle, irresponsible, uneducated, and a burden to the decent and taxpaying element of the area. Within northeastern Oklahoma, these 'Indians' are the Tribal Cherokees, and their communities are marked by high rates of unemployment, pitifully low cash incomes, and a disproportionate representation on relief agency rolls. Perhaps the major respect in which the Cherokee Indians differ from groups like the Sioux of Pine Ridge is that the latter, being situated on a well-known federal reservation, are the recipients of myriads of programs from a multiplicity of federal, private, and local agencies, whereas the Cherokee are still mainly the targets of welfare workers, sheriffs, and aggressive entrepreneurs.[9]

In this essay we wish to focus on the schools attended by Indian children in the cases where they are the preponderant element of the school population. This condition is realized not only on reservations, where the federal government operates a special school system under the administration of the Bureau of Indian Affairs, but also in other regions by virtue of covert systems of segregation. As in the case of Negro/white segregation, the basis is usually ecological. Thus, in northeastern Oklahoma the rural concentrations of Tribal Cherokee along the stream beds in the hill country predispose toward a segregated system at the elementary levels. But the guiding principle is social, so that there is reverse busing of Tribal Cherokee children living in towns and of middle-class white children living in the countryside. Within the rural elementary schools, the Indian children confront educators who are ethnically and linguistically alien, even when they appear to be neighbors (of Cherokee or non-Cherokee descent) from an adjacent or similar geographic area.

Such classrooms may be denominated as 'cross-cultural', although the ingredients contributed by each party seem to be weighted against the Indian pupils. The nature and layout of the school campus, the structure and spatial divisions of the school buildings, the very chairs and their array, all these are products of the greater society and its culture—indeed, they may at first glance seem so conventional that they fail to register with the academic observer the significance of their presence within a cross-cultural transaction. Equally conventional, and almost more difficult to apprehend as significant, is the temporal structure: the school period, the school day;

and the school calendar. The spatial and temporal grid by which the lives of the Indian pupils are organized is foreign to their native traditions, manifesting as it does the symbolic structure of the society which has encompassed them.

The observer thus anticipates that the classroom will be the arena for an unequal clash of cultures. Since the parental society is fenced out of the school, whatever distinctive traditions have been transmitted to their children will not be 'taught out' of them; and the wealth, power, and technical supremacy of the greater society will smash and engulf these traditionalized folk. Forced to attend school, the Indian children there must face educators who derive their financial support, their training and ideology, their professional affiliation and bureaucratic status, from a complex of agencies and institutions based far outside the local Indian community. The process is designed to be unidirectional; the children are to be 'educated' and the Indian communities thus to be transformed. Meanwhile, neither the educator nor the agencies for which he is a representative are presumed to be altered—at least by the learning process.

Cherokees in the classroom

The classrooms where Indian students and a white teacher create a complex and shifting sequence of interactions exhibit as many varieties of reality and illusion as there are possible observers. One such illusion—in the eyes of the white educator—is that the Cherokee are model pupils. Within their homes they have learned that restraint and caution is the proper mode of relating to others; therefore in the classroom the teacher finds it unnecessary to enforce discipline. As early as the second grade, the children sit with perfect posture, absorbed in their readers, rarely talking—and then only in the softest of tones—and never fidgeting. Even when they are marking time, unable to understand what is occurring within the classroom, or bored by what they are able to understand, they make themselves unobtrusive while keeping one ear attuned to the educational interchange. They respect competence in scholastic work, and their voluntary activities both in and out of school are organized surprisingly often and with great intensity about such skills. Eager to learn, they devote long periods of time to their assignments, while older and more experienced students instruct their siblings in the more advanced arithmetic they will be encountering at higher grade levels.

To the alien observer (whether local teacher or otherwise), the Cherokee children seem to love to 'play school'. The senior author, for example, recalls talking during one recess period with an elderly white woman who had devoted many years to teaching in a one-room school situated in an isolated rural Cherokee community and who now was responsible for the intermediate grades in a more consolidated enterprise that still was predominantly Cherokee.

'You just have to watch these children,' she said. 'If you don't pay no mind, they'll stay in all recess. They like to play school.' And, as if to illustrate her point, she excused herself, went back into the school building, and returned with a straggle of children. 'They told me they had work they wanted to do, but it is too nice for them to stay inside. ... You know, I forgot how noisy students were until I went to the County Seat for a teachers' meeting. It's time for me to ring the bell now. If I don't they will come around and remind me pretty soon.'

Given the seeming dedication of her pupils, the naïve observer might have judged this woman an exceedingly skilled and effective teacher. Yet in reality, she was a rather poor teacher, and at the time of graduation the pupils of her one-room school knew scarcely any English—a fact so well known that parents said of her, 'She don't teach them anything!'

Like many of her white colleagues, this woman was interpreting Cherokee conduct from within her own culture, as is evident in her description of the intensive involvement of her pupils in learning tasks as *'playing school'*. In kindred fashion, other teachers describe the silence of the students as timidity or shyness, and their control and restraint as docility. Most teachers are unable to perceive more than their own phase of the complex reality which occurs within their classrooms because they are too firmly set within their own traditions, being the products of rural towns and of small state teachers' colleges, and now working within and limited by a tightly-structured institutional context. Certainly, one benefit of teaching Indians in rural schools is that the educators are sheltered from observation and criticism. Except for their own consciences and professional ideologies, no one cares about, guides or supervises their performance, and little pressure is exerted to encourage them to enlarge their awareness of classroom realities.

Even for ourselves—who have had much experience in observing Indian classrooms—many hours of patient and careful watching were required, plus the development of some intimacy with the local community, before we began to appreciate the complexities of interaction within the Cherokee schoolroom. The shape assumed by the clash of cultures was a subtle one. At first, it could be appreciated most easily in the frustration of the teachers; the war within the classrooms was so cold that its daily battles were not evident, except at the close of the day as the teachers assessed their lack of pedagogical accomplishment. Those teachers who defined their mission as a 'teaching out' of native traditions were failing to make any headway; and some of these good people had come to doubt their ability to work with such difficult and retiring children (actually, as we soon discovered, their classes contained a fair share of youngsters who were eager, alert, intelligent, and industrious). A few teachers had resigned themselves to marking time, while surrendering all notions of genuine instruction.

As these phenomena began to impress themselves

upon us, we began to discern in these classrooms an active social entity that we came to call 'The Cherokee School Society'. Later still, we were surprised to discover in other classrooms, which we came to call 'Intercultural Classrooms', that this Society remained latent and that instead the teacher and students were constructing intercultural bridges for communication and instruction (these will be discussed in the next section).

In order to comprehend the complexity of classroom interaction, we need to remind ourselves that the children who perform here as pupils have been socialized (or enculturated) within the world of the Tribal Cherokee as fully and extensively as have any children of their age in other communities. In short, we just disregard the material poverty of the Tribal Cherokee families and their lower-class status and avoid any of the cant about 'cultural deprivation' or 'cultural disadvantage'. These children are culturally alien, and for the outsider (whether educator or social researcher) to enter into their universe is as demanding as the mastering of an utterly foreign tongue. In the compass of a brief article, we can do no more than indicate a few of the more striking evidences of this distinctive cultural background.

Even in the first grade, Cherokee children exhibit a remarkable propensity for precision and thoroughness. Asked to arrange a set of colored matchsticks into a pyramidal form, the children became so thoroughly involved in maintaining an impeccable vertical and horizontal alignment that they were oblivious to the number learning which they are supposed to acquire via this digital exercise. These six-year-olds do not resolve the task by leaving it at the level of achievement for which their physical dexterity would suffice, but continue to manipulate the sticks in a patient effort to create order beyond the limitations of the material and their own skills. As they mature, the Cherokee students continue this patient and determined ordering of the world, but as a congregate activity that is more often directed at social than physical relationships. At times, this orientation is manifested in an effort toward a precision in social affairs that is startling to witness in persons so young (here, sixth graders):

The teacher has asked about the kinds of things which early pioneers would say to each other in the evening around the campfire as they were traveling.
Jane: 'Save your food.'
Teacher: 'That's preaching.'
Jane and Sally (together): 'No.'
Jane: 'That is just to tell you.' (The tone of voice makes her sound just like a teacher.)
The teacher agrees, and his acquiescent tone makes him sound like the student. He continues, 'They would get you in a room. . . .'
Jane interrupts: 'Not in a room.'
Teacher: 'In around a campfire then.' He

continues by asking if everyone would be given a chance to speak or just representatives.
Dick: 'That would take all night; they might forget.' Jane and Sally agree that representatives would be the right way.

The foregoing is as significant for the form of the interaction, as it is revealing of the students' concern for the precise reconstruction of a historical event. The students have wrought a reversal of roles, so that *their* standards of precision and *their* notions of social intercourse emerge as normative for the discussion.

Although this kind of exchange may be rare—actually it is typical only of the Intercultural Classroom—we have cited it here, as reflecting many of the norms of Cherokee students. As healthy children, they are oriented towards the world of their elders, and they see their adult goal as participating in the Cherokee community of their parents. In this sense, the art of relating to other persons so that learning, or other co-operative efforts, may proceed fruitfully and without friction becomes more important to them than the mastery of particular scholastic tasks, whose relevance in any case may be dubious. In the matrix of the classroom they learn to sustain, order, and control the relationships of a Cherokee community; in so doing they are proceeding towards adult maturity and responsibility. According to these norms, the educational exchange is voluntary for both students and teachers and is governed by a mutual respect.

In any educational transaction, the Cherokee School Society is actively judging the competence of the teacher and allowing him a corresponding function as leader. Their collective appraisal does not tolerate the authoritarian stance assumed by some educators ('You must learn this!') but rather facilitates the emergence of a situation in which the teacher leads because he knows ('I am teaching you this because you are indicating that you wish to learn . . .'). A consequence of this configuration (or, in the eyes of an unsympathetic observer, a symptom) is that the Cherokee students may organize themselves to resist certain categories of knowledge that the school administration has formally chosen to require of them.

We must bear in mind that within the Tribal Cherokee community, the reading or writing of English, calculating arithmetically, and even speaking English have minor employment and minimal utility. By the intermediate grades, the students perceive that, with no more than a marginal proficiency in spoken or written English, their elders are nonetheless leading satisfactory lives *as Cherokees*. Attempts to exhort them towards a high standard of English proficiency and a lengthy period of time-serving in school are likely to evoke a sophisticated negative reaction. After one such educational sermon, a ten-year-old boy bluntly pointed out to his teacher that a Cherokee adult, greatly admired within the local community—and senior kin to many of the pupils present—had only a fifth-grade education. When the teacher attempted to evade this rebuttal by suggesting that the students would, as adults, feel inferior because they lacked a lengthy education and could not speak good English, the pupils were again able to rebut. To the teacher's challenge, 'Who would you talk to?' the same boy responded, 'To other Cherokee!'

Orienting themselves toward the community of their elders, the Cherokee students respond to the pressures of the alien educators by organizing themselves as The Cherokee School Society. As the teacher molds the outer forms of class procedure, the children exploit his obtuseness as a white alien to construct the terms on which they will act as students. But, while among the Oglala Sioux this transformation is effected with a wondrous boldness and insouciance,[10] here among the Cherokee it is with an exquisite social sensibility. A gesture, an inflection in voice, a movement of the eye is as meaningful as a large volume of words would be for their white peers. By the upper elementary grades, the result is a multiple reality according to which the adolescent Cherokee appear now as quiet and shy, or again as stoical and calm, or yet again (apparent only after prolonged observation) as engaged in the most intricate web of sociable interaction. Such delicacy of intercourse, so refined a sensibility, reflects and requires a precision of movement, a neat and exact ordering of the universe.

Interestingly, the Cherokee School Society does not reject the curricular tasks formulated by the alien educational administrators. In fact, the pupils proceed with their usual patient intensity to labor at assignments that can have no bearing on their tradition or experience. The fact that they are unable to relate these materials meaningfully to life within the Cherokee community acts as an increasing barrier to their mastery of them. In particular, the fact that most students have acquired no more than rudimentary proficiency in spoken English means that the involved patterns of the printed language in the advanced texts are beyond their most diligent endeavors; neither the language nor the topics can be deciphered.

So far, we have emphasized that the Cherokee students are interested in learning and that, from the viewpoint of the educator, they are docile pupils. Yet the cultural differences noted, and the basic social separateness and lack of communication, ensure that conflicts will develop and become more intensive as the students mature. The school cannot proceed along the trackways established by educational authority, nor can it be switched by the students into becoming an adjunct of the rural Cherokee community. Hence, as the children mature, the tension within the schoolroom becomes more extreme. Since the participants are one adult and many children, and since the latter are imbued with a cultural standard of nonviolence and passive resistance, open confrontations do not occur. Instead, what typically happens is that, by the seventh and eighth grades, the students have surrounded themselves with a wall of silence impenetrable by the outsider, while sheltering a rich emotional communion among themselves. The silence is positive, not simply negative or withdrawing, and it shelters them so that, among other things, they can pursue their scholastic interests in their own style and pace. By their silence they exercise control over the teacher and maneuver him toward a mode of participation that meets their standards, as the following instance illustrates:

Teacher: 'Who was Dwight David Eisenhower?' Silence.

Teacher: 'Have you heard of him, Joan?' She moves her eyes from his stare and smiles briefly.

Very quickly, the teacher jumps to the next person. There is something in his voice that is light and not deadly serious or moralistic in the way that is customary of him. He is just having fun, and this comes through so that the kids have picked it up. They respond to the tone, not to the question, 'Alice?'

Alice leans back in her chair; her blank stare into space has disappeared, and her eyes are averted. She blushes. Now, she grins.

The teacher does not wait, 'Wayne?'

Wayne is sitting straight, and his face wears a cockeyed smile that says he knows something. He says nothing.

Seeing the foxy grin, the teacher shifts again, 'Wayne, you know?' This is a question and that makes all the difference. There is no challenge, no game-playing, and the interrogation mark challenges Wayne's competency. But Wayne maintains the foxy grin and shakes his head, negative.

Quickly, the teacher calls on another, 'Jake?' He bends his head down and grins but says nothing.

Teacher (in authoritative tone): 'Nancy, tell me.' But she says nothing, keeping her head lowered, although usually she answers when called upon. The teacher switches tones again, so that what he is asking of Nancy has become a command. Perhaps he catches this, for he switches again to the lighter tone, and says: 'Tell me, Debra.'

The only one in the room who doesn't speak Cherokee, Debra answers in a flat voice: 'President.'

As soon as the answer is given, there are many covert smiles, and Alice blushes. They all knew who he was.

To most educators and observers, such an incident is perplexing. Who within that classroom really is exercising authority? Are the students deficient in their comprehension either of English or of the subject matter? Are they, perhaps, flexing their social muscles and mocking the teacher—because they don't like the lesson, they don't like him to act as he is acting, or why? For the Cherokee School Society has created within the formal confines of the institutional classroom another social edifice, their own 'classroom', so that at times there appears to be not simply a clash of cultural traditions but a cold war between rival definitions of the classroom. Such tension is not proper within Cherokee tradition, since the Tribal Cherokee value harmonious social relationships and frown upon social conflict.[11] Moderate disagreement is resolved by prolonged discussion interspersed, wherever possible, by joking and jesting, while severe disagreement leads to withdrawal from the conflict-inducing situation. Given the compulsory nature of school attendance, however, the students cannot withdraw from the classroom, much as they might wish to, and the teacher can withdraw only by losing his job and his income. Thus, an unmanageable tension may develop if the teacher is unable to recognize the Cherokee pupils as his peers who, through open discussion, may share with him in the decisions as to the organizing and operating of the school.

The unresolved conflict of cultural differences typifies these classrooms. Within them, there is little pedagogy, much silence, and an atmosphere that is apprehended by Indians (or observers of kindred sensibility) as ominous with tension. The following incident, participated in by Dumont, exhibits all these features in miniature:

> The classroom was small and the teacher had begun to relate a joke to Dumont. Not far away were seated four teenage Cherokee, and the teacher decided to include them within the range of his ebullience: 'Boys, I want to tell you a joke. . . . ' It was one of those that played upon the stoical endurance of Indians in adapting to the whimsical wishes of whites, and to narrate it in the classroom context was highly ironic. The plot and phrasing were simple, and easily apprehended by the students. But when the teacher had finished, they merely continued looking toward him, with their eyes focused, not upon him, but fixed at some point above or to the side of his eyes. As he awaited their laughter, their expressions did not alter but they continued to stare at the same fixed point and then gradually lowered their heads to their work.

The Cherokee School Society maintains a rigid law of balance that says, in effect, we will change when the teacher changes. If the teacher becomes involved in appreciating the ways of his students, then they will respond with an interest in his ways. Needless to say, the older the students become, the higher their grade-level, the less is the likelihood that this reciprocity will be initiated by their educators. There is thus a deep tragedy, for it is the students who lose and suffer the most. Yet the School Society is their technique for protecting themselves in order to endure the alien intrusiveness of the teacher and the discourtesy and barbarity of the school. Occasionally, observer and students experience a happier interlude, for some teachers are able to enter into a real intercultural exchange. Unfortunately, they are as rare as they are remarkable. And they are sometimes unaware of their truly prodigious achievements in establishing what we term the Intercultural Classroom.

The Intercultural Classroom

Within the Intercultural Classroom, Tribal Cherokee students do such remarkable things as engaging in lengthy conversations with the teacher about academic subjects. For this to occur, the teacher must be responsive to the distinctive norms and expectations of the students; but, strikingly, he need not abide by these nor accept norms as long as he is able to persuade the students of his willingness to learn about them and to accommodate to them. This attitude places the teacher on a plane or parity such that he must learn from his students the most rudimentary Cherokee cultural prescriptions. Naturally, both parties experience conflicts in this reshuffling of teacher/learner roles. Certainly, such interaction is not what the teacher has been trained to sustain. Yet there arise structured devices for reducing these conflicts.

For instance, to bridge the social breaches that are always opening, the Cherokee students urge forward one of their members—not always the same person—to mediate and harmonize. Then if the teacher, by an unconscious presumption, disrupts the harmonious flow of class activity, it is the mediator whose deft maneuver reduces the intensity of the tension and relaxes the participants. In a sense, what the mediator does is to restore parity between teacher and students by removing the nimbus of authority from the teacher, thus allowing the students to work out with the teacher a compromise which redirects class activities and so permits them to regain their proper tempo. The teacher is freed to pursue the subject matter, but as scholastic assistant rather than classroom tyrant. With this in mind, let us examine the sequence of events which ended in a conversational repartee already quoted:

> They are reading about important men in history and have just finished with a section about adult educators.
>
> Teacher (referring to the observers): 'We have two distinguished educators here. Does this make you feel proud?'
>
> It is quiet for the first time in the room. It is likely that the students are all thinking, how could we be proud of educators! As observer, I am uneasy and expectant; I wonder who will break the silence and how he will handle the delicate situation.
>
> John: 'I don't like schools myself.'(!)
>
> Teacher: 'Would you quit school if you could?' (He's asking for it!)
>
> John (a firm answer): 'Yes.'
>
> Teacher: 'Suppose that your dad came and said you could quit, but he brought you a shovel

and said, "Dig a ditch from here to Brown's house," since you weren't going to school.'

John: 'Okay.'

Another student: 'He might learn something.' Everyone finds this humorous; the class is in good spirits and is moving along.

John, too, is quick to reply: 'Might strike gold.' The topic has been discussed earlier in class. (The interaction develops and others become involved, including the more reticent students.)

Here it is John who has played, and most successfully, the role of mediator. The teacher had ventured into a delicate area that had the potential of disrupting the classroom atmosphere. The responding silence was a token of the social peril, and John, who so often among his peers had assumed the mediating role, moved forward first, boldly countering with a declaration as strong as the teacher's. As a consequence, he redefined the structure of the interaction and became the initiator of the exchange, while the teacher merely sustained it. A cultural bridge was thereby constructed, accessible alike to students and teacher; and John's 'Okay' is his consent to the conditions of the structure.

The mediating role becomes less necessary as the teacher grows more attuned to the interactional norms of Indian society; it becomes more difficult (if more essential) if the teacher insists on maintaining a tyrannical control over the classroom. Yet, even as the teacher is attuned, some function is reserved for a mediator, for the teacher tends to proceed in terms of work to be done by an abstract student, while the mediator explores how the task can be redefined within the framework of the Cherokee student. His is a work of adaptation, and insofar as he is successful, the classroom becomes *intercultural*—a locus where persons of different cultural traditions can engage in mutually beneficial transactions without affront to either party.

What must the teacher do to foster the emergence of an intercultural classroom within the cross-cultural situation? The answer would require another essay at least as long as the present one, but it may be helpful to quote the remarks of one teacher in the region:

'I can't follow a lesson plan, and I just go along by ear. I've taught Cherokee students for six years in high school, and this is my first [year] in elementary school.' Referring then to his experiences as a high school coach, he continued, 'The thing you have to do, if you get a team, is that you got to get them to co-operate. . . .'

At first glance, this appears at odds with our earlier assertions about the spontaneous emergence of the Cherokee School Society, not to mention contradictory to the conventional notions that Indians will not compete with each other. But what he is explaining is that unless the teacher chooses to recognize the social nature of the classroom and to work toward integrating his teaching with that life, he will not be able to elicit active learning experiences from his pupils. Or, to put it negatively, if the teacher does not work with his Indian students as a social group, their union will be directed toward other goals. Yet the teacher can secure their response only if he 'gets them' to co-operate; he cannot 'make them' do so.

Conclusion

The foregoing report provides the basis for judgments and hypotheses on a variety of levels. On the practical level, it would seem that ethnic integration is not an essential precondition for satisfactory education of groups from a low socio-economic background. The Tribal Cherokee certainly are impoverished and poorly educated. Nevertheless, we would predict that the consolidation of rural schools into larger, better-staffed, and better-equipped schools in northeastern Oklahoma may actually lead to deterioration rather than improvement of the educational condition. Given the ethos of the Tribal Cherokee, consolidation may mean the irremediable loss of many opportunities for assisting their children educationally.

On the methodological level, we are reminded of how sociologically valuable it is for researchers to focus on the frontier situation 'where peoples meet'.[12] The resulting accommodations, adaptations, and divisions of labor are an enlightening and fascinating phenomenon, which especially deserves to be studied as a corrective to those theoretical systems which regard the national society as an integrated social system. On the methodological level also, our study illustrates anew the value of ethnographic observations of classroom activities. Basic and simple as it may seem, and unpretentious in the face of modern testing procedures, direct observation still has much to teach us.[13]

Finally, on the substantive level, the research reported here cautions against the erosion of our conceptual armamentarium when researchers allow their research problems to be defined by educational administrations. When that happens, the educational situation of peoples such as the Indians tends to be conceived in terms of individual pupils and their 'cultural deprivation'. The researcher then is asked to assist the adminstration in raising these disadvantaged individuals to the point where they can compete in school in the same fashion as do white middle-class children. Our research is a reminder that such styles of conceptualization neglect the social nature of the classrooms and the social ties among the pupils. They also neglect the tension between teacher and pupils as a social group, and the struggles that occur when the teacher presses for individualistic achievement at the expense of group solidarity.[14]

Notes

1 Cf. Rosalie H. Wax and Murray L. Wax, American Indian Education for What? *Midcontinent America Studies Journal* 6 (2) 1965, 164–70; reprinted in Stuart Levine and Nancy O. Lurie (eds), *The American Indian Today*, Deland, Florida: Everett Edwards 1968, 163–9.

2 For an enlightening account of the mission schools for American Indians, see the chapter, 'Nurseries of Morality' in Robert F. Berkhofer, Jr, *Salvation and the Savage; An analysis of Protestant Missions and American Indian Response, 1787–1862*, University of Kentucky Press 1965, 20–43.

3 Unfortunately, some of the anthropological textbooks on American Indians are guilty of the same static imagery, as they present particular tribes in 'the ethnographic present'. Conspicuous and happy exceptions are such books as Edward H. Spicer, *Cycles of Conquest*, University of Arizona Press 1962, and Fred Eggan, *The American Indian*, Chicago: Aldine 1966. Cf. Murray L. Wax, The white man's burdensome 'business': a review essay on the change and constancy of literature on the American Indians, *Social Problems* 16 (1) 1968, 106–13.

4 *The Indian: America's Unfinished Business*, compiled by William A. Brophy and Sophie D. Aberle, University of Oklahoma Press 1966, 3–4.

5 While missionaries have always included a small number of individuals who have patiently tried to understand the language and culture of their alien flock, and while some few missionaries have been excellent ethnographers, the majority, particularly on the North American continent, have had quite the opposite attitude. Today, missionary activity on the world scene has become increasingly sophisticated and culturally humble (as evidenced by *Practical Anthropology*), yet it is noteworthy how slowly this has affected labors among American Indians. Despite a century (or even several!) of mission activity among some tribes, the church in many instances remains a mission, detached from tribal influence or control, and the clergyman continues to be a person who is culturally alien and socially isolated and who regards his task as preaching but not learning.

6 An excellent brief summary and bibliography of the history of research on Indian education is found in the presentation by Philleo Nash, *Proceedings* of the National Research Conference on American Indian Education, edited by Herbert A. Aurbach, Kalamazoo, Michigan: The Society for the Study of Social Problems, 1967, 6–30. In order to discuss the history of Indian education research, Nash had to deal with some of the major changes of policy as well. The conference *Proceedings* also contain a summary review by William H. Kelly of current research on Indian education and other helpful discussions and bibliographies. See also Willard W. Beatty, Twenty Years of Indian Education, in David A. Baerreis (ed.), *The Indian in Modern America*, Madison: State Historical Society of Wisconsin 1956, 16–49; Evelyn C. Adams, *American Indian Education*, New York: King Crowns Press 1946; Harold E. Fey and D'Arcy McNickle, *Indians and Other Americans*, New York: Harper 1959, chapter 12. And of course the Meriam Report included an intensive assessment of the goals and achievements of Indian education: Lewis Meriam and Associates, *The Problem of Indian Administration*, Baltimore: Johns Hopkins Press 1928, especially 346–429.

7 We take the term 'Tribal Cherokee' from the research reports of Albert Wahrhaftig, which, in addition to whatever information may be inferred from the tables of the US Census, constitute the best recent source on the condition of the Cherokee of Oklahoma. See, e.g. his 'Social and Economic Characteristics of the Cherokee Population of Eastern Oklahoma' and 'The Tribal Cherokee Population of Eastern Oklahoma', both produced under sponsorship of the Carnegie Cross-cultural Education Project of the University of Chicago, 1965 (mimeographed): and Community and the Caretakers, *New University Thought* 4 (4) 1966/7, 54–76. See also Murray L. Wax, 'Economy, Ecology, and Educational Achievement', Indian Education Research Project of the University of Kansas, Lawrence 1967 (mimeographed), and Angie Debo, *The Five Civilized Tribes of Oklahoma; Report on Social and Economic Conditions*, Philadelphia: Indian Rights Association 1951.

8 Responding to contact and intermarriage with the European invaders, the Cherokee were one of several tribes noteworthy during the eighteenth century for their adoption of foreign techniques. By 1827 they had organized themselves as a Cherokee Nation, complete with an elective bicameral legislature and a national superior court. Meantime, Sequoyah had been perfecting his syllabary, and in 1828 there began the publication of the *Cherokee Phoenix*, a bilingual weekly. Developments of this character led to the Cherokee and several neighboring tribes of the southeastern US being called 'the Civilized Tribes'; nevertheless, this did not protect them from the greed of the white settlers, particularly in Georgia. When the Indian nations would not cede their lands peaceably, Andrew Jackson employed federal troops to herd the Indian peoples westward into the region which subsequently was to become Oklahoma. There the survivors of the terrible journey ('the Trail of Tears') incorporated themselves once again as a Cherokee Nation and remained such until dissolved by act of Congress early in the present century. Today, books, museums, and pageants commemorate these events and highlight for the tourists the high-cultural aspects of upper-status life in the Cherokee Nation. Judged by that historical standard, the life of contemporary Tribal Cherokee constitutes a blot on a record otherwise cherished by Oklahomans of Cherokee descent.

9 Cf. Murray L. Wax and Rosalie H. Wax, The Enemies of the People, in Howard S. Becker *et al.* (eds), *Institutions and the Person; Essays Presented to Everett C. Hughes*, Chicago: Aldine Press 1968, 101–18.

10 Cf. Murray L. Wax, Rosalie H. Wax, and Robert V. Dumont, Jr, *Formal Education in an American Indian Community*, Kalamazoo, Michigan: The Society for the Study of Social Problems 1964, chapter 6.

11 See the discussions of 'The Harmony Ethic' in John Gulick, *Cherokees at the Crossroads*, Institute for Research in Social Science, University of North Carolina 1960, 135–9 *et passim*.

12 Everett C. Hughes and Helen M. Hughes, *Where Peoples Meet; Ethnic and Racial Frontiers*, Chicago: Free Press 1952.

13 Consider, for example, the impact and contribution of such recent books which rely either on direct observation or participation observation of classrooms as John Holt, *How Children Fail*, New York: Delta 1964; Harry F. Wolcott, *A Kwakiutl Village and School*, New York: Holt, Rinehart & Winston 1967; Wax, Wax and Dumont, op. cit.; Estelle Fuchs, *Pickets at the Gates*, New York: Free Press 1966; G. Alexander Moore, *Realities of the Urban Classroom; Observations in Elementary Schools*, New York: Doubleday Anchor 1967; Elizabeth M. Eddy, *Walk the White Line*, New York: Doubleday Anchor, 1967.

14 Such phenomena were clearly noted by Willard Waller in his *Sociology of Teaching*, first published in 1932, reprinted by Science Editions, Wiley 1965. It is unfortunate to see the neglect of such elementary sociological considerations in much of the more recent literature of the 'sociology of education'.

13 Making the scene

David J. Bennett and Judith D. Bennett

All social interaction is affected by the physical container within which it occurs. The various elements of the container establish a world of meaning through the arrangement of non-verbal symbolism. For this reason, the common practice in the social sciences of focusing on behavior without reference to the physical setting would seem to ignore an important dimension of the total picture of interaction.

As in the case of spoken language and even gestural conduct, there must be a consensus upon meaning for this symbolism to play a relevant part in social situations. The container imposes both physical and symbolic limitations upon behavior. Its sheer physical dimension limits the range of possible movement. We do not neck in the back of churches; we do in movie theaters.

Recently, some work has been done in exploring the relation between the physical and interactional worlds of human beings. The more obvious effects of the physical setting as the background against which interaction takes place have been dealt with as 'regions' by Erving Goffman;[1] the physical territory as a generator of behavior has been hypothesized by Robert Ardrey;[2] the physical container as a variable matrix of interaction within different cultural frameworks has been studied by Edward T. Hall;[3] others[4] have concerned themselves with the variable effects of physical containers. However, with the possible exception of Hall, this area has not been dealt with systematically.

While very few systematic studies exist, the practice of dealing with the physical environment by deliberately manipulating it and its constituent parts and dimensions to secure some desired social effect has long been a practice of those professions concerned with environmental design: architects, planners, industrial designers, interior decorators, stage managers,

and others. These people, however, have not developed quantitative techniques for analyzing physical settings as symbolic frameworks within which social interaction proceeds. Rather, their work is guided by tradition, 'common sense' and accumulated, but unsystematized, experience. They assume causal relationships between certain physical arrangements and specific social 'end results'.[5] Whether these assumed relationships are valid has yet to be determined. Yet, there are some physical arrangements that have occurred with remarkable consistency around the world throughout human history.

The physical building or space which forms the symbolic edifice of superhuman power, whether God, Hero, or State, seems to have the following universal characteristics: (1) tremendous size in relation to other buildings, or, when diminutive in actual size, as in the case of some shrines in both Oriental and Occidental civilizations, a scale, i.e. a relation of the elements of the object to the whole, which suggests tremendous size; (2) an expression of great stability, durability, and immutability, often achieved by symmetry, and, when not, by a highly stylized arrangement of objects or parts of the whole; (3) a carefully organized progression of spaces (be it the entrance to an ancient Egyptian royal tomb, the path through the Acropolis at Athens, the forecourt to a Shinto shrine, the road to Versailles, or the monumental steps up to almost any seat of judgment of any time or place in the Western world) arranged so that they are experienced as a linear sequence of events invested with awesome meaning. Similarly, other symbolic-physical arrangements seemingly have the same cross-cultural uniformity. Authority is usually physically elevated.

Components and dimensions of the scene

In order to analyze the specific relationships which obtain between physical environment and social behavior, it is necessary to establish precisely which

Source: *Social Psychology through Symbolic Interaction*, ed. Gregory Stone and Harvey Farberman, Waltham, Mass.: Ginn-Blaisdell (1970), 190–6.

elements of the environment or scene may affect human conduct. Such elements may have isolated effects or may affect human conduct in interaction with one another. We have made a preliminary attempt to list such elements, and our attempt has generated the following six components or dimensions of any scene:

1 The *container*—the fixed external enclosure of human interaction.
2 The *props*—physical objects which adhere to persons in the enclosure or to the enclosure itself, including dress and furnishings.
3 The *actors*—persons involved in, peripheral to, or spectators to the transactions carried on in the enclosure.

These components have been dealt with, one way or another, in the works we have cited earlier. Taken together, they are what most social psychologists have considered when they have included aspects of the scene in their analysis of social interaction. The following three elements have seldom been considered in such analyses:

4 The *modifiers*—elements of light, sound, color, texture, odor, temperature, and humidity which serve to affect the emotional tone or mood of the interaction.
5 *Duration*—the objective time in measurable units (minutes, hours, etc.) during which the interaction occurs, as well as the anticipated time the interaction will require.
6 *Progression*—the order of events which precede and follow, or are expected to follow, the interaction and have some bearing upon it.

These latter three terms, as can be seen, do not deal with objects, but with action or modifiers of action. In most European grammars, as Whorf notes, these are verbs or adverbs in the object-action conception of reality demanded by the rules of syntax.[6] As such, they add a critical dimension to the enclosure within which interaction transpires, but, more important, they lend the interaction a certain affect or mood. We can understand such affects by imagining four situations occurring within enclosures, each of identical dimensions, with three constant props and the same number of actors.

Behavioral consequences of scenes

The scene is a room only large enough to accommodate one table with sufficient space to move around it. Two men are seated at opposite sides of the table. Without changing the arrangement of the men, the chairs, and the table, let us show how the entire context of interaction—its symbolic significance—can be altered by manipulating other components and dimensions of the scene.

Situation one: The walls, floor, and ceiling of the room are concrete and plaster, unpainted and bare of any decoration. There is a single bare, bright electric bulb suspended above the table as the only source of light. The table and chairs are wood, bare, hard, and smooth. The temperature is relatively low (say 60 degrees Fahrenheit), and the relative humidity is high, making the room chilly and damp. There is a slight odor of mildew. The predominant colors are gray and white.

Situation two: Now the walls are hung with dark red drapes. The floor is thickly carpeted, and the ceiling painted a soft off-white. The light source is a light cove around the ceiling which gives off a soft, diffuse, dim light. The table is covered with a white cloth and the chairs are upholstered with a nappy material. The temperature and humidity are a little above the American Standard Engineering 'comfort range' (68 degrees Fahrenheit and 45 per cent relative humidity), making the room feel a little warm and humid. There is a slightly 'stuffy' odor in the room. The predominant colors are dark red, off-white, and a muted gold.

Situation three: The ceiling is a luminous fluorescent ceiling such as may be found in many contemporary office buildings. Three of the walls are smooth white plaster; the fourth, a chromatic blue. The floor is covered with a dark gray carpet. The table is very low, its top no more than sixteen inches above the floor. Its base is polished steel, its top is glass. The chairs are polished steel frames fitted with black leather cushions. The room is cool and dry and, for all intents and purposes, 'odorless'.

Situation four: The ceiling is an off-white plaster. The walls, also plaster, are painted beige. The floor is a vinyl asbestos tile of a light brown color with a green oval woven area rug. The light source is a floor-to-ceiling pole light with three shaded fixtures. The table is a dark grained wood, and the chairs are wood frame with green upholstered seats and backs. The temperature and relative humidity are within the 'comfort range'. There is no discernible odor.

What is significant about the four situations presented above is not that a precise description of their meaning can be made—it cannot—but that they are presented in the expectation that the reader will respond to each one differently despite the fact that: (1) the dimension of the enclosure, the arrangement of people and objects (although the appearance of chairs and tables are modified) remain unchanged; (2) the reader knows nothing specific about either the people or the nature of the interaction; (3) the description of the situations is incomplete, having not included the elements of sound (although the quality of sound is implied), duration, or progression. Also, the situations, each a carefully contrived ensemble of mutually reinforcing conventionalized elements in conventionalized combinations, probably will evoke grossly predictable responses from specific audiences, presuming cultural, age, and socio-economic homogeneity.

We may describe these four situations as settings for the following interactions. The reader, although he will be able to supply alternatives, will find it difficult to reject these possibilities:

Situation one—an interrogation
Situation two—a social conversation
Situation three—an interview
Situation four—indeterminate (could be any one of the above).

All of these interpretations apply, remember, to the same enclosure, the same number of objects, and the same number of people. The fourth scene is indeterminate, we would assert, because of the relative neutrality, in symbolic terms, of the modifying elements which ordinarily enhance mood or affect. That the reader may be able to supply alternative interpretations of the interaction taking place in any of the situations we have presented is not an indication of the symbolic imprecision, in any absolute sense, of our descriptions. In fact, the situations are of a generalized type. Each can accommodate a number—but a *finite* number—of different interactions in the context of our culture. It is important to note that, whatever number of events may occur in each of these situations, that number could probably be counted or estimated while the number which could *not* occur is probably beyond measure or estimate. We have mentioned that, among other elements of the situation, we have ignored matters of duration and progression. These seem to us to be of seminal importance, and we wish now to speculate about their possible impact on these situated interactions.

Duration. The expected duration of an interrogation has no objective time unit. Instead, it is a function of the relative definitions of the situation formulated by the interrogated and the interrogator. Both may, for separate reasons, want it over 'quickly' (a subjective time unit). However, if the interrogated's aim is resistance, he may wish to extend it indefinitely, while the interrogator's desire may be a rapid termination of the encounter. The opposite may also be the case. In any event, the interrogation is a situation in which the duration of the situation is highly significant for the actor's conception of its meaning, even without some prior established expectation about the objective time of duration. For the interrogated, this is part of the terror.

In contrast, a social conversation or an interview present situations in which actors usually have distinct and mutual expectations about how long the encounter will last, and they are prepared to engage one another for that length of time. The job interviewer who conducts an interview with, let us say, a potential secretary over a four-hour period will be violating a norm so flagrantly that the applicant may well redefine the situation as an interrogation.[7] In other words, time can affect the definition, including the mood of the situation.

We enter a situation with a learned expectation of its duration and are prepared to participate for that length of time. If that expectation is not met, our definition of the situation will be altered, and our ability to sustain the appropriate mood of the encounter will be seriously tested. As Hall observed, our expectations in this regard vary widely from one culture to the next. In the unitary linear treatment of time which characterizes the 'American way of life', time units, in discrete segments and in highly conventionalized sequences, are a salient feature of the way we give form and meaning to the sensational chaos of experience.

Progression. Like duration, progression is another dimension of the meaning of a situation. Having acquired expectations about the sequence of events both in space (one expects the invisible part of a road around a curve to *be there*, if one can see the continuation of the road in the distance and, often, if one cannot) and in time, we extend the isolated scene into a sequential pattern in order to increase our understanding of its scope. Progression, as sequence, affects both the meaning of the scope of the interaction and the interaction itself. To descend into a shaft in the earth and then step through an opening into outer space constitutes a break in environmental sequence for which our original definitions of that situation have left us unprepared. Kafka's *The Trial* achieves its sense of strangeness and distortion in part from the deliberate deletion of key transitional scenes so that both the protagonist and the audience—the observers and vicarious actors—lose confidence in their ability to predict what will happen next. Here, the factor of continuity emphasizes the overriding importance progression has in establishing the meaning of a situation.[8] Progression, therefore, is an ordered sequence of events within an ordered sequence of scenes which is related to learned expectations, i.e. the taken-for-granted dimensions of everyday conduct.

Social interaction, then, takes place in a physical world full of objects, their modifiers, movement, and change—not in a vacuum. What is more, this physical world, differentially arranged and modified, is not so ambiguous in its relation to social interaction that its effects cannot be measured or estimated by analytical inquiry. Nor is this world so incidental that it can continue to be ignored.

A paradigm for the analysis of the components and dimensions of scenes

Although this treatment of the subject has been necessarily brief and tentative, too exploratory to establish a comprehensive scheme which will embrace all alternative possibilities, we can propose the following paradigm as a point of departure for the initial investigation of those effects on social interaction perpetrated by the scene:

The Setting

Basic physical container as it might affect social interaction	Number and arrangement of props and persons in the encounter
1 Natural, man-made, or both.	1 Physical objects which are not part of the space, but are in it and are taken into account in the interaction, e.g. furniture, automobiles, etc.
2 Interior, exterior, or both.	2 Number of people who act as participants and their measurable spatial relation to each other.
3 Meaningful size in relation to type of interaction (too large? too small? not culturally significant?).	3 Number of people who act as spectators and their spatial relation to the other participants and to each other.
4 Single or multiple spaces.	4 Number of people who are neither participants nor observers, but who occupy the same significant area and who, by being present, affect interaction.
5 Connected or disconnected.	
6 Relative proximity (measured in real time, subjective time, means of locomotion).	
7 Salient features, scale, size, multiple levels, etc.	

Modifiers

Light	Sound	Color	Texture	Odor	Relative temperature and humidity
Source(s)	Volume	Hues	Location	Source(s)	
Intensity	Pitch	Location	Mixture	Mixture	
Direction	Intensity	Mixture		Permanence	
Color	Duration	Chromatic			
	Source	intensities			
	Direction				

Duration

Objective time span measured against conventional and/or subjective expectations.

Progression

The actual sequence of events implied by the scene and considered significant by those persons encountering one another on the scene.

From this rough diagram a list of questions may be drawn which adds another dimension to the existing set of questions about the meaning of behavior. Obviously, as the questions are asked and a body of quantitative information is assembled, an assessment can be made of what is or is not significant about physical environment as it applies to social interaction, and a more comprehensive and sophisticated scheme will evolve. Until such time, this scheme, or one like it, can serve as a point of departure from which an initial investigation can be made into the unexplored dimensions of non-verbal, non-gestural, symbolic reality.

Notes

1 Erving Goffman, *The Presentation of Self in Everyday Life* (Garden City: Doubleday Anchor 1959), and *Behavior in Public Places* (Collier-Macmillan 1963).

2 Robert Ardrey, *The Territorial Imperative* (Collins 1966).

3 Edward T. Hall, *The Hidden Dimension* (Garden City: Doubleday 1966).

4 In searching the literature for studies and discussions of how the physical container affects social behavior, we find two areas which are indirectly related to our problem. The first of these is the work of the transactional psychologists concerned with the nature of perception. See, for example, Franklin P. Kilpatrick (ed.), *Exploration in Transactional Psychology* (New York University Press 1961). Many of the studies in this collection deal with the ways in which the perception of objects occurs. In addition, there is an excellent bibliography in that volume. From the developmental perspective, Piaget

has dealt with the problem of how children learn to organize external reality. See Jean Piaget, *The Child's Construction of Reality*, Routledge & Kegan Paul 1955.

5 Note well that the process of assuming a causal relationship between physical form and meaning may act to bring about that very relationship. Thus, the recurring use of great scale (monumental buildings) to symbolize super-human authority finally dictates that, if one wishes to symbolize super-human authority, one must use great scale.

6 Benjamin Lee Whorf, *Language, Thought and Reality* (New York: John Wiley 1959), 207–19; 233–45.

7 Edward T. Hall, *The Silent Language* (New York: Doubleday 1959), had discussed at length cultural differences in the perception and meaning of time.

8 One reason that a film like *Last Year at Marienbad* is so disorienting is that it violates our expectations of progression. By externalizing the random order of events which we have learned to accept as the unique characteristic of thought, memory, and imagination and making them appear to be happening 'out there', the hermetic seal between internal and external experience is broken and our ability to predict within our conventionalized framework is destroyed.

14 Pedagogy and sociology

Émile Durkheim

I regard as the prime postulate of all pedagogical speculation that education is an eminently social thing in its origins as in its functions, and that, therefore, pedagogy depends on sociology more closely than on any other science. And since this idea will dominate all my teaching, as it already dominated the similar instruction that I formerly gave at another university, it seemed to me appropriate to use this first lecture to set it forth specifically in order that you might be better able to follow its ultimate applications. There can be no question of demonstrating it explicitly in the course of only a single lecture. A principle so general, the implications of which are so extensive, can be verified only progressively, successively as one gets into detailed facts and as one sees how it is applied to them. But what is possible now is to give you an overview of the whole; to indicate to you the principal reasons for its acceptance from the first step of the inquiry, even if only provisionally and subject to the necessary verification; finally, to mark out its scope as well as its limits—and this will be the object of this first lecture.

It is all the more necessary immediately to call your attention to this fundamental axiom because it is not very generally known. Until recently—and there are still exceptions—modern pedagogues agreed almost unanimously that education is an eminently individual thing, and, consequently, on making of pedagogy an immediate and direct corollary of psychology alone. For Kant as for Mill, for Herbart as for Spencer, the object of education would be above all to realize, in each individual, but carrying them to their highest possible point of perfection, the attributes distinctive of the human species in general. They stated as a truism that there is one education and one alone, which, to the exclusion of any other, is suitable for all men indiscriminately, whatever may be the historical

Source: *Education and Sociology*, New York: Free Press (1956), 114–16, 123–34.

and social conditions on which they depend—and it is this abstract and unique ideal that the theorists of education propose to determine. They assumed that there is *one* human nature, the forms and properties of which are determinable once and for all, and the pedagogical problem consisted of investigating how the educational influence should be exercised on human nature so defined. No doubt, no one has ever thought that man is, at the outset, as soon as he enters life, all that he can and should be. It is quite clear that the human being is formed only progressively in the course of a slow growth which begins at birth and is completed only at maturity. But they supposed that this growth is only a realization of potentialities and only brings to light the latent energies which existed, fully formed, in the physical and mental organism of the child. The educator, then, would have nothing essential to add to the work of nature. He would create nothing new. His role would be limited to preventing these existing potentialities from becoming atrophied through disuse, or from deviating from their normal direction, or from developing too slowly. Therefore, conditions of time and place, the state of the social milieu, lose all interest for pedagogy. Since man carries in himself all the potentialities of his development, it is he and he alone who must be observed when one undertakes to determine in what direction and in what manner this development should be guided. What is important is to know what his native faculties are and what their nature is. Now, the science which has as its object the description and explanation of the individual man is psychology. It seems, then, that it should suffice for all the needs of the pedagogue.

In sum, education, far from having as its unique or principal object the individual and his interests, is above all the means by which society perpetually recreates the conditions of its very existence. Can society survive only if there exists among its members a sufficient homogeneity? Education perpetuates and reinforces this homogeneity by fixing in advance, in the mind of the child, the essential similarities that collective life presupposes. But, on the other hand, without a certain diversity, would all co-operation be impossible? Education assures the persistence of this necessary diversity by becoming itself diversified and by specializing. It consists, then, in one or another of its aspects, of a systematic socialization of the young generation. In each of us, it may be said, there exist two beings which, while inseparable except by abstraction, remain distinct. One is made up of all the mental states which apply only to ourselves and to the events of our personal lives. This is what might be called the individual being. The other is a system of ideas, sentiments, and practices which express in us, not our personality, but the group or different groups of which we are part; these are religious beliefs, moral beliefs and practices, national or occupational traditions, collective opinions of every kind. Their totality forms the social being. To constitute this being in each of us is the end of education.

It is here, moreover, that are best shown the importance of its role and the fruitfulness of its influence. Indeed, not only is this social being not given, fully formed, in the primitive constitution of man, but it has not resulted from it through a spontaneous development. Spontaneously, man was not inclined to submit to a political authority, to respect a moral discipline, to dedicate himself, to be self-sacrificing. There was nothing in our congenital nature that predisposed us to become servants of divinities, symbolic emblems of the society, to render them worship, to deprive ourselves in order to do them honor. It is society itself which, to the degree that it is firmly established, has drawn from within itself those great moral forces before which man has felt his inferiority. Now, if one leaves aside the vague and indefinite tendencies which can be attributed to heredity, the child, on entering into life, brings to it only his nature as an individual. Society finds itself, so to speak, with each new generation, faced with a *tabula rasa*, very nearly, on which it must build anew. To the egoistic and asocial being that has just been born it must, as rapidly as possible, add another, capable of leading a social and moral life. Such is the work of education, and you can readily see its great importance. It is not limited to developing the individual organism in the direction indicated by nature, to eliciting the hidden potentialities which need only be manifested. It creates in man a new man, and this man is made up of all the best in us, of all that gives value and dignity to life. This creative quality is, moreover, a special prerogative of human education Anything else is what animals receive, if one can apply this name to the progressive training to which they are subjected by their parents. It can, indeed, foster the development of certain instincts that lie dormant in the animal; but such training does not initiate it into a new life. It facilitates the play of

natural functions; but it creates nothing. Taught by its mother, the young animal learns more quickly how to fly or build its nest; but it learns almost nothing from its parents that it would not have been able to discover through its own individual experience. This is because animals either do not live under social conditions, or form rather simple societies which function through instinctive mechanisms that each individual carries within himself, fully formed, from birth. Education, then, can add nothing essential to nature, since the latter is adequate for everything, for the life of the group as well as that of the individual. By contrast, among men the aptitudes of every kind that social life presupposes are much too complex to be able to be contained, somehow, in our tissues, to take the form of organic predispositions. It follows that they cannot be transmitted from one generation to another by way of heredity. It is through education that the transmission is effected.

A ceremony found in many societies clearly demonstrates this distinctive feature of human education and shows, too, that man was aware of it very early. It is the initiation ceremony. It takes place when education is completed; generally, too, it brings to a close a last period in which the elders conclude the instruction of the young man by revealing to him the most fundamental beliefs and the most sacred rites of the tribe. Once this is accomplished, the person who has undergone it takes his place in the society; he leaves the women, among whom he had passed his whole childhood; henceforth, his place is among the warriors; at the same time, he becomes conscious of his sex, all the rights and duties of which he assumes from then on. He has become a man and a citizen. Now, it is a belief universally diffused among all these peoples that the initiate, by the very fact of initiation, has become an entirely new man: he changes his personality, he takes another name, and we know that the name was not then considered as a simple verbal sign, but as an essential element of the person. Initiation was considered as a second birth. The primitive mind conceives of this transformation symbolically, imagining that a spiritual principle, a sort of new soul, has come to be incarnated in the individual. But if we separate from this belief the mythical forms in which it is enveloped, do we not find under the symbol this idea, obscurely glimpsed, that education has had the effect of creating a new being in man? It is the social being.

However, it will be said, if one can indeed conceive that the distinctively moral qualities, because they impose privations on the individual, because they inhibit his natural impulses, can be developed in us only under an outside influence, are there not others which every man wishes to acquire and seeks spontaneously? Such are the divers qualities of the intelligence which allow him better to adapt his behavior to the nature of things. Such, too, are the physical qualities and everything that contributes to the vigor and health of the organism. For the former, at least, it seems that education, in developing them, may only assist the development of nature itself, only lead the individual to a state of relative perfection toward which he tends by himself, although he attains it more rapidly thanks to the co-operation of society.

But what demonstrates, despite appearances, that here as elsewhere education answers above all to external, that is social, necessities, is that there are societies in which these qualities have not been cultivated at all, and that in every case they have been understood very differently in different societies. The advantages of a solid intellectual culture have been far from recognized by all peoples. Science and the critical mind, that we rate so high today, were for a long time held in suspicion. Do we not know a great doctrine which proclaims happy the poor in spirit? And we must guard against believing that this indifference to knowledge had been artificially imposed on men in violation of their nature. By themselves, they had then no desire for science, quite simply because the societies of which they were part did not at all feel the need of it. To be able to live they needed, above all, strong and respected traditions. Now, tradition does not arouse, but tends rather to preclude, thought and reflection. It is not otherwise with respect to physical qualities. Where the state of the social milieu inclines the public conscience towards asceticism, physical education will be spontaneously relegated to the background. Something of this sort took place in the schools of the Middle Ages. Similarly, following currents of opinion, this same education will be understood very differently. In Sparta its main object was to harden the limbs to fatigue; in Athens it was a means of making bodies beautiful to the sight; in the time of chivalry it was required to form agile and supple warriors; today it no longer has any but a hygienic end, and is concerned above all with limiting the dangerous effects of a too intense intellectual culture. Thus, even those qualities which appear at first glance so spontaneously desirable, the individual seeks only when society invites him to, and he seeks them in the fashion that it prescribes for him.

You see to what degree psychology by itself is an inadequate resource for the pedagogue. Not only, as I showed you at the start, is it society that outlines for the individual the ideal which he should realize through education, but more, in the individual nature there are no determinate tendencies, no defined states which are like a first aspiration to this ideal, which can be regarded as its internal and anticipated form. There is no doubt that there exist in us very general aptitudes without which it would evidently be unrealizable. If man can learn to sacrifice himself, it is because he is not incapable of sacrifice; if he has been able to submit himself to the discipline of science, it is because it was not unsuitable to him. Through the very fact that we are an integral part of the universe, we care about something other than ourselves; there is in us, therefore, a primary impersonality which prepares for disinterestedness. Similarly, by the fact that we

think, we have a certain tendency to know. But between these vague and confused predispositions (mixed, besides, with all kinds of contrary predispositions) and the very definite and very particular form that they take under the influence of society, there is an abyss. It is impossible for even the most penetrating analysis to perceive in advance, in these indistinct potentialities, what they are to become once the collectivity has acted upon them. For the latter is not limited to giving them a form that was lacking in them; it adds something to them. It adds to them its own energy, and by that very fact it transforms them and draws from them effects which had not been contained in them in primitive form. Thus, even though the individual mind would no longer have any mystery for us, even though psychology would be a real science, it would not teach the educator about the end that he should pursue. Sociology alone can either help us to understand it, by relating it to the social conditions on which it depends and which it expresses, or help us to discover it when the public conscience, disturbed and uncertain, no longer knows what it should be.

But if the role of sociology is predominant in the determination of the ends that education should follow, does it have the same importance with respect to the choice of means?

Here psychology clearly comes into its own. If the pedagogic ideal expresses, above all, social necessities, they can, however, be realized only in and by individuals. In order that it may be more than just a mental construct, an idle injunction of the society to its members, it is necessary to find the way to make the conscience of the child conform to it. Now, the conscience has its own laws which one must know to be able to modify it, if at least one wishes to be spared the empirical gropings which it is precisely the object of pedagogy to reduce to a minimum. To be able to stimulate activity to develop in a given direction, one must also know what its causes are and what their nature is; for it is on this condition that it will be possible to exert the appropriate influence, based on knowledge. Is it a matter, for example, of arousing either patriotism or the sense of humanity? We shall know all the better how to shape the moral sensibility of our pupils in one or the other direction, when we shall have more complete and more precise notions about the totality of phenomena that are called tendencies, habits, desires, emotions, etc., of the divers conditions on which they depend, of the form that they take in the child. According to whether one sees in such tendencies a product of agreeable or disagreeable experiences that the species has been able to have, or indeed, on the contrary, a primitive fact prior to the affective states which accompany their functioning, one will have to treat them in very different ways in order to regulate their development. Now it is up to psychology, and more specifically, child psychology, to resolve these questions. If it is incompetent to fix the end, or rather the ends, of education, there is no doubt that it has a useful role to play in the establishment of methods. And since no method can be applied in the same fashion to different children, it is psychology, too, that should help us to cope with the diversity of intelligence and character. We know, unfortunately, that we are still far from the time when it will truly be in a condition to satisfy this desideratum.

There could be no question, then, of not recognizing the services which the science of the individual can render to pedagogy, and we shall acknowledge its role. But even in that circle of problems in which it can usefully enlighten the pedagogue, it cannot do without the co-operation of sociology.

First, because the ends of education are social, the means by which these ends can be attained must necessarily have the same character. And indeed, among all the pedagogical institutions there is perhaps not one which is not analogous to a social institution the principal traits of which it reproduces, in a smaller and abridged form. There is a discipline in the school as in the community. The rules which set his duties for the schoolboy are comparable to those which prescribe his conduct for the adult man. The rewards and punishments that are attached to the first are not unlike the rewards and punishments that sanction the second. Do we teach children science ready-made? But the science that is growing teaches itself, too. It does not remain enclosed in the brains of those who conceive it, but it becomes truly operative only on the condition of being communicated to other men. Now, this communication, which sets in motion a whole network of social mechanisms, constitutes an instruction which, in order to address itself to the adult, does not differ in nature from that which the pupil receives from his teacher. Is it not said, besides, that the scientists are teachers for their peers, and is the name of schools not given to the groups that are formed around them? One could multiply examples. This is why, indeed, as the scholastic life is only the germ of social life, as the latter is only the consequence and the blossoming of the former, it is impossible for the principal procedures by which the one operates not to be found in the other. One can foresee, then, what sociology, the science of social institutions, contributes to our understanding of what pedagogical institutions are or to our conjectures on what they should be. The better we understand society, the better shall we be able to account for all that happens in that social microcosm that the school is. On the contrary, you see with what prudence and within what limits it is appropriate to use the data of psychology, even with respect to the determination of methods. By itself alone, it could not provide us with the necessary elements for the construction of a technique which, by definition, has its prototype not in the individual, but in the collectivity.

Moreover, the social conditions on which pedagogical ends depend do not limit their influence to this. They also affect the conception of methods; for the nature of the end implies, in part, that of the means. When society, for example, is oriented in an individualistic direction, all the educational procedures which can have the effect of doing violence to the individual, of ignoring his inner spontaneity, will seem intolerable and will be disapproved. By contrast, when, under pressure of lasting or transitory circumstances, it feels the need of imposing on everyone a more rigorous conformity, everything that can provoke excessive initiative of the intelligence will be proscribed. In fact, every time that the system of educational methods has been profoundly transformed, it has been under the influence of one of those great social currents the effect of which has made itself felt throughout the entire collective life. It is not as a consequence of psychological discoveries that the Renaissance opposed a whole set of new methods to those that the Middle Ages had practiced. But it is because, as a result of the changes that had come about in the structure of European societies, a new conception of man and of his place in the world had emerged. In like manner, the pedagogues who, at the end of the eighteenth century or at the beginning of the nineteenth, undertook to substitute the inductive method for the abstract method, were above all the reflection of the aspirations of their time. Neither Basedow, nor Pestalozzi, nor Froebel were very good psychologists. What their theory expresses above all is that respect for inner liberty, that horror for any restriction, that love of man and consequently of the child, which are at the base of our modern individualism.

Thus, under whatever aspect one considers education, it appears to us everywhere with the same character. Whether it is a matter of the ends that it follows or the means that it employs, it is social needs that it answers; it is collective ideas and sentiments that it expresses. No doubt, the individual himself finds some benefit in it. Have we not expressly recognized that we owe to education the best in us? But this is because the best in us is of social origin. It is always to the study of society, then, that we must return; it is only there that the pedagogue can find the principles of his speculation. Psychology will indeed be able to indicate to him what is the best way to proceed in order to apply these principles to the child, once they are stated; but it will hardly help us to discover them.

I add, in closing, that if there was ever a time and a country in which the sociological point of view was indicated, in a particularly urgent fashion, for pedagogues, it is certainly our country and our time. When a society finds itself in a state of relative stability, of temporary equilibrium, as, for example, French society in the seventeenth century; when, consequently, a system of education is established which, while it lasts, is not contested by anyone, the only pressing questions which are put are questions of application. No serious doubt arises either over the end to attain or over the general orientation of methods; there can, then, be controversy only over the best way to put them into practice, and these are difficulties which psychology can settle. I do not have to tell you that this intellectual and moral security is not of our century; this is at the same time its trouble and its greatness. The profound transformations which contemporary societies have undergone or which they are in process of undergoing, necessitate corresponding transformations in the national education. But although we may be well aware that changes are necessary, we do not know what they should be. Whatever may be the private convictions of individuals or factions, public opinion remains undecided and anxious. The pedagogical problem is, then, posed for us with greater urgency than it was for the men of the seventeenth century. It is no longer a matter of putting verified ideas into practice, but of finding ideas to guide us. How to discover them if we do not go back to the very source of educational life, that is to say, to society? It is society that must be examined; it is society's needs that must be known, since it is society's needs that must be satisfied. To be content with looking inside ourselves would be to turn our attention away from the very reality that we must attain; this would make it impossible for us to understand anything about the forces which influence the world around us and ourselves with it. I do not believe that I am following a mere prejudice or yielding to an immoderate love for a science which I have cultivated all my life, in saying that never was a sociological approach more necessary for the educator. It is not because sociology can give us ready-made procedures which we need only use. Are there, in any case, any of this sort? But it can do more and it can do better. It can give us what we need most urgently; I mean to say a body of guiding ideas that may be the core of our practice and that sustain it, that give a meaning to our action, and that attach us to it; which is the necessary condition for this action to be fruitful.

15   The rise of the child-saving movement: a study in social policy and correctional reform[1]

Anthony Platt

Studies of crime and delinquency have, for the most part, focused on their psychological and environmental origins. Correctional research has traditionally encompassed the relationship between prisoners and prison-management, the operation of penal programs, the implementation of the 'rehabilitative ideal' and, in recent years, the effectiveness of community-based corrections. On the other hand, we know very little about the social processes by which certain types of behavior come to be defined as 'criminal' or about the origins of penal reforms.[2] If we intend rationally to assess the nature and purposes of correctional policies, it is of considerable importance to understand how laws and legislation are passed, how changes in penal practices are implemented, and what interests are served by such reforms.

This paper analyzes the nature and origins of the reform movement in juvenile justice and juvenile corrections at the end of the nineteenth century. Delinquency raises fundamental questions about the objects of social control, and it was through the child-saving movement that the modern system of delinquency-control emerged in the United States. The child-savers were responsible for creating a new legal institution for penalizing children (juvenile court) and a new correctional institution to accommodate the needs of youth (reformatory). The origins of 'delinquency' are to be found in the programs and ideas of these reformers, who recognized the existence and carriers of delinquent norms.

Images of delinquency

The child-saving movement, like most moral crusades, was characterized by a 'rhetoric of legitimization',[3] built on traditional values and imagery. From the medical profession, the child-savers borrowed the imagery of pathology, infection, and treatment; from

Source: *Annals of the American Academy* (January 1969), 381, 21–38.

the tenets of Social Darwinism, they derived their pessimistic views about the intractability of human nature and the innate moral defects of the working class; finally, their ideas about the biological and environmental origins of crime may be attributed to the positivist tradition in European criminology and to anti-urban sentiments associated with the rural, Protestant ethic.

American criminology in the last century was essentially a practical affair. Theoretical concepts of crime were imported from Europe, and an indiscriminating eclecticism dominated the literature. Lombrosian positivism and Social Darwinism were the major sources of intellectual justification for crime workers. The pessimism of Darwinism, however, was counterbalanced by notions of charity, religious optimism, and the dignity of suffering which were implicit components of the Protestant ethic.

Before 1870 there were only a few American textbooks on crime, and the various penal organizations lacked specialized journals. Departments of law and sociology in the universities were rarely concerned with more than the description and classification of crimes. The first American writers on crime were physicians, like Benjamin Rush and Isaac Ray, who were trained according to European methods. The social sciences were similarly imported from Europe, and American criminologists fitted their data to the theoretical framework of criminal anthropology. Herbert Spencer's writings had an enormous impact on American intellectuals, and Cesare Lombroso, perhaps the most significant figure in nineteenth-century criminology, looked for recognition in the United States when he felt that his experiments had been neglected in Europe.[4]

Although Lombroso's theoretical and experimental studies were not translated into English until 1911, his findings were known by American academics in the early 1890's, and their popularity, like that of Spencer's works, was based on the fact that they confirmed popular assumptions about the character and existence of a 'criminal class'. Lombroso's original theory suggested the existence of a criminal type distinguishable from noncriminals by observable physical anomalies of a degenerative or atavistic nature. He proposed that the criminal was a morally inferior human species, characterized by physical traits reminiscent of apes, lower primates, and savage tribes. The criminal was thought to be morally retarded and, like a small child, instinctively aggressive and precocious unless restrained.[5] It is not difficult to see the connection between biological determinism in criminological literature and the principles of 'natural selection'; both of these theoretical positions automatically justified the 'eradication of elements that constituted a permanent and serious danger'.[6]

Nature versus nurture

Before 1900, American writers were familiar with Lombroso's general propositions but had only the briefest knowledge of his research techniques.[7] Although the emerging doctrines of preventive criminology implied human malleability, most American penologists were preoccupied with the intractability of the 'criminal classes'. Hamilton Wey, an influential physician at Elmira Reformatory, argued before the National Prison Association in 1881 that criminals were 'a distinct type of human species', characterized by flat-footedness, asymmetrical bodies, and 'degenerative physiognomy'.[8]

Literature on 'social degradation' was extremely popular during the 1870's and 1880's, though most such 'studies' were little more than crude polemics, padded with moralistic epithets and preconceived value judgments. Richard Dugdale's series of papers on the Jukes family, which became a model for the case-study approach to social problems, was distorted almost beyond recognition by anti-intellectual supporters of hereditary theories of crime.[9] Confronted by the evidence of Darwin, Galton, Dugdale, Caldwell, and many other disciples of the biological image of man, correctional professionals were compelled to admit that 'a large proportion of the unfortunate children that go to make up the great army of criminals are not born right.'[10] Reformers adopted the rhetoric of Darwinism in order to emphasize the urgent need for confronting the 'crime problem' before it got completely out of hand. A popular proposal was the 'methodized registration and training' of potential criminals, 'or these failing, their early and entire withdrawal from the community'.[11]

The organization of correctional workers through national representatives and their identification with the professions of law and medicine operated to discredit the tenets of Darwinism and Lombrosian theory. Correctional workers did not think of themselves merely as the custodians of a pariah class. The self-image of penal reformers as doctors rather than guards and the domination of criminological research

in the United States by physicians helped to encourage the acceptance of 'therapeutic' strategies in prisons and reformatories. As Arthur Fink has observed:[12]

> The role of the physician in this ferment is unmistakable. Indeed, he was the dynamic agent. . . . Not only did he preserve and add to existing knowledge—for his field touched all borders of science—but he helped to maintain and extend the methodology of science.

Perhaps what is more significant is that physicians furnished the official rhetoric of penal reform. Admittedly, the criminal was 'pathological' and 'diseased', but medical science offered the possibility of miraculous cures. Although there was a popular belief in the existence of a 'criminal class' separated from the rest of mankind by a 'vague boundary line', there was no good reason why this class could not be identified, diagnosed, segregated, changed, and controlled.[13]

By the late 1890's, most correctional administrators agreed that hereditary theories of crime were over-fatalistic. The superintendent of the Kentucky Industrial School of Reform told delegates to a national conference on corrections that heredity is 'unjustifiably made a bugaboo to discourage efforts at rescue. We know that physical heredity tendencies can be neutralized and often nullified by proper counteracting precautions.'[14] E. R. L. Gould, a sociologist at the University of Chicago, similarly criticized biological theories of crime for being unconvincing and sentimental. 'Is it not better', he said, 'to postulate freedom of choice than to preach the doctrine of the unfettered will, and so elevate criminality into a propitiary sacrifice?'[15]

Charles Cooley was one of the first sociologists to observe that criminal behavior depended as much upon social and economic circumstances as it did upon the inheritance of biological traits. 'The criminal class', he said, 'is largely the result of society's bad workmanship upon fairly good material.' In support of this argument, he noted that there was a 'large and fairly trustworthy body of evidence' to suggest that many 'degenerates' could be converted into 'useful citizens by rational treatment'.[16]

Urban disenchantment

Another important influence on nineteenth-century criminology was a disenchantment with urban life—an attitude which is still prevalent in much 'social problems' research. Immigrants were regarded as 'unsocialized', and the city's impersonality compounded their isolation and degradation. 'By some cruel alchemy,' wrote Julia Lathrop, 'we take the sturdiest of European peasantry and at once destroy in a large measure its power to rear to decent livelihood the first generation of offspring upon our soil.'[17] The city symbolically embodied all the worst features of industrial life. A member of the Massachusetts Board of Charities observed:[18]

Children acquire a perverted taste for city life
and crowded streets; but if introduced when young
to country life, care of animals and plants, and
rural pleasures, they are likely . . . to be healthier
in mind and body for such associations.

Programs which promoted rural and primary group
concepts were encouraged because slum life was regarded as unregulated, vicious, and lacking social
rules. Its inhabitants were depicted as abnormal and
maladjusted, living their lives in chaos and conflict.[19]
It was consequently the task of social reformers to
make city life more wholesome, honest, and free from
depravity. Beverley Warner told the National Prison
Association in 1898[20] that philanthropic organizations
all over the country were

making efforts to get the children out of the
slums, even if only once a week, into the radiance
of better lives. . . . It is only by leading the
child out of sin and debauchery, in which it has
lived, into the circle of life that is a repudiation
of things that it sees in its daily life, that it can
be influenced.

Although there was a wide difference of opinion
among experts as to the precipitating causes of crime,
it was generally agreed that criminals were abnor-
mally conditioned by a multitude of biological and
environmental forces, some of which were permanent
and irreversible. Biological theories of crime were
modified to incorporate a developmental view of
human behavior. If, as it was believed, criminals are
conditioned by biological heritage and brutish living
conditions, the prophylactic measures must be taken
early in life. Criminals of the future generations
must be reached. 'They are born to crime,' wrote the
penologist Enoch Wines in 1880, 'brought up for it.
They must be saved.'[21]

Maternal justice

The 1880's and 1890's represented for many middle-
class intellectuals and professionals a period of
discovery of the 'dim attics and damp cellars in
poverty-stricken sections of populous towns' and of
'innumerable haunts of misery throughout the land'.[22]
The city was suddenly discovered to be a place of
scarcity, disease, neglect, ignorance, and 'dangerous
influences'. Its slums were the 'last resorts of the pen-
niless and the criminal'; here humanity reached its
lowest level of degradation and despair.[23]

The discovery of problems posed by 'delinquent'
youth was greatly influenced by the role of feminist
reformers in the child-saving movement. It was widely
agreed that it was a woman's business to be involved
in regulating the welfare of children, for women were
considered the 'natural caretakers' of wayward children. Women's claim to the public care of children had
some historical justification during the nineteenth century, and their role in child-rearing was considered

paramount. Women were regarded as better teachers
than men and were also more influential in child-
training at home. The fact that public education also
came more under the direction of women teachers in
the schools increased the predominance of women in
the raising of children.[24]

Child-saving was a predominantly feminist movement, and it was regarded even by antifeminists as
female domain. The social circumstances behind this
appreciation of maternalism were women's emancipation and the accompanying changes in the character
of traditional family life. Educated middle-class
women now had more leisure time but a limited
choice of careers. Child-saving was a reputable task
for women who were allowed to extend their housekeeping functions into the community without denying
antifeminist stereotypes of woman's nature and place.
'It is an added irony,' writes Christopher Lasch in his
study of American intellectualism,[25]

that the ideas about woman's nature to which
some feminists still clung, in spite of their
opposition to the enslavement of woman in the
home, were these very clichés which had so long
been used to keep her there. The assumption that
women were morally purer than men, better
capable of altruism and self-sacrifice, was the
core of the myth of domesticity against which the
feminists were in revolt. . . . [F]eminist and
anti-feminist assumptions seemed curiously to
coincide.

Child-saving may be understood as a crusade
which served symbolic and status functions for native,
middle-class Americans, particularly feminist groups.
Middle-class women at the turn of the century
experienced a complex and far-reaching status revolution. Their traditional functions were dramatically
threatened by the weakening of domestic roles and
the specialized rearrangement of family life.[26] One
of the main forces behind the child-saving movement
was a concern for the structure of family life and the
proper socialization of young persons, since it was
these concerns that had traditionally given purpose to
a woman's life. Professional organizations—such as
settlement houses, women's clubs, bar associations
and penal organizations—regarded child-saving as a
problem of women's rights, whereas their opponents
seized upon it as an opportunity to keep women in
their proper place. Child-saving organizations had
little or nothing to do with militant supporters of the
suffragette movement. In fact, the new role of social
worker was created by deference to antifeminist
stereotypes of a 'woman's place'.

A woman's place

Feminist involvement in child-saving was endorsed by
a variety of penal and professional organizations.
Their participation was usually justified as an extension of their housekeeping functions so that they

did not view themselves, nor were they regarded by others, as competitors for jobs usually performed by men. Proponents of the 'new penology' insisted that reformatories should resemble home life, for institutions without women were likely to do more harm than good to inmates. According to G. E. Howe, the reformatory system provided 'the most ample opportunities for woman's transcendent influence'.[27]

Female delegates to philanthropic and correctional conferences also realized that correctional work suggested the possibility of useful careers. Mrs W. P. Lynde told the National Conference of Charities and Correction in 1879 that children's institutions offered the 'truest and noblest scope for the public activities of women in the time which they can spare from their primary domestic duties.'[28] Women were exhorted by other delegates to make their lives meaningful by participating in welfare programs, volunteering their time and services, and getting acquainted with less privileged groups. They were told to seek jobs in institutions where 'the woman-element shall pervade ... and soften its social atmosphere with motherly tenderness.'[29]

Although the child-savers were responsible for some minor reforms in jails and reformatories, they were more particularly concerned with extending governmental control over a whole range of youthful activities that had previously been handled on an informal basis. The main aim of the child-savers was to impose sanctions on conduct unbecoming youth and to disqualify youth from enjoying adult privileges. As Bennett Berger has commented, 'adolescents are not made by nature but by being excluded from responsible participation in adult affairs, by being rewarded for dependency, and penalized for precocity.'[30]

The child-saving movement was not so much a break with the past as an affirmation of faith in traditional institutions. Parental authority, education at home, and the virtues of rural life were emphasized because they were in decline at this time. The child-saving movement was, in part, a crusade which, through emphasizing the dependence of the social order on the proper socialization of children, implicitly elevated the nuclear family and, more especially, the role of women as stalwarts of the family. The child-savers were prohibitionists, in a general sense, who believed that social progress depended on efficient law enforcement, strict supervision of children's leisure and recreation, and the regulation of illicit pleasures. What seemingly began as a movement to humanize the lives of adolescents soon developed into a program of moral absolutism through which youth was to be saved from movies, pornography, cigarettes, alcohol, and anything else which might possibly rob them of their innocence.

Although child-saving had important symbolic functions for preserving the social prestige of a declining elite, it also had considerable practical significance for legitimizing new career openings for women. The new role of social worker combined elements of an old and partly fictitious role—defenders of family life—and elements of a new role—social servant. Social work was thus both an affirmation of cherished American values and an instrumentality for women's emancipation.

Juvenile court

The essential preoccupation of the child-saving movement was the recognition and control of youthful deviance. It brought attention to, and thus 'invented', new categories of youthful misbehavior which had been hitherto unappreciated. The efforts of the child-savers were institutionally expressed in the juvenile court, which, despite recent legislative and constitutional reforms, is generally acknowledged as their most significant contribution to progressive penology.

The juvenile-court system was part of a general movement directed towards removing adolescents from the criminal-law process and creating special programs for delinquent, dependent, and neglected children. Regarded widely as 'one of the greatest advances in child welfare that has ever occurred', the juvenile court was considered 'an integral part of total welfare planning'.[31] Charles Chute, an enthusiastic supporter of the child-saving movement, claimed:[32]

No single event has contributed more to the welfare of children and their families. It revolutionized the treatment of delinquent and neglected children and led to the passage of similar laws throughout the world.

The juvenile court was a special tribunal created by statute to determine the legal status of children and adolescents. Underlying the juvenile-court movement was the concept of *parens patriae* by which the courts were authorized to handle with wide discretion the problems of 'its least fortunate junior citizens'.[33] The administration of juvenile justice differed in many important respects from the criminal-court processes. A child was not accused of a crime but offered assistance and guidance; intervention in his life was not supposed to carry the stigma of criminal guilt. Judicial records were not generally available to the press or public, and juvenile-court hearings were conducted in relative privacy. Juvenile-court procedures were typically informal and inquisitorial. Specific criminal safeguards of due process were not applicable because juvenile proceedings were defined by statute as civil in character.[34]

The original statutes enabled the courts to investigate a wide variety of youthful needs and misbehavior. As Joel Handler has observed, 'the critical philosophical position of the reform movement was that no formal, legal distinctions should be made between the delinquent and the dependent or neglected.[35] Statutory definitions of 'delinquency' encompassed (1) acts that would be criminal if committed by adults; (2) acts that violated county, town, or municipal ordinances; and (3) violations or vaguely defined catch-alls

—such as 'vicious or immoral behavior', 'incorrigibility' and 'truancy'—which 'seem to express the notion that the adolescent, if allowed to continue, will engage in more serious conduct.'[36]

The juvenile-court movement went far beyond a concern for special treatment of adolescent offenders. It brought within the ambit of governmental control a set of youthful activities that had been previously ignored or dealt with on an informal basis. It was not by accident that the behavior selected for penalizing by the child-savers—sexual license, drinking, roaming the streets, begging, frequenting dance halls and movies, fighting, and being seen in public late at night—was most directly relevant to the children of lower-class migrant and immigrant families.

The juvenile court was not perceived by its supporters as a revolutionary experiment, but rather as a culmination of traditionally valued practices.[37] The child-saving movement was 'antilegal', in the sense that it derogated civil rights and procedural formalities, while relying heavily on extra-legal techniques. The judges of the new court were empowered to investigate the character and social life of predelinquent as well as delinquent children; they examined motivation rather than intent, seeking to identify the moral reputation of problematic children. The requirements of preventive penology and child-saving further justified the court's intervention in cases where no offense had actually been committed, but where, for example, a child was posing problems for some person in authority such as a parent or teacher or social worker.

The personal touch

Judges were expected to show the same professional competence as doctors and therapists. The sociologist Charles Henderson wrote:[38]

> A careful study of individuals is an essential
> element in wise procedure. The study must
> include the physical, mental and moral peculiarities
> and defects of the children who come under the
> notice of the courts. Indeed we are likely to
> follow the lead of those cities which provide for a
> careful examination of all school children whose
> physical or psychical condition is in any way or
> degree abnormal, in order to prevent disease,
> correct deformity and vice, and select the proper
> course of study and discipline demanded by the
> individual need.

Juvenile court judges had to be carefully selected for their skills as expert diagnosticians and for their appreciation of the 'helping' professions. Miriam Van Waters, for example, regarded the juvenile court as a 'laboratory of human behavior' and its judges as 'experts with scientific training' and specialists in 'the art of human relations'. It was the judge's task to 'get the whole truth about a child' in the same way that a 'physician searches for every detail that bears on the condition of a patient.'[39]

The child-savers' interest in preventive strategies and treatment programs was based on the premise that delinquents possess innate or acquired characteristics which predispose them to crime and distinguish them from law-abiding youths. Delinquents were regarded as constrained by a variety of biological and environmental forces, so that their proper treatment involved discovery of the 'cause of the aberration' and application of 'the appropriate corrective or antidote'.[40] 'What the trouble is with the offender,' noted William Healy, 'making him what he is, socially undesirable, can only be known by getting at his mental life, as it is an affair of reactive mechanisms.'[41]

The use of terms like 'unsocialized', 'maladjusted' and 'pathological' to describe the behavior of delinquents implied that 'socialized' and 'adjusted' children conform to middle-class morality and participate in respectable institutions.[42] The failure empirically to demonstrate psychological differences between delinquents and nondelinquents did not discourage the child-savers from believing that rural and middle-class values constitute 'normality'. The unique character of the child-saving movement was its concern for predelinquent offenders—'children who occupy the debatable ground between criminality and innocence'—and its claim that it could transform potential criminals into respectable citizens by training them in 'habits of industry, self-control and obedience to law'.[43] This policy justified the diminishing of traditional procedures in juvenile court. If children were to be rescued, it was important that the rescuers be free to provide their services without legal hindrance. Delinquents had to be saved, transformed, and reconstituted. 'There is no essential difference', said Frederick Wines, 'between a criminal and any other sinner. The means and methods of restoration are the same for both.'[44]

The reformatory system

It was through the reformatory system that the child-savers hoped to demonstrate that delinquents were capable of being converted into law-abiding citizens. The reformatory was initially developed in the United States during the middle of the nineteenth century as a special form of prison discipline for adolescents and young adults. Its underlying principles were formulated in Britain by Matthew Davenport Hill, Alexander Maconochie, Walter Crofton and Mary Carpenter. If the United States did not have any great penal theorists, it at least had energetic penal administrators who were prepared to experiment with new programs. The most notable advocates of the reformatory plan in the United States were Enoch Wines, Secretary of the New York Prison Association; Theodore Dwight, the first Dean of Columbia Law School; Zebulon Brockway, Superintendent of Elmira Reformatory in New York; and Frank Sanborn,

Secretary of the Massachusetts State Board of Charities.

The reformatory was distinguished from the traditional penitentiary by its policy of indeterminate sentencing, the 'mark' system, and 'organized persuasion' rather than 'coercive restraint'. Its administrators assumed that abnormal and troublesome individuals could become useful and productive citizens. Wines and Dwight, in a report to the New York legislature in 1867,[45] proposed that the ultimate aim of penal policy was reformation of the criminal, which could only be achieved

by placing the prisoner's fate, as far as possible,
in his own hand, by enabling him, through
industry and good conduct to raise himself,
step by step, to a position of less restraint; while
idleness and bad conduct, on the other hand,
keep him in a state of coercion and restraint.

But, as Brockway observed at the first meeting of the National Prison Congress in 1870, the 'new penology' was tough-minded and devoid of 'sickly sentimentalism. . . . Criminals shall either be cured, or kept under such continued restraint as gives guarantee of safety from further depredations.'[46]

Reformatories, unlike penitentiaries and jails, theoretically repudiated punishments based on intimidation and repression. They took into account the fact that delinquents were 'either physically or mentally below the average.' The reformatory system was based on the assumption that proper training can counteract the impositions of poor family life, a corrupt environment, and poverty, while at the same time toughening and preparing delinquents for the struggle ahead. 'The principle at the root of the educational method of dealing with juvenile crime,' wrote William Douglas Morrison, 'is an absolutely sound one. It is a principle which recognizes the fact that the juvenile delinquent is in the main, a product of adverse individual and social conditions.'[47]

The reformatory movement spread rapidly through the United States, and European visitors crossed the Atlantic to inspect and admire the achievements of their pragmatic colleagues. Mary Carpenter, who visited the United States in 1873, was generally satisfied with the 'generous and lavish expenditures freely incurred to promote the welfare of the inmates, and with the love of religion'. Most correctional problems with regard to juvenile delinquents, she advised, could be remedied if reformatories were built like farm schools or 'true homes'. At the Massachusetts Reform School, in Westborough, she found an 'entire want of family spirit', and, in New York, she complained that there was no 'natural life' in the reformatory. 'All the arrangements are artificial,' she said; 'instead of the cultivation of the land, which would prepare the youth to seek a sphere far from the dangers of large cities, the boys and young men were being taught trades which will confine them to the great centers of an over-crowded population.' She found similar conditions in Philadelphia where 'hundreds of youth were there congregated under lock and key', but praised the Connecticut Reform School for its 'admirable system of agricultural training.'[48] If she had visited the Illinois State Reformatory at Pontiac, she would have found a seriously overcrowded 'minor penitentiary' where the inmates were forced to work ten hours a day manufacturing shoes, brushes, and chairs.

To cottage and country

Granted the assumption that 'nurture' could usually overcome most of nature's defects, reformatory-administrators set about the task of establishing programs consistent with the aim of retraining delinquents for law-abiding careers. It was noted at the Fifth International Prison Congress, held in Paris in 1895, that reformatories were capable of obliterating hereditary and environmental taints. In a new and special section devoted to delinquency,[49] the Congress proposed that children under twelve years

should always be sent to institutions of
preservation and unworthy parents must be
deprived of the right to rear children. . . . The
preponderant place in rational physical training
should be given to manual labor, and particularly
to agricultural labor in the open air, for both
sexes.

The heritage of biological imagery and Social Darwinism had a lasting influence on American criminology, and penal reformers continued to regard delinquency as a problem of individual adjustment to the demands of industrial and urban life. Delinquents had to be removed from contaminating situations, segregated from their 'miserable surroundings', instructed and 'put as far as possible on a footing of equality with the rest of the population.'[50]

The trend from congregate housing in the city to group living in the country represented a significant change in the organization of penal institutions for young offenders. The family or cottage plan differed in several important respects from the congregate style of traditional prisons and jails. According to William Letchworth, in an address delivered before the National Conference of Charities and Correction in 1886:[51]

A fault in some of our reform schools is their
great size. In the congregating of large numbers,
individuality is lost. . . . These excessive
aggregations are overcome to a great extent in
the cottage plan. . . . The internal system of the
reformatory school should be as nearly as
practicable as that of the family, with its refining
and elevating influences; while the awakening of
the conscience and the inculcation of religious
principles should be primary aims.

The new penology emphasized the corruptness and

artificiality of the city; from progressive education, it inherited a concern for naturalism, purity, and innocence. It is not surprising, therefore, that the cottage plan also entailed a movement to a rural location. The aim of penal reformers was not merely to use the countryside for teaching agricultural skills. The confrontation between corrupt delinquents and unspoiled nature was intended to have a spiritual and regenerative effect. The romantic attachment to rural values was quite divorced from social and agricultural realities. It was based on a sentimental and nostalgic repudiation of city life. Advocates of the reformatory system generally ignored the economic attractiveness of city work and the redundancy of farming skills. As one economist cautioned reformers in 1902:[52]

> Whatever may be said about the advantages of farm life for the youth of our land, and however much it may be regretted that young men and women are leaving the farm and flocking to the cities, there can be no doubt that the movement city-ward will continue. . . . There is great danger that many who had left the home [that is, reformatory], unable to find employment in agricultural callings, would drift back to the city and not finding there an opportunity to make use of the technical training secured in the institution, would become discouraged and resume their old criminal associations and occupations.

The 'new' reformatory suffered, like all its predecessors, from overcrowding, mismanagement, 'boodleism', under-staffing, and inadequate facilities. Its distinctive features were the indeterminate sentence, the movement to cottage and country, and agricultural training. Although there was a decline in the use of brutal punishments, inmates were subjected to severe personal and physical controls: military exercise, 'training of the will', and long hours of tedious labor constituted the main program of reform.

Summary and conclusions

The child-saving movement was responsible for reforms in the ideological and institutional control of 'delinquent' youth. The concept of the born delinquent was modified with the rise of a professional class of penal administrators and social servants who promoted a developmental view of human behavior and regarded most delinquent youth as salvageable. The child-savers helped to create special judicial and correctional institutions for the processing and management of 'troublesome' youth.

There has been a shift during the last fifty years or so in official policies concerning delinquency. The emphasis has shifted from one emphasizing the criminal nature of delinquency to the 'new humanism' which speaks of disease, illness, contagion, and the like. It is essentially a shift from a legal to a medical emphasis. The emergence of a medical emphasis is of considerable significance, since it is a powerful rationale for organizing social action in the most diverse behavioral aspects of our society. For example, the child-savers were not concerned merely with 'humanizing' conditions under which children were treated by the criminal law. It was rather their aim to extend the scope of governmental control over a wide variety of personal misdeeds and to regulate potentially disruptive persons.[53] The child-savers' reforms were politically aimed at lower-class behavior and were instrumental in intimidating and controlling the poor.

The child-savers made a fact out of the norm of adolescent dependence. 'Every child is dependent,' wrote the Illinois Board of Charities in 1899, 'even the children of the wealthy. To receive his support at the hands of another does not strike him as unnatural, but quite the reverse.'[54] The juvenile court reached into the private lives of youth and disguised basically punitive policies in the rhetoric of 'rehabilitation.'[55] The child-savers were prohibitionists, in a general sense, who believed that adolescents needed protection from even their own inclinations.

The basic conservatism of the child-saving movement is apparent in the reformatory system which proved to be as tough-minded as traditional forms of punishment. Reformatory programs were unilateral, coercive, and an invasion of human dignity. What most appealed to correctional workers were the paternalistic assumptions of the 'new penology', its belief in social progress through individual reform, and its nostalgic preoccupation with the 'naturalness' and intimacy of a preindustrial way of life.

The child-saving movement was heavily influenced by middle-class women who extended their housewifely roles into public service. Their contribution may also be seen as a 'symbolic crusade' in defense of the nuclear family and their positions within it. They regarded themselves as moral custodians and supported programs and institutions dedicated to eliminating youthful immorality. Social service was an instrumentality for female emancipation, and it is not too unreasonable to suggest that women advanced their own fortune at the expense of the dependency of youth.

This analysis of the child-saving movement suggests the importance of (1) understanding the relationship between correctional reforms and related changes in the administration of criminal justice, (2) accounting for the motives and purposes of those enterprising groups who generate such reforms, (3) investigating the methods by which communities establish the formal machinery for regulating crime, and (4) distinguishing between idealized goals and enforced conditions in the implementation of correctional reforms.

Implications for corrections and research

The child-saving movement illustrates a number of important problems with the quality and purposes of correctional research and knowledge. The following discussion will draw largely upon the child-saving movement in order to examine its relevance for contemporary issues.

Positivism and progressivism

It is widely implied in the literature that the juvenile court and parallel reforms in penology represented a progressive effort by concerned reformers to alleviate the miseries of urban life and to solve social problems by rational, enlightened, and scientific methods. With few exceptions, studies of delinquency have been parochial and inadequately descriptive, and they show little appreciation of underlying political and cultural conditions. Historical studies, particularly of the juvenile court, are, for the most part, self-confirming and support an evolutionary view of human progress.[56]

The positivist heritage in the study of social problems has directed attention to (1) the primacy of the criminal actor rather than the criminal law as the major point of departure in the construction of etiological theory, (2) a rigidly deterministic view of human behavior, and (3) only the abnormal features of deviant behavior.[57] The 'rehabilitative ideal' has so dominated American criminology that there have been only sporadic efforts to undertake sociolegal research related to governmental invasion of personal liberties. But, as Francis Allen has suggested:[58]

Even if one's interests lie primarily in the problems of treatment of offenders, it should be recognized that the existence of the criminal presupposes a crime and that the problems of treatment are derivative in the sense that they depend upon the determination by law-giving agencies that certain sorts of behavior are crimes.

The conservatism and 'diluted liberalism'[59] of much research on delinquency results from the fact that researchers are generally prepared to accept prevailing definitions of crime, to work within the premises of the criminal law, and to concur at least implicitly with those who make laws as to the nature and distribution of a 'criminal' population. Thus, most theories of delinquency are based on studies of convicted or imprisoned delinquents. As John Seeley has observed in another context, professional caution requires us 'to *take* our problems rather than *make* our problems, to accept as constitutive of our "intake" what is held to be "deviant" in a way that concerns enough people in that society enough to give us primary protection'.[60] Money, encouragement, co-operation from established institutions, and a market for publications are more easily acquired for studies of the socialization or treatment of delinquents than for studies of how laws, law-makers, and law-enforcers, contribute to the 'registration' of delinquency.

Law and its implementation have been largely dismissed as irrelevant topics for inquiry into the 'causes' of delinquency. According to Herbert Packer, it is typical that the National Crime Commission ignored the fundamental question of: 'What is the criminal sanction good for?'[61] Further research is needed to understand the dynamics of the legislative and popular drive to 'criminalize'.[62] Delinquency legislation for example, as has been noted earlier, was not aimed merely at reducing crime or liberating youth. The reform movement also served important symbolic and instrumental interests for groups who made hobbies and careers out of saving children.

Policy research

Correctional research in this country has been dominated by persons who are intimately concerned with crime and its control. The scholar-technician tradition in corrections, especially with regard to delinquency, has resulted in the proliferation of 'agency-determined' research whereby scholarship is catered to institutional interests.[63] Much of what passes under the label of 'research' takes the form of 'methods engineering', produced in the interest of responsible officials and management.[64] It is only rarely, as in Erving Goffman's study of 'total institutions', that sympathetic consideration is given to the perceptions and concerns of subordinates in the correctional hierarchy.[65]

There are many historical and practical reasons why corrections has been such a narrow and specialized field of academic interest. First, corrections has been intellectually influenced by the problematic perspective of scholar-technicians, which limits the scope of 'research' to local, policy issues. In the last century especially, penology was the exclusive domain of philanthropists, muckrakers, reformers, and missionaries. Secondly, the rise of the 'multiversity' and of federal-grant research has given further respectability to applied research in corrections, to the extent that social science and public policy are inextricably linked.[66] Nevertheless, such research is minimal when compared, for example, with that done under the auspices of the Defense Department.[67] It is quite true, as the National Crime Commission reports, that research in corrections has been unsystematic, sporadic, and guided primarily by 'intuitive opportunism'.[68] Thirdly, it should be remembered that correctional institutions are politically sensitive communities which resist intrusions from academic outsiders unless the proposed research is likely to serve their best interests.[69] Research which undermines policy is generally viewed as insensitive and subversive, aside from the fact that it helps to justify and harden administrators' suspicions of 'intellectuals'. The lack of critical research is, no doubt, also due to 'the reluctance of scholars to address the specific problems faced by those charged with the perplexing task of controlling and rehabilitating offenders'.[70]

Politics and corrections

Correctional institutions have been generally regarded as distinct, insulated social organizations. Their relationship to the wider society is viewed in a bureaucratic, civil-service context, and their population is defined in welfare terms. Prisons and their constituency are stripped of political implications, seemingly existing in an apolitical vacuum. Corrections as an academic specialization has focused on the prison community to the neglect of classical interest in the relationship between political decision-making and social policies. As Hans Mattick has observed:[71]

> There is very little appreciation . . . that this 'contest between good and evil,' and the whole 'drama of crime,' is taking place within the larger arena of our political system and this, in part, helps to determine public opinion about the nature of crime, criminals and how they are dealt with.

As the gap between social deviance and political marginality narrows, it becomes increasingly necessary to examine how penal administrators are recruited, how 'new' programs are selected and implemented, and how local and national legislatures determine correctional budgets. The crisis caused by white racism in this country also requires us to appreciate in what sense prisons and jails may be used as instrumentalities of political control in the 'pacification' of black Americans. Similarly, it furthers our understanding of 'delinquency' if we appreciate the motives and political interests of those reformers and professionals who perceive youth as threatening and troublesome.

Faith in reform

The child-saving movement further illustrates that corrections may be understood historically as a succession of reforms. Academics have demonstrated a remarkably persistent optimism about reform, and operate on the premise that they can have a humanitarian influence on correctional administration. As Irving Louis Horowitz has observed, to the extent that social scientists become involved with policy-making agencies, they are committed to an elitist ideology:[72]

> They come to accept as basic the idea that men who really change things are at the top. Thus, the closer to the top one can get direct access, the more likely will intended changes be brought about.

There is little evidence to support this faith in the ultimate wisdom of policy-makers in corrections. The reformatory was not so much an improvement on the prison as a means of extending control over a new constituency; probation and parole became instruments of supervision rather than treatment; halfway houses have become a means of extending prisons into communities rather than democratically administered sanctuaries; group therapy in prisons has justified invasion of privacy and coercive treatment on the dubious grounds that prisoners are psychologically unfit; community-based narcotics programs, such as the nalline clinic, disguise medical authoritarianism in the guise of rehabilitation. Nevertheless, the optimism continues, and this is nowhere more apparent than in the National Crime Commission's Task Force Report on Corrections, which reveals that, in Robert Martinson's words, correctional policy consists of 'a redoubling of efforts in the face of persistent failure'.[73]

Finally, we have neglected to study and appreciate those who work in corrections. Like the police and, to an increasing extent, teachers and social workers, correctional staffs are constrained by the ethic of bureaucratic responsibility. They are society's 'dirty-workers', technicians working on people. As Lee Rainwater has observed:[74]

> The dirty-workers are increasingly caught between the silent middle class, which wants them to do the dirty work and keep quiet about it, and the objects of that dirty work, who refuse to continue to take it lying down. . . . These civilian colonial armies find their right to respect from their charges challenged at every turn, and often they must carry out their daily duties with fear for their physical safety.

Correctional workers are required to accommodate current definitions of criminality and to manage victims of political expediency and popular fashion—drug users, drunks, homosexuals, vagrants, delinquents and 'looters'. They have minimal influence on law-makers and rarely more than ideological rapport with law enforcers. They have no clear mandate as to the purpose of corrections, other than to reduce recidivism and reform criminals. They have to live with the proven failure of this enterprise and to justify their role as pacifiers, guards, warehouse-keepers and restrainers.[75] They are linked to a professional system that relegates them to the lowest status in the political hierarchy but uses them as a pawn in electoral battles. They are doomed to annual investigations, blue-ribbon commissions, ephemeral research studies, and endless volumes of propaganda and muckraking. They live with the inevitability of professional mediocrity, poor salaries, uncomfortable living conditions, ungrateful 'clients', and tenuous links with established institutions. It is understandable that they protect their fragile domain from intrusive research which is not supportive of their policies.

Notes

1 This paper is adapted from part of the author's book, *The Child-Savers; The Invention of Delinquency*, University of Chicago Press 1969.

2 This perspective is influenced by Howard S. Becker, *Outsiders; Studies in the Sociology of Deviance* (Collier-Macmillan 1963).

3 This term is used by Donald W. Ball, An abortion clinic ethnography, *Social Problems*, **14** (1967), 293–301.

4 See Lombroso's Introduction to Arthur MacDonald, *Criminology* (New York: Funk and Wagnall 1893).

5 Marvin E. Wolfgang, Cesare Lombroso, in Hermann Mannheim (ed.), *Pioneers in Criminology* (London: Stevens 1960), 168–227.

6 Leon Radzinowicz, *Ideology and Crime* (London: Heinemann Educational Books 1966), 55.

7 See, for example, Arthur MacDonald, *Abnormal Man* (Washington, DC: US Government Printing Office 1893); and Robert Fletcher, *The New School of Criminal Anthropology* (Washington, DC: Judd and Detwiler 1891).

8 Hamilton D. Wey, A plea for physical training of youthful criminals, in National Prison Association, *Proceedings of the Annual Congress* (Boston 1888), 181–93.

9 Richard L. Dugdale, Hereditary pauperism, as illustrated in the 'Jukes' family, in Annual Conference of Charities, *Proceedings* (Saratoga 1877), 81–99; *The Jukes; A Study in Crime, Pauperism, Disease, and Heredity* (New York: G. P. Putnam 1877).

10 Sarah B. Cooper, The kindergarten as child-saving work, in National Conference of Charities and Correction, *Proceedings* (Madison 1883), 130–8.

11 I. N. Kerlin, The moral imbecile, in National Conference of Charities and Correction, *Proceedings* (Baltimore 1890), 244–50.

12 Arthur E. Fink, *Causes of Crime; Biological Theories in the United States, 1800–1915* (Perpetua 1962), 247.

13 See, for example, Illinois, Board of State Commissioners of Public Charities, *Second Biennial Report* (Springfield: State Journal Steam Print 1873), 195–6.

14 Peter Caldwell, The duty of the state to delinquent children, National Conference of Charities and Correction, *Proceedings* (New Haven 1895), 134–43.

15 E. R. L. Gould, The statistical study of hereditary criminality, National Conference of Charities and Correction, *Proceedings* (New Haven 1895), 134–43.

16 Charles H. Cooley, 'Nature v. nurture' in the making of social careers, National Conference of Charities and Correction, *Proceedings* (Grand Rapids, Michigan 1896), 399–405.

17 Julia Lathrop, The development of the probation system in a large city, *Charities*, **13** (January 1905), 348.

18 Clara T. Leonard, Family homes for pauper and dependent children, Annual Conference of Charities, *Proceedings* (Chicago 1879), 174.

19 William Foote Whyte, Social disorganization in the slums, *American Sociological Review*, **8** (1943), 34–9.

20 Beverley Warner, Child-saving, in National Prison Association, *Proceedings of the Annual Congress* (Indianapolis 1898), 377–8.

21 Enoch C. Wines, *The State of Prisons and of Child-Saving Institutions in the Civilized World* (Cambridge, Mass.: Harvard University Press 1880), 132.

22 William P. Letchworth, Children of the state, National Conference of Charities and Correction, *Proceedings* (St Paul, Minn. 1886), 138. The idea that intellectuals *discovered* poverty as a result of their own alienation from the centers of power has been fully treated by Richard Hofstadter, *The Age of Reform* (Cape 1962); and Christopher Lasch, *The New Radicalism in America, 1889–1963; The Intellectual as a Social Type* (Chatto & Windus 1966).

23 R. W. Hill, The children of Shinbone Alley, National Conference of Charities and Correction, *Proceedings* (Omaha 1887), 231.

24 Robert Sunley, Early nineteenth-century American literature on child-rearing, in Margaret Mead and Martha Wolfenstein (eds), *Childhood in Contemporary Cultures* (University of Chicago Press 1955), 152; see also Orville G. Brim, *Education for Child-Rearing* (Collier-Macmillan 1965), 321–49.

25 Lasch, op. cit., 53–4.

26 Talcott Parsons and Robert F. Bales, *Family; Socialization and Interaction Process* (Routledge & Kegan Paul 1956), 3–33.

27 G. E. Howe, The family system, National Conference of Charities and Correction, *Proceedings* (Cleveland 1880), 212–13.

28 W. P. Lynde, Prevention in some of its aspects, Annual Conference of Charities, *Proceedings* (Chicago 1879), 167.

29 Clara T. Leonard, Family homes for pauper and dependent children, in ibid., 175.

30 Bennett Berger, review of Frank Musgrove, *Youth and the Social Order*, *American Sociological Review*, **32**, 1021.

31 Charles L. Chute, The juvenile court in retrospect, *Federal Probation*, **13** (September 1949), 7; Harrison A. Dobbs, In defense of juvenile courts, ibid., 29.

32 Charles L. Chute, Fifty years of the juvenile court, in *National Probation and Parole Association Yearbook* (1949), 1.

33 Gustav L. Schramm, The Juvenile Court Idea, *Federal Probation*, **13** (September 1949), 21.

34 Monrad G. Paulsen, Fairness to the juvenile offender, *Minnesota Law Review*, **41** (1957), 547–67. Note: Rights and rehabilitation in the juvenile courts, *Columbia Law Review*, **67** (1967), 281–341.

35 Joel F. Handler, The juvenile court and the adversary system: problems of function and form, *Wisconsin Law Review* (1965), 9.

36 Joel F. Handler and Margaret K. Rosenheim, Privacy and welfare: public assistance and juvenile justice, *Law and Contemporary Problems*, **31** (1966), 377–412.

37 A reform movement, according to Herbert Blumer, is differentiated from a revolution by its inherent respectability and acceptance of an existing social order. 'The primary function of the reform movement is probably not so much the bringing about of social change, as it is to reaffirm the ideal values in a given society.'—Herbert Blumer, Collective behavior, in Alfred McClung Lee (ed.), *Principles of Sociology* (New York: Barnes and Noble, 1963), 212–13.

38 Charles R. Henderson, Theory and practice of juvenile courts, National Conference of Charities and Correction, *Proceedings* (Portland 1904), 358–9.

39 Miriam Van Waters, The socialization of juvenile

court procedure, *Journal of Criminal Law and Criminology*, **12** (1922), 61, 69.

40 Illinois, Board of State Commissioners of Public Charities, *First Biennial Report* (Springfield: Illinois Journal Printing Office 1871), 180.

41 William Healy, The psychology of the situation: a fundamental for understanding and treatment of delinquency and crime, in Jane Addams (ed.), *The Child, The Clinic and The Court* (New York: New Republic Inc. 1925), 40.

42 C. Wright Mills, The professional ideology of social pathologists, in Bernard Rosenberg, Israel Gerver and F. William Howton (eds), *Mass Society in Crisis* (Collier-Macmillan 1964), 92–111.

43 Illinois, Board of State Commissioners of Public Charities, *Sixth Biennial Report* (Springfield: H. W. Rokker 1880), 104.

44 Frederick H. Wines, Reformation as an end in prison discipline, National Conference of Charities and Correction, *Proceedings* (Buffalo 1888), 198.

45 Max Grünhut, *Penal Reform* (Clarendon Press 1948), 90.

46 This speech is reprinted in Zebulon Reed Brockway, *Fifty Years of Prison Service* (New York: Charities Publication Committee 1912), 389–408.

47 William Douglas Morrison, *Juvenile Offenders* (New York: Appleton 1897), 274–5.

48 Mary Carpenter, Suggestions on reformatory schools and prison discipline, founded on observations made during a visit to the United States, National Prison Reform Congress, *Proceedings* (St Louis 1874), 157–73.

49 Negley K. Teeters, *Deliberations of the International Penal and Penitentiary Congresses, 1872–1935* (Philadelphia: Temple University Book Store 1949), 97–102.

50 Morrison, op. cit., 60, 276.

51 William P. Letchworth, Children of the State. National Conference of Charities and Correction, *Proceedings* (St Paul, Minnesota, 1886), 151, 156.

52 M. B. Hammond's comments at the Illinois Conference of Charities (1901), reported in Illinois, Board of State Commissioners of Public Charities, *Seventeenth Biennial Report* (Springfield: Phillips Brothers 1902), 232–3.

53 This thesis is supported by a European study of family life, Phillipe Ariès, *Centuries of Childhood* (Cape 1962).

54 Illinois, Board of State Commissioners of Public Charities, *Fifteenth Biennial Report* (Springfield: Phillips Brothers 1899), 62–72.

55 Francis A. Allen, *The Borderland of Criminal Justice* (University of Chicago Press, 1964), *passim*.

56 See, for example, Herbert H. Lou, *Juvenile Courts in the United States* (Chapel Hill: University of North Carolina 1927); Negley K. Teeters and John Otto Reinemann, *The Challenge of Delinquency* (New York: Prentice-Hall 1950); Katherine L. Boole, The juvenile court: its origin, history and procedure' (unpublished doctoral dissertation, University of California, Berkeley 1928). One notable exception is Paul W. Tappan, *Delinquent Girls in Court* (New York: Columbia University Press, 1947).

57 David Matza, *Delinquency and Drift* (Wiley 1964).

58 Allen, op. cit., 125.

59 This phrase and its perspective are taken from C. Wright Mills (ed.), *Images of Man* (New York: George Braziller 1960), 5.

60 John R. Seeley, The making and taking of problems: Toward an ethical stance, *Social Problems*, **14** (1967), 384–5.

61 Herbert L. Packer, A patchy look at crime, *New York Review of Books*, **17** (October 12, 1967).

62 Sanford H. Kadish, The crisis of over-criminalization, Annals of the American Academy, **374** (November 1967), 157–70.

63 Herbert Blumer, Threats from agency-determined researching: the case of Camelot, in Irvin Louis Horowitz (ed.), *The Rise and Fall of Project Camelot* (Cambridge, Mass.: MIT Press 1967), 153–74.

64 See, for example, Daniel Glaser, *The Effectiveness of a Prison and Parole System* (New York: Bobbs-Merrill 1964).

65 Erving Goffman, *Asylums* (New York: Anchor Books, 1961).

66 Clark Kerr, *The Uses of the University* (New York: Anchor Books 1961).

67 'Approximately 15 per cent of the Defense Department's annual budget is allocated for research, compared with one per cent of the total federal expenditure for crime control.'—US, President's Commission on Law Enforcement and Administration of Justice (National Crime Commission), *The Challenge of Crime in a Free Society* (the General Report) (Washington, DC: US Government Printing Office 1967), 273.

68 US, President's Commission on Law Enforcement and Administration of Justice (National Crime Commission), *Task Force Report; Corrections* (Washington, DC: US Government Printing Office 1967), 13.

69 Controversial studies of official institutions run the risk of hampering further academic investigations, as was apparently the case with Jerome Skolnick's study of a California police department, *Justice without Trial* (Wiley 1966).

70 *The Challenge of Crime in a Free Society*, 183.

71 Hans W. Mattick (ed.), The Future of Imprisonment in a Free Society, *Key Issues*, **2** (1965), 5.

72 Horowitz (ed.), op. cit., 353.

73 Robert Martinson, The age of treatment: some implications of the custody treatment dimension, *Issues in Criminology*, **2** (Fall 1966), 291.

74 Lee Rainwater, The Revolt of the Dirty-Workers, *Trans-action*, **5** (November 1967), 2.

75 Henry McKay's 'Report on the Criminal Careers of Male Delinquents in Chicago' concludes that 'the behavior of significant numbers of boys who become involved in illegal activity is not redirected toward conventional activity by the institutions created for that purpose.'—US, President's Commission on Law Enforcement and Administration of Justice (National Crime Commission), *Task Force Report; Juvenile Delinquency and Youth Crime* (Washington, DC: US Government Printing Office 1967), 113.

16 Identity as a problem in the sociology of knowledge

Peter L. Berger

It is through the work of George Herbert Mead and the Meadian tradition of the 'symbolic-interactionist' school that a theoretically viable social psychology has been founded. Indeed, it may be maintained that in this achievement lies the most important *theoretical* contribution made to the social sciences in America. The perspectives of the Meadian tradition have become established within American sociology far beyond the school that explicitly seeks to represent them. Just as it was sociologists who 'discovered' Mead at the University of Chicago and diffused his ideas beyond the latter's confines, so the social psychology constituted on this foundation continues to be the one to which sociologists gravitate most naturally in their theoretical assumptions, a 'sociologist's psychology', despite the later competition from psychoanalysis and learning theory.[1] By contrast, the sociology of knowledge has remained marginal to the discipline in this country, still regarded widely as an unassimilated European import of interest only to a few colleagues with a slightly eccentric penchant for the history of ideas.[2] This marginality of the sociology of knowledge is not difficult to explain in terms of the historical development of sociological theory in this country. All the same, it is rather remarkable that the theoretical affinity between the sociology of knowledge and social psychology in the Meadian tradition has not been widely recognized. One might argue that there has been an implicit recognition in the linkage of social psychology, by way of role theory and reference group theory, with the psychology of cognitive processes, particularly in the work of Robert Merton, Muzafer Sherif and Tamotsu Shibutani.[3] In the case of Merton, however, the discussion of the cognitive implications of social-psychological processes occurs in a curious segregation from the treatment of the sociology of knowledge, while in the cases of Sherif and Shibutani there appears to be no conscious connection with the sociology of knowledge at all.

Source: *Archives européennes de sociologie* (1966), 7, 105–15.

Understandable historically, this segregation is theoretically deplorable. Social psychology has been able to show how the subjective reality of individual consciousness is socially constructed. The sociology of knowledge, as Alfred Shutz has indicated, may be understood as the sociological critique of consciousness, concerning itself with the social construction of reality in general.[4] Such a critique entails the analysis of both 'objective reality' (that is, 'knowledge' about the world, as objectivated and taken for granted in society) and its subjective correlates (that is, the modes in which this objectivated world is subjectively plausible or 'real' to the individual). If these shorthand descriptions of the two sub-disciplines are allowed, then integration between them is not an exotic miscegenation but a bringing together of two partners by the inner logic of their natures. Obviously this paper cannot develop the details of such a project of theoretical integration, but it may indicate some general directions and implications.

Social psychology has brought about the recognition that the sphere of psychological phenomena is continuously permeated by social forces, and more than that, is decisively shaped by the latter. 'Socialization' means not only that the self-consciousness of the individual is constituted in a specific form by society (which Mead called the 'social genesis of the self'), but also that psychological reality is in an ongoing dialectical relationship with social structure. Psychological reality refers here, *not* to scientific or philosophical propositions *about* psychological phenomena, but to the manner in which the individual apprehends himself, his processes of consciousness and his relations with others. Whatever its anthropological-biological roots, psychological reality arises in the individual's biography in the course of social processes and is only maintained (that is, maintained in consciousness *as* 'reality') by virtue of social processes. Socialization not only ensures that the individual is 'real' to himself in a certain way, but that he will ongoingly respond to his experience of the world with the cognitive and emotive patterns appropriate to this 'reality'. For example, successful socialization shapes a self that apprehends itself exclusively and in a taken-for-granted way in terms of one or the other of two socially defined sexes, that 'knows' this self-apprehension to be the only 'real' one, and rejects as 'unreal' any contrary modes of apprehension or emotionality. Self and society are inextricably interwoven entities. Their relationship is dialectical because the self, once formed, may act back in its turn upon the society that shaped it (a dialectic that Mead expressed in his formulation of the 'I' and the 'me'). The self exists by virtue of society, but society is only possible as many selves continue to apprehend themselves and each other with reference to it.[5]

Every society contains a repertoire of identities that is part of the 'objective knowledge' of its members. It is 'known' as a matter 'of course' that there are men and women, that they have such-and-such psychological traits and that they will have such-and-such psychological reactions in typical circumstances. As the individual is socialized, these identities are 'internalized'. They are then not only taken for granted as constituents of an objective reality 'out there' but as inevitable structures of the individual's own consciousness. The objective reality, as defined by society, is subjectively appropriated. In other words, socialization brings about symmetry between objective and subjective reality, objective and subjective identity. The degree of this symmetry provides the criterion of the successfulness of socialization. The psychological reality of the successfully socialized individual thus *verifies* subjectively what his society has objectively defined as real. He is then no longer required to turn outside himself for 'knowledge' concerning the nature proper of men and women. He can obtain that result by simple introspection. He 'knows who he is'. He feels accordingly. He can conduct himself 'spontaneously', because the firmly internalized cognitive and emotive structure makes it unnecessary or even impossible for him to reflect upon alternative possibilities of conduct.[6]

This dialectic between social structure and psychological reality may be called the fundamental proposition of any social psychology in the Meadian tradition. Society not only defines but also creates psychological reality. The individual *realizes* himself in society—that is, he recognizes his identity in socially defined terms and these definitions *become reality* as he lives in society. This fundamentally Meadian dialectic makes intelligible the social-psychological scope of W. I. Thomas's concept of the 'definition of the situation' as well as of Merton's of the 'self-fulfilling prophecy'.[7]

The sociology of knowledge is concerned with a related but broader dialectic—that between social structure and the 'worlds' in which individuals live, that is, the comprehensive organizations of reality within which individual experience can be meaning-fully interpreted.[8] Every society is a world-building enterprise. Out of the near-infinite variety of individual symbolizations of experience society constructs a universe of discourse that comprehends and objectivates them. Individual experience can then be understood as taking place in an intelligible world that is inhabited also by others and about which it is possible to communicate with others. Individual meanings are objectivated so that they are accessible to everyone who co-inhabits the world in question. Indeed, this world is apprehended as 'objective reality', that is, as reality that is shared with others and that exists irrespective of the individual's own preferences in the matter. The socially available definitions of such a world are thus taken to be 'knowledge' about it and are continuously verified for the individual by social situations in which this 'knowledge' is taken for granted. The socially constructed world becomes the world *tout court*—the only real world, typically the only world that one can seriously conceive of. The individual is thus freed of the necessity of reflecting anew about the meaning of each step in his unfolding experience. He can simply refer to 'common sense' for such interpretation, at least for the great bulk of his biographical experience.[9]

Language is both the foundation and the instrumentality of the social construction of reality.[10] Language focalizes, patterns and objectivates individual experience. Language is the principal means by which an individual is socialized to become an inhabitant of a world shared with others and also provides the means by which, in conversation with these others, the common world continues to be plausible to him.[11] On this linguistic base is erected the edifice of interpretative schemes, cognitive and moral norms, value systems and, finally, theoretically articulated 'world views' which, in their totality, form the world of 'collective representations' (as the Durkheimian school put it) of any given society.[12] Society *orders* experience. Only in a world of social order can there develop a 'collective consciousness' which permits the individual to have a subjectively meaningful life and protects him from the devastating effects of *anomie*, that is, from a condition in which the individual is deprived of the social ordering processes and thus deprived of meaning itself. It is useful to remind oneself of the linguistic base of all social order whenever one theorizes about the latter, because language makes particularly clear just what is meant by the social construction of an objectively real world. Language is undeniably a social invention and a linguistic system cannot be credited with an ontological status apart from the society that invented it. Nevertheless, the individual learns his language (especially, of course, his native language) as an objective reality.[13] He cannot change it at will. He must conform to its coercive power. Typically, he is unable to conceive of either the world or of himself except through the conceptual modalities which it provides. But this facticity, externality and coerciveness of language (the very traits that constitute the Durkheimian *choseïté*, or thing-like character, of social phenomena) extends to all the objectivations of society. The subjective consequence is that the individual 'finds himself' (that is, apprehends himself as placed, willy-nilly) in the social world as much as in nature.

It is important to stress that the social construction of reality takes place on both the pre-theoretical and the theoretical levels of consciousness, and that, therefore, the sociology of knowledge must concern itself with both. Probably because of the German intellectual situation in which the sociology of knowledge was first developed, it has hitherto interested itself predominantly in the theoretical side of the phenomenon—the problem of the relationship of society and 'ideas'.[14] This is certainly an important problem. But only very few people are worried over 'ideas', while everyone lives in some sort of a world. There is thus a sociological dimension to the human activity of world-building in its totality, not only in that segment of it in which intellectuals manufacture theories, systems of thought and *Weltanschauungen*. Thus, in the matter under discussion here, the sociology of knowledge has an interest not only in various theories *about* psychological phenomena (what one may call a sociology of psychology) but also in these phenomena themselves (what one may then, perhaps impertinently, call a sociological psychology.)

The relationship between a society and its world is a dialectic one because, once more, it cannot be adequately understood in terms of a one-sided causation.[15] The world, though socially constructed, is not a mere passive reflection of the social structures within which it arose. In becoming 'objective reality' for its inhabitants it attains not only a certain autonomy with respect to the 'underlying' society but even the power to act back upon the latter. Men invent a language and then find that its logic imposes itself upon them. And men concoct theories, even theories that may start out as nothing but blatant explications of social interests, and then discover that these theories themselves become agencies of social change. It may be seen, then, that there is a theoretically significant similarity between the dialectics of social psychology and of the sociology of knowledge, the dialectic through which society generates psychological reality and the dialectic through which it engages in world-building. Both dialectics concern the relationship between objective and subjective realities, or more precisely, between socially objectivated reality and its subjective appropriation. In both instances, the individual internalizes facticities that appear to him as given outside himself and, having internalized them to become given contents of his own consciousness, externalizes them again as he continues to live and act in society.[16]

These considerations, especially in the compressed form in which they have had to be presented here, may at first seem to be excessively abstract. Yet, if one asks about the combined significance of these root perspectives of social psychology and the sociology of knowledge for the sociological understanding of identity, one may answer in a rather simple statement: *Identity, with its appropriate attachments of psychological reality, is always identity within a specific, socially constructed world.* Or, as seen from the viewpoint of the individual: *One identifies oneself, as one is identified by others, by being located in a common world.*

Socialization is only possible if, as Mead put it, the individual 'takes the attitude' of others, that is, relates to himself as others have first related to him. This process, of course, extends to the establishment of identity itself, so that one may formulate that social identification both precedes and produces self-identification. Now, it is possible that the Meadian process of attitude- and role-taking occurs between individuals who do not share a common world—for instance, between Columbus and the very first American Indians he met in 1492. Even they, however, soon identified each other within a world which they inhabited together, or more accurately, they together established such a world as they dealt with each other. Socializing each other in terms of this world, they could then take on the attitudes and roles appropriate within it. Columbus and his Spaniards, being (like parents in this respect) the stronger party, had the edge in this game of 'naming'—the others had to identify themselves in the Spaniard's terms, namely as *Indios*, while the Spaniards were probably little tempted to identify themselves with the mythological creatures as which they in turn were first identified by the others. In other words, the American Indian identified himself by locating himself in the Spaniard's world, though, to be sure, that world was itself modified as he became its co-inhabitant. In the more normal cases of socialization, occurring between individuals who already co-inhabit the same world, it is even easier to see how identification entails location in that world from the beginning. The parents give their child a name and then deal with him in terms appropriate to this identification. The literal act of 'naming', of course, is already location in this sense (its exactitude depending upon the culture— 'John Smith' being less satisfactory as an 'address' than 'Ivan Ivanovitch', 'Village-Idiot', and so forth). However, as the full implications of the name and its location unfold in the course of socialization, the child appropriates the world in which he is thus located in the same process in which he appropriates his identity—a moral universe as he identifies himself as a 'good baby', a sexual universe as a 'little boy', a class universe as a 'little gentleman'—and so on. One may expand the Meadian phrase, then, by saying that the individual takes the world of others as he takes their attitudes and roles. Each role implies a world. The self is always located in a world. The *same* process of socialization generates the self and internalizes the world to which this self belongs.

The same reasoning applies to psychological reality in general. Just as any particular psychological reality is attached to a socially defined identity, so it is located in a socially constructed world. As the individual identifies and locates himself in the world of his society, he finds himself the possessor of a pre-defined assemblage of psychological processes, both 'conscious' and 'unconscious' ones, and even some with somatic effects. The 'good baby' feels guilty after a temper tantrum, the 'little boy' channels his erotic fantasies towards little girls, the 'little gentle-man' experiences revulsion when someone engages in public nose-picking—and this revulsion may, under the proper conditions, affect his stomach to the point of vomitation. Every socially constructed world thus contains a repertoire of identities and a corresponding psychological system. The social definition of identity takes place as part of an overarching definition of reality. The internalization of the world, as it occurs in socialization, imposes upon consciousness a psycho-logical as well as cognitive structure, and (to a degree which has as yet not been adequately clarified scienti-fically) even extends into the area of physiological processes.[17] Pascal indicated the root problem of the sociology of knowledge when he observed that what is truth on one side of the Pyrenees is error on the other. The same observation applies to the good conscience and the bad (including the 'unconscious' mani-festations of the latter), to the libidinously interesting and the libidinously indifferent, as well as to what upsets and what relaxes the gastric juices. And, of course, a French identity differs appreciably from a Spanish one.[18]

A third dialectic may be analysed if one now turns to the theoretical level of consciousness—that be-tween psychological reality and psychological models. Men not only experience themselves. They also ex-plain themselves. While these explanations differ in their degrees of sophistication, it would be difficult to conceive of a society without some theoretical explication of the psychological nature of man. Whether such explication takes the form of proverbial wisdom, mythology, metaphysics or scientific general-ization is, of course, a different question. What all these forms have in common is that they systematize the experience of psychological reality on a certain level of abstraction. They constitute psychological models, by means of which individual psychological processes can be compared, typified and thus 'pre-pared for treatment'. For example, individuals in a society may have all kinds of visionary experiences. Both the individuals themselves and those with whom they live are faced with the question of what these experiences signify. A psychological model that 'explains' such occurrences allows them to compare any particular experience with the several species codified in the model. The experience may then be classified in terms of this typology—as a case of demon pos-session, say, or as a mark of sacred status, or as merely crazy in a profane mode. This application of the psychological model (the 'diagnosis') then permits a decision on what to do about the occurrence (the

therapy') to exorcize the individual, to beatify him, or possibly to award him the role of buffoon and of menace to disobedient children. In other words, the psychological model locates individual experience and conduct within a comprehensive theoretical sys-tem.[19]

It goes without saying that each psychological model is embedded in a more general theoretical formulation of reality. The model is part of the society's general 'knowledge about the world', raised to the level of theoretical thought. Thus a psychological model that contains a typology of possession belongs to a religious conception of the world as such and a psychological theory of 'mental illness', as understood by contemporary psychiatry, is located in a much wider 'scientific' conception of the world and of man's place in it. *Psychological 'knowledge' is always part of a general 'knowledge about the world'*—in this proposition lies the foundation of what, a little earlier, was called the sociology of psychology. The import of this proposition can be conveyed by referring to the psychiatric concept of 'reality orientation'. A psy-chiatrist may decide that a certain individual is not adequately 'oriented to reality' and, therefore, 'mentally ill'. The sociologist may then accept this description, but must immediately ask, '*which reality?*' Just as cultural anthropology has been able to demon-strate that the manifestations of the Freudian 'pleasure principle' vary from one society to another, so the sociology of knowledge must insist on a similar socio-cultural relativization of the Freudian 'reality prin-ciple'.[20]

This sociological perspective has far-reaching implications for the analysis of psychological theories. As has been indicated, every socially constructed world contains a psychological model. If this model is to retain its plausibility, it must have some empirical relationship to the psychological reality objectivated in the society. A demonological model is 'unreal' in contemporary society. The psychoanalytic one is not. It is important to stress once again the matter of empirical verification. Just as the individual can verify his socially assigned identity by introspection, so the psychological theoretician can verify his model by 'empirical research'. If the model corresponds to the psychological reality as socially defined and produced, it will quite naturally be verified by empirical investi-gation of this reality. This is not quite the same as saying that psychology is self-verifying. It rather says that the data discovered by a particular psycho-logy belong to the same socially constructed world that has also produced that psychology.

Once more, the relationship between psychological reality and psychological model is a dialectic one. The psychological reality produces the psychological model, insofar as the model is an empirically verifiable representation of the reality. Once formed, however, the psychological model can act back upon the psy-chological reality. The model has *realizing* potency, that is, it can create psychological reality as a 'self-fulfilling prophecy'. In a society in which demonology is socially established, cases of demon possession will empirically multiply. A society in which psychoanalysis is institutionalized as 'science' will become populated by people who, in fact, evince the processes that have been theoretically attributed to them. It should be clear that this self-fulfilling character of psychological models is grounded in the same dialectic of socialization that Mead first formulated with incisive clarity and which can be summarized by saying that men become that as which they are addressed.

The purpose of these brief considerations has been to indicate what theoretical gains might be expected from an integration of the approaches of social psychology in the Meadian tradition and the sociology of knowledge. This is obviously not the place to discuss the methodological issues or the numerous possibilities of empirical exploration arising from such integration.[21] Suffice it to say, in conclusion, that the theoretical viewpoint expressed here implies a serious reconsideration of the relationship between the two disciplines of sociology and psychology. This relationship has been characterized, at least in this country, by a theoretically unjustified timidity on the side of the sociologists and by a spirit of oecumenical tolerance that may have beneficial consequences for interdepartmental amity, but which has not always been conducive to clear sociological thinking.

Notes

1 On the 'diffusion' of Meadian social psychology among American sociologists, cf. Anselm Strauss (ed.), *George Herbert Mead on Social Psychology* (University of Chicago Press 1964), vii sqq. For a critique of this Meadian 'establishment', from a psychoanalytically oriented viewpoint, cf. Dennis Wrong, The oversocialized conception of man in modern sociology, *Psychoanalysis and the Psychoanalytic Review*, **39** (1962), 53 sqq.

2 Among American sociologists, the sociology of knowledge has remained rather narrowly associated with its conception by Karl Mannheim, who served as its principal 'translator' from the context of German *Geisteswissenschaft* to that of English-speaking social science. The writings of Max Scheler on *Wissenssoziologie* (the term was coined by him) remain untranslated today. American sociologists have also, in the main, remained unaffected by the development of the sociology of knowledge in the work of Alfred Schutz, not to mention recent contributions in the positivistic tradition (mainly by sociologists writing in German) and by Marxists (mainly in France). For the Mannheim-oriented reception of the sociology of knowledge in America, cf. Robert Merton, *Social Theory and Social Structure* (Collier-Macmillan 1957), 439 sqq., and Talcott Parsons, An approach to the sociology of knowledge, *Transactions of the Fourth World Congress of Sociology* (Louvain: International Sociological Association 1959). For a conception of the sub-discipline more in the line of Scheler than of Mannheim (and with which the present writer would not associate himself fully, either), cf. Werner Stark, *The Sociology of Knowledge* (Routledge & Kegan Paul 1958).

3 Cf. Merton, op. cit., 225 sqq.; Muzafer Sherif and Carolyn Sherif, *An outline of Social Psychology* (Harper 1956); Tamotsu Shibutani, Reference groups and social control, in Arnold Rose (ed.), *Human Behaviour and Social Processes* (Routledge & Kegan Paul 1962), 128 sqq.

4 This understanding of the scope of the sociology of knowledge, a much broader one than that of the Mannheim-oriented approach, has been strongly influenced by the work of Alfred Schutz. Cf. Alfred Schutz, *Der sinnhafte Aufbau der sozialen Welt* (Vienna: Springer 1960); *The Problem of Social Reality* (The Hague: Nijhoff 1962); *Studies in Social Theory* (The Hague: Nijhoff 1964).

5 This dialectic between self and society can also be formulated in Marxian terms. Cf., for example, Joseph Gabel, *La fausse Conscience* (Paris: Éditions de Minuit 1962), and Jean-Paul Sartre, *Search for a Method* (New York: Knopf 1963). For an attempt at integrating certain Marxian categories within a non-Marxian sociology of knowledge, cf. Peter Berger and Stanley Pullberg, Reification and the sociological critique of consciousness, *History and Theory*, **4** (1965).

6 On the social structuring of conduct, cf. Arnold Gehlen, *Urmensch und Spätkultur* (Bonn: Athenaeum 1956), where Gehlen proposes a biologically grounded theory of social institutions. On this very suggestive theory, which to date has remained practically unknown to American sociologists, also cf. Arnold Gehlen, *Anthropologische Forschung* (Hamburg: Rowohlt 1961), and *Studien zur Anthropologie und Soziologie* (Neuwied/Rhein: Luchterhand 1963).

7 Thomas's well-known dictum on the 'real consequences' of social definition was presumably intended, and has been generally understood as intending, to say that once a 'reality' has been defined, people will act *as if* it were indeed so. To this important proposition must be added an understanding of the *realizing* (that is, reality-producing) potency of social definition. This social-psychological import of Thomas's 'basic theorem' was developed by Merton, op. cit., 421 sqq. The sociology of knowledge, as this paper tries to indicate, would extend this notion of the social construction of 'reality' even further.

8 Cf. Schutz, *The Problem of Social Reality*, 207 sqq.

9 Cf. ibid., 3 sqq.

10 Cf. ibid., 287 sqq. Also, cf. Ernst Cassirer, *An Essay on Man* (New Haven: Yale University Press 1962), 109 sqq. The problem of language and 'reality', neglected by American sociologists, has been extensively discussed in American cultural anthropology; see the influence of Edward Sapir and the controversy over the so-called 'Whorf hypothesis'. It has been a central problem for sociologists and cultural anthropologists in France ever since the Durkheim school. Cf. Claude Lévi-Strauss, *The Savage Mind* (Weidenfeld & Nicolson 1966).

11 On the maintenance of 'reality' by means of the 'con-

versational apparatus', cf. Peter Berger and Hansfried Kellner, Marriage and the construction of reality (this volume).

12 One may say that the Durkheimian theory of 'collective consciousness' is the positive side of the theory of *anomie*. The *locus classicus* of this is, of course, Durkheim's *Elementary Forms of the Religious Life*. For important developments of this (all of great relevance for the sociology of knowledge), cf. Marcel Granet, *La Pensée chinoise* (Paris: Albin Michel 1950); Maurice Halbwachs, *Les Cadres sociaux de la mémoire* (Paris: PUF 1952); Marcel Mauss, *Sociologie et anthropologie* (Paris: PUF 1960).

13 The fullest evidence on the 'objectivity' of the child's language learning is to be found in the work of Jean Piaget.

14 The fixation of the sociology of knowledge on the theoretical level of consciousness is well expressed in the sub-title of the previously cited work by Stark—'An Essay in Aid of a Deeper Understanding of the History of Ideas'. The present writer would consider Schutz's work as essential for arriving at a broader conception of the sub-discipline. For a broader approach based on Marxian pre-suppositions, cf. Henri Lefebvre, *Critique de la vie quotidienne* (Paris: L'Arche, 1958–61). For a discussion of the possibility of using Pareto for a critique of pre-theoretical consciousness in society, cf. Brigitte Berger, Vilfredo Pareto's Sociology as a Contribution to the Sociology of Knowledge (Unpublished doctoral dissertation—Graduate Faculty, New School for Social Research, New York, 1964).

15 This problem is, of course, dealt with by Marx in his well-known conception of sub- and super-structure. The present writer would argue that, at least in Marx's early writings (as in the Economic and Philosophic Manuscripts of 1844), the relationship between the two is clearly a dialectic one. In later Marxism, the dialectic is lost in a mechanistic understanding of sub- and super-structure in which the latter becomes a mere epiphenomenon (Lenin—a 'reflection') of the former. On this 'reification' of Marxism in Communist ideology (perhaps one of the great ironies in the history of ideas), cf., for example, Joseph Gabel, *Formen der Entfremdung* (Frankfurt: Fischer 1964), 53 sqq. Probably the most important work, within the Marxian tradition, which has tried to recapture the original dialectic in dealing with this problem is Georg Lukacs's *Geschichte und Klassenbewusstsein* (1923), now virtually unobtainable in German, but available in an excellent French translation—*Histoire et conscience de classe* (Paris: Éditions de Minuit 1960).

16 The overarching dialectic of socialization indicated here can be analysed in terms of three 'moments'—externalization, objectivation and internalization. The dialectic is lost whenever one of these 'moments' is excluded from social theory. Cf. Berger and Pullberg, op. cit.

17 For indications of the intriguing possibilities of such a 'socio-somatics', cf. Georg Simmel's discussion of the 'sociology of the senses', in his *Sociology* (Collier-Macmillan 1964), 483 sqq. Also, cf. Mauss' essay on the 'techniques of the body', in his op. cit., 365 sqq.

18 It is not intended here to propose a 'sociologistic' view of reality as *nothing but* a social construction. Within the sociology of knowledge, however, it is possible to bracket the final epistemological questions.

19 On the sociology-of-knowledge implications of diagnostic typologies, cf. Eliot Freidson, *The Sociology of Medicine* (Oxford: Blackwell 1963), 124 sqq.

20 For a critique of the contemporary concept of 'mental illness', coming from within psychiatry itself, cf. Thomas Szasz, *The Myth of Mental Illness* (New York: Hosber-Harper 1961).

21 Cf. Peter L. Berger and Thomas Luckmann, *The Social Construction of Reality* (Allen Lane, Penguin Press 1967).

17 Situated actions and vocabularies of motive

C. Wright Mills

The major reorientation of recent theory and observation in sociology of language emerged with the overthrow of the Wundtian notion that language has as its function the 'expression' of prior elements within the individual. The postulate underlying modern study of language is the simple one that we must approach linguistic behavior, not by referring it to private states in individuals, but by observing its social function of co-ordinating diverse actions. Rather than expressing something which is prior and in the person, language is taken by other persons as an indicator of future actions.[1]

Within this perspective there are suggestions concerning problems of motivation. It is the purpose of this paper to outline an analytic model for the explanation of motives which is based on a sociological theory of language and a sociological psychology.[2]

As over against the inferential conception of motives as subjective 'springs' of action, motives may be considered as typical vocabularies having ascertainable functions in delimited societal situations. Human actors do vocalize and impute motives to themselves and to others. To explain behavior by referring it to an inferred and abstract 'motive' is one thing. To analyze the observable lingual mechanisms of motive imputation and avowal, as they function in conduct, is quite another. Rather than fixed elements 'in' an individual, motives are the terms with which interpretation of conduct *by social actors* proceeds. This imputation and avowal of motives by actors are social phenomena to be explained. The differing reasons men give for their actions are not themselves without reasons.

First, we must demarcate the general conditions under which such motive imputation and avowal seem to occur.[3] Next, we must give a characterization of motive in denotable terms and an explanatory paradigm of why certain motives are verbalized rather than others. Then, we must indicate mechanisms of the linkage of vocabularies of motive to systems of action.

Source: *American Sociological Review* (1940), 5 (6), 439–52.

What we want is an analysis of the integrating, controlling, and specifying functions a certain type of speech fulfills in socially situated actions.

The generic situation in which imputation and avowal of motives arise, involves, first, the *social* conduct of the (stated) programs of languaged creatures, i.e. programs and actions oriented with reference to the actions and talk of others; second, the avowal and imputation of motives is concomitant with the speech form known as the 'question'. Situations back of questions typically involve *alternative* or *unexpected* programs or actions of which phases analytically denote 'crises'.[4] The question is distinguished in that it usually elicits another *verbal* action, not a motor response. The question is an element in *conversation*. Conversation may be concerned with the factual features of a situation as they are seen or believed to be or it may seek to integrate and promote a set of diverse social actions with reference to the situation and its normative pattern of expectations. It is in this latter assent and dissent phase of conversation that persuasive and dissuasive speech and vocabulary arise. For men live in immediate acts of experience and their attentions are directed outside themselves until acts are in some way frustrated. It is then that awareness of self and of motive occur. The 'question' is a lingual index of such conditions. The avowal and imputation of motives are features of such conversations as arise in 'question' situations.

Motives are imputed or avowed as answers to questions interrupting acts or programs. Motives are words. Generically, to what do they refer? They do not denote any elements 'in' individuals. They stand for anticipated situational consequences of questioned conduct. Intention or purpose (stated as a 'program') *is* awareness of anticipated consequence; motives are names for consequential situations, and surrogates for actions leading to them. Behind questions are possible alternative actions with their terminal consequences. 'Our introspective words for motives are rough, shorthand descriptions for certain typical patterns of discrepant and conflicting stimuli.'[5]

The model of purposive conduct associated with Dewey's name may briefly be stated. Individuals confronted with 'alternative acts' perform one or the other of them on the basis of the differential consequences which they anticipate. This nakedly utilitarian schema is inadequate because: (a) the 'alternative acts' of *social* conduct 'appear' most often in lingual form, as a question, stated by one's self or by another; (b) it is more adequate to say that individuals act in terms of anticipation of *named* consequences.

Among such names and in some technologically oriented lines of action there may appear such terms as 'useful', 'practical', 'serviceable', etc., terms so 'ultimate' to the pragmatists, and also to certain sectors of the American population in these delimited situations. However, there are other areas of population with different vocabularies of motives. The choice of lines of action is accompanied by representations, and selection among them, of their situational termini. Men discern situations with particular vocabularies, and it is in terms of some delimited vocabulary that they anticipate consequences of conduct.[6] Stable vocabularies of motives link anticipated consequences and specific actions. There is no need to invoke 'psychological' terms like 'desire' or 'wish' as explanatory, since they themselves must be explained socially.[7] Anticipation is a subvocal or overt naming of terminal phases and/or social consequences of conduct. When an individual names consequences, he elicits the behaviors for which the name is an integrative cue. In a *social* situation, implicit in the names for consequences is the social dimension of motives. Through such vocabularies, types of societal controls operate. Also, the terms in which the question is asked often will contain both alternatives: 'Love or Duty?' 'Business or Pleasure?' Institutionally different situations have different *vocabularies of motive* appropriate to their respective behaviors.

This sociological conception of motives as relatively stable lingual phases of delimited situations is quite consistent with Mead's program to approach conduct socially and from the outside. It keeps clearly in mind that 'both motives and actions very often originate not from within but from the situation in which individuals find themselves'.[8] It translates the question of 'why'[9] into a 'how' that is answerable in terms of a situation and its typical vocabulary of motives, i.e. those which conventionally accompany that type situation and function as cues and justifications for normative actions in it.

It has been indicated that the question is usually an index to the avowal and imputation of motives. Max Weber defines motive as a complex of meaning, which appears to the actor himself or to the observer to be an adequate ground for his conduct.[10] The aspect of motive which this conception grasps is its intrinsically social character. A satisfactory or adequate motive is one that satisfies the questioners of an act or program, whether it be the other's or the actor's. As a word, *a motive tends to be one which is to the actor and to the other members of a situation an unquestioned answer to questions concerning social and lingual conduct.* A stable motive is an ultimate in justificatory conversation. The words which in a type situation will fulfill this function are circumscribed by the vocabulary of motives acceptable for such situations. Motives are accepted justifications for present, future, or past programs or acts.

To term them justification is *not* to deny their efficacy. Often anticipation of acceptable justifications will control conduct. ('If I did this, what could I say? What would they say?') Decisions may be, wholly or in part, delimited by answers to such queries.

A man may begin an act for one motive. In the course of it, he may adopt an ancillary motive. This does not mean that the second apologetic motive is inefficacious. The vocalized expectation of an act, its 'reason', is not only a mediating condition of the act but it is a proximate and controlling condition for which the term 'cause' is not inappropriate. It may strengthen the act of the actor. It may win new allies for his act.

When they appeal to others involved in one's act, motives are strategies of action. In many social actions, others must agree, tacitly or explicitly. Thus, acts often will be abandoned if no reason can be found that others will accept. Diplomacy in choice of motive often controls the diplomat. Diplomatic choice of motive is part of the attempt to motivate acts for other members in a situation. Such pronounced motives undo snarls and integrate social actions. Such diplomacy does not necessarily imply intentional lies. It merely indicates that an appropriate vocabulary of motives will be utilized—that they are conditions for certain lines of conduct.[11]

When an agent vocalizes or imputes motives, he is not trying to *describe* his experienced social action. He is not merely stating 'reasons'. He is influencing others —and himself. Often he is finding new 'reasons' which will mediate action. Thus, we need not treat an action as discrepant from 'its' verbalization, for in many cases, the verbalization is a new act. In such cases, there is not a discrepancy between an act and 'its' verbalization, but a difference between two disparate actions, motor-social and verbal.[12] This additional (or '*ex post facto*') lingualization may involve appeal to a vocabulary of motives associated with a norm with which both members of the situation are in agreement. As such, it is an integrative factor in *future* phases of the original social action or in other acts. By resolving conflicts, motives are efficacious. Often if 'reasons' were not given, an act would not occur, nor would diverse actions be integrated. Motives are common grounds for mediated behaviors.

Perry summarily states the Freudian view of motives 'as the view that the real motives of conduct are those which we are ashamed to admit either to ourselves or to others.'[13] One can cover the facts by merely saying that scruples (i.e. *moral* vocabularies of motive) are often efficacious and that men will alter and deter their acts in terms of such motives. One of the components of a 'generalized other', as a mechanism of societal control, is vocabularies of acceptable motives. For example, a business man joins the Rotary Club and proclaims its public-spirited vocabulary.[14] If this man cannot act out business conduct without so doing, it follows that this vocabulary of motives is an important factor in his behavior.[15] The long acting out of a role, with its appropriate motives, will often induce a man to become what at first he merely sought to appear. Shifts in the vocabularies of motive that are utilized later by an individual disclose an important aspect of various integrations of his actions with concomitantly various groups.

The motives actually used in justifying or criticizing an act definitely link it to situations, integrate one man's action with another's, and line up conduct with norms. The societally sustained motive-surrogates of situations are both constraints and inducements. It is a hypothesis worthy and capable of test that typal vocabularies of motives for different situations are significant determinants of conduct. As lingual segments of social action, motives orient actions by enabling discrimination between their objects. Adjectives such as 'good', 'pleasant' and 'bad' promote action or deter it. When they constitute components of a vocabulary of motives, i.e. are typical and relatively unquestioned accompaniments of typal situations, such words often function as directives and incentives by virtue of their being the judgments of others as anticipated by the actor. In this sense will be able to influence [himself or others].[16] The 'control' of others is not usually direct but rather through manipulations of a field of objects. We influence a man by naming his acts or imputing motives to them—or to 'him'. The motives accompanying institutions of war, e.g. are not 'the causes' of war, but they do promote continued integrated participation, and they vary from one war to the next. Working vocabularies of motive have careers that are woven through changing institutional fabrics.

Genetically, motives are imputed by others before they are avowed by self. The mother controls the child: 'Do not do that, it is greedy.' Not only does the child learn what to do, what not to do, but he is given standardized motives which promote prescribed actions and dissuade those proscribed. Along with rules and norms of action for various situations, we learn vocabularies of motives appropriate to them. These are the motives we shall use, since they are a part of our language and components of our behavior.

The quest for 'real motives' set over against 'mere rationalization' is often informed by a metaphysical view that the 'real' motives are in some way biological. Accompanying such quests for something more real and back of rationalization is the view held by many sociologists that language is an external manifestation or concomitant of something prior, more genuine, and 'deep' in the individual. 'Real attitudes' versus 'mere verbalization' or 'opinion' implies that at best we only infer from his language what 'really' is the individual's attitude or motive.

Now what *could we possibly* so infer? Of precisely *what* is verbalization symptomatic? We cannot *infer* physiological processes from lingual phenomena. All we can infer and empirically check[17] is another verbalization of the agent's which we believe was orienting and controlling behavior at the time the act was performed. The only social items that can 'lie deeper' are other lingual forms.[18] The 'Real Attitude or Motive' is not something different in kind from the verbalization of the 'opinion'. They turn out to be only relatively and temporally different.

The phrase 'unconscious motive' is also unfortunate. All it can mean is that a motive is not explicitly vocalized, but there is no need to infer unconscious motives from such situations and then posit them in individuals as elements. The phrase is informed by persistence of the unnecessary and unsubstantiated notion that 'all action has a motive', and it is promoted by the observation of gaps in the relatively frequent verbalization in everyday situations. The facts to which this phrase is supposedly addressed are covered by the statements that men do not always explicitly articulate motives, and that *all* actions do not pivot around language. I have already indicated the conditions under which motives are typically avowed and imputed.

Within the perspective under consideration, the verbalized motive is not used as an index of something in the individual but *as a basis of inference for a typal vocabulary of motives of a situated action*. When we ask for the 'real attitude' rather than the 'opinion', for the 'real motive', rather than the 'rationalization', all we can meaningfully be asking for is the controlling speech form which was incipiently or overtly presented in the performed act or series of acts. There is no way to plumb behind verbalization into an individual and directly check our motive-mongering, but there is an empirical way in which we can guide and limit, in given historical situations, investigations of motives. That is by the construction of typical vocabularies of motives that are extant in types of situations and actions. Imputation of motives may be controlled by reference to the typical constellation of motives which are observed to be societally linked with classes of situated actions. Some of the 'real' motives that have been imputed to actors were not even known to them. As I see it, motives are circumscribed by the vocabulary of the actor. The only source for a terminology of motives is the vocabularies of motives actually and usually verbalized by actors in specific situations.

Individualistic, sexual, hedonistic, and pecuniary vocabularies of motives are apparently now dominant in many sections of twentieth-century urban America. Under such an ethos, verbalization of alternative conduct in these terms is least likely to be challenged among dominant groups. In this milieu, individuals are skeptical of Rockefeller's avowed religious motives for his business conduct because such motives are not *now* terms of the vocabulary conventionally and prominently accompanying situations of business enterprise. A medieval monk writes that he gave food to a poor but pretty woman because it was 'for the glory of God and the eternal salvation of his soul'. Why do we tend to question him and impute sexual motives? Because sex is an influential and widespread motive in our society and time. Religious vocabularies of explanation and of motives are now on the wane. In a society in which religious motives have been debunked on a rather wide scale, certain thinkers are skeptical of those who ubiquitously proclaim them. Religious motives have lapsed from selected portions of modern populations and other motives have become 'ultimate' and operative. But from the monasteries of medieval Europe we have no evidence that religious vocabularies were not operative in many situations.

A labor leader says he performs a certain act because he wants to get higher standards of living for the workers. A business man says that this is rationalization, or a lie; that it is really because he wants more money for himself from the workers. A radical says a college professor will not engage in radical movements because he is afraid for his job, and besides, is a 'reactionary'. The college professor says it is because he just likes to find out how things work. What is reason for one man is rationalization for another. The variable is the accepted vocabulary of motives, the ultimates of discourse, of each man's dominant group about whose opinion he cares. *Determination of such groups, their location and character, would enable delimitation and methodological control of assignment of motives for specific acts.*

Stress on this idea will lead us to investigations of the compartmentalization of operative motives in personalities according to situation and the general types and conditions of vocabularies of motives in various types of societies. The motivational structures of individuals and the patterns of their purposes are relative to societal frames. We might, e.g., study motives along stratified or occupational lines. Max Weber has observed:[19]

> that in a free society the motives which induce people to work vary with ... different social classes. ... There is normally a graduated scale of motives by which men from different social classes are driven to work. When a man changes ranks, he switches from one set of motives to another.

The lingual ties which hold them together react on persons to constitute frameworks of disposition and motive. Recently, Talcott Parsons has indicated, by reference to differences in actions in the professions and in business, that one cannot leap from 'economic analysis to ultimate motivations; the institutional patterns *always* constitute one crucial element of the problem.'[20] It is my suggestion that we may analyze, index, and gauge this element by focusing upon those specific verbal appendages of variant institutionalized actions which have been referred to as vocabularies of motive.

In folk societies, the constellations of motives connected with various sectors of behavior would tend to be typically stable and remain associated only with their sector. In typically primary, sacred, and rural societies, the motives of persons would be regularly compartmentalized. Vocabularies of motives ordered to different situations stabilize and guide behaviour and expectation of the reactions of others. In their appropriate situations, verbalized motives are not typically questioned.[21] In secondary, secular, and urban structures, varying and competing vocabularies of motives operate co-terminally and the situations to which they are appropriate are not clearly demarcated. Motives once unquestioned for defined situations are now questioned. Various motives can release similar acts in a given situation. Hence, variously situated persons are confused and guess which motive 'activated' the person. Such questioning has resulted intellectually in such movements as psychoanalysis with its dogma of rationalization and its systematic motive-mongering. Such intellectual phenomena are underlaid by split and conflicting sections of an individuated society which is characterized by the existence of competing vocabularies of motive. Intricate constellations of motives, for example, are components of business enterprise in America. Such patterns have encroached on the old style vocabulary of the virtuous relation of men and women: duty, love, kindness. Among certain classes, the romantic, virtuous, and pecuniary motives are confused. The asking of the question: 'Marriage for love or money?' is significant, for the pecuniary is now a constant and almost ubiquitous motive, a common denominator of many others.[22]

Back of 'mixed motives' and 'motivational conflicts' are competing or discrepant situational patterns and their respective vocabularies of motive. With shifting and interstitial situations, each of several alternatives may belong to disparate systems of action which have differing vocabularies of motives appropriate to them. Such conflicts manifest vocabulary patterns that have overlapped in a marginal individual and are not easily compartmentalized in clear-cut situations.

Besides giving promise of explaining an area of lingual and societal fact, a further advantage of this view of motives is that with it we should be able to give sociological accounts of other theories (terminologies) of motivation. This is a task for the sociology of knowledge. Here I can refer only to a few theories. I have already referred to the Freudian terminology of motives. It is apparent that these motives are those of an upper bourgeois patriarchal group with strong sexual and individualistic orientation. When introspecting on the couches of Freud, patients used the only vocabulary of motives they knew; Freud got his hunch and guided further talk. Mittenzwey has dealt with similar points at length.[23] Widely diffused in a postwar epoch, psychoanalysis was never popular in France where control of sexual behavior is not puritanical.[24] To converted individuals who have become accustomed to the psychoanalytic terminology of motives, all others seem self-deceptive.[25]

In like manner, to many believers in Marxism's terminology of power, struggle, and economic motives, all others, including Freud's, are due to hypocrisy or ignorance. An individual who has assimilated thoroughly only business congeries of motives will attempt to apply these motives to all situations, home and wife included. It should be noted that the business terminology of motives has its intellectual articulation, even as psychoanalysis and Marxism have.

It is significant that since the Socratic period many 'theories of motivation' have been linked with ethical and religious terminologies. Motive is that in man which leads him to do good or evil. Under the aegis of religious institutions, men use vocabularies of moral motives: they call acts and programs 'good' and 'bad', and impute these qualities to the soul. Such lingual behavior is part of the process of social control. Institutional practices and their vocabularies of motive exercise control over delimited ranges of possible situations. One could make a typal catalog of religious motives from widely read religious texts, and test its explanatory power in various denominations and sects.[26]

In many situations of contemporary America, conduct is controlled and integrated by *hedonistic* language. For large population sectors in certain situations, pleasure and pain are now unquestioned motives. For given periods and societies, these situations should be empirically determined. Pleasure and pain should not be reified and imputed to human nature as underlying principles of all action. Note that hedonism as a psychological and an ethical doctrine gained impetus in the modern world at about the time when older moral-religious motives were being debunked and simply discarded by 'middle-class' thinkers. Back of the hedonistic terminology lay an emergent social pattern and a new vocabulary of motives. The shift of unchallenged motives which gripped the communities of Europe was climaxed when, in reconciliation, the older religious and the hedonistic terminologies were identified: the 'good' is the 'pleasant.' The conditioning situation was similar in the Hellenistic world with the hedonism of the Cyrenaics and Epicureans.

What is needed is to take all these *terminologies* of motive and locate them as *vocabularies* of motive in historic epochs and specified situations. Motives are of no value apart from the delimited societal situations for which they are the appropriate vocabularies. They must be situated. At best, socially unlocated *terminologies* of motives represent unfinished attempts to block out social areas of motive imputation and avowal. Motives vary in content and character with historical epochs and societal structures.

Rather than interpreting actions and language as external manifestations of subjective and deeper lying elements in individuals, the research task is the locating of particular types of action within typal frames of normative actions and socially situated clusters of motive. There is no explanatory value in subsuming various vocabularies of motives under some terminology or list. Such procedure merely confuses the task of explaining specific cases. The languages of situations as given must be considered a valuable portion of the data to be interpreted and related to their conditions. To simplify these vocabularies of motive into a socially abstracted terminology is to destroy the legitimate use of motive in the explanation of social actions.

Notes

1 See C. Wright Mills, Bibliographical appendices, Section I, 4: Sociology of language, in *Contemporary Social Theory*, Barnes, Becker & Becker (eds), New York 1940.

2 See G. H. Mead, Social psychology as counterpart of physiological psychology, *Psychol. Bull.* (1909), **6**, 401–8; Karl Mannheim, *Man and Society in an Age of Reconstruction* (Routledge & Kegan Paul 1940); L. V. Wiese-Howard Becker, *Systematic Sociology*, part I, New York 1932; J. Dewey, All psychology is either biological or social psychology, *Psychol. Rev.*, **24**, 276.

3 The importance of this initial task for research is clear. Most researches on the verbal level merely ask abstract questions of individuals, but if we can tentatively delimit the situations in which certain motives *may* be verbalized, we can use that delimitation in the construction of *situational* questions, and we shall be *testing* deductions from our theory.

4 On the 'question' and 'conversation' see G. A. DeLaguna, *Speech: Its Function and Development*, New Haven, 1927, 37 (and index). For motives in crises, see J. M. Williams, *The Foundations of Social Science*, New York, 1920, 435ff.

5 K. Burke, *Permanence and Change*, New York 1936, 45. I am indebted to this book for several leads which are systematized into the present statement.

6 See such experiments as C. N. Rexroad's Verbalization in Multiple Choice Reactions, *Psychol. Rev.* (1926), **33**, 458.

7 Cf. J. Dewey, Theory of valuation, *Int. Ency. of Unified Science*, New York, 1939.

8 K. Mannheim, *Man and Society*, London, 1940, 249.

9 Conventionally answerable by reference to 'subjective factors' within individuals. R. M. MacIver, The Modes of the question why, *J. Soc. Phil.* (April 1940). Cf. also his The Imputation of motives, *Amer. J. Sociol.* (July 1940).

10 *Wirtschaft und Gesellschaft*, Tubingen 1922, 5: '"Motiv" heisst ein Sinnzusammenhang, Welcher dem Handlenden selbst oder dem Beobachtenden als sinnhafter

"Grund" eines Verhaltens in dem Grade heissen, als die Beziehung seiner Bestandteile von uns nach den durchschnittlichen Denk- und Gefühlsgewohnheiten als typischer (wir pflegen in sagen: "richtiger") Sinzusammenhand bejaht Wird.'

11 Of course, since motives are communicated, they may be lies; but, this must be proved. Verbalizations are not lies merely because they are socially efficacious. I am here concerned more with the social function of pronounced motives than with the sincerity of those pronouncing them.

12 See F. Znaniecki, *Social Actions*, New York, 1936, 30.

13 *General Theory of Value*, New York, 1936, 292–3.

14 Ibid., 392.

15 The 'profits motive' of classical economics may be treated as an ideal-typical vocabulary of motives for delimited economic situations and behaviors. For late phases of monopolistic and regulated capitalism, this type requires modification; the profit and commercial vocabularies have acquired other ingredients. See N. R. Danielian's *AT & T*, New York, 1940, for a suggestive account of the *non-economic* behavior and motives of business bureaucrats.

16 *Social Actions*, 73.

17 Of course, we could infer or interpret constructs posited in the individual, but these are not easily checked and they are not explanatory.

18 Which is not to say that, physiologically, there may not be cramps in the stomach wall or adrenalin in the blood, etc., but the character of the 'relation' of such items to social action is quite moot.

19 Paraphrased by K. Mannheim, op. cit., 316–17.

20 The motivation of economic activities, in C. W. M. Hart, *Essays in Sociology*, Toronto, 1940, 67.

21 Among the ethnologists, Ruth Benedict has come up to the edge of a genuinely sociological view of motivation. Her view remains vague because she has not seen clearly the identity of differing 'motivations' in differing cultures with the varied extant and approved vocabularies of motive. 'The intelligent understanding of the relation of the individual to his society ... involves always the understanding of the types of human motivations and capacities capitalized in his society', Configurations of culture in North America, *Amer. Anthrop.* (Jan.–Mar. 1932), 25; see also *Patterns of Culture*, Boston 1935, 242–3. She turns this observation into a quest for the unique 'genius' of each culture and stops her research by words like 'Apollonian'. If she would attempt constructively to observe the vocabularies of motives which precipitate acts to perform, implement programs, and furnish approved motives for them in circumscribed situations, she would be better able to state precise problems and to answer them by further observation.

22 Also motives acceptably imputed and avowed for one system of action may be diffused into other domains and gradually come to be accepted by some as a comprehensive portrait of *the* motive of men. This happened in the case of the economic man and his motives.

23 Kuno Mittenzwey, Zur Sociologie der psychoanalystischer Erkenntnis, in Max Scheler (ed.), *Versuche zu einer Sociologie des Wissens*, Munich 1924, 365–75.

24 This fact is interpreted by some as supporting Freudian theories. Nevertheless, it can be just as adequately grasped in the scheme here outlined.

25 See K. Burke's acute discussion of Freud, op. cit., Part I.

26 Moral vocabularies deserve a special statement. Within the viewpoint herein outlined many snarls concerning 'value-judgments', etc., can be cleared up.

18 Social-class variations in the teacher–pupil relationship

Howard S. Becker

The major problems of workers in the service occupations are likely to be a function of their relationship to their clients or customers, those for whom or on whom the occupational service is performed.[1] Members of such occupations typically have some image of the 'ideal' client, and it is in terms of this fiction that they fashion their conceptions of how their work ought to be performed, and their actual work techniques. To the degree that actual clients approximate this ideal the worker will have no 'client problem'.

In a highly differentiated urban society, however, clients will vary greatly, and ordinarily only some fraction of the total of potential clients will be 'good' ones. Workers tend to classify clients in terms of the way in which they vary from this ideal. The fact of client variation from the occupational ideal emphasizes the intimate relation of the institution in which work is carried on to its environing society. If that society does not prepare people to play their client roles in the manner desired by the occupation's members there will be conflicts, and problems for the workers in the performance of their work. One of the major factors affecting the production of suitable clients is the cultural diversity of various social classes in the society. The cultures of particular social-class groups may operate to produce clients who make the worker's position extremely difficult.

We deal here with this problem as it appears in the experience of the functionaries of a large urban educational institution, the Chicago public school system, discussing the way in which teachers in this system observe, classify and react to class-typed differences in the behavior of the children with whom they work. The material to be presented is thus relevant not only to problems of occupational organization but also to the problem of differences in the educational opportunities available to children of various social classes. Warner, Havighurst, and Loeb,[2] and Hollingshead[3] have demonstrated the

Source: *Journal of Education Sociology* (1952), *25* (4), 451–65.

manner in which the schools tend to favor and select out children of the middle classes. Allison Davis has pointed to those factors in the class cultures involved which make lower-class children less and middle-class children more adaptable to the work and behavioral standards of the school.[4] This paper will contribute to knowledge in this area by analyzing the manner in which the public school teacher reacts to these cultural differences and, in so doing, perpetuates the discrimination of our educational system against the lower-class child.

The analysis is based on sixty interviews with teachers in the Chicago system.[5] The interviews were oriented around the general question of the problems of being a teacher and were not specifically directed toward discovering feelings about social-class differences among students. Since these differences created some of the teachers' most pressing problems they were continually brought up by the interviewees themselves. They typically distinguished three social-class groups with which they, as teachers, came in contact: (1) a bottom stratum, probably equivalent to the lower-lower and parts of the upper-lower class; (2) an upper stratum, probably equivalent to the upper-middle class; and (3) a middle stratum, probably equivalent to the lower-middle and parts of the upper-lower class. We will adopt the convention of referring to these groups as lower, upper and middle groups, but it should be understood that this terminology refers to the teachers' classification of students and not to the ordinary sociological description.

We will proceed by taking up the three problems that loomed largest in the teachers' discussion of adjustment to their students: (1) the problem of *teaching* itself, (2) the problem of *discipline*, and (3) the problem of the *moral acceptability* of the students. In each case the variation in the form of and adjustment to the problem by the characteristics of the children of the various class groups distinguished by teachers is discussed.

A basic problem in any occupation is that of performing one's given task successfully, and where this involves working with human beings their qualities are a major variable affecting the ease with which the work can be done. The teacher considers that she has done her job adequately when she has brought about an observable change in the children's skills and knowledge which she can attribute to her own efforts:

> Well, I would say that a teacher is successful when she is putting the material across to the children, when she is getting some response from them. I'll tell you something. Teaching is a very rewarding line of work, because you can see those children grow under your hands. You can see the difference in them after you've had them for five months. You can see where they've started and where they've got to. And it's all yours. It really is rewarding in that way, you can see results and know that it's your work that brought those results about.

She feels that she has a better chance of success in this area when her pupils are interested in attending and working hard in school, and are trained at home in such a way that they are bright and quick at school work. Her problems arise in teaching those groups who do not meet these specifications, for in these cases her teaching techniques, tailored to the 'perfect' student, are inadequate to cope with the reality, and she is left with a feeling of having failed in performing her basic task.

Davis has described the orientations towards education in general, and school work in particular, of the lower and middle classes:[6]

> Thus, our educational system, which next to the family is the most effective agency in teaching good work habits to middle class people, is largely ineffective and unrealistic with underprivileged groups. Education fails to motivate such workers because our schools and our society both lack *real rewards* to offer underprivileged groups. Neither lower class children or adults will work hard in school or on the job just to please the teacher or boss. They are not going to learn to be ambitious, to be conscientious, and to study hard, as if school and work were a fine character-building game, which one plays just for the sake of playing. They can see, indeed, that those who work hard at school usually have families that already have the occupations, homes, and social acceptance that the school holds up as the rewards of education. The underprivileged workers can see also that the chances of their getting enough education to make their attainment of these rewards in the future at all probable is very slight. Since they can win the rewards of prestige and social acceptance in their own slum groups

without much education, they do not take very seriously the motivation taught by the school.

As these cultural differences produce variations from the image of the 'ideal' student, teachers tend to use class terms in describing the children with whom they work.

Children of the lowest group, from slum areas, are characterized as the most difficult group to teach successfully, lacking in interest in school, learning ability, and outside training:

> They don't have the right kind of study habits. They can't seem to apply themselves as well. Of course, it's not their fault; they aren't brought up right. After all the parents in a neighborhood like that really aren't interested. . . . But as I say, those children don't learn very quickly. A great many of them don't seem to be really interested in getting an education. I don't think they are. It's hard to get anything done with children like that. They simply don't respond.

In definite contrast are the terms used to describe children of the upper groups:

> In a neighborhood like this there's something about the children, you just feel like you're accomplishing so much more. You throw an idea out and you can see that it takes hold. The children know what you're talking about and they think about it. Then they come in with projects and pictures and additional information, and it just makes you feel good to see it. They go places and see things, and they know what you're talking about. For instance, you might be teaching social studies or geography. . . . You bring something up and a child says, 'Oh my parents took me to see that in a museum.' You can just do more with material like that.

Ambivalent feelings are aroused by children of the middle group. While motivated to work hard in school they lack the proper out-of-school training:

> Well, they're very nice here, very nice. They're not hard to handle. You see, they're taught respect in the home and they're respectful to the teacher. They want to work and do well. . . . Of course, they're not too brilliant. You know what I mean. But they are very nice children and very easy to work with.

In short, the differences between groups make it possible for the teacher to feel successful at her job only with the top group; with the other groups she feels, in greater or lesser measure, that she has failed.

These differences in ability to do school work, as perceived by teachers, have important consequences. They lead, in the first place, to differences in actual teaching techniques. A young high school teacher contrasted the techniques used in 'slum' schools with those used in 'better' schools:

At S—, there were a lot of guys who were just waiting till they were sixteen so they could get out of school. L—, everybody—well, a very large percentage, I'll say—was going on to secondary school, to college. That certainly made a difference in their classroom work. You had to teach differently at the different schools. For instance, at S—, if you had demonstrations in chemistry they had to be pretty flashy, lots of noise and smoke, before they'd get interested in it. That wasn't necessary at L—. Or at S— if you were having electricity or something like that you had to get the static electricity machine out and have them all stand around and hold hands so that they'd all get a little jolt.

Further, the teacher feels that where these differences are recognized by her superiors there will be a corresponding variation in the amount of work she is expected to accomplish. She expects that the amount of work and effort required of her will vary inversely with the social status of her pupils. This teacher compared schools from the extremes of the class range:

So you have to be on your toes and keep up to where you're supposed to be in the course of study. Now, in a school like the D— [slum school] you're just not expected to complete all that work. It's almost impossible. For instance, in the second grade we're supposed to cover nine spelling words a week. Well, I can do that up here at the K— ['better' school], they can take nine new words a week. But the best class I ever had at the D— was only able to achieve six words a week and they had to work pretty hard to get that. So I never finished the year's work in spelling. I couldn't. And I really wasn't expected to.

One resultant of this situation—in which less is expected of those teachers whose students are more difficult to teach—is that the problem becomes more aggravated in each grade, as the gap between what the children should know and what they actually do know becomes wider and wider. A principal of such a school describes the degeneration there of the teaching problem into a struggle to get a few basic skills across, in a situation where this cumulative effect makes following the normal program of study impossible:

The children come into our upper grades with very poor reading ability. That means that all the way through our school everybody is concentrating on reading. It's not like at a school like S— [middle group] where they have science and history and so on. At a school like that they figure that from first to fourth you learn to read and from fifth to eighth you read to learn. You use your reading to learn other material. Well, these children don't reach that second stage while they're with us. We have to plug along

getting them to learn to read. Our teachers are pretty well satisfied if the children can read and do simple number work when they leave here. You'll find that they don't think very much of subjects like science, and so on. They haven't got any time for that. They're just trying to get these basic things over. . . . That's why our school is different from one like the S—.

Such consequences of teachers' differential reaction to various class groups obviously operate to further perpetuate those class-cultural characteristics to which they object in the first place.

Discipline is the second of the teacher's major problems with her students. Willard Waller pointed to its basis when he wrote: 'Teacher and pupil confront each other in the school with an original conflict of desires, and however much that conflict may be reduced in amount, or however much it may be hidden, it still remains.'[7] We must recognize that conflict, either actual or potential, is ever present in the teacher–pupil relationship, the teacher attempting to maintain her control against the children's efforts to break it.[8] This conflict is felt even with those children who present least difficulty; a teacher who considered her pupils models of good behavior nevertheless said:

But there's that tension all the time. Between you and the students. It's hard on your nerves. Teaching is fun, if you enjoy your subject, but it's the discipline that keeps your nerves on edge, you know what I mean? There's always that tension. Sometimes people say, 'Oh, you teach school. That's an easy job, just sitting around all day long.' They don't know what it's really like. It's hard on your nerves.

The teacher is tense because she fears that she will lose control, which she tends to define in terms of some line beyond which she will not allow the children to go. Wherever she may draw this line (and there is considerable variation), the teacher feels that she has a 'discipline' problem when the children attempt to push beyond it. The form and intensity of this problem are felt to vary from one social-class group to another, as might be expected from Davis's description of class emphases on aggression:[9]

In general, middle-class aggression is taught to adolescents in the form of social and economic skills which will enable them to compete effectively at that level. . . . In lower-class families, physical aggression is as much a normal, socially approved and socially inculcated type of behavior as it is in frontier communities.

These differences in child training are matched by variation in the teachers' reactions.

Children in 'slum' schools are considered most difficult to control, being given to unrestrained behavior and physical violence. The interviews are filled with descriptions of such difficulties. Miriam Wagenschein, in a parallel study of the beginning school teacher, gave this summary of the experiences of these younger teachers in lower-class schools:[10]

> The reports which these teachers give of what *can be* done by a group of children are nothing short of amazing. A young white teacher walked into her new classroom and was greeted with the comment, 'Another damn white one.' Another was 'rushed' at her desk by the entire class when she tried to be extremely strict with them. Teachers report having been bitten, tripped, and pushed on the stairs. Another gave an account of a second grader throwing a milk bottle at the teacher and of a first grader having such a temper tantrum that it took the principal and two policemen to get him out of the room. In another school, following a fight on the playground, the principal took thirty-two razor blades from children in a first grade room. Some teachers indicated fear that they might be attacked by irate persons in the neighborhoods in which they teach. Other teachers report that their pupils carry long pieces of glass and have been known to threaten other pupils with them, while others jab each other with hypodermic needles. One boy got angry with his teacher and knocked in the fender of her car.

In these schools a major part of the teacher's time must be devoted to discipline; as one said: 'It's just a question of keeping them in line.' This emphasis on discipline detracts from the school's primary function of teaching, thus discriminating, in terms of available educational opportunity, against the children of these schools.

Children of the middle group are thought of as docile, and with them the teacher has least difficulty with discipline:

> Those children were much quieter, easier to work with. When we'd play our little games there was never any commotion. That was a very nice school to work in. Everything was quite nice about it. The children were easy to work with . . .

Children of the upper group are felt hard to handle in some respects, and are often termed 'spoiled', 'over-indulged' or 'neurotic'; they do not play the role of the child in the submissive manner teachers consider appropriate. One interviewee, speaking of this group, said:

> I think most teachers prefer not to teach in that type of school. The children are more pampered and, as we say, more inclined to run the school for themselves. The parents are very much at fault. The children are not used to taking orders at home and naturally they won't take them at school either.

Teachers develop methods of dealing with these discipline problems, and these tend to vary between social-class groups as do the problems themselves. The basic device used by successful disciplinarians is to establish authority clearly on the first meeting with the class:

> You can't ever let them get the upper hand on you or you're through. So I start out tough. The first day I get a new class in, I let them know who's boss. . . . You've got to start off tough, then you can ease up as you go along. If you start out easy-going, when you try to get tough they'll just look at you and laugh.

Having once established such a relation, it is considered important that the teacher be consistent in her behavior so that the children will continue to respect and obey her:

> I let them know I mean business. That's one thing you must do. Say nothing that you won't follow through on. Some teachers will say anything to keep kids quiet, they'll threaten anything. Then they can't or won't carry out their threats. Naturally, the children won't pay any attention to them after that. You must never say anything that you won't back up.

In the difficult 'slum' schools, teachers feel the necessity of using stern measures, up to and including physical violence (nominally outlawed):

> Technically you're not supposed to lay a hand on a kid. Well, they don't, technically. But there are a lot of ways of handling a kid so that it doesn't show—and then it's the teacher's word against the kid's, so the kid hasn't got a chance. Like dear Mrs —. She gets mad at a kid, she takes him out in the hall. She gets him stood up against the wall. Then she's got a way of chucking the kid under the chin, only hard, so that it knocks his head back against the wall. It doesn't leave a mark on him. But when he comes back in that room he can hardly see straight, he's so knocked out. It's really rough. There's a lot of little tricks like that that you learn about.

Where such devices are not used, there is recourse to violent punishment, 'tongue lashings'. All teachers, however, are not emotionally equipped for such behavior and must find other means:

> The worst thing I can do is lose my temper and start raving. . . . You've got to believe in that kind of thing in order for it to work. . . . If you don't honestly believe it, it shows up and the children know you don't mean it and it doesn't do any good anyway. . . . I try a different approach myself. Whenever they get too rowdy I go to the piano and . . . play something and we have rhythms or something until they sort of settle down. . . . That's what we call 'softsoaping' them. It seems to work for me. It's about the only thing I can do.

Some teachers may also resort to calling in the parents, a device whose usefulness is limited by the fact that such summonses are most frequently ignored. The teacher's disciplinary power in such a school is also limited by her fear of retaliation by the students: 'Those fellows are pretty big, and I just think it would take a bigger person than me to handle them. I certainly wouldn't like to try.'

In the school with children of the middle group no strong sanctions are required, mild reprimands sufficing:

Now the children at Z— here are quite nice to teach. They're pliable, yes, that's the word, they're pliable. They will go along with you on things and not fight you. You can take them any place and say to them, 'I'm counting on you not to disgrace your school. Let's see that Z— spirit.' And they'll behave for you. . . . They can be frightened, they have fear in them. They're pliable, flexible, you can do things with them. They're afraid of their parents and what they'll do to them if they get into trouble at school. And they're afraid of the administration. They're afraid of being sent down to the principal. So that they can be handled.

Children of the upper group often act in a way which may be interpreted as 'misbehavior' but which does not represent a conscious attack on the teacher's authority. Many teachers are able to disregard such activity by interpreting it as a natural concomitant of the 'brightness' and 'intelligence' of such children. Where such an interpretation is not possible the teachers feel hampered by a lack of effective sanctions:

I try different things like keeping them out of a gym period or a recess period. But that doesn't always work. I have this one little boy who just didn't care when I used those punishments. He said he didn't like gym anyway. I don't know what I'm going to do with him.

The teacher's power in such schools is further limited by the fact that the children are able to mobilize their influential parents so as to exert a large degree of control over the actions of school personnel.

It should be noted, finally, that discipline problems tend to become less important as the length of the teacher's stay in a particular school makes it possible for her to build a reputation which coerces the children into behaving without attempting any test of strength:[11]

I have no trouble with the children. Once you establish a reputation and they know what to expect, they respect you and you have no trouble. Of course, that's different for a new teacher, but when you're established that's no problem at all.

The third area of problems has been termed that of *moral acceptability*, and arises from the fact that some actions of one's potential clients may be offensive in terms of some deeply felt set of moral standards; these clients are thus morally unacceptable. Teachers find that some of their pupils act in such a way as to make themselves unacceptable in terms of the moral values centered on health and cleanliness, sex and aggression, ambition and work, and the relations of age groups.

Children of the middle group present no problem at this level, being universally described as clean, well dressed, moderate in their behavior, and hard working. Children from the 'better' neighborhoods are considered deficient in the important moral traits of politeness and respect for elders:

Here the children come from wealthy homes. That's not so good either. They're not used to doing work at home. They have maids and servants of all kinds and they're used to having things done for them, instead of doing them themselves. . . . They won't do anything. For instance, if they drop a piece of cloth on the floor, they'll just let it lay, they wouldn't think of bending over to pick it up. That's janitor's work to them. As a matter of fact, one of them said to me once: 'If I pick that up there wouldn't be any work for the janitor to do.' Well it's pretty difficult to deal with children like that.

Further, they are regarded as likely to transgress what the teachers define as moral boundaries in the matter of smoking and drinking; it is particularly shocking that such 'nice' children should have such vices.

It is, however, the 'slum' child who most deeply offends the teacher's moral sensibilities; in almost every area mentioned above these children, by word, action, or appearance, manage to give teachers the feeling that they are immoral and not respectable. In terms of physical appearance and condition they disgust and depress the middle-class teacher. Even this young woman, whose emancipation from conventional morality is symbolized in her habitual use of the argot of the jazz musician, was horrified by the absence of the toothbrush from the lives of her lower-class students:

It's just horribly depressing, you know. I mean, it just gets you down. I'll give you an example. A kid complained of a toothache one day. Well, I thought I could take a look and see if I could help him or something so I told him to open his mouth. I almost wigged when I saw his mouth. His teeth were all rotten, every one of them. Just filthy and rotten. Man, I mean, I was really shocked, you know. I said, 'Don't you have a toothbrush?' He said no, they were only his baby teeth and Ma said he didn't need a toothbrush for that. So I really got upset and looked in all their mouths. Man, I never saw anything like it. They were all like that, practically. I asked how many had toothbrushes, and about a quarter of them had them. Boy, that's terrible. And I don't dig that crap about baby teeth either, because they start getting molars when they're six, I know that. So I gave them a talking to, but what good does it do? The kid's mouth was just rotten. They never heard of a toothbrush or going to a dentist.

These children, too, are more apt than the other groups to be dishonest in some way that will get them into trouble with law enforcement officials. The early (by middle-class standards) sexual maturity of such children is quite upsetting to the teacher:

One thing about these girls is, well, some of them are not very nice girls. One girl in my class I've had two years now. She makes her money on the side as a prostitute. She's had several children. . . . This was a disturbing influence on the rest of the class.

Many teachers reported great shock on finding that words which were innocent to them had obscene meanings for their lower-class students:[12]

I decided to read them a story one day. I started reading them 'Puss in Boots' and they just burst out laughing. I couldn't understand what I had said that had made them burst out like that. I went back over the story and tried to find out what it might be. I couldn't see anything that would make them laugh. I couldn't see anything at all in the story. Later one of the other teachers asked me what had happened. She was one of the older teachers. I told her that I didn't know; that I was just reading them a story and they thought it was extremely funny. She asked me what story I read them and I told her 'Puss in Boots.' She said, 'Oh, I should have warned you not to read that one.' It seems that Puss means something else to them. It means something awful—I wouldn't even tell you what. It doesn't mean a thing to us.

Warner, Havighurst, and Loeb note that 'unless the middle-class values change in America, we must expect the influence of the schools to favor the values of material success, individual striving, thrift, and social mobility.'[13] Here again, the 'slum' child violates the teacher's moral sense by failing to display these virtues:

Many of these children don't realize the worth of an education. They have no desire to improve themselves. And they don't care much about school and schoolwork as a result. That makes it very difficult to teach them.

That kind of problem is particularly bad in a school like —. That's not a very privileged school. It's very under-privileged, as a matter of fact. So we have a pretty tough element there, a bunch of bums, I might as well say it. That kind you can't teach at all. They don't want to be there at all, and so you can't do anything with

them. And even many of the others—they're simply indifferent to the advantages of education. So they're indifferent, they don't care about their homework.

This behavior of the lower-class child is all the more repellent to the teacher because she finds it incomprehensible; she cannot conceive that any normal human being would act in such a way. This teacher stresses the anxiety aroused in the inexperienced teacher by her inability to provide herself with a rational explanation for her pupils' behavior:

We had one of the girls who just came to the school last year and she used to come and talk to me quite a bit. I know that it was just terrible for her. You know, I don't think she'd ever had anything to do with Negroes before she got there and she was just mystified, didn't know what to do. She was bewildered. She came to me one day almost in tears and said, 'But they don't want to learn, they don't even want to learn. Why is that?' Well, she had me there.

It is worth noting that the behavior of the 'better' children, even when morally unacceptable, is less distressing to the teacher, who feels that, in this case, she can produce a reasonable explanation for the behavior. An example of such an explanation is the following:

I mean, they're spoiled, you know. A great many of them are only children. Naturally, they're used to having their own way, and they don't like to be told what to do. Well, if a child is in a room that I'm teaching he's going to be told what to do, that's all there is to it. Or if they're not spoiled that way, they're the second child and they never got the affection the first one did, not that their mother didn't love them, but they didn't get as much affection, so they're not so easy to handle either.

We have shown that school teachers experience problems in working with their students to the degree that those students fail to exhibit in reality the qualities of the image of the ideal pupil which teachers hold. In a stratified urban society there are many groups whose life-style and culture produce children who do not meet the standards of this image, and who are thus impossible for teachers like these to work with effectively. Programs of action intended to increase the educational opportunities of the under-privileged in our society should take account of the manner in which teachers interpret and react to the cultural traits of this group, and the institutional consequences of their behavior.[14] Such programs might profitably aim at producing teachers who can cope effectively with the problems of teaching this group and not, by their reactions to class differences, perpetuate the existing inequities.

A more general statement of the findings is now in

order. Professionals depend on their environing society to provide them with clients who meet the standards of their image of the ideal client. Social class cultures, among other factors, may operate to produce many clients who, in one way or another, fail to meet these specifications and therefore aggravate one or another of the basic problems of the worker–client relation (three were considered in this paper).

In attacking this problem we touch on one of the basic elements of the relation between institutions and society, for the differences between ideal and reality place in high relief the implicit assumptions which institutions, through their functionaries, make about the society around them. All institutions have embedded in them some set of assumptions about the nature of the society and the individuals with whom they deal, and we must get at these assumptions, and their embodiment in actual social interaction, in order fully to understand these organizations. We can, perhaps, best begin our work on this problem by studying those institutions which, like the school, make assumptions which have high visibility because of their variation from reality.

Notes

1 See Howard S. Becker, The professional dance musician and his audience, *American Journal of Sociology* (September 1951), 57, 136–44, for further discussion of this point.

2 W. Lloyd Warner, Robert J. Havighurst and Martin B. Loeb, *Who Shall be Educated?* (New York: Harper 1944).

3 August de B. Hollingshead, *Elmtown's Youth; The Impact of Social Class on Adolescents* (Wiley 1949).

4 Allison Davis, *Social-Class Influences upon Learning* (Cambridge, Mass.: Harvard University Press 1950).

5 The entire research has been reported in Howard S. Becker, Role and career problems of the Chicago public school teacher, doctoral dissertation, University of Chicago 1951.

6 Allison Davis, 'The motivation of the underprivileged worker', in William F. Whyte (ed.), *Industry and Society* (New York: McGraw-Hill 1947), 99.

7 Willard Waller, *Sociology of Teaching* (Wiley 1965), 197.

8 Although all service occupations tend to have such problems of control over their clients, the problem is undoubtedly aggravated in situations like the school where those upon whom the service is being performed are not there of their own volition, but rather because of the wishes of some other group (the parents, in this case).

9 Allison Davis, *Social-Class Influence upon Learning*, 34–5.

10 Miriam Wagenschein, Reality shock, master's thesis, University of Chicago, 1950, 58–9.

11 This is part of the process of job adjustment described in detail in Howard S. Becker, The career of the Chicago public school teacher, *American Journal of Sociology* (March 1952), vol. 57.

12 Interview by Miriam Wagenschein. The lack of common meanings in this situation symbolizes the great cultural and moral distance between teacher and 'slum' child.

13 Warner, Havighurst and Loeb, op. cit., 172.

14 One of the important institutional consequences of these class preferences is a constant movement of teachers away from lower-class schools, which prevents these schools from retaining experienced teachers and from maintaining some continuity in teaching and administration.

Section III Learning and its organization in school

It is a too frequently disregarded truism that learning is a process which takes place over time. Schools recognize this in so far as they structure the time which pupils spend with them in a number of ways. They allocate the time available, to various areas of knowledge each of which is itself broken down into more easily assimilable parts. These are then placed in a particular sequence and decreed to be taken at a particular pace. The areas of knowledge, their relative value as evidenced by the time allotted to them, the sequence in which they are mastered and the pace at which they are mastered, all tend to become hallowed by continuous usage to a point where alternatives begin to appear to be unnatural.

Of these four areas, only the creation of a sequence of learning can in any way be justified in terms which transcend the values in any particular ideology of education. That is to say, the creation of 'subjects', the value placed on them, and the pace at which they can or must be learned, all have a more or less direct relationship with ideology and will all vary from ideology to ideology. There is, however, one sequence of activities and experiences which must be followed if learning is to be achieved. This sequence is outlined in Howard Becker's well-known paper 'Becoming a marihuana user'. This paper might well have the alternative title of 'Learning to smoke pot', for it does give us a basic sequence of activities necessary to learning in a social setting. In order to learn to use it in a way which will produce real effects, it is necessary to recognize these effects and connect them with using the drug, and to learn to enjoy the sensations one perceives. Parallels with more formal and approved subject areas seem to be pretty clear, as do the limits to inferring any 'objective' sequence of learning from the formulation. We cannot, for instance, infer from it that it is necessary, say, to learn the future tense before the perfect tense when tackling a foreign language.

The other consequence of the clear recognition that learning is a process that takes place over time, is that in order to understand the process we have to recognize that people change over time and that what they learn, and the way they learn, changes too.

The other paper in this section by Howard Becker, 'Personal change in adult life', addresses itself to this problem. Becker rejects both the view of people as basically unchanging (a view neatly summed up by Anselm Strauss, by analogy with an egg—however we cook an egg it remains essentially an egg*) and the view that sees behaviour as basically an expression of an underlying system of values, with any changes that do occur being regarded as superficial. Instead, he suggests that people do change, and he looks at personal change through the process of situational adjustment 'in which individuals take on the characteristics required by the situations they participate in'. Since he regards personal change as normal, personal stability, of course, becomes problematic; this is investigated through the concept of commitment, 'in which externally unrelated interests of the person become linked in such a way as to constrain future behaviour'.

The ideas contained in the two papers by Becker are brought together in the extract from Julius Roth's work on career timetables. Here we see how conceptions of the pacing and sequencing of activities, and the way individuals structure time, vary not only between careers but at different stages of the same career. Additionally, the degree of control an individual has over his timetable in any particular career varies at different stages of the same career as well as between different careers. Roth also shows that many careers have built-in testing points, performance at which determines which branch of the career the individual will follow; the parallel with our education system is too obvious to require further comment.

The paper by Cicourel and Kitsuse shows the way in

* Anselm L. Strauss, *Mirrors and Masks*, San Francisco: Sociology Press, 1969, 90–1.

which careers in schools, including deviant careers, are produced and bureaucratized by the school. The division of pupils into different career lines in the school is seen to give rise to the different 'career cultures' because the academic separation of pupils leads to their social and ecological separation within the school. The paper is representative of a recent school of sociological theory, known as the 'labelling' or 'societal reaction' school, which looks to the interaction between the individual and society, and society's definition of the value of behaviour, as a necessary starting point in the analysis of the causes of deviant behaviour.

Young and Brandis place some broad types of careers available in schools, and the criteria of allocation to them, in a more structural context. The authors put forward some likely consequences for secondary schools in England and Wales, and for the careers to be provided for pupils in them, of changes in the pattern of secondary education. They suggest that in some contexts, moral criteria—the pupil's 'state of grace or disgrace', his 'worthiness' and so on, may become the criteria for admission to various streams in the schools. They go on to argue that the system of streaming itself arises in response to the problems the school faces as a result of the pressures arising from the reorganization of secondary education.

The message implicit in many of the papers in this section seems to be that personal and institutional change is inevitable and that attempts to narrowly confine and control these processes create tensions in individuals and problems for organizations.

The two papers which complete this section focus on this problem of change. In 'Ritual in education', Bernstein, Elvin and Peters analyse the changing basis and strength of ritual, which they see as having facilitated essentially conservative régimes in English schools. They examine the relationship between these changes in the forms, functions and strength of rituals in education, and the occupational structure, and look at some likely implications for the structure of the school resulting from these changes.

This theme is the central one of the final paper in this section 'Open schools, open society?' In it Bernstein looks at the implications for schools of a general shift which he perceives as taking place in their basis of social integration, from mechanical to organic solidarity, or from 'closed' to 'open' schools. These changes are examined in a number of areas of school life, but they can be summarized as deriving from a change from 'purity of categories' (values, curriculum, teachers, teaching groups, etc.) to the mixing of categories. This is a change from certainty to ambiguity, from homogeneity to heterogeneity, which it is suggested may be symptomatic of basic changes in British society.

19 Personal change in adult life[1]

Howard S. Becker

People often exhibit marked change—in their attitudes, beliefs, behavior and style of interaction—as they move through youth and adulthood. Many social scientists, and others interested in explaining human behavior, think that human beings are governed by deep and relatively unchanging components of the personality or self, so that important changes at late stages in the life cycle are viewed as anomalies that need to be explained away. They may trace the roots of behavior to personality components formed in early childhood—needs, defenses, identifications, and the like—and interpret change in adulthood as simply a variation on an already established theme. Or they may, more sociologically, see the sources of everyday behavior in values established in the society, inculcated in the young during childhood, and maintained thereafter by constraints built into major communal institutions. Like the personality theorists, those who use values as a major explanatory variable see change in adulthood as essentially superficial, a new expression of an unchanging underlying system of values. In either case, the scientist wishes to concern himself with basic processes that will explain lasting trends in individual behavior.

Both these approaches err by taking for granted that the only way we can arrive at generalized explanations of human behavior is by finding some unchanging components in the self or personality. They err as well in making the prior assumption that human beings are essentially unchanging, that changes which affect only such 'superficial' phenomena as behavior without affecting deeper components of the person are trivial and unimportant.

There are good reasons to deny these assumptions. Brim, for instance, has persuasively argued that there are no 'deep' personality characteristics, traits of character which persist across any and all situations and social roles.[2] In any case, it is clearly a useful strategy to explore the theoretical possibilities opened

Source: *Sociometry* (March 1964), 27 (1), 40–53.

up by considering what might be true if we look in other directions for generalizeable explanations of human behavior.

A good many studies are now available which suggest that an appropriate area in which further explanations might be sought is that of social structure and its patterned effects on human experience. Two of these seem of special importance, and I devote most of what I have to say to them. The process of *situational adjustment*, in which individuals take on the characteristics required by the situations they participate in, provides an entering wedge into the problem of change. It shows us one example of an explanation which can deal with superficial and immediate changes in behavior and at the same time allow us to make generalized theories about the processes involved. The process of *commitment*, in which externally unrelated interests of the person become linked in such a way as to constrain future behavior, suggests an approach to the problem of personal stability in the face of changing situations. Before dealing with these processes, however, I will consider a problem of definition which reveals a further influence of social structure, this time an influence on the very terms in which problems of socialization are cast.

The eye of the beholder

Many of the changes alleged to take place in adults do not take place at all. Or, rather, a change occurs but an optical illusion causes the outside observer to see it as a change quite different in kind and magnitude from what it really is. The observer (a layman or a social scientist looking at the phenomenon from a layman's point of view), through a semantic transformation, turns an observable change into something quite different.

Take, for example, the commonly asserted proposition that the professional education of physicians stifles their native idealism and turns it into a profound professional cynicism.[3] Educated laymen believe this, and scientific studies have been carried out to test the proposition.[4] Observed changes in the behavior of fledgling physicians attest to its truth. Doctors are in fact inclined to speak with little reverence of the human body; they appear to be and probably are to a large extent unmoved in the emotional way a layman would be by human death; their standards are not as high as the layman thinks they ought to be, their desire for wealth stronger than it ought to be.

People describe these changes with reference to an unanalyzed conception of idealism and cynicism. It would not be unfair to describe the conception as the perspective of a disgruntled patient, who feels that the doctor he has to deal with is thinking about other things than the patient's welfare. The perspective of the disgruntled patient itself draws on some very general lay conceptions which suggest that those who deal with the unpleasant and the unclean—in this case, with death and disease—must of necessity be cynical, since 'normal people' prefer what is pleasant and clean and find the unclean repulsive.

It is typically the case in service occupations, however, that the practitioners who perform the service have a perspective quite different from the clients, patients or customers for whom they perform it.[5] They understand the techniques used by professionals, the reasons for their use in one case and not in another, the contingencies of the work situation and of work careers which affect a man's judgment and behavior, and the occupational ethos and culture which guide him. The client understands nothing of this. In an effort to make sense of his experience with those who serve him, he may resort to the folk notions I have already mentioned, reasoning that people who constantly deal with what decent people avoid may be contaminated: some of the dirt rubs off. The client is never sure that the practitioner has his best interests at heart and tends to suspect the worst.

But why should we assess and evaluate the change that takes place in the doctor as he goes through professional school from the point of view of his patient? Suppose we look at it instead from the characteristic perspective of the medical profession. If we do this, we find (as we would find if we studied the views of almost any occupation toward the institutions which train people for entrance into them) that medical schools are typically regarded as too idealistic. They train students to practice in ways that are not 'practical', suited to an ideal world but not to the world we live in. They teach students to order more laboratory tests than patients will pay for, to ignore the patients' requests for 'new' drugs or 'popular' treatments,[6] but do not teach students what to do when the waiting room holds more patients than can be seen during one's office hours. Similarly, people often complain of schools of education that they train prospective teachers in techniques that are not adapted to the situation the teacher will really have to deal with; they idealistically assume that the teacher can accomplish ends which in fact cannot be gained in the situations she will face. They do not tell the teacher how to teach a fifteen-year-old fifth grader, nor do they tell her what to do when she discovers a pupil carrying a switchblade knife.

It is a paradox. In one view, professional training makes physicians less idealistic, in the other, more idealistic. Where does the truth lie? I have already noted that many of the changes seen as signs of increasing cynicism in the young physician do in fact take place. It can equally be demonstrated that the changes which make him seem too idealistic also take place. The medical students we studied at the University of Kansas expected, when they graduated, to practice in ways that would be regarded as hopelessly idealistic by many, if not most, medical practitioners. They proposed to see no more than twenty patients a day: they proposed never to treat a disease without having first made a firm diagnosis. These beliefs, inculcated by a demanding faculty, are just the opposite of the cynicism supposed to afflict the new physician.[7]

The lesson we should learn from this is that personality changes are often present only in the eye of the beholder. Changes do take place in people, but the uninformed outsider interprets the change wrongly. Just as doctors acquire new perspectives and ideas as a result of their medical training, any adult may acquire new perspectives and ideas. But it would be a mistake to assume that these changes represent the kind of fundamental changes suggested by such polar terms as 'idealism' and 'cynicism'. We learn less by studying the students who are alleged to have lost their idealism than we do by studying those who claim they have become cynical.

Even so, adults do change. But we must make sure, not only by our own observation but also by careful analysis of the terms we use to describe what we see, that the changes we try to explain do in fact take place. Parenthetically, an interesting possibility of transferring concepts from the study of adults to the study of socialization of children lies in defining the character of the changes that take place as children develop. Is it too farfetched to say that the definitions ordinarily used are excessively parochial in that they are all arrived at from the adult point of view? What would our theories look like if we made a greater effort to capture the child's point of view? What does he think is happening to him? How does his conception of the process differ from that of the adults who bring him up and those who study his growing up?

Situational adjustment

One of the most common mechanisms in the development of the person in adulthood is the process of situational adjustment. This is a very gross conception, which requires analytic elaboration it has not yet received. But the major outlines are clear. The person, as he moves in and out of a variety of social situations, learns the requirements of continuing in each situation and of success in it. If he has a strong desire to continue, the ability to assess accurately what is required, and can deliver the required performance, the individual turns himself into the kind of person the situation demands.

Broadly considered, this is much the same as Brim's notion of learning adult roles. One learns to be a doctor or a policeman, learns the definitions of the statuses involved and the appropriate behavior with respect to them. But the notion of situational adjustment is more flexible than that of adult role learning. It allows us to deal with smaller units and make a finer analysis. We construct the process of learning an adult role by analyzing sequences of smaller and more numerous situational adjustments. We should have in our minds the picture of a person trying to meet the expectations he encounters in immediate face-to-face situations: doing well in today's chemistry class, managing to be poised and mature on tonight's date, surmounting the small crises of the moment. Sequences and combinations of small units of adjustment produce the larger units of role learning.

If we view situational adjustment as a major process of personal development, we must look to the character of the situation for the explanation of why people change as they do. We ask what there is in the situation that requires the person to act in a certain way or to hold certain beliefs. We do not ask what there is in him that requires the action or belief. All we need to know of the person is that for some reason or another he desires to continue his participation in the situation or to do well in it. From this we can deduce that he will do what he can to do what is necessary in that situation. Our further analysis must adjust itself to the character of the situation.

Thus for example, in our present study of college undergraduates,[8] we find that they typically share a strong desire to get high grades. Students work very hard to get grades and consider them very important, both for their immediate consequences and as indicators of their own personal ability and worth. We need not look very deeply into the student to see the reason for his emphasis on grades. The social structure of the campus coerces students to believe that grades are important because, in fact, they are important. You cannot join a fraternity or sorority if your grades do not meet a certain minimum standard. You cannot compete for high office in important campus organizations if your grades are not high enough. As many as one-fourth of the students may not be able to remain in school if they do not raise their grades in the next semester. For those who are failing, low grades do not simply mean blocked access to the highest campus honors. Low grades, for these unfortunates, mean that every available moment must be spent studying, that the time the average student spends dating, playing, drinking beer or generally goofing off must be given over to the constant effort to stay in school. Grades are the currency with which the economy of campus social life operates. Only the well-to-do can afford the luxuries; the poor work as hard as they can to eke out a marginal existence.

The perspectives a person acquires as a result of situational adjustments are no more stable than the situation itself or his participation in it. Situations occur in institutions: stable institutions provide stable situations in which little change takes place. When the institutions themselves change, the situations they provide for their participants shift and necessitate development of new patterns of belief and action. When, for instance, a university decides to up-grade its academic program and begins to require more and different kinds of work from its students, they must adjust to the new contingencies with which the change confronts them.

Similarly, if an individual moves in and out of given situations, is a transient rather than a long-term participant, his perspectives will shift with his movement. Wheeler has shown that prisoners become more 'prisonized' the longer they are in prison; they are more likely to make decisions on the basis of criminal than of law-abiding values. But he has also shown that if you analyze prisoners' responses by time still to be served, they become more law-abiding the nearer they approach release.[9] This may be interpreted as a situational shift. The prisoner is frequently sorry that he has been caught and is in a mood to give up crime; he tends to respect law-abiding values. But when he enters prison he enters an institution which, in its lower reaches, is dominated by men wedded to criminal values. Studies of prisons have shown that the most influential prisoners tend to have stable criminal orientations and that inmate society is dominated by these perspectives.[10] In order to 'make out' in the prison, the new inmate discovers that he must make his peace with this criminally oriented social structure, and he does. As he approaches release, however, he realizes that he is going back into a world dominated by people who respect the law and that the criminal values which stand him in such good stead in prison society will not work as well outside. He thereupon begins to shed the criminal values appropriate to the prison and renew his attachment to the law-abiding values of the outside world.

We discovered the same process in the medical school, where students gave up a naïve idealistic approach to the problems of medicine for an approach that was specifically oriented toward getting through school. As they approached the end of their schooling, they relinquished their attachment to these school-specific values and once more returned to their concern with problems that would arise in the outer world, albeit with a new and more professional approach than they would have been capable of before.

We find a similar change in college students, when we observe them in the Spring of their last college year. They look back over the four years of school and wonder why they have not spent their time better, wonder if college has been what they wanted. This concern reflects their preoccupation, while in school, with the pursuit of values that are valuable primarily within the confines of the collegiate community: grades, office in campus organizations, and the like. (Even though they justify their pursuit of these ends in part on the basis of their utility in the outside world, students are not sure that the pursuit of other ends, less valued on the campus, might not have even more usefulness for the future.) Now that they are leaving for the adult community, in which other things will be valuable, they find it hard to understand their past concerns as they try, retrospectively, to assess the experience they have just been through.

Situational adjustment is very frequently not an individual process at all, but a collective one. That is, we are not confronted with one person undergoing change, but with an entire cohort, a 'class' of people, who enter the institution and go through its socializing program together. This is most clearly the case in those institutions which typically deal with 'batches' of people.[11] Schools are perhaps the best example, taking in a class of students each year or semester who typically go through the entire training program as a unit, leaving together at the end of their training.

But situational adjustment may have a collective character even where people are not processed in groups. The individual enters the institution alone, or with a small group, but joins a larger group there already, who stand ready to tell him how it is and what he should do, and he will be followed by others for whom he will perform the same good turn.[12] In institutions where people are acted upon in groups by socializing agents, much of the change that takes place—the motivation for it and the perceived desirability of different modes of change—cannot be traced to the predilections of the individual. It is, instead, a function of the interpretive response made by the entire group, the consensus the group reaches with respect to its problems.

The guidelines for our analysis can be found in Sumner's analysis of the development of folkways.[13] A group finds itself sharing a common situation and common problems. Various members of the group experiment with possible solutions to those problems and report their experiences to their fellows. In the course of their collective discussion, the members of the group arrive at a definition of the situation, its problems and possibilities, and develop consensus as to the most appropriate and efficient ways of behaving. This consensus thenceforth constrains the activities of individual members of the group, who will probably act on it, given the opportunity.

The collective character of socialization processes has a profound effect on their consequences. Because the solutions the group reaches have, for the individual being socialized, the character of 'what everyone knows to be true', he tends to accept them. Random variation in responses that might arise from differences in prior experiences is drastically reduced. Medical students, for instance, began their training with a variety of perspectives on how one ought to approach academic assignments. The pressure generated by their inability to handle the tremendous amount of work given them in the first year anatomy course forced them to adopt collectively one of the many possible solutions to the problem, that of orienting their studying to learning what the faculty was likely to ask about in examinations. (Where the situation does not coerce a completely collective response, variation due to differences in background and experience remains. Irwin and Cressey[14] argue that the behavior of prisoners, both in prison and after release, varies depending on whether the convict was previously a member of the criminal underworld.)

In addition, where the response to problematic situations is collective, members of the group involved develop group loyalties that become part of the environment they must adjust to. Industrial workers are taught by their colleagues to restrict production in order that an entire work group may not be held to the higher production standard one or two people might be able to manage.[15] Medical students, similarly, find that they will only make it harder for others, and eventually for themselves, if they work too hard and 'produce' too much.[16]

One major consequence of the collective character of situational adjustment, a result of the factors just mentioned, is that the group being socialized is able to deviate much more from the standards set by those doing the socializing than would be possible for an individual. Where an individual might feel that his deviant response was idiosyncratic, and thus be open to persuasion to change it, the member of a group knows that there are many who think and act just as he does and is therefore more resistant to pressure and propaganda. A person being socialized alone, likewise, is freer to change his ways than one who is constrained by his loyalties to fellow trainees.

If we use situational adjustment as an explanation for changes in persons during adulthood, the most interesting cases for analysis are the negative cases, those instances in which people do not adjust appropriately to the norms implicit or explicit in the situation. For not everyone adjusts to the kind of major situational forces I have been discussing. Some prison inmates never take on criminal values; some college students fail to adopt campus values and therefore do not put forth their full effort in the pursuit of grades. In large part, cases in which it appears that people are not adjusting to situational pressures are cases in which closer analysis reveals that the situation is actually not the same for everyone involved in the institution. A job in the library may effectively remove the prisoner from the control of more criminally oriented prisoners; *his* situation does not constrain him to adopt criminal values. The political rewards owed a student's living group may require a campus organization to give him an office his grade point average would otherwise make it difficult for him to attain.

More generally, it is often the case that subgroups in an institution will often have somewhat different life situations. College, for instance, is clearly one thing for men, another for women; one thing for members of fraternities and sororities, another for independents. We only rarely find an institution as monolithic as the medical school, in which the environment is, especially during the first two years, exactly alike for everyone. So we must make sure that we have discovered the effective environment of those whose personal development we want to understand.

Even after removing the variation in personal change due to variation in the situation, we will find a few cases in which people sturdily resist situational pressures. Here we can expect to find a corresponding weakness in the desire to remain in the situation or to do well in it, or a determination to remain in the situation only on one's terms or as long as one can get what one wants out of it. Many institutions have enough leeway built into them for a clever and determined operator to survive without much adjustment.

Commitment

The process of situational adjustment allows us to account for the changes people undergo as they move through various situations in their adult life. But we also know that people exhibit some consistency as they move from situation to situation. Their behavior is not infinitely mutable, they are not infinitely flexible. How can we account for the consistency we observe?

Social scientists have increasingly turned to the concept of commitment for an explanation of personal consistency in situations which offer conflicting directives. The term has been used to describe a great variety of social-psychological mechanisms, such a variety that it has no stable meaning. Nevertheless, I think we can isolate at least one process referred to by the term commitment, a process which will help explain a great deal of behavioral consistency.[17]

Briefly, we can say a person is committed when we observe him pursuing a consistent line of activity in a sequence of varied situations. Consistent activity persists over time. Further, even though the actor may engage in a variety of disparate acts, he sees them as essentially consistent; from his point of view they serve him in pursuit of the same goal. Finally, it is a distinguishing mark of commitment that the actor rejects other situationally feasible alternatives, choosing from among the available courses of action that which best suits his purpose. In so doing, he often ignores the principle of situational adjustment, pursuing his consistent line of activity in the face of a short-term loss.

The process of commitment consists in the linking of previously extraneous and irrelevant lines of action and sets of rewards to a particular line of action under study. If, for instance, a person refuses to change jobs, even though the new job would offer him a higher salary and better working conditions, we should suspect that his decision is a result of commitment, that other sets of rewards than income and working conditions have become attached to his present job so that it would be too painful for him to change. He may have a large pension at stake, which he will lose if he moves; he may dread the cost of making new friends and learning to get along with new working associates; he may feel that he will get a reputation for being flighty and erratic if he leaves his present job. In each instance, formerly extraneous interests have become linked to keeping his present job. I have elsewhere described this process metaphorically as the making of side-bets.[18]

The committed person has acted in such a way as to involve other interests of his, originally extraneous to the action he is engaged in, directly in that action. By his own actions . . . he has staked something of value to him, something originally unrelated to his present line of action, on being consistent in his present behavior. The consequences of inconsistency will be so expensive that inconsistency . . . is no longer a feasible alternative.

A person may make side-bets producing commitments consciously and deliberately or he may acquire them or have them made for him almost without his knowledge, becoming aware that he is committed only when he faces a difficult decision. Side-bets and commitments of the latter type, made by default, arise from the operation of generalized cultural expectations, from the operation of impersonal bureaucratic arrangements, from the process of individual adjustment to social positions, and through the need to save face.

One way of looking at the process of becoming an adult is to view it as a process of gradually acquiring, through the operation of all these mechanisms, a variety of commitments which constrain one to follow a consistent pattern of behavior in many areas of life. Choosing an occupation, getting a job, starting a family—all these may be seen as events which produce lasting commitments and constrain the person's behavior. Careful study might show that the operation of the process of commitment accounts for the well-known fact that juvenile delinquents seldom become adult criminals, but rather turn into respectable conventional, law-abiding lower-class citizens. It may be that the erratic behavior of the juvenile delinquent is erratic precisely because the boy has not yet taken any actions which commit him more or less permanently to a given line of endeavor.

Viewing commitment as a set of side-bets encourages us to inquire into the kind of currency with which bets are made in the situation under analysis. What things are valuable enough to make side-bets that matter with? What kinds of counters are used in the game under analysis? Very little research has been done on this problem, but I suspect that erratic behavior and 'random' change in adult life result from situations which do not permit people to become committed because they deny to them the means, the chips, with which to make side-bets of any importance.

Members of medical faculties complain, for instance, that students' behavior toward patients is erratic. They do not exhibit the continued interest in or devotion to the patient's welfare supposed to characterize the practicing physician. They leave the hospital at five o'clock, even though a patient assigned to them is in critical condition. Their interest in a surgical patient disappears when the academic schedule sends them to a medical ward and a new set of student duties. The reason for students' lack of interest and devotion becomes clear when we consider their frequent complaint that they are not allowed to exercise medical responsibility, to make crucial decisions or carry out important procedures. Their behavior toward patients can be less constrained than that of a practicing physician precisely because they are never allowed to be in a position where they can make a mistake that matters. No patient's life or welfare depends on them: they need not persist in any particular pattern of activity since deviation costs nothing.[19]

The condition of being unable to make important side-bets and thus commit oneself may be more widespread than we think. Indeed, it may well be that the age at which it becomes possible to make lasting and important side-bets is gradually inching up. People cannot become committed to a consistent line of activity until later in life. As divorce becomes more frequent, for instance, the ability to make a lasting commitment by getting married becomes increasingly rare. In studying the possibilities of commitment afforded by social structures, we discover some of the limits to consistent behavior in adult life.

(It might be useful to apply similar concepts in studies of child socialization. It is likely, for instance, that children can seldom commit themselves. Our society, particularly, does not give them the means with which to make substantial side-bets, nor does it think it appropriate for children to make committing side-bets. We view childhood and youth as a time when a person can make mistakes that do not count. Therefore, we would expect children's behavior to be flexible and changeable, as in fact it seems to be.)

Situational adjustment and commitment are closely related, but by no means identical, processes. Situational adjustment produces change; the person shifts his behavior with each shift in the situation. Commitment produces stability; the person subordinates immediate situational interests to goals that lie outside the situation. But a stable situation can evoke a well-adjusted pattern of behavior which itself becomes valuable to the person, one of the counters that has meaning in the game he is playing. He can become committed to preserving the adjustment.

We find another such complementary relationship between the two when we consider the length of time one is conventionally expected to spend in a situation, either by oneself or by others, and the degree to which the present situation is seen as having definite connections to important situations anticipated at some later stage of development. If one sees that his present situation is temporary and that later situations will demand something different, the process of adjustment will promote change. If one thinks of the present situation as likely to go on for a long time, he may resist what appear to him temporary situational changes because the strength of the adjustment has committed him to maintaining it. This relationship requires a fuller analysis than I have given it here.

Conclusion

The processes we have considered indicate that social structure creates the conditions for both change and stability in adult life. The structural characteristics of institutions and organizations provide the framework of the situations in which experience dictates the expediency of change. Similarly, they provide the counters with which side-bets can be made and the links between lines of activity out of which commitment grows. Together, they enable us to arrive at general explanations of personal development in adult life without requiring us to posit unvarying characteristics of the person, either elements of personality or of 'value structure'.

A structural explanation of personal change has important implications for attempts to deliberately mold human behavior. In particular, it suggests that we need not try to develop deep and lasting interests, be they values or personality traits, in order to produce the behavior we want. It is enough to create situations which will coerce people into behaving as we want them to and then to create the conditions under which other rewards will become linked to continuing this behavior. A final medical example will make the point. We can agree, perhaps, that surgeons ought not to operate unless there is a real need to do so: the problem of 'unnecessary surgery' has received a great deal of attention both within and outside the medical profession. We might achieve our end by inculcating this rule as a basic value during medical training; or we might use personality tests to select as surgeons only those men whose own needs would lead them to exercise caution. In fact, this problem is approaching solution through a structural innovation: the hospital tissue committee, which examines all tissue removed at surgery and disciplines those surgeons who too frequently remove healthy tissue. Surgeons, whatever their values or personalities, soon learn to be careful when faced with the alternative of exposure or discipline.

Notes

1 A slightly different version of this paper was presented at the Social Science Research Council Conference on Socialization Through the Life Cycle, New York, 17 May 1963.

2 Orville G. Brim, Jr, Personality as role-learning, in Ira Iscoe and Harold Stevenson (eds), *Personality Development in Children* (Austin: University of Texas Press, 1960), 127–59.

3 This problem is discussed at greater length in Howard S. Becker and Blanche Geer, The fate of idealism in medical school, *American Sociological Review* (Feb. 1958), **23**, 50–6, and in Howard S. Becker, Blanche Geer, Everett C. Hughes and Anselm L. Strauss, *Boys in White; Student Culture in Medical School* (University of Chicago Press 1961), 419–33.

4 See Leonard D. Eron, Effect of Medical Education on Medical Students, *Journal of Medical Education* (Oct. 1955), **10**, 559–66; and Richard Christie and Robert K. Merton, Procedures for the sociological study of the values climate of medical schools, ibid. (1958), **33** (2), 125–53.

5 See, for a discussion of this point, Howard S. Becker, *Outsiders; Studies in the Sociology of Deviance* (Collier-Macmillan 1963), 82 ff. and Everett C. Hughes, *Men and their Work* (Collier-Macmillan 1958), *passim*.

6 See Eliot Freidson, *Patients' Views of Medical Practice* (New York: Russell Sage Foundation 1961), 200–2.

7 Becker *et al.*, *Boys in White*, 426–8.

8 Statements about college students are based on preliminary analysis of the data collected in a study of undergraduates at the University of Kansas in which I collaborated with Blanche Geer and Everett C. Hughes. A monograph reporting our findings is in preparation. The study was supported by the Carnegie Corporation of New York.

9 Stanton Wheeler, Socialization in correctional communities, *American Sociological Review* (Oct. 1961), **26**, 697–712.

10 See Donald R. Cressey (ed.), *The Prison: Studies in Institutional Organization and Change* (Holt, Rinehart and Winston 1961) and Richard A. Cloward *et al.*, *Theoretical Studies in Social Organization of the Prison* (New York: Social Science Research Council 1960).

11 See Erving Goffman's use of this idea in *Asylums: Essays on the Social Situation of Mental Patients and Other Inmates* (Garden City: Doubleday 1961), 6 and *passim* (available in Penguin Books).

12 See Anselm L. Strauss, *Mirrors and Masks; The Search for Identity* (New York: Free Press 1959) and Howard S. Becker and Anselm L. Strauss, Careers, personality and adult socialization, *American Journal of Sociology* (Nov. 1956), **62**, 253–63.

13 William Graham Sumner, *Folkways* (Boston: Ginn 1907, also NEL 1965). See also Albert K. Cohen, *Delinquent Boys; The Culture of a Gang* (Collier-Macmillan 1955); and Richard A. Coward and Lloyd E. Ohlin, *Delinquency and Opportunity; A Theory of Delinquent Gangs* (Routledge & Kegan Paul 1960).

14 John Irwin and Donald R. Cressey, Thieves, convicts and the inmate culture, *Social Problems* (Fall 1962), **10**, 142–55. See also Howard S. Becker and Blanche Geer, Latent culture: a note on the theory of latent social roles (in the present volume).

15 Donald Roy, Quota restriction and goldbricking in a machine shop, *American Journal of Sociology* (Mar. 1952), **57**, 427–42.

16 Becker *et al.*, *Boys in White*, 297–312.

17 Howard S. Becker, Notes on the concept of commitment, *American Journal of Sociology* (July 1960), **66**, 32–40.

18 Ibid., 35.

19 Becker *et al.*, *Boys in White*, 254–73.

20 The study of the career timetables

Julius A. Roth

People will not accept uncertainty. They will make an effort to structure it no matter how poor the materials they have to work with and no matter how much the experts try to discourage them.

One way to structure uncertainty is to structure the time period through which uncertain events occur. Such a structure must usually be developed from information gained from the experience of others who have gone or are going through the same series of events. As a result of such comparisons, norms develop for entire groups about when certain events may be expected to occur. When many people go through the same series of events, we speak of this as a career and of the sequence and timing of events as their career timetable. . .

I contend that it may be worthwhile to study career timetables in a variety of areas (in most cases probably as part of a broader study of a career), including areas where a timetable structure now seems obscure. In this chapter I review the dimensions and issues of such a study, note some cautions and qualifications that one might watch for, and make a tentative effort to point out the definitions and boundaries of career timetables.

Conditions for timetable norms

From an examination of the careers illustrated in this book, the following conditions appear to be necessary for timetables to develop:

1 The series of events or conditions under scrutiny must be thought of in terms of a career—a series of related and definable stages or phases of a given sphere of activity that a group of people goes through in a progressive fashion (that is, one step leads to another) in a given direction or on the way to a more or less definite and recognizable end-point or goal or series of goals. This means that there must be a group definition of success or attainment of a goal. Such definitions may be provided by movement through an institutional hierarchy (business executive careers, academic careers); through a series of contingencies moving in a given direction (the private practice physician getting a better clientele, better office location, better hospital appointments; the school-teacher getting better school assignments or more desirable courses to teach); escape from an undesirable situation (the patient getting out of a hospital, the prisoner getting out of jail, the draftee getting out of the army); or development in a given direction (children developing toward independent adulthood).

2 There must be an interacting (not necessarily face-to-face) group of people with access to the same body of clues for constructing the norms of a timetable. . .

Splitting up blocks of time

Everyone, even the backward mental hospital patient, makes use of various devices to break up the days, weeks, months, and years of his life into smaller units. Such division of large masses into smaller blocks occurs not only in relation to time. We divide books into chapters, chapters into sections, sections into subsections and paragraphs. We divide academic disciplines into specialty areas, topics, and courses so that the subject matter may be viewed a little at a time. When a long series of digits must be memorized, people invariably break the series up into groups of a few digits each and memorize the digits in these groups rather than as an undifferentiated series of digits. These examples are perhaps all different aspects of the same psychological phenomenon.

However, although the splitting of time periods into smaller units probably always goes with the development of timetable norms, this process in itself does not make a career timetable. The units into

Source: Julius A. Roth, *Timetables*, Indianapolis: Bobbs Merrill (1963), 93–5, 98–100, 104–10, 112–13.

which the chronic patient breaks up his days and weeks show no discernible direction or movement toward discharge from the hospital or other goal. The life prisoner can look forward to Sunday as a welcome break in a dreary routine, but the succession of Sundays does not lead him anywhere. The division of time into units with recurring markers may make one's life more psychologically manageable, but it does not in itself make a career timetable. For such a timetable to develop, the reference points must move in some definable direction or toward some recognizable goal.

The meaning of reference points

In all timetables we find dividing points for events that serve as signposts for progress in a given direction (toward discharge or graduation or adulthood, attaining family security or racial equality or a certain occupational position). In retrospect, such signposts may also serve as reference points from which one may predict and measure further progress.

Reference points may be more or less clear-cut and stable. If they are prescribed in detail and rigidly adhered to, as in the career of pupils in our school system, one's movement through the timetable is almost completely predictable. As the reference points become less rigid and less clear cut, they must be discovered and interpreted through observation and through interaction with others of one's career group. The more unclear the reference points are, the harder it is for members of a career group to know where they stand in relation to others and the more likely it is that they will attend to inappropriate clues and thus make grossly inaccurate predictions concerning future progress. The degree of stability is related in part to the changes in timetables through time. Such changes may be gradual and almost imperceptible or they may occur quickly, as in military careers in time of war, occupational careers during economic expansion or depression, and disease careers at a time of drastic changes in treatment methods.

The meanings of such reference points are learned by members of the group through observation of the experience of other members and through the communication of experiences, ideals, myths, and hopes among the members of the group. During a time of rapid change in the timetable when the changes are not made explicit, such information will contain many contradictions and thus make the construction of stable and reliable timetable norms more difficult. We may conceive of an extreme situation where rapidity of change and lack of explicit information may make the development of group timetable norms impossible. Not that members of the group will not keep trying, but that their judgments will so often be so far wrong that they lose confidence in their ability to make predictions of their future. None of the careers we have used as illustrations approaches this extreme, and it is difficult to invent a realistic group traversing the same career line without some fairly accurate norms of progress. In any case, the stability of norms is relative. They are more stable (and more accurately predictive) for Valentine Hospital TB patients than for Dover Sanatorium patients, for railroad firemen and engineers than for airline pilots; but in no case do they seem to be completely absent.[1]

Shifting time perspectives

Another aspect of a career timetable that deserves attention is the change that may occur in timetable perspectives during the course of the career. We have seen in the case of the long-term hospital patient how the timetable norms lengthen with increasing duration of hospitalization, at least up to a certain point. The patient frequently starts out identifying himself with those who are in for a short time. Only after he himself has passed this stage does he begin to think of himself as staying the 'average' time, and then he even advances the average somewhat when he stays longer until it becomes obvious that he is being kept 'overtime'.

We may wonder whether the same process occurs in other careers. The new executive trainee fresh out of college fancies himself, let us say, a department head by age thirty and revises this expectation upward only when he reaches thirty without being near this goal. The average, he finds from observation, seems to be between ages thirty-five and forty, so he still has plenty of time. When he has not reached this level by forty, he may note that in a number of cases other men did not reach the department-head level until forty-five, so he still has a chance. Only when he is approaching fifty without making the grade does he finally admit that he is clearly behind schedule.

Do such shifts in perspectives occur in occupational groups, with parents observing and directing their children's development, with families trying to keep pace with the social and economic advancement of their social circle, or on the part of politicians striving to work their way up through a hierarchy of public offices? And what is the attitude toward those who are very far ahead or very far behind the timetable norms? Do such attitudes have the effect of moving the actual careers of individuals closer to the group norms as they do in the case of tuberculosis and polio patients?

Shifting perspectives are probably more common in some types of careers than in others. We may expect a lag in the norms when a career timetable is changing rapidly, as with the airline pilots whose career stages are being slowed up or with middle-class children whose developmental timetable is being speeded up. Perhaps a lack of explicitness in timetable bench marks also makes such shifting of perspectives during the course of one's career more likely.

Handling failure

A career timetable is, as I mentioned earlier, a tight production schedule which not all those following the career path can keep up with. Some fall so far behind and have so little chance of catching up—either in the reasonably near future, or ever—that the normal timetable no longer applies to them except to show how much they have fallen by the wayside.

The proportion of such 'failures' varies widely from one career line to another. In some—for example, public school pupils—it is a small proportion of the total; in others—for example, nursing home inmates—it is a majority. In some cases the definition of failure is sharp and unmistakable and is symbolized by shifting the person to a different social and/or geographical location—for example, the patient moved from an intensive treatment unit to a chronic service. In other cases, failure to keep up to the mark in the promotion system is never clearly established, and there is an accumulation of borderline cases who may or may not be considered failures depending upon slight differences of interpretation of their career experiences—for example, business executive careers, where it is often not clear whether many of the men in intermediate positions have been left behind or are still in the running, but on the slow side of the norm.

There must be some provision in every career line for those who cannot keep up to the mark, especially those who are being left hopelessly behind to the point where they become a class apart. In some career lines, the failures may be uncompromisingly shucked off—airline piloting seems to approach this extreme. In other career lines, however, the total society or some organized part of it has made a commitment to a given category of its members that cannot easily be rejected. Care and treatment of the ill and education of the young are typical of such career lines in the United States. Those who cannot possibly approach the normal timetable of recovery or learning must still be cared for, but in a different way and with a different set of expectations. A 'chronic sidetrack' is created for them. They are still pupils, but in an ungraded class or a special school. They are still patients, but receiving largely maintenance care rather than active treatment. They are still part of the domain occupied by their career group, but no longer part of the forward-moving promotion system.

There are intermediate ways of dealing with timetable failures. In many universities and in large, well-established businesses there is often an obligation to provide a job for the professor or executive even when he is no longer considered useful to the organization. Because of the nature of the relationship, the unwanted incumbents cannot be moved off to a dead-end sidetrack in as blatant a manner as can the public hospital patient or the public school pupil who is considered hopeless. (However, systems of compulsory retirement with loopholes for excepting individuals who are still wanted sometimes operate as such a sidetrack at the upper age range.) The sidetracking in such cases must operate more subtly, often with the notion of failure or rejection denied or obscured by a consolation prize.

An important issue to investigate, then, in any study of a career timetable is the manner in which failure is handled, both by those who suffer the failure and by others who play a part in the control of their career timetables. When a number of studies dealing with this issue has been made, we may be able to specify in more detail the conditions under which different modes of handling failure are applied. For example, does a firm commitment by a public agency to provide long-term service to a given category of people invariably lead to the development of chronic sidetracks? Under what conditions can an organization frankly reject those who cannot be maintained in the promotion system? (For instance, does obvious danger in a career activity, such as piloting aircraft, give the authorities the right to be ruthless in getting rid of the unwanted?) On the other hand, under what conditions must the indications of failure be more indirect and subtle? In what ways can the definition of failure be affected and manipulated by the person whose career is directly involved? When, for example, can a person dodge being sidetracked by switching to a different social or organizational career line—different job, different social class aspirations, different institutional treatment program?

Bargaining over the timetable

When a career is part of a service or authority relationship, each of the two (or more) groups concerned attempts to structure the same series of events. If the nature of the relationship is more than a unique or fleeting one, each party to the relationship will develop timetable norms that are somewhat different from each other because their goals, their criteria of success or progress, and their conceptions of proper timing are more or less different from each other. If the relationship is to continue, bargaining and accommodation must take place. The two parties inevitably influence each other's timetables, often simply as a result of anticipating the reactions of the other to given decisions, procedures, rules, or other actions.

Thus, the parent attempts to some extent to impose upon his children his conception of the proper timetable of development, but he must make compromises in response to the spoken and unspoken pressures from his children and his anticipation of how they will feel about the demands that he will make on them. At the same time, children are trying to do some things before they are expected to or allowed to and are trying to avoid doing some other things at the time when they should. The children too modify some of their behavior and some of their pressures so as to avoid conflict with the parents. Thus both parents and children are constantly making compromises about the times when they believe certain events or stages of development should occur.

Of course, there are limiting cases where the room for bargaining over the timetable is narrowed to the vanishing point. Where we have the imposition of a standardized timetable as a massive bureaucratic procedure—as in compulsory military service—this limit is approached. Under what conditions does the highly standardized timetable appear? Certainly, the degree of control plays a part. The controlling authority must have the power to impose a timetable without compromise. Not only must the draftee serve his time whether he likes it or not, but his superiors usually have no power to modify the total time or its sequence except under certain specific circumstances (e.g. certain kinds of illness). Giving the underdogs' superiors discretionary power to modify their subordinates' career timetables immediately opens the door to wholesale bargaining.[2]

However, power to control the underdogs is certainly not the only factor leading to standardized timetables. The degree of uncertainty of outcome plays a part, but it is not clear just what that part is. If the outcome of treatment of disease, training for a job, control of sexual behavior, or the rehabilitation of criminals is highly uncertain, it may seem to be a good reason for considerable leeway in timing the sequence of events in each of these careers and thus promoting a wider area of bargaining between superior and subordinate, professional and client, or two parties engaged in a joint series of acts. However, sometimes the effect is quite the opposite—a standardized timetable is imposed or maintained as a way of avoiding the disruptive consequences of uncertainty and widespread bargaining. Thus, the outcome of academic education in terms of test performance of pupils is highly variable and uncertain, yet the public school system imposes one of the most rigid, unvarying timetables of progress in a career that we can find in our society. Hospital physicians, too, sometimes impose standard time points in areas where uncertainty is greatest: for example, the sequence of giving passes after admission or surgery. Perhaps standardization results from a combination of a high degree of uncertainty and a powerful authority to impose a timetable without compromise. However, this question can only be addressed with more assurance after there have been further studies of career timetables in a variety of areas differing in certainty, power of authority, and perhaps other factors. In any study of a career timetable, there should be an effort not only to determine to what extent and in what ways the timetable is or is not standardized, but also what there is about the career and bargaining situation that produces or prevents standardization.

Another aspect of the timetable that deserves attention is the use of testing points. These, too, must be imposed by an authority on subordinates or underdogs and thus become part of the bargaining relationship to the extent that the subordinates can influence the evaluation of their performance or the use to which information about their performance is put. The executive who knows he is being evaluated for a crucial decision about his future promotion potentialities may contrive to control the communication system in such a way that he makes his performance look better than it is to his bosses.

We must be careful, however, to see whether the apparent testing points perform a definite function in affecting the career timetable or whether they are merely empty formalities. A good example of the latter is our public school system, which, despite a standard series of scholastic testing points, promotes and graduates the vast majority of pupils 'on time' regardless of performance, on the grounds that it would be psychologically damaging to the pupils to be separated from their age group. Occupations in which seniority reigns supreme may operate in a similar way.

The selection of career boundaries is to some extent arbitrary. We select those which suit our purpose. Child development, for example, is a rather broad career category, and for certain purposes we may want to focus on the timetable of subdivisions of child development—linguistic development, sexual development, development of social group formation—recognizing that they are to some degree related and will affect one another. Of course, the selection of career boundaries cannot be completely arbitrary. The category used must have meaning to the people whose behavior is being studied; otherwise, it could scarcely be used as an explanatory device for that behavior.

If one wishes to apply a timetable analysis to the whole of a person's life, one must realize that each person is operating on a number of timetables simultaneously. The amount of pressure the long-term patient brings to bear to influence his treatment timetable may depend on his occupational or family timetables. A man may be a parent concerned with measuring the development of his children in terms of the expectations about child development in his social group and at the same time be a professor measuring his success in his professional career by reference to the expectations of his occupational colleague group. His career stage will affect the school where he chooses to teach, which in turn will affect the kinds of schools, neighborhood, and companions to which his children will be exposed at a given stage of their development. (It may also work the other way around—the stage of development of the professor's children may determine his place of residence, which will partly determine the kind of occupational position he can obtain at a given point in his professional career.) If the focus is on individual development, the interactions between timetables may be of more interest than the separately analyzed career timetables.

140   *Julius A. Roth*

Notes

1 Where we have professional–client or boss–subordinate relationships, it is not only the underdog, but also his superior, who is confused by sharp changes in timetable contingencies. When treatment methods undergo a sudden shift, not only do the patients have greater difficulty anticipating their future careers, but the physicians also become much more doubtful about when patients should be given privileges or be discharged—until a new set of norms to accompany the new treatment has been worked out. When a corporation is drastically reorganized, not only is the junior executive's timetable thrown into temporary confusion, but his bosses also have much greater difficulty deciding when their subordinates are 'ready' for promotion under the new circumstances.

2 This point is often recognized by hospital medical directors who try to reduce the pressure for concessions from patients by prohibiting their ward doctors from giving patients passes, privileges, or discharges other than those prescribed by a standardized timetable unless the exception is approved by the director or medical board. The difficulty with this solution for the physicians is that is poses another dilemma for them: it prevents the ward doctor from exercising his independent expert judgment in treating his patients and thus makes him somewhat less of a physician according to the values held by the medical profession. In fact, this solution can be used only when the ward doctors are interns or residents-in-training or unlicensed foreign physicians working under a restrictive contract.

21 Becoming a marihuana user

Howard S. Becker

An unknown, but probably quite large, number of people in the United States use marihuana. They do this in spite of the fact that it is both illegal and disapproved.

The phenomenon of marihuana use has received much attention, particularly from psychiatrists and law enforcement officials. The research that has been done, as is often the case with research on behavior that is viewed as deviant, is mainly concerned with the question: why do they do it? Attempts to account for the use of marihuana lean heavily on the premise that the presence of any particular kind of behavior in an individual can best be explained as the result of some trait which predisposes or motivates him to engage in that behavior. In the case of marihuana use, this trait is usually identified as psychological, as a need for fantasy and escape from psychological problems the individual cannot face.[1]

I do not think such theories can adequately account for marihuana use. In fact, marihuana use is an interesting case for theories of deviance, because it illustrates the way deviant motives actually develop in the course of experience with the deviant activity. To put a complex argument in a few words: instead of the deviant motives leading to the deviant behavior, it is the other way around; the deviant behavior in time produces the deviant motivation. Vague impulses and desires—in this case, probably most frequently a curiosity about the kind of experience the drug will produce—are transformed into definite patterns of action through the social interpretation of a physical experience which is in itself ambiguous. Marihuana use is a function of the individual's conception of marihuana and of the uses to which it can be put, and this conception develops as the individual's experience with the drug increases.[2]

The research reported in this paper deals with the career of the marihuana user. Here we will look at

Source: *American Journal of Sociology* (November 1953), 59, 41–58.

the development of the individual's immediate physical experience with marihuana. In later work we consider the way he reacts to the various social controls that have grown up around use of the drug. What we are trying to understand here is the sequence of changes in attitude and experience which lead to *the use of marihuana for pleasure*. This way of phrasing the problem requires a little explanation. Marihuana does not produce addiction, at least in the sense that alcohol and the opiate drugs do. The user experiences no withdrawal sickness and exhibits no ineradicable craving for the drug.[3] The most frequent pattern of use might be termed 'recreational'. The drug is used occasionally for the pleasure the user finds in it, a relatively casual kind of behavior in comparison with that connected with the use of addictive drugs. The report of the New York City Mayor's Committee on Marihuana emphasizes this point:[4]

A person may be a confirmed smoker for a prolonged period, and give up the drug voluntarily without experiencing any craving for it or exhibiting withdrawal symptoms. He may, at some time later on, go back to its use. Others may remain infrequent users of the cigarette, taking one or two a week, or only when the 'social setting' calls for participation. From time to time we had one of our investigators associate with a marihuana user. The investigator would bring up the subject of smoking. This would invariably lead to the suggestion that they obtain some marihuana cigarettes. They would seek a 'tea-pad', and if it was closed the smoker and our investigator would calmly resume their previous activity, such as the discussion of life in general or the playing of pool. There were apparently no signs indicative of frustration in the smoker at not being able to gratify the desire for the drug. We consider this point highly significant since it is so contrary to the experience of users of other narcotics. A similar situation occurring in one addicted to the use of morphine, cocaine or heroin would result in a compulsive attitude on the part of the addict to obtain the drug. If unable to secure it, there would be obvious physical and mental manifestations of frustration. This may be considered presumptive evidence that there is not true addiction in the medical sense associated with the use of marihuana.

In using the phrase 'use for pleasure', I mean to emphasize the noncompulsive and casual character of the behavior. (I also mean to eliminate from consideration here those few cases in which marihuana is used for its prestige value only, as a symbol that one is a certain kind of person, with no pleasure at all being derived from its use.)

The research I am about to report was not so designed that it could constitute a crucial test of the theories that relate marihuana use to some psychological trait of the user. However, it does show that psychological explanations are not in themselves sufficient to account for marihuana use and that they are, perhaps, not even necessary. Researchers attempting to prove such psychological theories have run into two great difficulties, never satisfactorily resolved, which the theory presented here avoids. In the first place, theories based on the existence of some predisposing psychological trait have difficulty in accounting for that group of users, who turn up in sizable numbers in every study,[5] who do not exhibit the trait or traits which are considered to cause the behavior. Second, psychological theories have difficulty in accounting for the great variability over time of a given individual's behavior with reference to the drug. The same person will at one time be unable to use the drug for pleasure, at a later stage be able and willing to do so, and still later again be unable to use it in this way. These changes, difficult to explain from a theory based on the user's needs for 'escape', are readily understandable as consequences of changes in his conception of the drug. Similarly, if we think of the marihuana user as someone who has learned to view marihuana as something that can give him pleasure, we have no difficulty in understanding the existence of psychologically 'normal' users.

In doing the study, I used the method of analytic induction. I tried to arrive at a general statement of the sequence of changes in individual attitude and experience which always occurred when the individual became willing and able to use marihuana for pleasure, and never occurred or had not been permanently maintained when the person was unwilling to use marihuana for pleasure. The method requires that *every* case collected in the research substantiates the hypothesis. If one case is encountered which does not substantiate it, the researcher is required to change the hypothesis to fit the case which has proven his original idea wrong.[6]

To develop and test my hypothesis about the genesis of marihuana use for pleasure, I conducted fifty interviews with marihuana users. I had been a professional dance musician for some years when I conducted this study and my first interviews were with people I had met in the music business. I asked them to put me in contact with other users who would be willing to discuss their experiences with me. Colleagues working on a study of users of opiate drugs made a few interviews available to me which contained, in addition to material on opiate drugs, sufficient material on the use of marihuana to furnish a test of my hypothesis.[7] Although in the end half of the fifty interviews were conducted with musicians, the other half covered a wide range of people, including laborers, machinists, and people in the professions. The sample is, of course, in no sense 'random'; it would not be possible to draw a random sample, since no one knows the nature of the universe from which it would have to be drawn.

In interviewing users, I focused on the history of the person's experience with marihuana, seeking major changes in his attitude toward it and in his actual use of it, and the reasons for these changes. Where it was possible and appropriate, I used the jargon of the user himself.

The theory starts with the person who has arrived at the point of willingness to try marihuana. (I discuss how he got there in the next chapter.) He knows others use marihuana to 'get high', but he does not know what this means in any concrete way. He is curious about the experience, ignorant of what it may turn out to be, and afraid it may be more than he has bargained for. The steps outlined below, if he undergoes them all and maintains the attitudes developed in them, leave him willing and able to use the drug for pleasure when the opportunity presents itself.

Learning the technique

The novice does not ordinarily get high the first time he smokes marihuana, and several attempts are usually necessary to induce this state. One explanation of this may be that the drug is not smoked 'properly', that is, in a way that insures sufficient dosage to produce real symptoms of intoxication. Most users agree that it cannot be smoked like tobacco if one is to get high:

Take in a lot of air, you know, and . . . I don't know how to describe it, you don't smoke it like a cigarette, you draw in a lot of air and get it deep down in your system and then keep it there. Keep it there as long as you can.

Without the use of some such technique[8] the drug will produce no effects, and the user will be unable to get high:

The trouble with people like that [who are not able to get high] is that they're just not smoking it right, that's all there is to it. Either they're not holding it down long enough, or they're getting too much air and not enough smoke, or the other way around or something like that. A lot of people just don't smoke it right, so naturally nothing's gonna happen.

If nothing happens, it is manifestly impossible for the user to develop a conception of the drug as an object which can be used for pleasure, and use will therefore not continue. The first step in the sequence of events that must occur if the person is to become a user is that he must learn to use the proper smoking technique so that his use of the drug will produce effects in terms of which his conception of it can change.

Such a change is, as might be expected, a result of the individual's participation in groups in which marihuana is used. In them the individual learns the proper way to smoke the drug. This may occur through direct teaching:

I was smoking like I did an ordinary cigarette. He said, 'No, don't do it like that.' He said, 'Suck it, you know, draw in and hold it in your lungs till you . . . for a period of time.'
I said, 'Is there any limit of time to hold it?'
He said, 'No, just till you feel that you want to let it out, let it out.' So I did that three or four times.

Many new users are ashamed to admit ignorance and, pretending to know already, must learn through the more indirect means of observation and imitation:

I came on like I had turned on [smoked marihuana] many times before, you know. I didn't want to seem like a punk to this cat. See, like I didn't know the first thing about it—how to smoke it, or what was going to happen, or what. I just watched him like a hawk—I didn't take my eyes off him for a second, because I wanted to do everything just as he did it. I watched how he held it, how he smoked it, and everything. Then when he gave it to me I just came on cool, as though I knew exactly what the score was. I held it like he did and took a poke just the way he did.

No one I interviewed continued marihuana use for pleasure without learning a technique that supplied sufficient dosage for the effects of the drug to appear. Only when this was learned was it possible for a conception of the drug as an object which could be used for pleasure to emerge. Without such a conception marihuana use was considered meaningless and did not continue.

Learning to perceive the effects

Even after he learns the proper smoking technique, the new user may not get high and thus not form a conception of the drug as something which can be used for pleasure. A remark made by a user suggested the reason for this difficulty in getting high and pointed to the next necessary step on the road to being a user:

As a matter of fact, I've seen a guy who was high out of his mind and didn't know it.
[How can that be, man?]
Well, it's pretty strange, I'll grant you that, but I've seen it. This guy got on with me, claiming that he'd never got high, one of those guys, and he got completely stoned. And he kept insisting that he wasn't high. So I had to prove to him that he was.

What does this mean? It suggests that being high consists of two elements: the presence of symptoms caused by marihuana use and the recognition of these symptoms and their connection by the user with his use of the drug. It is not enough, that is, that the effects be present; alone, they do not automatically provide the experience of being high. The user must be able to point them out to himself and consciously connect them with having smoked marihuana before he can have this experience. Otherwise, no matter what actual effects are produced, he considers that the drug has had no effect on him: 'I figured it either had no effect on me or other people were exaggerating its effect on them, you know. I thought it was probably psychological, see.' Such persons believe the whole thing is an illusion and that the wish to be high leads the user to deceive himself into believing that something is happening when, in fact, nothing is. They do not continue marihuana use, feeling that 'it does nothing' for them.

Typically, however, the novice has faith (developed from his observation of users who do get high) that the drug actually will produce some new experience and continues to experiment with it until it does. His failure to get high worries him, and he is likely to ask more experienced users or provoke comments from them about it. In such conversations he is made aware of specific details of his experience which he may not have noticed or may have noticed but failed to identify as symptoms of being high:

I didn't get high the first time. . . . I don't think I held it in long enough. I probably let it out, you know, you're a little afraid. The second time I wasn't sure, and he [smoking companion] told me, like I asked him for some of the symptoms or something, how would I know, you know. . . . So he told me to sit on a stool. I sat on—I think I sat on a bar stool—and he said, 'Let your feet hang', and then when I got down my feet were real cold, you know.
And I started feeling it, you know. That was the first time. And then about a week after that, sometime pretty close to it, I really got on. That was the first time I got on a big laughing kick, you know. Then I really knew I was on.

One symptom of being high is an intense hunger. In

the next case the novice becomes aware of this and gets high for the first time:

> They were just laughing the hell out of me because like I was eating so much. I just scoffed [ate] so much food, and they were just laughing at me, you know. Sometimes I'd be looking at them, you know, wondering why they're laughing, you know, not knowing what I was doing. [Well, did they tell you why they were laughing eventually?] Yeah, yeah, I come back, 'Hey, man, what's happening?' Like, you know, like I'd ask, 'What's happening?' and all of a sudden I feel weird, you know. 'Man, you're on, you know. You're on pot [high on marihuana].' I said, 'No, am I?' Like I don't know what's happening.

The learning may occur in more indirect ways:

> I heard little remarks that were made by other people. Somebody said, 'My legs are rubbery', and I can't remember all the remarks that were made because I was very attentively listening for all these cues for what I was supposed to feel like.

The novice, then, eager to have this feeling, picks up from other users some concrete referents of the term 'high' and applies these notions to his own experience. The new concepts make it possible for him to locate these symptoms among his own sensations and to point out to himself a 'something different' in his experience that he connects with drug use. It is only when he can do this that he is high. In the next case, the contrast between two successive experiences of a user makes clear the crucial importance of the awareness of the symptoms in being high and re-emphasizes the important role of interaction with other users in acquiring the concepts that make this awareness possible:

> [Did you get high the first time you turned on?] Yeah, sure. Although, come to think of it, I guess I really didn't. I mean, like that first time it was more or less of a mild drunk. I was happy. I guess, you know what I mean. But I didn't really know I was high, you know what I mean. It was only after the second time I got high that I realized I was high the first time. Then I knew that something different was happening.
>
> [How did you know that?] How did I know? If what happened to me that night would of happened to you, you would've known, believe me. We played the first tune for almost two hours —one tune! Imagine man! We got on the stand and played this one tune, we started at nine o'clock. When we got finished I looked at my watch, it's a quarter to eleven. Almost two hours on one tune. And it didn't seem like anything.
>
> I mean, you know, it does that to you. It's like you have much more time or something.

Anyway, when I saw that, man, it was too much. I knew I must really be high or something if anything like that could happen. See, and then they explained to me that that's what it did to you, you had a different sense of time and everything. So I realized that that's what it was. I knew then. Like the first time, I probably felt that way, you know, but I didn't know what's happening.

It is only when the novice becomes able to get high in this sense that he will continue to use marihuana for pleasure. In every case in which use continued, the user had acquired the necessary concepts with which to express to himself the fact that he was experiencing new sensations caused by the drug. That is, for use to continue, it is necessary not only to use the drug so as to produce effects but also to learn to perceive these effects when they occur. In this way marihuana acquires meaning for the user as an object which can be used for pleasure.

With increasing experience the user develops a greater appreciation of the drug's effects; he continues to learn to get high. He examines succeeding experiences closely, looking for new effects, making sure the old ones are still there. Out of this there grows a stable set of categories for experiencing the drug's effects whose presence enables the user to get high with ease.

Users, as they acquire this set of categories, become connoisseurs. Like experts in fine wines, they can specify where a particular plant was grown and what time of year it was harvested. Although it is usually not possible to know whether these attributions are correct, it is true that they distinguish between batches of marihuana, not only according to strength, but also with respect to the different kinds of symptoms produced.

The ability to perceive the drug's effects must be maintained if use is to continue; if it is lost, marihuana use ceases. Two kinds of evidence support this statement. First, people who become heavy users of alcohol, barbiturates, or opiates do not continue to smoke marihuana, largely because they lose the ability to distinguish between its effects and those of the other drugs.[9] They no longer know whether the marihuana gets them high. Second, in those few cases in which an individual uses marihuana in such quantities that he is always high, he is apt to feel the drug has no effect on him, since the essential element of a noticeable difference between feeling high and feeling normal is missing. In such a situation, use is likely to be given up completely, but temporarily, in order that the user may once again be able to perceive the difference.

Learning to enjoy the effects

One more step is necessary if the user who has now learned to get high is to continue use. He must learn to enjoy the effects he has just learned to experience. Marihuana-produced sensations are not automatically or necessarily pleasurable. The taste for such experience is a socially acquired one, not different in kind from acquired tastes for oysters or dry martinis. The user feels dizzy, thirsty; his scalp tingles; he misjudges time and distances. Are these things pleasurable? He isn't sure. If he is to continue marihuana use, he must decide that they are. Otherwise, getting high, while a real enough experience, will be an unpleasant one he would rather avoid.

The effects of the drug, when first perceived, may be physically unpleasant or at least ambiguous:

> It started taking effect, and I didn't know what was happening, you know, what it was, and I was very sick. I walked around the room, walking around the room trying to get off, you know; it just scared me at first, you know. I wasn't used to that kind of feeling.

In addition, the novice's naïve interpretation of what is happening to him may further confuse and frighten him, particularly if he decides, as many do, that he is going insane:

> I felt I was insane, you know. Everything people done to me just wigged me. I couldn't hold a conversation, and my mind would be wandering, and I was always thinking, oh, I don't know, weird things, like hearing music different. . . . I get the feeling that I can't talk to anyone. I'll goof completely.

Given these typically frightening and unpleasant first experiences, the beginner will not continue use unless he learns to redefine the sensations as pleasurable:

> It was offered to me, and I tried it. I'll tell you one thing. I never did enjoy it at all. I mean it was just nothing that I could enjoy. [Well, did you get high when you turned on?] Oh, yeah, I got definite feelings from it. But I didn't enjoy them. I mean I got plenty of reactions, but they were mostly reactions of fear. [You were frightened?] Yes. I didn't enjoy it. I couldn't seem to relax with it, you know. If you can't relax with a thing, you can't enjoy it, I don't think.

In other cases the first experiences were also definitely unpleasant, but the person did become a marihuana user. This occurred, however, only after a later experience enabled him to redefine the sensations as pleasurable:

> [This man's first experience was extremely unpleasant, involving distortion of spatial relationships and sounds, violent thirst, and panic produced by these symptoms.] After the first time I didn't turn on for about, I'd say, ten months to a year. . . . It wasn't a moral thing; it

was because I'd gotten so frightened, bein' so high. An' I didn't want to go through that again, I mean, my reaction was, 'Well, if this is what they call bein' high, I don't dig [like] it.' . . . So I didn't turn on for a year almost, accounta that . . .

> Well, my friends started, an' consequently I started again. But I didn't have any more, I didn't have that same initial reaction, after I started turning on again.

[In interaction with his friends he became able to find pleasure in the effects of the drug and eventually became a regular user.]

In no case will use continue without a redefinition of the effects as enjoyable.

This redefinition occurs, typically, in interaction with more experienced users who, in a number of ways, teach the novice to find pleasure in this experience which is at first so frightening.[10] They may reassure him as to the temporary character of the unpleasant sensations and minimize their seriousness, at the same time calling attention to the more enjoyable aspects. An experienced user describes how he handles newcomers to marihuana use:

> Well, they get pretty high sometimes. The average person isn't ready for that, and it is a little frightening to them sometimes. I mean, they've been high on lush [alcohol], and they get higher that way than they've ever been before, and they don't know what's happening to them. Because they think they're going to keep going up, up, up till they lose their minds or begin doing weird things or something. You have to like reassure them, explain to them that they're not really flipping or anything, that they're gonna be all right. You have to just talk them out of being afraid. Keep talking to them, reassuring, telling them it's all right. And come on with your own story, you know: 'The same thing happened to me. You'll get to like that after awhile.' Keep coming on like that; pretty soon you talk them out of being scared. And besides they see you doing it and nothing horrible is happening to you, so that gives them more confidence.

The more experienced user may also teach the novice to regulate the amount he smokes more carefully, so as to avoid any severely uncomfortable symptoms while retaining the pleasant ones. Finally, he teaches the new user that he can 'get to like it after a while'. He teaches him to regard those ambiguous experiences formerly defined as unpleasant as enjoyable. The older user in the following incident is a person whose tastes have shifted in this way, and his remarks have the effect of helping others to make a similar redefinition:

> A new user had her first experience of the effects of marihuana and became frightened and hysterical. She 'felt like she was half in and half out of the room' and experienced a number of alarming physical symptoms. One of the more

experienced users present said, 'She's dragged because she's high like that. I'd give anything to get that high myself. I haven't been that high in years.'

In short, what was once frightening and distasteful becomes, after a taste for it is built up, pleasant, desired, and sought after. Enjoyment is introduced by the favorable definition of the experience that one acquires from others. Without this, use will not continue, for marihuana will not be for the user an object he can use for pleasure.

In addition to being a necessary step in becoming a user, this represents an important condition for continued use. It is quite common for experienced users suddenly to have an unpleasant or frightening experience, which they cannot define as pleasurable, either because they have used a larger amount of marihuana than usual or because the marihuana they have used turns out to be of a higher quality than they expected. The user has sensations which go beyond any conception he has of what being high is and is in much the same situation as the novice, uncomfortable and frightened. He may blame it on an overdose and simply be more careful in the future. But he may make this the occasion for a rethinking of his attitude towards the drug and decide that it no longer can give him pleasure. When this occurs and is not followed by a redefinition of the drug as capable of producing pleasure, use will cease.

The likelihood of such a redefinition occurring depends on the degree of the individual's participation with other users. Where this participation is intensive, the individual is quickly talked out of his feeling against marihuana use. In the next case, on the other hand, the experience was very disturbing, and the aftermath of the incident cut the person's participation with other users to almost zero. Use stopped for three years and began again only when a combination of circumstances, important among which was a resumption of ties with users, made possible a redefinition of the nature of the drug:

It was too much, like I only made about four pokes, and I couldn't even get it out of my mouth, I was so high, and I got real flipped. In the basement, you know, I just couldn't stay in there anymore. My heart was pounding real hard, you know, and I was going out of my mind; I thought I was losing my mind completely. So I cut out of this basement, and this other guy, he's out of his mind, told me, 'Don't, don't leave me, man. Stay here.' And I couldn't.

I walked outside, and it was five below zero, and I thought I was dying, and I had my coat open; I was sweating, I was perspiring. My whole insides were all . . . and I walked about two blocks away, and I fainted behind a bush. I don't know how long I laid there, I woke up, and I was feeling the worst, I can't describe it at all, so I made it to a bowling alley, man, and I was

trying to act normal, I was trying to shoot pool, you know, trying to act real normal, and I couldn't lay and I couldn't stand up and I couldn't sit down, and I went up and laid down where some guys that spot pins lay down, and that didn't help me, and I went down to a doctor's office. I was going to go in there and tell the doctor to put me out of my misery . . . because my heart was pounding so hard, you know. . . . So then all week-end I started flipping, seeing things there and going through hell, you know, all kinds of abnormal things. . . . I just quit for a long time then.

[He went to a doctor who defined the symptoms for him as those of a nervous breakdown caused by 'nerves' and 'worries'. Although he was no longer using marihuana, he had some recurrences of the symptoms, which led him to suspect that 'it was all his nerves'.] So I just stopped worrying, you know; so it was about thirty-six months later I started making it again. I'd just take a few pokes, you know. [He first resumed use in the company of the same user-friend with whom he had been involved in the original incident.]

A person, then, cannot begin to use marihuana for pleasure, or continue its use for pleasure, unless he learns to define its effects as enjoyable, unless it becomes and remains an object he conceives of as capable of producing pleasure.

In summary, an individual will be able to use marihuana for pleasure only when he goes through a process of learning to conceive of it as an object which can be used in this way. No one becomes a user without (1) learning to smoke the drug in a way which will produce real effects; (2) learning to recognize the effects and connect them with drug use (learning, in other words, to get high); and (3) learning to enjoy the sensations he perceives. In the course of this process he develops a disposition or motivation to use marihuana which was not and could not have been present when he began use, for it involves and depends on conceptions of the drug which could only grow out of the kind of actual experience detailed above. On completion of this process he is willing and able to use marihuana for pleasure.

He has learned, in short, to answer 'Yes' to the question: 'Is it fun?' The direction his further use of the drug takes depends on his being able to continue to answer 'Yes' to this question and, in addition, on his being able to answer 'Yes' to other questions which arise as he becomes aware of the implications of the fact that society disapproves of the practice: 'Is it expedient?' 'Is it moral?' Once he has acquired the ability to get enjoyment by using the drug, use will continue to be possible for him. Considerations of morality and expediency, occasioned by the reactions of society, may interfere and inhibit use, but use continues to be a possibility in terms of his conception of the drug. The act becomes impossible only when the ability to enjoy the experience of being high is lost, through a change in the user's conception of the drug occasioned by certain kinds of experience with it.

Notes

1 See, as examples of this approach, the following: Eli Marcovitz and Henry J. Meyers, The marihuana addict in the army, *War Medicine* (December 1944), **6**, 382–91; Herbert S. Gaskill, Marihuana, an intoxicant, *American Journal of Psychiatry* (September 1945), **102**, 202–4; Sol Charen and Luis Perelman, Personality Studies of Marihuana Addicts, *American Journal of Psychiatry* (March 1946), **102**, 674–82.

2 This theoretical point of view stems from George Herbert Mead's discussion of objects in *Mind, Self, and Society* (University of Chicago Press 1934), 277–80.

3 Cf. Rogers Adams, Marihuana, *Bulletin of the New York Academy of Medicine* (November 1962), **18**, 705–30.

4 The New York City Mayor's Committee on Marihuana, *The Marihuana Problem in the City of New York* (Lancaster, Pennsylvania: Jacques Cattell Press 1944), 12–13.

5 Cf. Lawrence Kolb, Marihuana, *Federal Probation* (July 1938), **2**, 22–5; and Walter Bromberg, Marihuana: a psychiatric study, *Journal of the American Medical Association* (1 July 1939), **113**, 11.

6 The method is described in Alfred R. Lindesmith, *Opiate Addiction* (Bloomington, Indiana: Principia Press 1947), chap. 1. There has been considerable discussion of this method in the literature. See particularly, Ralph H. Turner, The Quest for Universals in Sociological Research, *American Sociological Review* (December 1953), **18**, 604–11, and the literature cited there.

7 I wish to thank Solomon Kobrin and Harold Finestone for making these interviews available to me.

8 A pharmacologist notes that this ritual is in fact an extremely efficient way of getting the drug into the blood stream. See R. P. Walton, *Marihuana; America's New Drug Problem* (Philadelphia: J. B. Lippincott 1938), 48.

9 'Smokers have repeatedly stated that the consumption of whiskey while smoking negates the potency of the drug. They find it very difficult to get "high" while drinking whiskey and because of that smokers will not drink while using the "weed".' (New York City Mayor's Committee on Marihuana, *The Marihuana Problem in the City of New York*, 13.)

10 Charen and Perelman, op. cit., 679.

22 Two types of streaming and their probable application in comprehensive schools

D. A. Young and W. Brandis

The comprehensive ideal embraces the desire to produce a citizenry able to meet on some common ground, despite differences in occupation. The hope is to provide many areas of shared educational experience, at the same time recognizing and providing for diversity, but valuing individual differences equally. Flexibility of organization is seen as a priority in order to be able to accommodate children who develop at different rates, and also to allow experiment and change.

Against this, the present system is seen as one which perpetuates social division, generates feelings of failure among many children, and elitist notions among others. It is castigated as being inflexible in organization and curriculum, and resistant to change.

Few of us would quarrel with the ideal. Such are the pressures on the comprehensive school, however, that we regard its accomplishment as unlikely.

The greatest source of pressure will be the level of academic attainment that it will be expected to meet. The evidence suggests that this will be at least as high as that required of grammar schools. This pressure will create problems which in their solution will create the conditions that will defeat the comprehensive ideal.

In January 1965 Pedley published in *The Observer* some figures showing the performance in both 'O' level and 'A' level of all LEAs, the fully comprehensive and the creamed comprehensive (those that had lost as many as five per cent of the most able pupils to local grammar schools). From his figures we derive the following:

For every 100 children entered for some 'O' levels by all LEAs, the fully comprehensive schools entered 121 (reasonable in view of the alleged wastage of talent that the present system allows, but still a higher level of attainment to be met). Surprisingly, however, the creamed comprehensive schools entered 172;

Source: University of London Institute of Education, *Bulletin* (new series) (August 1967), 11.

evidence of very great pressure. At 'A' level, for every 100 entered by all LEAs, the fully comprehensive entered 150, while the creamed comprehensive entered 115. This suggests that the fully comprehensive (the future pattern) is trying to meet a level of attainment even higher than present grammar schools.

We suggest that two major problems will arise out of trying to meet such a programme. The first problem will be that of having insufficient children disposed to pursue their studies up to these levels particularly up to 'A' level. The second will be that of having too few children with the obvious capacity to attain these academic standards.

The following diagram illustrates four possible positions in which a school might find itself:

Capacity and disposition of pupils in a particular school in relation to other schools

	Capacity +	
Dispo-sition to stop on at school	(2) High capacity Low disposition	High capacity (1) High disposition
−		+
	(4) Low capacity Low disposition	Low capacity (3) High disposition
	−	

A school in position 2 would have the problem of retaining its pupils; typically this would be a school with a large proportion of its pupils from the working class. A school in position 3 would have the problem of obtaining optimum performance from children who, on the evidence of intelligence tests, might not be expected to reach high levels of attainment. This would be the unusual case of a school with a large proportion of middle-class children, but with a relatively low over-all average IQ. Our argument is that because of the high level of academic attainment required of comprehensive schools, they will tend to be pushed into position 4, giving rise to both problems at once. In order to solve both these problems, the solutions devised by schools in positions 2 and 3 will have to be applied.

The questions to be answered are: in what ways do schools in positions 2 and 3 overcome their problems and with what consequences? If these questions can be answered, perhaps some tentative suggestions might be made as to the possible structure of comprehensive schools.

The answer is that both will stream[1] but on distinctly different principles leading to different consequences. Each school will try to derive maximum benefit from the positive characteristic of its children. (A good deal has been said about streaming as it applies to the purely technical aspects of teaching, but little or nothing has been said about streaming as a method of organizing a school to meet particular problems.)

We would expect the school with the problem of retention to stream on capacity. From the teacher's point of view, it might seem self-evident that the best thing to do in such circumstances is to get the brightest children together in one class and, within the limits of justice, concentrate on these children. But in doing so, something else happens, of which the teachers might not be aware. A system of prestige is created within the school with the children in the 'C' stream serving as a point of reference for the children in higher streams, particularly the 'A' stream. The child in the 'A' stream can compare his position favourably with the 'C' stream child; he is made aware that he has gifts which at present give him prestige, and in future will lead to superior occupational opportunity, if he will comply with the demands of the school. The important point is that his superior position and opportunity are mediated to him through the constant presence of the 'C' stream children. This serves to create a tension between the 'A' stream children and their wider environment which may be attracting them out of the school. The school has improved its competitive position by giving these children something to lose, which in turn acts as a lever to keep them in the school. The school has assigned success and failure, as distinct from its being achieved. Such a system does not require a child to be deeply involved in the school, to accept its value system, but rather invites him to use its instrumental facilities. In this way it does not insist on values that might be alien to the working-class child— its appeal is to the children's calculation, and as such, is acceptable to children from different backgrounds.

Since the streaming is based on intelligence, the differences in prestige of the streams does not carry with it any moral judgment. Intelligence is not of the child's own making. Thus the 'C' stream children are seen as unfortunate rather than culpable. The 'C' stream child is left with a defence; although failure has been thrust upon him, he does not have to accept it as personal. He can point to the fact that it was through no fault of his own; he is left with his anger intact.

In practice, this anger, plus the fact that they also realize the potential of education as a source of superior occupational reward, may well bring them back to the educational system through other institutions at a later stage. Although denied access to the higher ranges of educational attainment at school, they are not finally alienated from the educational system. But their temporary denial is necessary to make the school work at optimal levels.

The two most important consequences of the method of streaming described above are (1) failure is not personalized; and (2) if intelligence is not associated with social class the working-class child has as much chance of access to the higher streams as the middle-class child, and will experience the same success. The association between social class and educational attainment disappears in this type of school.

The second problem situation described, that of a school having children with a relatively low average IQ, requires a different solution. Again the solution will be to try to maximize the benefit to be gained from the positive characteristic of the children. Confronted with this situation, the teacher might feel that it was self-evident that the best thing to do was to get together the children showing a willingness to work hard and stay on at school. But again in creating these groups, an extra tension is produced which serves to produce optimum performance from the children. Here again it is a question of prestige, but this time based on recognition of worthiness, which is displayed by willingness to work consistently and enter into school life. But in this system the recognition can be withdrawn. The teachers retain the ability to promote and demote the children through the streams, and can create a tension within an individual class as well as that between streams. The 'A' stream is in what we might call, somewhat fancifully, a state of 'grace', and to remain in this condition requires a constant effort on the part of the child. The 'C' stream is in a state of disgrace, because that which is required of the child is assumed to be within his control: effort. The different streams are given different moral evaluations, and it is the 'C' stream child's fault that he finds himself in such a lowly position. Here a high level of involvement in the school's value system is demanded: the school is not merely an instrument to help obtain future occupational reward, it also insists on the intrinsic value of school life. We might say that in such a school the child has not only an academic career, but also a moral one, and the school insists that these are related.

The consequences of this kind of streaming are: (1) failure does tend to be personalized, the 'C' streamer having no ready defence; (2) it serves to alienate the working-class child, since it appeals to, and insists on, a middle-class value system. The working-class child, even if he finds himself in the 'A' stream, tends to do very badly when compared with middle-class levels of attainment. (3) Since intelligence is played down, it bears little relation to educational attainment (it is not associated with stream).

These are the two solutions adopted, and in practice they appear to work, giving both types of school highly respectable levels of academic attainment.

To return to the comprehensive school: on our argument they will often find themselves faced with both problems. Hence we might expect them to apply both solutions. The consequences of this will be that:

1 Low IQ and low moral evaluation will be confounded since the lower streams will not only contain children with relatively low IQ, but also those seen as making insufficient effort.

2 This will lead to the personalization of failure, which will fall on children with relatively low IQ (not the case in the grammar school described). This is not a situation that arises frequently in the present system, because segregation at 11+ leaves children going to the secondary modern school with a defence; puts them into a school that has a subculture which mediates to them realistic occupational and academic aspirations.[2] It also removes them from the visible presence of successful children, and protects them from being used as a lever to make the higher streams maintain a high level of industry.

3 Consequent on personalized failure and its visible nature, the school will lead to social divisions at least as great as at present, but now loaded with a moral tone. Children of low status will avoid contact with children of high status, particularly when they are being used as a lever to make the latter work. Comprehensive schools may well be aware of the problem and use many methods to camouflage the situation; e.g. horizontal settings across the school, other aggregates of children than those that attend lessons at a given academic level. But all sociological evidence suggests that the primary prestige hierarchy (the academic one, with its associations with future occupational placement) will intrude into them all and confound the purpose for which they were created. Aside from this, the 'horizontal settings' concept, with its view of many routes to many kinds of success, accepts the naïve view that there is 'rough justice in nature'—that all of us have a talent that compensates for deficiencies. But the evidence shows that talents are not only differentially evaluated, but also unevenly distributed. On the whole, 'horizontal settings' create further areas in which the academically successful can succeed, and the others can fail anew, leading to greater social division. This may well lead to greater delinquency since it increases frustration.

4 The position of the working-class child will be diminished. We have argued that streaming based on willingness to work and exhortation is alienative to the working-class child, but it also involves the possibility of re-evaluation leading to re-selection (indeed it is part of the claims of the comprehensive system that mobility is possible and will happen). The prediction is that working-class children will figure prominently among the demoted, while the middle-class children will be promoted much more often. So even if that aspect of streaming based on capacity puts a working-class child high in the streaming order, the second aspect of streaming may well lead to his falling down through the streams.

5 Since it is part of the comprehensive school ideology that the final selection process should be delayed as long as possible, a common curriculum (at different levels perhaps) will have to be maintained: the race for certification must be protracted. This means that options created by the 11+, which settled the broad lines of occupational destiny, to pursue different and relevant courses for those not going to grammar schools, will be finally lost. This is despite the fact that we know that these children will suffer unremedied deficiencies in a wider sense than the narrowly academic, running from inefficient use of the social services to impoverishment of their general social experience. The comprehensive school may protest that it is part of its philosophy to recognize diversity, but how can it be successful if it is using the low-status children as a lever, concentrating so much of its resources on formal academic success?

6 It will become more difficult to determine how much is spent on whom. At least we know that more is spent on the grammar school pupil—the accounts will be obscured in a comprehensive school.

7 The discussion centred on the means of allocation to occupational inequality will reduce attention to these inequalities. If they are unjust, not merely in terms of material reward, but intrinsic satisfactions, tinkering with the means to inequality is no remedy for inequality. What will happen is that the means will be given a *prima facie* rationality which will make it more difficult for the denied to complain. We must accept the point that the educational system can produce only minimal changes in the world of work, and that while it accepts the task of being a selection agency for occupation, it is crippled in its wider social functions.

8 While it is accepted that comprehensive schools may well raise the level of aspiration of their pupils, may be more productive of 'O' and 'A' levels, the concept of inflation applies equally to examination certificates as to money; the coinage will be debased.

To be fully realized, the comprehensive ideal requires an attenuation of the relationship between school career and occupational placement. It must free itself of its function as a selection agency for occupation. Only then can it succeed and avoid the destructive distortions described above. Unfortunately there seems to be little hope of this.

Notes

1 The theory contained in this paper has grown out of a study of grammar schools, but may be applied to wider contexts. The empirical basis was contained in papers delivered by Professor Hilde Himmelweit to the Eugenic Society in 1965 (to be published), and by D. A. Young, A theory of early leaving among grammar school boys, to the British Psychological Society in 1964.

2 How well this works depends on the degree to which the school resists the development of an aggressive 'A' stream policy of 'O' and 'A' level.

23 The social organization of the high school and deviant adolescent careers

Aaron V. Cicourel and John I. Kitsuse

Everett C. Hughes has suggested that a study of careers—'of the moving perspective in which persons orient themselves with reference to the social order, and of the typical sequences and concatenations of office—may be expected to reveal the nature and "working constitution" of society'.[1] Erving Goffman has applied this conception of career in his analysis of the status of the mental patient which examines the 'moral aspects of career—that is, the regular sequence of changes that career entails in the person's self and in his framework of imagery for judging himself and others'.[2] Our usage of the concept of career follows Hughes's lead by focusing on the 'working constitution' of social organizations and, like Goffman, we shall direct our attention to the day-to-day interaction between adolescents and others in several organizational settings. We shall not, however, be concerned with the consequences of these interactions for the adolescent's self-concept. Rather, we are concerned with the consequences of the daily activities of the organizational personnel for the differentiation of the adolescent population within a given social organization, namely the high school.[3] A central problem here is that of identifying the environment of verbal and nonverbal objects to which such personnel attend and orient their actions.

The conception of adolescent careers as a product of organizational activities refers to decisions that lead to a student's transfer from one high school status to any other within the system. We have applied this conception in two empirical studies, directing investigation to the various ways students come into routine and special contact with school personnel, the basis for singling students out for such contacts, the organizationally structured situations in which such decisions were made, and the organizationally defined

actions which follow such decisions *vis-à-vis* adolescents so classified.[4] The gathering of these data was directed by an understanding of the personnel's conceptions for dealing with adolescents in the routine activities of the organization, and their use of the 'vocabulary and syntax of everyday language'.[5]

The descriptions of the 'vocabulary and syntax' employed by the school personnel, parents, the police, and peer groups identify the variety of social types which are recognized as significant within the different organizations. In Schutz's terms, the social types are the common sense constructs employed by persons in everyday life to interpret and classify adolescent behavior. The consequences of the actions oriented by the application of the social types produce what we have called 'adolescent careers'. Thus, 'adolescent career' is a 'construct of the second degree' and may be defined as the product of the social typing, classifying and processing of adolescents by the personnel of any social organization or set of organizations.

The focus upon the processing of deviants by social agencies distinguishes the present approach to the study of deviance from those which attempt to explain rates of deviant behavior by investigating the motivational 'sources' of deviant behavior, whether they are conceived to be psychological or social structural in origin. From the view of deviance followed here, the motivational processes which presumably lead to deviant behavior are conceptually independent of the social processes by which the members of the social organization *impute* motives and perceive regularities in their construction of the deviant, the grounds for such decisions, and the subsequent treatment of persons so defined.

The first task of the sociologist is to provide for the range of adolescent behaviors observed and interpreted by the personnel of the school and other organizations, and the social processes whereby adolescents come to be defined and classified as social types. The second task is to determine the consequences of such processes

Source: *Deviance: The Interactionist Perspective*, ed. Earl Rubington and Martin Weinberg, New York: Macmillan (1968), 124–35.

for any given adolescent's career within the specified organizations.

The school system may be conceived as an organization which produces, in the course of its activities, a variety of adolescent careers including the delinquent. Because the school occupies a strategic position as a coordinating agency between the activities of the family, the police, and the peer group *vis-à-vis* adolescents, it also provides a 'clearing house' which receives and releases information from and to other agencies concerning adolescents. In the following discussion of the school system as an institutionalized differentiator of adolescent careers, we suggest how the interpretations and actions of parents, police and peer group may affect the activation, maintenance and alteration of various careers within the high school.

The organizational structure of the school and its activities create a variety of 'adolescent problems' which are identified in the vocabulary and syntax of its personnel. The 'problems' may be grouped under three rough headings: Those pertaining to (1) the students' academic activities, (2) student infractions of rules of conduct and (3) the emotional problems of students. School personnel frequently refer to those they consider 'academic problems' as 'over-achievers', 'under-achievers', 'normal-achievers' and 'opportunity students'. Among the labels applied to students in the second category are 'trouble-makers', 'hoods' and 'delinquents'. In the third category are students who are considered 'nervous', 'withdrawn and unsocial' and 'isolates'.[6] The reader should note that any given student may be the object of several social type designations by the same teacher, by different teachers or by other students. Consequently, it is possible for a student to have several careers concurrently or consecutively within the high school organization.

The typing of students in the three problem areas provides the bases for a variety of careers. Any one of these careers may begin even prior to the student's enrollment in the school. For example, in the highly bureaucratized urban school system, the student's transfer to the high school may be preceded by a biography of records and comments documenting his social as well as academic performance in the elementary and junior high school. A review of such biographies by the admissions personnel of the high school results in a student being typed as an 'academic problem', for example, and thus initiates a career of the 'academic failure', 'drop-out', 'slow-learner' etc.

Academic careers

The social typing of the adolescent *vis-à-vis* his career within the high school often is based on the student's prior biography and the tests administered to the new cohort of freshmen. Students are usually given preliminary counseling on the basis of some personnel's interpretations of the test results and other information, frequently while those students are still in the junior high school. These initial organizational activities may result in the following classification of students: (1) The student may be defined as an 'underachiever' if his test scores are considered higher than his prior achievement measured by course grades. (2) Conversely, if the student is achieving higher than the 'ability' his test scores indicate, he may be labeled an 'over-achiever'. (3) The student may be classified as an 'opportunity student' if his record in class and on the entrance tests is consistently poor. (4) The student may be labeled a 'normal-achiever'.[7]

Concomitant with the social typing with reference to 'academic problems' is the classification of students as 'college', 'vocational' or 'business-secretarial' (often designated 'commercial') on the basis of their declared choice of curricula. The declaration of this choice may be the outcome of the student's interaction with his parents, with whom he is instructed by the school personnel to consult regarding the decision, and his peers. In the middle and upper-middle income groups, parents, peers, and the student himself frequently assume that college follows high school as a matter of course. It is important to bear in mind, however, that from an organizational point of view, the differentiation of students in this regard is not decided solely by criteria internal to the high school system (e.g. by achievement scores) but is also affected by considerations which may be independent of those which the personnel might consider relevant. For example, parents may insist that their child be placed in an academic program regardless of his prior academic record. Thus, in principle, a student has the right, on the approval of his parents, to choose between the curricula, a right which he, however, may not know he has.

Even where the right is invoked, the classification of the student as an 'academic problem' by the school personnel may have major consequences for the organizational processing of his declared choice of curriculum. If an 'under-achiever', 'over-achiever' or an 'opportunity student' declares his decision to follow a college-preparatory curriculum, the counselor may decide that he is 'not college material' or 'not adequately motivated' and thus unlikely to successfully complete such a curriculum. In such circumstances, the counselor frequently attempts to persuade the student or his parents to change to the vocational curriculum, or he may refuse to allow the student to enroll in certain elective courses because the courses may be considered 'too difficult' for him. On the other hand, a student whose test results and class performance are consistently high but who declares the choice of a non-college curriculum, may be counseled into the college-preparatory courses in case he should change his mind. Our study of the high school suggests, however, that school personnel are more likely to view middle and upper income adolescents as 'natural' college prospects than lower income students with comparable academic records.[8]

Such counseling activity may have consequences for the student's family relations as well as those with his peers. When parents are informed of the counselor's advice, either directly by the school or via the student, they may request a conference. In such conferences, parents are advised of their child's performance on achievement tests, the ability group in which he will be placed, and the possible difficulties he may encounter in gaining admission to certain colleges. The counselor may indirectly suggest that the parent's aspiration for the child is 'unrealistic' and that his ability is not as great as they may have assumed.

Counseled in this manner, the parents may now be able to 'see' that their child has 'bad study habits', 'he fools around too much', 'he hangs around with the wrong crowd' etc. These retrospective interpretations[9] of their child's behavior and activities may be revealed to school personnel along with additional information that 'we've had some problems at home' or that 'he has had difficulties' in the past and thus add support to the school's interpretation of his 'problem'. Other parental responses to the interview may take the form of requests that the school 'put the pressure on him', give him counseling, find him a tutor, 'let us know if there's anything we can do'. Organizationally the variety of parental response may lead to the typing of students as 'over-anxious', 'behavior problem', 'rebellious', 'ambitious parents', etc.

While the counselor's activities are 'officially' advisory in nature, the career consequences of his advice vary with the organizationally defined position of counselors within the school system. In schools where the 'search for talent' has stimulated and intensified counseling services, counselors are authorized and in some instances prescribed to control the student's access to alternative courses of action. A student whose record is interpreted by the counselor to indicate low ability but who nevertheless insists on following a college-preparatory curriculum may be assigned by the counselor to courses which do not carry college entrance credit. The consequences of such counselor action often do not become apparent to the student or his parents until he makes application for admission to a college when he is a senior in high school.

The differentiation of students which results from their declaration of curriculum choice has organizational consequences other than those which affect his academic career. One of these is that his declaration reduces the probable as well as possible interaction between him and his peers who have elected other curricula. Aside from factors such as differences in interests or socio-economic backgrounds which operate to reduce the interaction between students enrolled in different curricula, the curricula establish routines which separate students ecologically and socially. College preparatory students are enrolled in different courses than their non-college peers, their classrooms are frequently located at opposite ends of the school buildings, their curricula demand different kinds and amounts of study at school as well as at home.

Further, the college/non-college differentiation is reflected in the membership of school-sponsored student organizations such as the honor society, language, science, home-making, auto and other course-related clubs.

The differentiations of students in these respects are not merely differences but they are evaluated as socially, culturally, as well as academically significant differences by school personnel. The differential valuation given by school personnel to the college and non-college preparatory curricula is a familiar 'problem' in educational philosophy and administration, and one which has been intensified by the 'search for talent'. The differential valuation is reflected not only in the status hierarchy of teachers (e.g. language and math instructors rank those who teach industrial and home-making courses), but also in the distinctions implicit in the teachers' conceptions of college and non-college preparatory students and their activities. The 'brighter', 'more ambitious' students from 'better family backgrounds' are enrolled in the college preparatory courses, they belong to the 'better groups', and they are engaged in more 'worthwhile' activities during and after school hours.

In middle-income urban and suburban communities where parents are strongly oriented to sending their children to college, college preparatory students receive intensive attention from school personnel in the form of counseling them about 'academic' and 'emotional' problems so as to salvage and develop their talent, i.e. get them into colleges. Thus, the occasions and frequency of interaction between college preparatory students and school personnel may have a significant effect upon the differentiation of their academic as well as other careers from those of the non-college preparatory students within the high school.

Academic careers are continually subject to change as a consequence of the routine review of the student's performance, conducted in most schools after each marking period, and especially after the recording of the final grade for a given semester. On these occasions the student's performance is compared with his tested ability, and marked discrepancies between the two may lead to a re-classification of students with preference to 'academic problems'. This review may verify the fact that 'over-achievers' are now performing more nearly up to their ability, or that 'normal-achievers' should be re-classified as 'under-achievers', etc.[10]

A student's academic career may also be altered by communications to school personnel from parents or from his peers. A parent may call one of the student's teachers to find out why no homework is assigned, and the teacher may check and find that the student's homework has been copied from one of his friends. This may in turn lead to the referral of the student to the principal's office for disciplinary action or to the counselor as an 'emotional problem'. A friend may report to a teacher or counselor that a student is 'real worried' about passing a course. If such a student has been typed previously as an 'over-achiever', he may be referred to the counselor, or the teacher may consult his superior about transferring the student to a 'less competitive' section. Similarly, the police or juvenile authorities may inform the school about a student's delinquent activities which can lead to changes in his academic status even in the absence of any prior academic difficulties.

Such routine and 'special' reviews of the student's performance are the occasions for classifying, confirming, and changing the academic status of students. We do not here impute malevolence or 'discrimination' to the actions of counselors, teachers, and other school personnel, for their activities may open as well as close future alternatives for students. The importance of investigating the consequences of the counseling system for the social typing of students which alter their careers is to be found in the counselor's and teachers' conceptions of what constitutes 'improvement', 'satisfactory performance', 'predictable failure', etc. These are sources of data for the investigation of how rates of college-going students, failures, drop-outs, etc. are organizationally produced.

'Delinquent' careers

The social typing of students with reference to infractions of conduct rules may launch students on 'delinquent' careers within the high school. Like academic careers, a review of the student's folder or biographical materials received from the junior high school, may lead admissions personnel to alert teachers, counselors and administrators to his history of 'difficulties'. The labeling of the student as a 'trouble maker', 'truant', 'fresh', etc. may provide the occasion for singling him out for special handling and treatment. For example, he may be more closely supervised, his academic progress more frequently reviewed, his parents requested to come in for conferences, counseling advised, etc. Thus, the student's cumulative folder and the interpretations and actions which may follow from it are important sources of data for the investigation of delinquent as well as academic careers.

Another context of organizational activity which may be consequential for the classification of a student as a 'conduct problem' is in the classroom where his behavior may be interpreted by the teacher as 'disruptive' and lead her to refer him to the counselor, principal or some other administrator. Official as well as 'unofficial' records of such actions leave their organizational traces and subsequent 'difficulties' with the student may be interpreted in the light of his organizational history. The student may be disciplined for behavior (or even imputed attitudes) that is overlooked or unnoticed among 'good' students, and he may be denied opportunities to participate in extracurricular athletics, student government activities, school-sponsored recreational programs, etc.

The school personnel's conceptions of the 'good' student are particularly relevant for an investigation of the social processes by which adolescents are typed as 'conduct problems'. Such conceptions may be so general that the adolescent's posture, walk, cut of hair, clothes, use of slang, manner of speech—or indeed, almost any aspect of the so-called 'adolescent behavior'—may be the basis for the typing of the student as a 'conduct problem'. The stylizations of such behaviors are often the characteristics which distinguish peer groups of different socioeconomic backgrounds, interests, academic orientations, etc. and as a consequence, the student's association with peers considered by school personnel to be 'rowdies', 'serious students', or 'active in school activities' may implicitly be taken as indicative of the type of student he is.[11]

Thus, peer group activities and the variety of types which are differentiated by them may have important career-defining consequences. The emphasis on 'peer group adjustment' and the conception of the 'well-rounded student', which has been promoted virtually as an educational principle in high schools, have made teachers, counselors, and other school personnel aware of and attentive to the variety of social type distinctions made by adolescents themselves. Students may characterize groups as well as individuals as 'square' or 'jock', 'brain', 'hippy', 'acid heads', 'hoody', etc. The evaluation and ranking of such individuals and groups among and between school personnel and adolescents may in some instances concur, in others be quite discrepant. Thus, the 'squares' or 'brains' may be considered 'nice' students by school personnel, but 'jerks' by some student groups; 'jocks' may be held in high esteem by some students and personnel for their athletic ability, but ignored or deprecated by others. The alignments and realignments of peer groups, and the inclusion and exclusion of students in their activities, may therefore become the occasion for parent-school communications, initiating counseling activity, instituting programs of closer supervision, transfer of students from one section to another, etc.

Delinquent careers are particularly sensitive to information from outside as well as from within the system. School attendance being compulsory in most states until the age of sixteen, the adolescent's school affiliation is (together with the family) one of the first institutions to which his conduct or misconduct is referred. Thus, the school is the agency to which the police, shopkeepers, civic organizations, welfare agencies, as well as parents go with their reports (if not complaints) concerning the actual or suspected delinquency of students.

The consequences for the school of variously delinquent students, whether or not these delinquencies occur within the school, are primarily organizational in contrast to the family's legal responsibility. Delinquent students are viewed by school personnel as 'disruptive', 'harmful influences' and bad for the 'reputation' of the school. This is particularly true when students are 'officially' defined and publicized as delinquent by police action. Thus, contacts between the police and adolescents, and the police-school communication which may follow from them, have major significance for the adolescent's career as a delinquent within the school system. When students are particularly troublesome in their misconduct, the school will often initiate police contacts to rid the organization of 'trouble-makers' despite a lack of legal violations.

Contacts between the police and adolescents may, of course, occur in a variety of situations and circumstances. The police may act on their own observations of the adolescent's behavior, on complaint from members of the community, on the request from an adolescent's parents, the school, or other social agencies. Police may classify adolescents with whom they come into contact as being of two general types: those whom they consider 'good kids' who rarely cause any trouble, and the 'trouble-makers' who constitute the bulk of their contacts with adolescents. Among the 'good kids' the police may differentiate between the 'quiet, studious kids who never cause any trouble' and those who might be referred to as 'good kids who cut up a little and need to be warned'. The police also distinguish between two types of 'trouble-makers': those referred to as 'wild kids who need a good kick in the ass' and those considered 'real no-good punks' headed for criminal careers.

The conceptions held by the police concerning adolescents may be critical for their interpretations and processing of cases which come to their attention. With reference to a given complaint or observation of adolescent behavior, the police officer's conception of the youth as a 'good kid' may lead him to define the behavior as a 'prank' attributable to 'letting off steam', 'spring fever', 'high spirits', etc. The adolescent may be dismissed with a strong warning which the officer does not record. Assuming that there is a 'reasonable' time lapse, from the officer's point of view, between the incident and any other similar event involving this adolescent, the police contact may be 'lost', organizationally speaking. On the other hand, should the police view the youth as a 'no-good punk', the adolescent may be processed and thus become an official case subject to various (usually negative) interpretations when he is in 'trouble' again.

Many aspects of police activities *vis-à-vis* adolescents may never affect the career-defining processes of the school system.[12] The contingencies of police-school contacts, however, vary with the policies and practices of police departments in this regard. In large cities, the police may assemble biographies on students containing records of traffic tickets issued to 'hot-rodders', warnings for curfew violations, boisterous conduct at drive-in theaters or malt shops, etc., which may not come to the attention of school authorities. But a court hearing usually leads to a probation department report containing a school evaluation. The referral of a student by the school to the police for action, or

inquiries to the school by the police in their investigation of a student's activities, may be the occasion for an exchange of information leading to the development of a new career for the student within the high school. For example, a student who, until that time, had been considered 'loud' or 'sullen' may now be typed as a 'trouble-maker', 'anti-social', 'delinquent', etc.

The organization of inter-agency communication is therefore a major source of data for the study of adolescent careers. In smaller towns and suburban communities, police may routinely contact the school for information concerning adolescents who come to their attention. In the more specialized police systems, trained juvenile officers have been added to the staff, and their activities lead to an increasing coordination of the records compiled by the school and other community agencies. A development in the coordination of police and school records is the addition to the school personnel of a 'security officer' (often a person with some previous experience in police work) to handle problems of traffic and parking violations, infractions of curfew, smoking, and other school rules. Where such personnel are employed, liaison between the school and police may be routinized through the 'security officer'. To the degree that information concerning students defined as 'delinquents' of various types, either by the police or school personnel, is routinely exchanged between the two organizations, the interpretations and actions of one agency can have important consequences for the adolescent's career in both systems.

The organizational actions which chart the course of delinquent careers may have consequences beyond the student's participation in the school system. Should he seek part-time employment after school hours, apply for a job or military service upon leaving the school, the student's record may be used as the basis for unfavorable or qualified letters of recommendation to prospective employers. The student's record may be reviewed when police direct inquiries to the school about some 'delinquent' action or his family or peer group may learn about his record when school personnel contact them in the course of investigating cases of stealing, fighting, smoking, vandalism, etc.

The consequences of social typing for differential interpretation and treatment of the behavior of individuals so typed are commonplace and quite obvious. What is not so obvious, and the central concern of this paper, are the interpretative rules utilized by the organizational personnel who decide what forms of behavior and what kinds of evidence warrant actions which define individuals as deviant within the system. Our description of the organizational actions that may lead to various careers, delinquent and others, is not intended to take issue with the justification of such actions or the bases on which they are taken. The point we are making is theoretical and methodological: In any investigation of how 'deviant' and 'non-deviant' populations are differentiated within a system, the rules of interpretation employed for evaluating the behavioral elements observed and classified in the day-to-day activities of the personnel must systematically be taken into account.

'Clinical' careers

The personnel available to many high schools include clinically trained persons such as psychiatrists, psychiatric social workers, and clinical psychologists whose primary responsibility is the handling of students who are considered 'emotionally disturbed' by teachers, parents, counselors, and others. In such schools, parents and often students are informed of the availability of clinical services as part of their orientation to the high school. Referral to the clinical service is the organizational basis for the activation of clinical careers.

A student may come to the attention of clinical personnel in several ways: (1) The student may have been an 'emotional case' in the junior high school, and a recommendation for further treatment may accompany his biographical records to the high school. (2) The fact that a student is undergoing privately financed treatment by a psychiatrist may be communicated to the high school by his therapist or parents. (3) In schools where all students are assigned a counselor, the counselor's routine contacts with his counselees may be the occasion for a referral to clinical personnel. (4) A student's behavior may be viewed as 'strange' by teachers in the classroom or on school grounds, by custodial and administrative staff or by other students, any one of whom may initiate the referral process. (5) The student's behavior at home or within the community (e.g. delinquent acts) may lead his parents and the personnel of other agencies to seek information or advice from school clinicians.

The organizational processing of students who are defined as 'emotionally disturbed' is likely to be more problematic than in the case of the 'academic' or 'conduct' problems for several reasons. Unlike the classification of the student as an 'academic problem', there is relatively little organizational control over the competence of the person who reports the behavior which is the occasion for initiating the process of classifying a student as 'emotionally disturbed'. Almost any person within the school as well as outside of it may report that a student has been observed behaving in a 'strange', 'bizarre' or 'crazy' manner. Since the common sense interpretation of such behavior is relative to the observer, there may be considerable disagreement as to the 'objectivity' of the observer. Here the classification of the student as 'emotionally disturbed' is similar to the 'conduct problem'.

Unlike the 'conduct problem', however, the organizational processing of students whose behaviors are reported to be 'strange' in various ways has become professionalized by the activities of counselors, clinical psychologists, psychiatrists and psychiatric social workers. The professional training and theoretical orientation of such personnel may be critical for determining the classification of the student as a 'clinical' case. A psychiatrist or social worker, for example, may interpret the reported behavior and the preliminary interview with the student as indicative of 'deep-seated problems', with the implication that he is 'sick' and in need of 'professional help'. On the other hand, a part-time teacher-counselor may interpret the 'same facts' as a 'situation problem' or as no problem at all.[13]

When such cases come to the attention of counseling personnel, parents may be routinely advised of their child's 'difficulties' and a conference suggested. Parental response to such a communication may be critical for the student's career as a 'clinical case'. If we assume that the parents' conceptions of their child are based on his performance at home, the routine accommodations within the family of a wide variety of behavior may insulate the parents from definitions of those behaviors as 'strange', 'peculiar', 'immature', etc. In the absence of intrusive communications from extra-familial sources such as neighbors, the police, school authorities, and welfare agencies, parental interpretations of their child's behavior as a 'problem'—emotional delinquent, or whatever—may be vague or non-existent. Thus, when parents are advised of their child's 'difficulties' they may be surprised as well as resentful, hostile, and often belligerent towards the communicating agency's suggestion that he is in need of psychotherapeutic treatment. In the face of such 'resistance' parents may be informed that referral of the child to some other agency, e.g. the juvenile courts, may be necessary in order to obtain parental agreement to the counselor's recommendations.

'Family co-operation' is particularly important for the school when a student has been organizationally defined as a 'clinical' case. Since the 'difficulty' in question may include reports of such behaviors as hysterical weeping, sexual exhibition, use of marihuana or LSD, verbal and physical abuse of school personnel, and the like, the content of the communication itself creates a 'touchy' problem in parent-school relations. The current psychological interpretations of such behaviors, furthermore, implicitly if not explicitly attribute major significance to early socialization or 'the family situation'. Although middle-income parents may be more receptive to such interpretations and their implications for the importance of 'family co-operation', the parental response of rejecting them as 'nonsense' may be quite frequent, or the parents may ignore the communications altogether. Since parental consent is required in most schools for referring students to psychiatrists or social workers for intensive or 'deep' therapy, their rejection of such recommendations precludes the school from officially 'treating' the student as a 'clinical' case. He may, nevertheless, be classified and recorded officially as a 'behavior' or 'conduct' problem and assigned to a counselor for more 'superficial' counseling for which parental consent may not be required.

The processing of any given type of deviant within an organization may be modified at any point by such factors as parental response to organizational definitions, introduction of information from outside agencies, review of prior records, etc. Empirical investigation of the above remarks must establish the behavioral environment within which exchanges between organizational personnel and adolescents take place in order to pinpoint the verbal and non-verbal properties by which organizational conceptions are initiated or changed *vis-à-vis* the generation of deviant categories.

Notes

1 E. C. Hughes, Institutional office and the person, *American Journal of Sociology* (November 1937), **43**, 404–13.

2 E. Goffman, The moral career of the mental patient, *Psychiatry* (May 1959), **22**, 123. Although Goffman proposes to move back and forth between the patient's conceptions of his self and those of others in the institutional environment, he does not present a conceptually clear way of handling the problem of systematically investigating the socially organized character of the conceptions that 'others' have of the mental patient. Clarity in the conceptual formulation of this problem is critical if the organizational features of career-defining interactions are to be distinguished from the variety of inter-personal transactions that the mental patient (or, in the context of the present discussion, the adolescent) encounters in everyday life.

3 A study of patient selection in a psychiatric out-patient clinic by Garfinkel deals explicitly with the social processes by which a population is differentiated within a social organization. The study is concerned with the socially organized and socially controlled ways in which a patient's transfer from one clinic status to a succeeding one is achieved by the decisions of patients and clinic personnel and thus affect the features of patient load and flow. The study provides a method for investigating the processes by which different rates of deviance are produced in an organizational setting. See *Studies in Ethnomethodology* (Prentice-Hall 1967). See also A. V. Cicourel, *The Social Organization of Juvenile Justice* (Wiley 1968).

4 Cf. A. V. Cicourel and J. I. Kitsuse, *The Educational Decision-Makers*, Indianapolis: Bobbs-Merrill, 1963.

5 A. Schutz, *Collected Papers, I; The Problem of Social Reality* (The Hague: Martinus Nijhoff 1962), 3–47.

6 The reader will note that we have ignored the social type identified by 'good student' or 'nice kid' who might be considered by the school personnel to have 'no problems'. The 'normal' adolescent would presumably be included in such a category. Our exclusion of this type of student follows from the present formulation which suggests that the so-called 'normal' adolescent would be a rare case. We shall attempt to explicate this position in the following discussion of the organizational differentiation of the student population. We do not deny, however, the theoretical and empirical relevance of the 'normal' adolescent, for any study of the processes of organizational differentiation would have to address the question of who is considered 'normal' and the extent to which such individuals are behaviorally different from those labeled variously deviant.

7 In so far as school personnel document 'academic problems' by the discrepancy between some presumed 'objective' measure(s) of the student's ability and his level of performance as indicated by course grades, the process by which the latter are assigned becomes a major contingency in the classification of students as 'problems'. In this connection, a recent study by William Chambliss suggests that teachers accommodate a student's poor performance when he is viewed as a 'right type' of student. See W. J. Chambliss, Two gangs: a study of societal responses to deviance and deviant careers, unpublished manuscript.

8 See A. V. Cicourel and J. I. Kitsuse, op. cit.

9 The notion of 'retrospective interpretations' is adapted from Karl Mannheim's discussion of the 'documentary method'. See On the interpretation of Weltanschauung, in *Essays on the Sociology of Knowledge*, trans. and ed. by P. Kecskemeti (New York: Oxford University Press 1952), 53–63. See also Garfinkel's discussion of the documentary method in *Studies in Ethnomethodology*.

10 On such occasions considerations such as the student's socio-economic status, his ethnic status and his reputation as a 'trouble-maker' can enter the decision-making definitions of academic careers.

11 The significance of deference, demeanor, and appearance in the processing of juvenile offenders is discussed in Irving Piliavin and Scott Briar, Police encounters with juveniles, *American Journal of Sociology* (Sept. 1964), **70**, 206–14.

12 The way in which the youth is processed through juvenile court can be independent of what has transpired prior to his appearance before this agency. Other personnel introduced into the situation such as social workers, judges, psychiatrists, psychologists, and the like, may interpret the youth's behaviour quite differently from those who have activated the career-defining process. See P. W. Tappan, *Juvenile Delinquency* (McGraw-Hill 1949), chs 8–15. A juvenile court judge may, on the counsel of a psychologist, psychiatrist, or social worker, dispose of a case in a manner which negates all previous interpretations of the youth's behavior. Thus, the differential conceptions held by the police, social workers, psychiatrists, judges, and so on, may lead to a re-definition of a youth as 'disturbed' rather than 'wild' or 'insecure' and 'in need of love' rather than vigorous discipline and 'a kick where it hurts'. *The behavioral content of a youth's activities, therefore, may not be as critical in such cases as the interpretations which are placed upon it by others*. It is necessary, however, to go beyond this formulation and attempt to specify the behavioral regularities which are identified as relevant by personnel who have day-to-day contact with adolescents.

13 The current trend toward psychological interpretations of adolescent 'problems' of which the organizational

provision for clinical services is one reflection, has given impetus to the view among some high school personnel that academic, conduct, and other problems are all reducible to 'emotional difficulties'. For example, an 'under-achiever' might be interpreted by the clinician to be an expression of the student's reaction to 'parental conflicts', a 'hood' is rebelling against the authority of the school, etc. From an organizational point of view, it is important to investigate whether and how the differentiation of the several problem areas are maintained within the same system. Cf. *The Educational Decision-Makers*, ch. 4.

24 Ritual in education

Basil Bernstein, H. L. Elvin and R. S. Peters

Ritual in animals generally refers to a rigid pattern of motor acts which function as signals controlling behaviour between animals in specific situations. Ritual in humans generally refers to a relatively rigid pattern of acts specific to a situation which construct a framework of meaning over and beyond the specific situational meanings. Here, the symbolic function of ritual is to relate the individual through ritualistic acts to a social order, to heighten respect for that order, to revivify that order within the individual and, in particular, to deepen acceptance of the procedures used to maintain continuity, order and boundary and which control ambivalence towards the social order.

Ritual will be considered as an expression in action as distinct from thought of man's active attitudes towards these non-empirical aspects of their reality, which are expressive of ultimate values.

First, we shall examine these notions as they relate to a school as a social form and, secondly, we shall examine the effect of changes in the function of the school on ritualizing processes.

The school as a social form

A school can be considered to transmit two cultures: an instrumental one and an expressive one. The instrumental culture consists of those activities, procedures and judgments involved in the acquisition of specific skills, especially those that are *vocationally* important.

The expressive culture consists of those activities, procedures and judgments involved in the transmission of values and their derived norms. We are talking about an expressive culture when we make pronouncements about the aims of education, for example.

The expressive culture of the school can be considered as the source of its shared values and is therefore cohesive in function; whilst the instrumental culture is potentially divisive. It is the expressive culture which is the major mechanism of social consensus and thus prone to ritualization.

These rituals may be divided into two main groups: consensual and differentiating.

Consensual rituals

These are the rituals which function so as to bind together all members of the school, staff and pupils as a moral community, as a distinct collectivity. These consensual rituals give the school continuity in time and place. They recreate the past in the present and project it into the future. These rituals also relate the school's values and norms to those held by, or alleged to be held by, certain dominant groups in the non-school society. The consensual rituals give the school its specific identity as a distinct and separate institution. They facilitate appropriate sentiments towards the dominant value system of the wider society. They assist in the integration of the various goals of the school within a coherent set of shared values, so that the values of the school can become internalized and experienced as a unity. In general the consensual rituals consist of assemblies and ceremonies of various kinds together with the consensual linements of dress, the imagery of signs, totems, scrolls and plaques for the revivifying of special historical contexts and other symbolic features. An important component of the consensual rituals is the rituals of punishment and reward.

Differentiating rituals

These are concerned to mark off groups within the school from each other, usually in terms of age, sex, age relation or social function. The differentiating rituals deepen local attachment behaviour to, and detachment behaviour from, specific groups; they also deepen respect behaviour to those in various positions of authority, and create order in time.

Source: *Philosophical Transactions of the Royal Society of London* B (1966), *251* (772), 429–36.

These two main types of rituals are major mechanisms for the internalizing and revivifying of social order. They function to maintain continuity, order, boundary and the control of dual loyalties and ambivalence. The rituals control questioning of the basis of the expressive culture and so are conditions for its effective transmission and reception. They buttress the formal authority relations and evoke respect through the ritualization of difference and similarity of function; they create continuity in individual and social time and relate the value system and its derived norms to an approved external order.

To give an illustration: the school is a community related to, but different from, kin and local community. It is a stage in the emancipation of the pupil towards his acceptance of a wider referent group. Problems of divided allegiance and relation on the part of pupil, kin and school are partly solved by ritualizing, so sharpening the boundaries between the different groups. The consensual rituals and their inductive subsets facilitate detachment behaviour from family and local community and attachment behaviour to the school. For parents these rituals transform the child into pupil. The consensual rituals of the school orient the pupil to special classes of behaviour and give him a specific consciousness of age, sex, school and kinship status. The separation of statuses—for example, in possessing a distinct school and family status—increases the degree of control the school can exert on both the pupil and the kin.

Within the school the problem of ordering, integrating and controlling the heterogeneous population is assisted by the differentiating rituals and their initiating or inducting subsets. There are at least four types of such differentiating rituals.

(1) *Age differentiating rituals*. These help to differentiate groups in time by marking out age status as of special significance. The age rituals often function as *rites de passage*. They may become sources of conflict where such *rites de passage* have been weakened in the non-school society. The age rituals often reinforce the class as the basic unit of social organization and in this way serve to regulate local attachment behaviour to persons, territory and property. They also serve to impersonalize the relations between different age groups, controlling and focusing clashes or crushes.

(2) *Age relation rituals*. These are essentially concerned with authority relations. Often the age groups are marked off from each other in terms of different approach behaviour to those in formal authority. A cluster of rituals normally group round the prefect system, marking it off as a separate system of social control. These rituals serve to increase distance and thus boundary between unequals. They strengthen commitment to basic values and control feelings of ambivalence and dual allegiance.

(3) *Sex rituals*. These are consensual in single sex schools but differentiating as far as the non-school society is concerned. Conceptions of the masculine are celebrated by such rituals. They cohere round sporting activities but may appear as approach behaviour to female members of staff or to visitors. In dual sex schools they become differentiating rituals reinforcing sex typing. In boys' schools and particularly in girls' schools, these rituals may also control sexual display behaviour. However, it is as well to remember that the black stockings of the 30s have become signs of sexual display in the 60s.

(4) *House rituals*. These are the rituals which delineate fictional communities within the school, and each community has its own set of consensual and differentiating rituals together with their inductive subsets. The whole is supported by the lineaments of dress, the imagery of signs, totems, the associations and sentiments invoked by scrolls, plaques, chants, etc.

One further point should perhaps be made. Cognitive difference between boys, as this finds expression in ability, is often transformed into a component of consensual ritual if it is related to the school, or into a component of the differentiating ritual if it is related to a particular class. Sporting prowess is similarly transformed. The consensual and differentiating rituals then function to assist in the creation of a unique identity for the school, in defining and regulating boundary behaviour, continuity, and order, and in controlling ambivalence and dual allegiances. These rituals both facilitate the transmission, reception and internalization of the values of the expressive culture and relate these usually to an approved value system outside of the school. The rituals also serve to prevent questioning of the values and of the social order which transmits them.

So far then we have been considering not what necessarily exists, for schools vary in the degree to which the expressive culture is ritualized, but the critical points of ritualization. The more a school resembles a total institution (that is where the life of the pupil is almost wholly spent in the school as in a boarding school) the greater the ritualizing of its expressive culture. It is also likely that day schools in countries with a single, explicit political or religious ideology are likely to display extensive ritualization, especially schools in those countries which are currently undergoing, or have recently undergone, rapid technological change. In this case ritualization within the school is a major means through which such single ideologies are transmitted and social cohesion maintained under conditions of rapid social change. The school itself symbolizes and celebrates the social order to come.

Industrialization and responsiveness to ritual in schools

In advanced industrialized societies the social purpose of the school becomes one of educating for diversity in social and economic function. In this situation it is worthwhile examining the forces which may have critical consequences for the pupil's responsiveness to consensual and differentiating rituals. We are thinking here particularly of the situation in Britain.

(1) Differentiating rituals

In the school these rituals tend to mark out specific groups in terms of age, sex, age relations, and house. The latter may perhaps be regarded as the school equivalent of community. The process of industrialization reduces the significance of the family as a determiner of occupational status. It affects age relations (authority relations) by dissolving customary boundaries, mutual spheres of freedom and control, and renders more implicit and informal the transfer of adult responsibilities to the young, so that effective regulation of the young becomes problematic. Moreover, family rituals, which mark out as of special social significance changes in age status, weaken. In fact, age as a social status comes to have an important achieved element. Early adolescents, by various accessories (cosmetics and dress) present themselves as middle adolescents in order to achieve youth group identity, whilst fifty-year-olds attempt to present themselves as members of a younger age group. Thus there is a compression in that part of the age span which is socially significant. At the same time sex typing of the young is reduced and sex status is less significant as a restriction on occupational function. The net effect of changes in the significance of age, sex, age relation, and family status for the ordering of social relations is to increase the possibility of innovation within a society and to widen the area of individual choice. At the same time this creates problems of assuring cultural continuity for those transmitting the society's culture and creates problems of boundary, order ambivalence and thus of identity in the young.

Further, age and sex tend to become less relevant as general social categories for distinguishing and separating groups within the school. This can be seen in the development of vertical integration in the primary school where children between the ages of five to seven years are placed together to form one educational group. At the secondary level on the other hand, and especially in comprehensive schools, children are placed in sets according to the single criterion of the ability they display in each subject. In this way the social unit for school organization becomes both less homogeneous in terms of age and sex and more differentiated. Further, the changes in age relations (authority relations) are likely to make the authority of the teacher in expressive spheres conditional rather than automatic.

Thus differentiating rituals in the school in terms of age, sex, age relation and house membership are not matched by adult-regulated differentiating rituals in similar areas in the family setting or community; the organizational procedure of the school makes its social unit often less homogeneous and the units themselves more differentiated; the authority of the teacher in expressive spheres becomes conditional.

(2) Consensual rituals

These are the rituals which, it was said, function so as to bind together all members of the school, staff and pupils as a moral community. They assist in the integration of the various goals of the school, within a coherent set of shared values, so that the values of the school can become internalized and experienced as a unity. In pluralistic industrialized societies, there is often considerable ambiguity in their central value systems. This can lead to a sharp discrepancy between the clarity of the value system of the school and the ambiguity in the value system of the society. This tends to weaken responsiveness to the school's expressive culture, and thus also to its ritualization. The need to exploit intellectual ability leads to overt and covert selection procedures in order to increase the proportion of children who pass examinations. This often leads to a sense of failure, and sometimes alienation in the children who are less able. This situation is further complicated by the task the school has (especially the grammar school), of assimilating the children of parents who do not share, or who often do not understand, the expressive culture of the school. Here the acceptance of the school's expressive culture may also require a reorientation of the normal procedures a pupil uses to relate in his family setting and local community.

Thus the response to the consensual rituals is likely to be weakened because of ambiguity in the society's central value systems, the divisive consequences of covert and overt selection procedures and the increase in the social heterogeneity of pupils at selective secondary schools.

It is likely that the social basis for the ritualization of the expressive culture of the school will be considerably weakened and the rituals may come to have the character of social routines. We might also expect a switch from the dominance of adult-imposed and regulated rituals to the dominance of rituals generated and regulated by youth. It would seem then for the reasons given that there is likely to be a marked change in the pupils' responsiveness to consensual and differentiating rituals whilst organizational changes in the schools may not facilitate their development.

(3) Ritual and changes in school structure

We have been considering how the expressive culture of the school is transmitted and we have suggested that a major means of its transmission is through its ritualization. We have indicated that the pupil's responsiveness to ritualization of the school's expressive culture is likely to be weakened in state schools in our contemporary, pluralistic society. We now want to consider changes in the structure of the school as a social form and the consequences for changes in the *means* through which the expressive culture is transmitted. Ritualization is likely to be highly developed in schools where pupils are ordered and grouped on the basis of a fixed attribute or an attribute which is thought to be fixed. This fixed attribute can be sex, age or IQ. If IQ is considered as a fixed attribute then this acts to produce divisions within an age/sex group. Thus if a fixed attribute is taken as a basis for ordering relationships within a school, then a fairly explicit vertical and horizontal form of social organization develops. We shall call such a structure a stratified one. This structure facilitates ritualization of the expressive culture and especially so, if the school is insulated from or can insulate itself from the community of which it is a part. This can often be facilitated through the ritualization of relationships at its boundaries. However, if the basis for ordering relationships among the pupils is not a fixed attribute, then the school structure ceases to be stratified and becomes differentiated. This is the case where cognitive ability is seen as a process rather than a substance, a process which does not develop in a uniform way in all pupils, nor in a uniform way in all subjects, but a process which can be shaped and modified by the social context. If cognitive ability is perceived in this way, then a school will not develop explicit vertical and horizontal organizing procedures. Ideally, pupils will achieve different positions in a range of groups or sets, membership in which is less likely to be related to age or sex but more likely to be related to special proficiency in a particular subject. The notion of education for diversity receives institutional embodiment in the differentiated school. The shift from stratified to differentiated schools may not always involve a change in the content of the expressive culture but it does involve a change in the *means* by which it is transmitted. As vertical and horizontal organizing procedures become less relevant then the structural basis for consensual and differentiating rituals becomes much weaker. The values of the expressive culture in stratified schools are translated through ritual into elements of its social structure, whereas in differentiated schools the values tend to be psychologized and issue in the form of interpersonal relations. This changes also the basis of social control.

Ritual involves a highly redundant form of communication in the sense that, given the social context, the messages are highly predictable. The messages themselves contain meanings which are highly condensed. Thus the major meanings in ritual are extra-verbal or indirect; for they are not made verbally explicit. Ritual is a form of restricted code. The expressive culture then in a stratified school is transmitted through a communication system which is verbally both highly condensed and highly redundant. The expressive culture of a differentiated school is likely to be transmitted, not through ritual and its restricted code, but through a communication system where the meanings are verbally elaborated, less predictable and therefore more individualized. If the basis for social control through ritual is extra-verbal or indirect, impersonal and non-rational, then the basis for social control where ritual is weakened is likely to be personal, verbally explicit and rational. A

major source of control in stratified schools is the internalizing of the social structure and the arousal and organization of sentiments evoked through ritual, signs, linements, heraldic imagery and totems. In differentiated schools there is likely to be a weakening of ritual and its supporting insignia. The social structure is then unlikely to be experienced as a unity and social control will come to rest upon inter-personal means. It will tend to become psychologized and to work through the verbal manipulation of motives and dispositions in an inter-personal context. We shall call this form of social control, this form of transmission of the expressive culture, *therapeutic*. In the differentiated school both teacher and taught are exposed and vulnerable in a way very different from their relationships in a stratified school. One might wonder whether the stratified, ritualized school does not evoke *shame* as a major controlling sentiment in the pupils, whereas the differentiated, personalized school might evoke *guilt* as the controlling sentiment. The stratified school is, perhaps, also more likely to communalize failure, whereas the differentiated school is more likely to individualize failure. Thus changes in school structure and in the means used to transmit the expressive culture may have important socializing consequences.*

This shift in school structure from stratified to differentiated can be understood as a shift from a social order resting upon *domination* to one resting upon *co-operation*. This shift itself is probably related to a similar shift in the character of work relations in an advanced industrialized society.† However, this shift in school structure entails not only problems of order, boundary, continuity and ambivalence for pupils but also a shift in consensus within the school from that based upon shared ends or values to that based upon shared means or skills. This possibility must finally be considered.

(4) The instrumental culture of the school and the basis of social consensus

The more the social purpose of education is to educate for diversity in economic and social function then the more likely it is that the school will shift from a stratified to a differentiated form. We have argued that the response to the expressive culture is likely to be weakened and social control to be based upon thera-

---

* It should be possible to distinguish *within* forms of stratified or differentiated schools in terms of the degree and kind of stratification or differentiation. Some stratified schools may well display differentiating features and differentiated schools may well have sections which are stratified.
† The shift from stratified to differentiated is not necessarily related to changes in the character of the occupational order. The American high school started as a differentiated form with a relatively weak instrumental culture and a strong expressive one. The function of the latter was that of integrating the large immigrant population into the American society. Further, one would not expect, for example, Soviet schools to display marked differentiating features, as such features would weaken the transmission and reception of the political ideology transmitted through the schools' expressive culture.

peutic rather than ritual procedures. Inasmuch as the school is a major instrument of the division of labour through its control over the occupational fate of its pupils it has taken on a pronounced bureaucratic function. Here it subordinates pupils' needs to the requirements of the division of labour through the examination system. The teacher–pupil relation, where the pupils are selected as potential examinees, often becomes almost one of contract with limited commitment on each side. Knowledge is rationally organized by the teacher and transmitted in terms of its examination efficiency. Control over such pupils stems from control over their occupational or higher educational fate. Such control is bureaucratic. The instrumental culture of the school is likely to be transmitted through bureaucratic procedures which effect curriculum, the transmission of knowledge and the quality of the pupil–teacher relation.

For the non-examination children the school functions not so much as a delicate instrument of the division of labour but much more as an instrument of social control regulating the behaviour of such pupils, their emotional sensitivities, their modes of social relation to what is considered acceptable to a section of the society to which the pupils often feel they do not really belong. The school is regulating style of life. The teacher here can be likened to a social worker concerned with the transmission of social skills. Indeed this conception of the role of teacher is explicitly recognized. The control over such pupils is not so much bureaucratic as it is therapeutic, resting upon personal, verbal, rational techniques. Conformity within the school is obtained through the transmission of occupational and social skills. Social order within the school comes to rest upon shared techniques or skills rather than upon shared values. Here we have a dominant instrumental culture transmitted either through bureaucratic or therapeutic procedures.

Educating for diversity of economic and social function in pluralistic societies often involves a strengthening of the instrumental and a weakening of the expressive culture of schools within the State system. Problems of continuity, order, boundary and ambivalence become socially active as the school moves to a differentiated form, or as stratified schools become de-ritualized. Pupils are then likely to generate their own consensual and differentiating rituals in order to assist in the development of a transitional identity. What is new is not this but that the organizational setting of the school, its focus upon attributes of selected pupils, its emphasis upon skills, the bureaucratization of learning, the individualizing of failure, are facilitating the dominance of the informal, autonomous youth group as the major source of shared values and sentiments. This shift from adult-imposed to the dominance of pupil-generated and regulated rituals is likely to weaken still further the transmission of the school's expressive culture.

Inasmuch as the school is more and more closely linked to the demands of the occupational system

the more probable it is that the tendencies discussed will be strengthened. Indeed the viability of the differentiated school may be lost so that it becomes simply a disguised form of the stratified type. In fact it may be that the only means available to weaken the dominance of the instrumental culture is to challenge the *élitist* assumptions and functions of the contemporary British University system. It is the small percentage of the age group which is at present in Britain attending higher education which is responsible for overt and covert selection procedures, the bureaucratization of knowledge, the divisive nature of the instrumental culture in all schools, stratified or so-called differentiated, and the shift of educational resources and rewards towards the *élite* pupils and away from the less successful. If the number of places at the higher levels of education were greater than the number of students available to fill them (which would make selection procedures less relevant) then the schools would at least possess a degree of autonomy over their procedures, curriculum and organization. Educating for diversity under contemporary social conditions inevitably reduces the possibilities of social consensus at the level of ends within the school. It may be that, in a period of heightened social change, continuity in the transmission of culture can only be obtained at the cost of a false yesterday or a mythical tomorrow.

Conclusion

We have attempted to analyse the role of consensual and differentiating rituals in British state schools with some reference to problems of continuity order, boundary and ambivalence. We have suggested that these rituals facilitate the transmission and internalization of the expressive culture of the school, create consensus, revivify the social order within the individual, deepen respect for and impersonalize authority relations. They also serve to prevent questioning of the values the expressive culture transmits. We have argued that the social basis for the transmission and response to ritual has been weakened within the school as a result of changes in age, sex, age relation and family status in the society and through changes in school organization and social composition. We have also suggested that educating for diversity in economic and social function under contemporary social conditions increases the dominance of the school's instrumental culture, which may switch the focus of ritual from the celebration of ends to that of means. We have argued that bureaucratic and therapeutic forms of social control may develop, and that this probably will facilitate youth-generated and regulated rituals which will tend to replace adult-imposed and regulated rituals as the source of shared values and sentiments. Finally, we have suggested that if the school is to be more than a passive mediator of, or at worst, an amplifier for, general social pressures, a way must be found for attenuating the relationship between the educational and the occupational system.

References

Douglas, M. (1966) *Purity and Danger*. Routledge & Kegan Paul.

Durkheim, E. (1915) *The Elementary Forms of the Religious Life*. Allen & Unwin.

Durkheim, E. (1961) *Moral Education*. Collier-Macmillan.

Fortes, D. C. *et al.* (1966) *Essays on the Ritual of Social Relations*. Manchester University Press.

Gerth, H. H. and Mills, C. W. (1948) *From Max Weber*. Routledge & Kegan Paul.

Goffman, E. (1961) *Asylums*. New York: Doubleday (also Penguin Books).

Waller, W. (1961) *The Sociology of Teaching*. Wiley.

25 Open schools, open society?

Basil Bernstein

There has been much talk among sociologists concerned with education about the possibilities of analysing the school as a complex organization. The approach to current changes in the structure of the contemporary school system, which I attempt in this article, was initially set out by Durkheim over seventy years ago in his book, *The Division of Labour in Society*. I shall interpret the changes in terms of a shift of emphasis in the principles of social integration from 'mechanical' to 'organic' solidarity. Such changes in social integration within schools are linked to fundamental changes in the character of the British educational system: a change from education in depth to education in breadth. I shall raise throughout this article the question of the relationship between the belief and moral order of the school, its social organization and its forms of social integration.

The concepts, mechanical and organic solidarity, can be used to indicate the emphasis within a society of one form of social integration rather than another. Organic solidarity is emphasized wherever individuals relate to each other through a complex interdependence of specialized social functions. Therefore organic solidarity presupposes a society whose social integration arises out of *differences* between individuals. These differences between individuals find expression which became crystallized into *achieved* poles. Mechanical solidarity is emphasized wherever individuals share a common system of belief and common sentiments which produce a detailed regulation of conduct. If social roles are achieved under organic solidarity, they are *assigned* or 'ascribed' under mechanical solidarity.

Wherever we have mechanical solidarity, according to Durkheim, punishment is necessary in order to revivify shared values and sentiments; i.e. punishment takes on a symbolic value over and beyond its specific utilitarian function. The belief system is made palpable in the symbolization of punishment. Durk-

Source: *New Society*, 14 September 1967, 351–3.

heim took what he called repressive (criminal) law as an index of mechanical solidarity.

Under conditions of organic solidarity, the concern is less to punish but more to reconcile conflicting claims. Social control, in conditions of organic solidarity, is concerned with the relationships between *individuals* which have in some way been damaged. Durkheim took what he called restitutive law (civil) as his index of organic solidarity. Here the system of social control becomes restitutive or reparative in function. Whereas under mechanical solidarity individuals confront one another indirectly—their confrontation being mediated by the belief system—under organic solidarity, in situations of social control, the belief system recedes into the background and the individuals confront one another directly.

Mechanical solidarity, according to Durkheim, arises in what he called a segmental society. He meant by this a type of society which could lose much of its personnel without damage to its continuity. Organic solidarity would correspond to the differentiated society, with diverse specialization of social roles; consequently the loss of a particular group of specialists might seriously impair the society. One can infer that segmental societies would make clear distinctions between inside and outside, whereas in differentiated societies the boundaries, as all symbolic boundaries, between inside and outside would become blurred.

Durkheim argued that a secondary cause of the division of labour arose out of the growing indeterminacy of the collective conscience (the value system). He said that sentiments would be aroused only by the infringement of highly general values, rather than by the minutiae of social actions. This, he said, would give rise to wider choice and so would facilitate individualism.

Organic solidarity refers to social integration at the level of individualized, specialized interdependent social roles, whereas mechanical solidarity refers to social integration at the level of shared beliefs. Under mechanical solidarity, there would be little tension between private beliefs and role obligations. In organic solidarity, the tensions between private belief and role obligations could be severe. This tension might be felt particularly by those individuals in socializing roles—for example, parents, teachers, probation officers, psychiatrists.

This is the shift of emphasis in the principles of social integration in schools—from mechanical to organic solidarity—that I shall be talking about. I am not concerned whether all the relationships I refer to are factually present in all schools. Clearly, some schools will have shifted not at all, others more; the shift may be more pronounced in the education of special groups of pupils or within different subjects. I am interested only in the general movement which at the moment may exist at the ideological rather than the substantive level. However, the list of shifts in emphasis may form a measure or scale of the change in the principles of social integration.

Consider, first, the forms of social control. In secondary schools there has been a move away from the transmission of common values through a ritual order and control based upon position or status, to more personalized forms of control where teachers and taught confront each other as individuals. The forms of social control appeal less to shared values, group loyalties and involvements; they are based rather upon the recognition of differences between individuals. And with this there has been a weakening of the symbolic significance and ritualization of punishment.

Look now at the division of labour of the school staff. Irrespective of the pupil/teacher ratios, the staff is now much larger. The division of labour is more complex from the point of view of the range of subjects taught. Within the main subjects, the hierarchy of responsibility has become more differentiated. The teacher's role itself has fragmented to form a series of specialized roles (vocational, counselling, housemaster, social worker and so on). Still within the broad category of the division of labour consider—very briefly, for the moment—the organization of pupils. The pupils' position in the new schools in 'principle' is less likely to be fixed in terms of sex, age or IQ, for ideally their position, within limits, is achieved in terms of their individual qualities.

Thus we find (a) a movement towards a more complex division of labour among the staff and a greater differentiation of the teacher's role: and (b) at the same time, the pupils' relationships with other pupils in principle arise from their expression of their education differences. This is good evidence of a shift towards organic solidarity.

Let us turn, next, to shifts in emphasis in the curriculum, pedagogy, the organization of teaching groups and teaching and pupil roles. Here we are at the heart of the instrumental order of the school: the transmission of skills and sensitivities.

Take the organization of teaching groups first.

Here we can begin to see a shift from a situation where the teaching group is a fixed structural unit of the school's organization (the form or class), to secondary schools where the teaching group is a flexible or variable unit of the social organization. The teaching group can consist of one, five, twenty, forty or even a hundred pupils and this number can vary from subject to subject. At the same time there has been an increase in the number of different teaching groups a pupil of a given age is in. The form or class tends to be weakened as a basis for relation and organization.

One can raise the level of abstraction and point out that space and time in the new schools, relative to the old, have (again within limits) ceased to have fixed references. Social spaces can be used for a variety of purposes and filled in a number of different ways. This potential is built into the very architecture.

Now for the changes in pedagogy. There is a shift—from a pedagogy which, for the majority of secondary school pupils, was concerned with the learning of standard operations tied to specific contexts—to a pedagogy which emphasizes the exploration of principles; from schools which emphasized the teacher as a solution-giver to schools which emphasize the teacher as a problem-poser or creator. Such a change in pedagogy (itself perhaps a response to changed concepts of skill in industry) alters the authority relationships between teacher and taught, and possibly changes the nature of the authority inherent in the subject. The pedagogy now emphasizes the *means* whereby knowledge is created and principles established, in a context of self-discovery by the pupils. The act of learning itself celebrates choice.

But what about the curriculum? I mean by curriculum the principles governing the selection of, and relation between, subjects. We are witnessing a shift in emphasis away from schools where the subject is a clear-cut definable unit of the curriculum, to schools where the unit of the curriculum is not so much a subject as an *idea*—say, topic-centred interdisciplinary inquiry. Such a shift is already under way at the university level.

Now, when the basis of the curriculum is an idea which is supra subject, and which governs the relationship between subjects, a number of consequences may follow. The subject is no longer dominant, but subordinate to the idea which governs a particular form of integration. If the subject is no longer dominant, then this could affect the position of teacher as specialist. His reference point may no longer be his subject or discipline. His allegiance, his social point of gravity, may tend to switch from his commitment to his subject to the bearing his subject has upon the *idea* which is relating him to other teachers.

In the older schools, integration between subjects, when it existed, was determined by the public examination system and this is one of the brakes on the shift I am describing. In the new schools, integration at the level of idea involves a new principle of social integration of staff: that of organic solidarity. This shift in the basis of the curriculum from subject to idea may point towards a fundamental change in the character of British education: a change from education in depth to education in breadth.

As a corollary of this, we are moving from secondary schools where the teaching roles were insulated from each other, where the teacher had an assigned area of authority and autonomy, to secondary schools where the teaching role is less autonomous and where it is a shared or co-operative role. There has been a shift from a teaching role which is, so to speak, 'given' (in the sense that one steps into assigned duties), to a role which has to be *achieved* in relation with other teachers. It is a role which is no longer made but *has to be made*. The teacher is no longer isolated from other teachers, as where the principle of integration is the relation of his subject to a public examination. The teacher is now in a complementary relation with other teachers at the level of his day-by-day teaching.

Under these conditions of co-operative, shared teaching roles, the loss of a teacher can be most damaging to the staff because of the interdependence of roles. Here we can begin to see the essence of organic solidarity as it affects the crucial role of teacher. The act of teaching itself expresses the organic articulation between subjects, teachers and taught. The form of social integration, in the central area of the school's function, is organic rather than mechanical.

How is the role of pupil affected? I said that, under mechanical solidarity, social roles were likely to be fixed and ascribed, aspirations would be limited, and individuals would relate to each other through common beliefs and shared sentiments. These beliefs and sentiments would regulate the details of social action. In the older secondary schools, individual choice was severely curtailed, aspirations were controlled through careful streaming, and streaming itself produced homogeneous groups according to an imputed similarity in ability. The learning process emphasized the teacher as solution-giver rather than problem-poser. The role of pupil was circumscribed and well defined.

Now there has been a move towards giving the pupil greater choice. Aspirations are likely to be raised in the new schools, partly because of changes in their social organization. The learning process creates greater autonomy for the pupil. The teaching group may be either a heterogeneous unit (unstreamed class) or a series of different homogeneous units (sets) or even both. The pupil's role is less clearly defined. Of equal significance, his role conception evolves out of a series of diverse contexts and relationships. The enacting of the role of pupil reveals less his similarity to others, but rather his difference from others.

I suggested earlier that, where the form of social integration was mechanical, the community would tend to become sealed off, self-enclosed and its boundary relationship would be sharply defined. Inside and outside would be clearly differentiated. These notions can apply to changes both within the school and to its relation to the outside.

Schools' boundary relations, both within and without, are now more open. This can be seen at many levels. First of all, the very architecture of the new schools points up their openness compared with the old schools. The inside of the institution has become visible. Of more significance, the boundary relation between the home and school has changed, and parents (their beliefs and socializing styles) are incorporated within the school in a way unheard of in the older schools. The range and number of non-school adults who visit the school and talk to the pupils have increased. The barrier between the informal teenage subcultures and the culture of the school has weakened: often the non-school age-group subculture becomes a content of a syllabus. The outside penetrates the new schools in other fundamental ways. The careful editing, specially for schools, of books, papers, films, is being replaced by a diverse representation of the outside both within the library and through films shown to the pupils.

Within the school, as we have seen, the insulation between forms and between teaching roles has weakened, and authority relationships are less formal. The diminishing of a one-to-one relation between a given activity, a given space and a given time—i.e. flexibility—must reduce the symbolic significance of particular spaces and particular times. The controls over flow in the new schools carry a different symbolic significance from the controls over flow in the old schools.

Let me summarize at a more general level the significance of these shifts of emphasis. There has been a shift from secondary schools whose symbolic orders point up or celebrate the idea of purity of categories—whether these categories be values, subjects in a curriculum, teaching groups or teachers—to secondary schools whose symbolic orders point up or celebrate the idea of mixture or diversity of categories. (These concepts have been developed by Mary Douglas in her book, *Purity and Danger*.) For example:

1 The mixing of categories at the level of values. Changes in the boundary relationships between the inside and the outside of the school lead to a value system which is more ambiguous and more open to the influence of diverse values from outside.

2 The mixing of categories at the level of curriculum. The move away from a curriculum where subjects are insulated and autonomous, to a curriculum which involves the subordination of subjects and their integration.

3 The mixing of categories at the level of the teaching group. Heterogeneous rather than homogeneous teaching groups and differentiated sets of pupils rather than fixed forms or classes.

The secondary schools celebrate diversity, not purity. This may be symptomatic of basic changes in the culture of our society, particularly changes in the the principles of social control. Until recently the British educational system epitomized the concept of purity of categories. At the apex of the system sat the lonely, specialized figure of the arts PhD; a dodo in terms of our current needs.

There was also the separation of the arts and the sciences, and within each the careful insulation between the 'pure' and the 'applied'. (Contrast all this with the United States.)

The concept of knowledge was one that partook of the 'sacred': its organization and dissemination was intimately related to the principles of social control. Knowledge (on this view) is dangerous, it cannot be exchanged like money, it must be confined to special well-chosen persons and even divorced from practical concerns. The forms of knowledge must always be bounded and well insulated from each other; there must be no sparking across the forms with unpredictable outcomes. Specialization makes knowledge safe and protects the vital principles of social order. Preferably knowledge should be transmitted in a context where the teacher has maximum control or surveillance, as in hierarchical school relationships or the university tutorial relation. Knowledge and the principles of social order are made safe if knowledge is subdivided, well insulated and transmitted by authorities who themselves view their own knowledge or disciplines with the jealous eye of a threatened priesthood. (This applies much more to the arts than to the sciences.)

Education in breadth, with its implications of mixture of categories, arouses in educational guardians an abhorrence and disgust like the sentiments aroused by incest. This is understandable because education in breadth arouses fears of the dissolution of the principles of social order. Education in depth, the palpable expression of purity of categories, creates monolithic authority systems serving élitist functions; education in breadth weakens authority systems or renders them pluralistic, and it is apparently consensual in function. One origin of the purity and mixing of categories may be in the general social principles regulating the mixing of diverse groups in society. But monolithic societies are unlikely to develop education in breadth, in school systems with pronounced principles of organic solidarity. Such forms of social integration are inadequate to transmit collective beliefs and values.

It might now be helpful to drop the terms mechanical and organic solidarity and refer instead to 'closed' and 'open' schools.

Individuals, be they teachers or taught, may be able (under certain conditions) to make their own roles in a way never experienced before in the public sector of secondary education. But staff and students are likely to experience a sense of loss of structure and, with this, problems of boundary, continuity, order and ambivalence are likely to arise. This problem of the relationship between the transmission of belief and social organization is likely to be acute in large-scale 'open' church schools. It may be that the open school with its organic modes of social integration, its personalized forms of social control, the indeterminacy of its belief and moral order (except at the level of very general values) will strengthen the adherence of the pupils to their age group as a major source of belief, relation and identity. Thus, is it possible that, as the open school moves further towards organic solidarity as its major principle of social integration, so the pupils may move further towards the 'closed' society of the age group? Are the educational dropouts of the fifties to be replaced by the moral dropouts of the seventies?

None of this should be taken in the spirit that yesterday there was order; today there is only flux. Neither should it be taken as a long sigh over the weakening of authority and its social basis. Rather we should be eager to explore changes in the forms of social integration in order to re-examine the basis for social control. This, as Durkheim pointed out decades ago, is a central concern of a sociology of education.

References

Bernstein, Basil, Elvin, H. L. and Peters, R. S. (1966) Ritual in education (in this volume).
Douglas, Mary (1966) *Purity and Danger*. Routledge & Kegan Paul.

Durkheim, Émile (1961) *Moral Education*. Collier-Macmillan.
Durkheim, Émile (1964) *The Division of Labour in Society*. Collier-Macmillan.

Section IV   Ideology in education: curriculum and selection

The readings in this section are concerned with the relationship between activities within the educational system and their ideological and political contexts. Through the concept of 'ideology' they explore the social distribution of knowledge and suggest ways in which this might be related to social structure.

The contribution of Marx to the sociology of knowledge centres on his theorizing of the relationships between the economic production of a society (its 'substructure'), its political and cultural production 'superstructure') and its theoretical production (sciences). He saw ideology (or culture) as an intellectual and symbolic system (or aggregate of systems), as a collection of answers to various basic questions. These questions sprang not from inside the ideological level, but from outside it—from the political and economic levels. He saw the distribution and differentiation of ideology and science in a society as important features of its distribution of power. The stratification (of power and income) which results from unequal access to control of economic means is related to the unequal distribution of 'knowledge'. Marx used the concept 'ideology' especially to signify the knowledge which is propagated by particular classes to preserve their self-interest. Social structure was, therefore, for Marx, central to any sociology of knowledge.

The concept of ideology, therefore, is related both to social structure and stratification and to the sociology of knowledge. It helps us to relate these two sorts of sociology by pointing to one way in which concerns about society at the national level enter into principles and prejudices which inform thinking in and about education. It thereby gives us a method of interpreting the *content* of education in terms of the social stratification approach and vice versa. Thus we may interpret ideology in terms of economics and politics and also the relevance of economics and politics to the educational system in terms of ideology. Since the educational system distributes and reproduces ideology, this is an appropriate method of analysis.

The readings from Mannheim, Marx and Engels are designed to introduce the concept of ideology. Swift sets out an approach to understanding the relations between the area of interaction between individuals and the processes which operate at the level of the whole society. Those from Eliot, Leavis, Vaizey, Holbrook and Montessori are designed to illustrate three out of the four ideologies of education which we hope will be useful to students in so far as they provide perspectives for analysis as well as descriptions of the social thinking which constitutes an integral part of education. The fourth is exemplified by two books which are set reading for enrolled students of the Open University: Raymond Williams's *The Long Revolution* and the *Letter to a Teacher* by the schoolchildren of Barbiana. The reading from Durkheim is included so as to focus the concept of ideology more sharply on the content of education: and those from Yeo, Jevons and Jackson illustrate its application. With the Coleman piece we return to a more traditional concern with the *distribution* of educational goods and services. This last piece will, we hope, be further illuminated by the perspectives on interaction, knowledge and ideology to be found in the previous readings.

26 Ideology and Utopia

Karl Mannheim

The previous chapter traced a process of which numerous examples can be found in social and intellectual history. In the development of a new point of view one party plays the pioneering role, while other parties, in order to cope with the advantage of their adversary in the competitive struggle, must of necessity themselves make use of this point of view. This is the case with the notion of ideology. Marxism merely discovered a clue to understanding and a mode of thought, in the gradual rounding out of which the whole nineteenth century participated. The complete formulation of this idea is not the sole achievement of any single group and is not linked exclusively with any single intellectual and social position. The role that Marxism played in this process was one that deserves a high rank in intellectual history and should not be minimized. The process, however, by which the ideological approach is coming into general use, is going on before our very eyes, and hence is subject to empirical observation.

It is interesting to observe that, as a result of the expansion of the ideological concept, a new mode of understanding has gradually come into existence. This new intellectual standpoint constitutes not merely a change of degree in a phenomenon already operating. We have here an example of the real dialectical process which is too often misinterpreted for scholastic purposes—for here we see indeed a matter of difference in degree becoming a matter of difference in kind. For as soon as all parties are able to analyse the ideas of their opponents in ideological terms, all elements of meaning are qualitatively changed and the word ideology acquires a totally new meaning. In the course of this all the factors with which we dealt in our historical analysis of the meaning of the term are also transformed accordingly. The problems of 'false consciousness' and of the nature of reality henceforth take on a different

Source: Karl Mannheim, *Ideology and Utopia*. Routledge (1936) (Routledge paperback, 1960), 67–74.

significance. This point of view ultimately forces us to recognize that our axioms, our ontology, and our epistemology have been profoundly transformed. We will limit ourselves in what follows to pointing out through what variations in meaning the conception of ideology has passed in the course of this transformation.

We have already traced the development from the particular to the total conception. This tendency is constantly being intensified. Instead of being content with showing that the adversary suffers from illusions or distortions on a psychological or experiential plane, the tendency now is to subject his total structure of consciousness and thought to a thoroughgoing sociological analysis.[1]

As long as one does not call his own position into question but regards it as absolute, while interpreting his opponents' ideal as a mere function of the social positions they occupy, the decisive step forward has not yet been taken. It is true, of course, that in such a case the total conception of ideology is being used, since one is interested in analysing the structure of the mind of one's opponent in its totality, and is not merely singling out a few isolated propositions. But since, in such an instance, one is interested merely in a sociological analysis of the opponent's ideas, one never gets beyond a highly restricted, or what I should like to call a special, formulation of the theory. In contrast to this special formulation, the general[2] form of the total conception of ideology is being used by the analyst when he has the courage to subject not just the adversary's point of view but all points of view, including his own, to the ideological analysis.

At the present stage of our understanding it is hardly possible to avoid this general formulation of the total conception of ideology, according to which the thought of all parties in all epochs is of an ideological character. There is scarcely a single intellectual position, and Marxism furnishes no exception to this rule, which has not changed through history and which even in the present does not appear in many forms. Marxism, too, has taken on many diverse appearances. It should not be too difficult for a Marxist to recognize their social basis.

With the emergence of the general formulation of the total conception of ideology, the simple theory of ideology develops into the sociology of knowledge. What was once the intellectual armament[3] of a party is transformed into a method of research in social and intellectual history generally. To begin with, a given social group discovered the 'situational determination' (*Seinsgebundenheit*) of its opponents' ideas. Subsequently the recognition of this fact is elaborated into an all-inclusive principle according to which the thought of every group is seen as arising out of its life conditions.[4] Thus, it becomes the task of the sociological history of thought to analyse without regard for party biases all the factors in the actually existing social situation which may influence thought. This sociologically oriented history of ideas is destined to provide modern men with a revised view of the whole historical process.

It is clear, then, that in this connection the conception of ideology takes on a new meaning. Out of this meaning two alternative approaches to ideological investigation arise. The first is to confine oneself to showing everywhere the interrelationships between the intellectual point of view held and the social position occupied. This involves the renunciation of every intention to expose or unmask those views with which one is in disagreement.

In attempting to expose the views of another, one is forced to make one's own view appear infallible and absolute, which is a procedure altogether to be avoided if one is making a specifically non-evaluative investigation. The second possible approach is nevertheless to combine such a non-evaluative analysis with a definite epistemology. Viewed from the angle of this second approach there are two separate and distinct solutions to the problem of what constitutes reliable knowledge —the one solution may be termed *relationism*, and the other *relativism*.

Relativism is a product of the modern historical-sociological procedure which is based on the recognition that all historical thinking is bound up with the concrete position in life of the thinker (*Standortsgebundenheit des Denkers*). But relativism combines this historical-sociological insight with an older theory of knowledge which was as yet unaware of the interplay between conditions of existence and modes of thought, and which modelled its knowledge after static prototypes such as might be exemplified by the proposition $2 \times 2 = 4$. This older type of thought, which regarded such examples as the model of all thought, was necessarily led to the rejection of all those forms of knowledge which were dependent upon the subjective stand-point and the social situation of the knower, and which were, hence, merely 'relative'. Relativism, then, owes its existence to the discrepancy between this newly-won insight into the actual processes of thought and a theory of knowledge which had not yet taken account of this new insight.

If we wish to emancipate ourselves from this relativism we must seek to understand with the aid of the sociology of knowledge that it is not epistemology in any absolute sense but rather a certain historically transitory type of epistemology which is in conflict with the type of thought oriented to the social situation. Actually, epistemology is as intimately enmeshed in the social process as is the totality of our thinking, and it will make progress to the extent that it can master the complications arising out of the changing structure of thought.

A modern theory of knowledge which takes account of the relational as distinct from the merely relative character of all historical knowledge must start with the assumption that there are spheres of thought in which it is impossible to conceive of absolute truth existing independently of the values and position of the subject and unrelated to the social context. Even a god could not formulate a proposition on historical subjects like $2 \times 2 = 4$, for what is intelligible in history can be formulated only with reference to problems and conceptual constructions which themselves arise in the flux of historical experience.

Once we recognize that all historical knowledge is relational knowledge, and can only be formulated with reference to the position of the observer, we are faced, once more, with the task of discriminating between what is true and what is false in such knowledge. The question then arises: which social standpoint *vis-à-vis* of history offers the best chance for reaching an optimum of truth? In any case, at this stage the vain hope of discovering truth in a form which is independent of an historically and socially determined set of meanings will have to be given up. The problem is by no means solved when we have arrived at this conclusion, but we are, at least, in a better position to state the actual problems which arise in a more unrestricted manner. In the following we have to distinguish two types of approach to ideological inquiry arising upon the level of the general-total conception of ideology: first, the approach characterized by freedom from value-judgments and, second, the epistemological and metaphysically oriented normative approach. For the time being we shall not raise the question of whether in the latter approach we are dealing with relativism or relationism.

The non-evaluative general total conception of ideology is to be found primarily in those historical investigations where, provisionally and for the sake of the simplification of the problem, no judgments are pronounced as to the correctness of the ideas to be treated. This approach confines itself to discovering the relations between certain mental structures and the life-situations in which they exist. We must constantly ask ourselves how it comes about that a given type of social situation gives rise to a given interpretation. Thus the ideological element in human thought, viewed at this level, is always bound up with the existing life-situation of the thinker. According to this view human thought arises, and operates, not in a social vacuum but in a definite social milieu.

We need not regard it as a source of error that all thought is so rooted. Just as the individual who participates in a complex of vital social relations with other men thereby enjoys a chance of obtaining a more precise and penetrating insight into his fellows, so a given point of view and a given set of concepts, because they are bound up with and grow out of a certain social reality, offer, through intimate contact with this reality, a greater chance of revealing its meaning. (The example cited earlier showed that the proletarian-socialistic point of view was in a particularly favourable position to discover the ideological elements in its adversaries' thought.) The circumstance, however, that thought is bound by the social- and life-situation in which it arises creates handicaps as well as opportunities. It is clearly impossible to obtain an inclusive insight into problems if the observer or thinker is confined to a given place in society. For instance, as has already been pointed out, it was not possible for the socialist idea of ideology to have developed of itself into the sociology of knowledge. It seems inherent in the historical process itself that the narrowness and the limitations which restrict one point of view tend to be corrected by clashing with the opposite points of view. The task of a study of ideology, which tries to be free from value-judgments, is to understand the narrowness of each individual point of view and the inter-play between these distinctive attitudes in the total social process. We are here confronted with an inexhaustible theme. The problem is to show how, in the whole history of thought, certain intellectual standpoints are connected with certain forms of experience, and to trace the intimate interaction between the two in the course of social and intellectual change. In the domain of morals, for instance, it is necessary to show not only the continuous changes in human conduct but the constantly altering norms by which this conduct is judged. Deeper insight into the problem is reached if we are able to show that morality and ethics themselves are conditioned by certain definite situations, and that such fundamental concepts as duty, transgression, and sin have not always existed but have made their appearance as correlatives of distinct social situations.[5] The prevailing philosophic view which cautiously admits that the content of conduct has been historically determined, but which at the same time insists upon the retention of eternal forms of value and of a formal set of categories, is no longer tenable. The fact that the distinction between the content and the forms of conduct was made and recognized is an important concession to the historical–sociological approach which makes it increasingly difficult to set up contemporary values as absolutes.

Having arrived at this recognition it becomes necessary also to remember that the fact that we speak about social and cultural life in terms of values is itself an attitude peculiar to our time. The notion of 'value' arose and was diffused from economics, where the conscious choice between values was the starting-point of theory. This idea of value was later transferred to the ethical, aesthetic, and religious spheres, which brought about a distortion in the description of the real behaviour of the human-being in these spheres. Nothing could be more wrong than to describe the real attitude of the individual when enjoying a work of art quite unreflectively, or when acting according to ethical patterns inculcated in him since childhood, in terms of conscious choice between values.

The view which holds that all cultural life is an orientation towards objective values is just one more illustration of a typically modern rationalistic disregard for the basic irrational mechanisms which govern man's relation to his world. Far from being permanently valid the interpretation of culture in terms of objective values is really a peculiar characteristic of the thought of our own time. But even granting for the moment that this conception had some merit, the existence of certain formal realms of values and their specific structure would be intelligible only with reference to the concrete situations to which they have relevance and in which they are valid.[6] There is, then, no norm which can lay claim to formal validity and which can be abstracted as a constant universal formal element from its historically changing content.

Today we have arrived at the point where we can see clearly that there are differences in modes of thought, not only in different historical periods but also in different cultures. Slowly it dawns upon us that not only does the content of thought change but also its categorical structure. Only very recently has it become possible to investigate the hypothesis that, in the past as well as in the present, the dominant modes of thought are supplanted by new categories when the social basis of the group, of which these thought-forms are characteristic, disintegrates or is transformed under the impact of social change.

Research in the sociology of knowledge promises to reach a stage of exactness if only because nowhere else in the realm of culture is the interdependence in the shifts of meaning and emphasis so clearly evident and precisely determinable as in thought itself. For thought is a particularly sensitive index of social and cultural change. The variation in the meaning of words and the multiple connotations of every concept reflect polarities of mutually antagonistic schemes of life implicit in these nuances of meaning.[7]

Nowhere in the realm of social life, however, do we encounter such a clearly traceable interdependence and sensitivity to change and varying emphasis as in the meaning of words. The word and the meaning that attaches to it is truly a collective reality. The slightest nuance in the total system of thought reverberates in the individual word and the shades of meaning it carries. The word binds us to the whole of past history and, at the same time, mirrors the totality of the present. When, in communicating with others, we seek a common level of understanding the word can be used to iron out individual differences of meaning. But, when necessary, the word may become an instrument in emphasizing the differences in meaning and the unique experiences of each individual. It may then serve as a means for detecting the original and novel increments that arise in the course of the history of culture, thereby adding previously imperceptible values to the scale of human experience. In all of these investigations use will be made of the total and general conception of ideology in its non-evaluative sense.

Notes

1 This is not meant to imply that for certain aspects of the struggles of everyday life the particular conception of ideology is inapplicable.

2 We add here another distinction to our earlier one of 'particular and total', namely that of 'special and general'. While the first distinction concerns the question as to whether single isolated ideas or the entire mind is to be seen as ideological, and whether the social situation conditions merely the psychological manifestations of concepts, or whether it even penetrates to the onological meanings, in the distinction of special *versus* general, the decisive question is whether the thought of all groups (including our own) or only that of our adversaries is recognized as socially determined.

3 Cf. the Marxist expression 'To forge the intellectual weapons of the proletariat.'

4 By the term 'situational determination of knowledge' I am seeking to differentiate the propagandistic from the scientific sociological content of the ideological concept.

5 Cf. Max Weber, *Wirtschaft und Gesellschaft*. Grundriss der Sozialökonomik, part iii, 794, dealing with the social conditions which are requisite to the genesis of the moral.

6 Cf. E. Lask, *Die Logik der Philosophie und die Kategorienlehre* (Tübingen 1911), uses the term *hingelten* in order to explain that categorical forms are not valid in themselves but only with reference to their always changing content which inevitably reacts upon their nature.

7 For this reason the sociological analysis of meanings will play a significant role in the following studies. We may suggest here that such an analysis might be developed into a symptomatology based upon the principle that in the social realm, if we can learn to observe carefully, we can see that each element of the situation which we are analysing contains and throws light upon the whole.

27 The German ideology

Karl Marx and Friedrich Engels

History is nothing but the succession of the separate generations, each of which exploits the materials, the capital funds, the productive forces handed down to it by all preceding generations and thus, on the one hand, continues the traditional activity in completely changed circumstances, and on the other, modifies the old circumstances with a completely changed activity. This can be speculatively distorted so that later history is made the goal of earlier history, e.g. the goal ascribed to the discovery of America is to further the eruption of the French Revolution. Thereby history receives its own special aims and becomes 'a person ranking with other persons' (to wit: 'Self-Consciousness, Criticism, the Unique', etc.), while what is designated with the words 'destiny', 'goal', 'germ', or 'idea' of earlier history is nothing more than an abstraction formed from later history, from the active influence which earlier history exercises on later history.

The further the separate spheres, which act on one another, extend in the course of this development, the more the original isolation of the separate nationalities is destroyed by the developed mode of production and intercourse and the division of labour between various nations naturally brought forth by these, the more history becomes world history. Thus, for instance, if in England a machine is invented, which deprives countless workers of bread in India and China, and overturns the whole form of existence of these empires, this invention becomes a world-historical fact. Or again, take the case of sugar and coffee which have proved their world-historical importance in the nineteenth century by the fact that the lack of these products, occasioned by the Napoleonic Continental System, caused the Germans to rise against Napoleon, and thus became the real basis of the glorious Wars of Liberation of 1813. From this it follows that this transformation of history into world history is not

indeed a mere abstract act on the part of the 'self-consciousness', the world spirit, or of any other metaphysical spectre, but a quite material, empirically verifiable act, an act the proof of which every individual furnishes as he comes and goes, eats, drinks and clothes himself.

The ideas of the ruling class are in every epoch the ruling ideas: i.e., the class which is the ruling *material* force of society is at the same time its ruling *intellectual* force. The class which has the means of material production at its disposal, has control at the same time over the means of mental production, so that thereby, generally speaking, the ideas of those who lack the means of mental production are subject to it. The ruling ideas are nothing more than the ideal expression of the dominant material relationships, the dominant material relationships grasped as ideas; hence of the relationships which make the one class the ruling one, therefore, the ideas of its dominance. The individuals composing the ruling class possess among other things consciousness, and therefore think. In so far, therefore, as they rule as a class and determine the extent and compass of an epoch, it is self-evident that they do this in its whole range, hence among other things rule also as thinkers, as producers of ideas, and regulate the production and distribution of the ideas of their age: thus their ideas are the ruling ideas of the epoch. For instance, in an age and in a country where royal power, aristocracy and bourgeoisie are contending for mastery and where, therefore, mastery is shared, the doctrine of the separation of powers proves to be the dominant idea and is expressed as an 'eternal law'.

The division of labour, which we already saw above as one of the chief forces of history up till now, manifests itself also in the ruling class as the division of mental and material labour, so that inside this class one part appears as the thinkers of the class (its active, conceptive ideologists, who make the perfecting of the illusion of the class about itself their chief

Source: Karl Marx and Friedrich Engels, *The German Ideology*. Lawrence & Wishart (1965), 60–5.

source of livelihood), while the others' attitude to these ideas and illusions is more passive and receptive, because they are in reality the active members of this class and have less time to make up illusions and ideas about themselves. Within this class this cleavage can even develop into a certain opposition and hostility between the two parts, which, however, in the case of a practical collision, in which the class itself is endangered, automatically comes to nothing, in which case there also vanishes the semblance that the ruling ideas were not the ideas of the ruling class and had a power distinct from the power of this class. The existence of revolutionary ideas in a particular period presupposes the existence of a revolutionary class; about the premises for the latter sufficient has already been said above.

If now in considering the course of history we detach the ideas of the ruling class from the ruling class itself and attribute to them an independent existence, if we confine ourselves to saying that these or those ideas were dominant at a given time, without bothering ourselves about the conditions of production and the producers of these ideas, if we thus ignore the individuals and world conditions which are the source of the ideas, we can say, for instance, that during the time that the aristocracy was dominant, the concepts honour, loyalty, etc. were dominant, during the dominance of the bourgeoisie the concepts freedom, equality, etc. The ruling class itself on the whole imagines this to be so. This conception of history, which is common to all historians, particularly since the eighteenth century, will necessarily come up against the phenomenon that increasingly abstract ideas hold sway, i.e. ideas which increasingly take on the form of universality. For each new class which puts itself in the place of one ruling before it, is compelled, merely in order to carry through its aim, to represent its interest as the common interest of all the members of society, that is, expressed in ideal form: it has to give its ideas the form of universality, and represent them as the only rational, universally valid ones. The class making a revolution appears from the very start, if only because it is opposed to a *class*, not as a class but as the representative of the whole of society; it appears as the whole mass of society confronting the one ruling class.* It can do this because, to start with, its interest really is more connected with the common interest of all other non-ruling classes, because under the pressure of hitherto existing conditions its interest has not yet been able to develop as the particular interest of a particular class. Its victory, therefore, benefits also many individuals of the other classes which are not winning a dominant position, but only in so far as it now puts these individuals in a position to raise them-

* [Marginal note by Marx] Universality corresponds to (1) the class versus the state, (2) the competition, world-wide intercourse, etc., (3) the great numerical strength of the ruling class, (4) the illusion of the *common* interests (in the beginning this illusion is true), (5) the delusion of the ideologists and the division of labour.

selves into the ruling class. When the French bourgeoisie overthrew the power of the aristocracy, it thereby made it possible for many proletarians to raise themselves above the proletariat, but only in so far as they became bourgeois. Every new class, therefore, achieves its hegemony only on a broader basis than that of the class ruling previously, whereas the opposition of the non-ruling class against the new ruling class later develops all the more sharply and profoundly. Both these things determine the fact that the struggle to be waged against this new ruling class, in its turn, aims at a more decided and radical negation of the previous conditions of society than could all previous classes which sought to rule.

This whole semblance, that the rule of a certain class is only the rule of certain ideas, comes to a natural end, of course, as soon as class rule in general ceases to be the form in which society is organized, that is to say, as soon as it is no longer necessary to represent a particular interest as general or the 'general interest' as ruling.

Once the ruling ideas have been separated from the ruling individuals and, above all, from the relationships which result from a given stage of the mode of production, and in this way the conclusion has been reached that history is always under the sway of ideas, it is very easy to abstract from these various ideas '*the* idea', the notion, etc. as the dominant force in history, and thus to understand all these separate ideas and concepts as 'forms of self-determination' on the part of *the* concept developing in history. It follows then naturally, too, that all the relationships of men can be derived from the concept of man, man as conceived, the essence of man, *Man*. This has been done by the speculative philosophers. Hegel himself confesses at the end of the *Geschichtsphilosophie* that he 'has considered the progress of the *concept* only, and has represented in history the 'true *theodicy*'. Now one can go back again to the producers of the 'concept', to the theorists, ideologists and philosophers, and one comes then to the conclusion that the philosophers, the thinkers as such, have at all times been dominant in history: a conclusion, as we see, already expressed by Hegel. The whole trick of proving the hegemony of the spirit in history (hierarchy Stirner calls it) is thus confined to the following three efforts.

No. 1. One must separate the ideas of those ruling for empirical reasons, under empirical conditions and as empirical individuals, from these actual rulers, and thus recognize the rule of ideas or illusions in history.

No. 2. One must bring an order into this rule of ideas, probe a mystical connection among the successive ruling ideas, which is managed by understanding them as 'acts of self-determination on the part of the concept' (this is possible because by virtue of their empirical basis these ideas are really connected with one another and because, conceived as *mere* ideas, they become self-distinctions, distinctions made by thought).

No. 3. To remove the mystical appearance of this

'self-determining concept' it is changed into a person —'Self-Consciousness'—or, to appear thoroughly materialistic, into a series of persons, who represent the 'concept' in history, into the 'thinkers', the 'philosophers', the ideologists, who again are understood as the manufacturers of history, as the 'council of guardians', as the rulers.* Thus the whole body of materialistic elements has been removed from history and now full rein can be given to the speculative steed.

Whilst in ordinary life every shopkeeper is very

* [Marginal note by Marx] Man=the 'rational human spirit'.

well able to distinguish between what somebody professes to be and what he really is, our historians have not yet won even this trivial insight. They take every epoch at its word and believe that everything it says and imagines about itself is true.

This historical method which reigned in Germany, and especially the reason why, must be understood from its connection with the illusion of ideologists in general, e.g. the illusions of the jurists, politicians (of the practical statesmen among them, too), from the dogmatic dreamings and distortions of these fellows; this is explained perfectly easily from their practical position in life, their job, and the division of labour.

28 A contribution to the critique of political economy

Karl Marx

In the social production which men carry on they enter into definite relations that are indispensable and independent of their will; these relations of production correspond to a definite stage of development of their material powers of production. The sum total of these relations of production constitutes the economic structure of society—the real foundation, on which rise legal and political superstructures and to which correspond definite forms of social consciousness. The mode of production in material life determines the general character of the social, political and spiritual processes of life. It is not the consciousness of men that determines their existence, but, on the contrary, their social existence that determines their consciousness. At a certain stage of their development, the material forces of production in society come in conflict with the existing relations of production, or—what is but a legal expression for the same thing—with the

Source: Karl Marx, *A Contribution to the Critique of Political Economy*, Chicago: Charles H. Kerr (1904), pp. 11–12.

property relations within which they had been at work before. From forms of development of the forces of production these relations turn into their fetters. Then comes the period of social revolution. With the change of the economic foundation the entire immense superstructure is more or less rapidly transformed. In considering such transformations the distinction should always be made between the material transformation of the economic conditions of production which can be determined with the precision of natural science, and the legal, political, religious, aesthetic or philosophic—in short ideological forms in which men become conscious of this conflict and fight it out. Just as our opinion of an individual is not based on what he thinks of himself, so can we not judge of such a period of transformation by its own consciousness; on the contrary, this consciousness must rather be explained from the contradictions of material life, from the existing conflict between the social forces of production and the relations of production.

29 Social class analysis

D. F. Swift

What consequences for the developing child follow from differences in social experience? Perhaps the neatest of the early British studies on this question was carried out by Fraser (1959), who showed that a whole range of environmental factors related with scholastic achievement at age eleven. All these could have been described as consequences of stratification (Swift 1966). By this we mean that differential access to income, prestige and power in society appears to induce styles of life which bear a clear relation to school achievement. The fact that the different social classes have different ways of living is too obvious to have to debate—it is one of the recurring themes in our literature. But these different styles of life are not simply settings within which people function. They are one way of describing *how* people function; that is, we can separate the members of different social strata according to the cognitive, cathectic and evaluative habits and skills they employ. Individually, the habits and skills will be a partial consequence of their social experience. And this will follow from their access to participation in the social process, which is based upon their position in the system of stratification.

Consequently, when we divide a population according to the occupation followed by the head of each family, we are not attempting to measure a single stimulus variable in the way that we might measure an electrical charge being applied to a rat in a maze. A much better analogy to the maze situation could be produced if we had a number of mazes comprising many different kinds of problems and hence different kinds of environments. One maze, perhaps, might be characterized as something which produces aggression, while another produces skill at manipulating certain kinds of objects, and so on. Whether it is the humidity, the sequence of electric

shocks, the heat, the density of inhabitants in the maze, the breed of rat, atmospheric pressure during gestation or whatever, which 'really' produces the condition is not known. Of course, the response of an experimental psychologist would be to point out that this is not the way to conduct an experiment. Each of these factors should be treated as an independent variable, while all the others were controlled. In analysis of social class, this means that each social class is to be looked upon as a unique association of variables. Within its context any single variable is related to another in ways which are dependent upon their joint positions in the matrix. To put it in the very simplest way, factor X might be found to influence ability Y in situation A, but to have no influence in situation B. A factor which is important to educational achievement in the lowest social class may be irrelevant in the middle stratum. This destroys our hope that a factor X can be isolated which is simply a cause of Y (Farber 1965; Swift 1967).

A vitally important methodological issue is raised here, because so much of our research is based upon an assumption that associations between factors and achievement will be linear and present in all other situations. Further point is added to this criticism by Child (1966), who showed that children of parents from the top and the bottom of the status continuum were significantly more introverted than children whose parents were in the middle of it.

The point underlying the theoretical perspective upon stratification is that *when we are concerned with describing the social environment of individuals and relating it to their development*, a social class must be looked upon as a summarizing variable and not an effective influencing factor. As one of the foremost exponents of social class analysis has written (Kohn 1963, 471):

social class has proved to be so useful a concept because it refers to more than simple educational

Source: D. F. Swift, Social class and educational adaptation, in *Educational Research in Britain*, ed. H. J. Butcher, London University Press (1968), vol. 1, 289–96.

level, or occupation, or any of the large number of correlated variables. It is so useful because it captures the reality that the intricate interplay of all these variables creates different basic conditions of life at different levels of the social order. Members of different social classes, by virtue of enjoying (or suffering) different conditions of life, come to see the world differently—to develop different conceptions of social reality, different aspirations and hopes and fears, different conceptions of the desirable.

Even this is an over-simplification, because social classes do not exist as discrete entities around which it is possible to draw clear boundaries. They are analytical abstractions from reality. In real life, the boundaries shade into each other and are obscured by the presence of other social abstractions describing other factors. While it is analytically reasonable to think of the subculture of a social class, we can equally well distinguish a subculture founded upon regional factors or sheer historical accident (Roach and Gursslin 1967). It would be a great mistake to equate, for example, the working-class fisherman subculture of Hull with the working-class miner subculture of south Wales. Nevertheless, Kahan *et al.* (1966) have produced some recent proof that the simple split between white-collar and manual jobs is a subjectively real one in the British population.

Similarly, a single occupational or income category will not necessarily produce a subculture in the accepted sense of the word. All bus conductors or all people earning £1,000–1,100 a year do not form a subculture. The problem, therefore, is to devise a criterion according to which the most meaningful collection of the relevant factors can be grouped. The two words 'meaningful' and 'relevant' are deliberately used here to emphasize the difficulties of the problem. The meaningfulness will depend upon the associations among the factors on the one hand, and between the factors and important aspects of social structure on the other. Relevance relates to the extent to which a factor actually does influence school achievement.

A great deal of the necessary research has not yet been done; but there are many pointers to the way in which we will have to move if we are to try and specify the mechanisms by which adaptation comes about. Two areas of research which promise increased understanding will be dealt with in the remaining sections. They are the views which people hold of education and the influence which linguistic forms are believed to have upon the development of cognitive skills.

The perception of education and aspiration

It is probably true that all groups, except those to be found in the more alienated of slum cultures, would tend to agree at the verbal level that education is a good thing. On the other hand, there is no doubt that the degree of conviction behind the statement varies enormously. The evidence of research shows fairly conclusively that the more highly parents value education, the more they will support their child's educational endeavours and the more likely he is to succeed (Banfield *et al.* 1966; Douglas 1964; Wall *et al.* 1962). Furthermore, the more the child succeeds, the more likely he is to go on succeeding (Robinson 1964). But this is a very crude way of describing a very subtle set of processes. What do we mean when we say education is a good thing? Clearly there are at least two kinds of criteria by which we can view its goodness: (a) education as an end in itself; and (b) education as a means to other ends. The stereotype in teaching folk-lore of an 'educogenic' environment contains an emphasis on the first aspect of judgment. On the other hand, most people actually have a view of education as a means to other ends. Education is for getting good jobs. In teaching children how to behave, it makes possible a quieter and more successful period of child-rearing for parents, and so on. We must also take into account differences, which are often based on class, in perception of what *success* actually is (Katz 1964; Lambert and Klineberg 1964). If we are to discover the mechanisms by which educational achievement is brought about, we will have to distinguish between the different conceptions of education and their relation to achievement motivation. Grossly we say that there are small sections of the middle classes where belief in education *as an end in itself* is more important to people than their knowledge that it is also a means to certain practical ends. Proportionately similar but numerically larger sections of the working class do not even conceive of it as a good thing, or are more likely to think of it as a bad thing, especially for girls.

We have seen that we must look for differences in ideas about what education is *for*; we can also expect to find differences in ideas about what it is. Obviously these two ways of 'seeing' education are related. Perhaps they are simply different aspects of the same generalized 'attitude towards education'. Nevertheless, we must be prepared for greatly differing pictures in the minds of parents about what actually goes on in education. Working-class students are often amused or annoyed by their parents' ideas of what happens to them at university. It is possible that if their parents really knew, many of them would be inclined to discourage their children from going at all.

A great deal of research has produced a large amount of evidence to show that middle-class children aspire to higher occupational and income levels than do those of the working class (Bruckman 1966; Jackson and Marsden 1961; Kahl 1953; Rosen 1956; Sewell *et al.* 1957; Stacey 1965; Swift 1967; R. H. Turner 1966). It is also probable that they try harder at *all* tasks, presumably because of the view of 'themselves in relation to task' which they are taught (Hyman 1953; Rosen and d'Andrade 1959). It has even been suggested (Davis 1948) that the child-rearing methods and stresses of middle-class life tend to produce a higher level of anxiety about all forms of achievement, but research has failed to confirm the hypothesis for Britain (Himmelweit 1955).

It is a truism, but an important one, to say that whether or not middle-class child-training produces generalized anxiety, it teaches the habits of responsibility (Clausen and Williams 1963; E. Cohen, 1965; Dale and Griffith 1966), restraint of physical aggression (Fraser 1959) and the extended time-span of attention to the world which is vitally necessary to educational adaptation (Campbell 1952; Elder 1965; Sugarman 1966). This is supported by an important rational process which inevitably follows from the 'instrumental' and individualistic life-orientations of middle-class parents (Bernstein 1965; Strauss 1962; Sugarman 1966). Their manifestations of love for the child are intelligently linked to the actual achievement of what are thought to be appropriate skills. From a different point of view this has been called emotional blackmail, but its success in achieving its short-term objective is undisputed.

In contrast, the child-training of the lower classes tends to emphasize unthinking acceptance of authority personified in the parents. Parents tend to rely upon physical punishment, which is often long delayed, inconsistent, vengeful and violent. Children tend to be unsupervised in play and allowed a great deal of unorganized freedom. This might be a much better way of convincing the children that their parents love them for themselves, since punishment, however violent, is irrationally and inconsistently related to behaviour; but it is not a particularly efficient way of encouraging the children to internalize the process of self-control. Authority, children learn, is partial, external and inexplicable. Such a set of ideas is likely to hinder rather than help the process of educational adaptation.

So far we have described some characteristics of social class subcultures and guessed how they might encourage or discourage the development of potentially adaptive cognitions, cathexes and evaluations in the child. To some extent this has fallen into the trap described earlier of assuming that single factors are linearly related to achievement throughout the stratification continuum. If we accept the criticism, we have to try to think in terms of matrices of factors rather than single ones. To some extent the folk-lore of teaching does this. There is a common stereotype of the educationally successful home, which is democratic, values learning as an end in itself, respects the authority of the teachers, supports school activities in a comprehending way, and so on. The problem with this stereotype is that it is unreal.

In order to emphasize that the characteristics of the 'good' family are seldom found in real life, Swift (1967) suggested a second ideal type which might very well turn out to have much greater applicability. This family is found in the upper working class, but predominates in the lower white collar. Both parents are dissatisfied with the status they have achieved. They feel themselves to be able, but are convinced that promotion or social mobility does not depend upon ability. Connections and qualifications are better explanations. Commitment to education is very strong, but it is different from that found in the stereotypical 'good' home where education is seen to be *intellectually* liberating. In this situation it is seen to be *socially* liberating. Educational certificates are only a means to an end of social mobility.

Discipline of the children is traditional as a result of the need to project or 'introject' (Argyle 1964; Argyle and Robinson 1962) frustrated ambitions on to the child. At the same time, parents will have some understanding of the financial and social rewards which are open to the socially mobile. They will also have an adequate understanding of what is involved in successful school adaptation, even though, for reasons which they can usually explain, they were only initially successful themselves. Finally, and perhaps most importantly, they will not have the common working-class view of the middle and upper middle classes; that is, they will not look upon people of these strata as basically different from themselves. All these attitudes provide a climate which is likely to produce a high degree of achievement motivation.

Modes of speech and cognitive skills

There is much more to successful adaptation than the desire to adapt; it is not only a question, that is, of holding positive evaluations and cathexes of education. Adaptation is a consequence of a series of implicit and explicit accepting decisions made by other members of the organization over a period of time. These decisions are evaluations based on many facets of social behaviour. Amongst them exhibited cognitive skills are clearly of the first importance. To put it crudely, the existing members of the group (school) will tend to value thinking and valuing skills which are most like the ones they possess themselves. From the point of view of social class analysis we have to ask how the different social classes encourage the development of those thinking skills which have a bearing on successful school adaptation. Research at this level of complexity is non-existent in Britain. However, one of the best developed and most widely accepted theories concerning such processes has been suggested by Bernstein (1964, 1965), who posits the existence of two types of 'linguistic code', elaborated and restricted. The elaborated code makes precise use of words to communicate meaning, and a person who speaks in this way develops habits and skills in thinking which encourage him to view the environment as a structure to be manipulated. The restricted code, on the other hand, requires its user to employ gesture, intonation and posture to communicate adequately. As a result of this, a more emotional, less predictable approach to coping with the environment is encouraged. Cognitive and social skills so produced tend to be of the kind which are not valued in education. It is not too misleading a generalization to say that the lower reaches of the status continuum are more likely to employ only a restricted code.

The crucial factor from an educational point of view is Bernstein's argument that for a child sensitive to an elaborated code 'school experience is one of symbolic and social development'. He suggests that the linguistic code mediates between the environment and the individual's experience of it, so as to channel the development of his thought in specific directions. In arguing that the user of the elaborated code learns to take an instrumental view of the world around him, Bernstein is concerned with very much more than modes of communication. He is describing the development of intelligent behaviour in which the linguistic code plays a part of unknown importance.

Unfortunately, Bernstein's work has received very little empirical validation. This has not been through lack of interest in a most persuasive theory, but because of the sheer complexity of the research which will be necessary. One such empirical test has been devised by Warren (1966), who reports 'a measure of support' for certain cognitive aspects of the theory. In addition, a great deal of social-psychological research is afoot, which promises an improvement in our present crudely conceived ideas about the development of cognitive style (Bruner *et al.* 1966; Triandis 1964).

Bernstein has argued that his theory does not *necessarily* evaluate the quality of symbolization which the restricted code is thought to produce: it 'carries its own aesthetic . . . will tend to develop a metaphoric range of considerable power, simplicity and directness, vitality and rhythm'. Nevertheless, it seems possible to argue that the conditions of life in some lower-class subcultures are intellectually *less* stimulating. They conduce to lower levels of intellectual efficiency and lower standards of judgment and reasoning. This can come about through inadequate conditions for physical functioning—poverty may still play a part. Again, there is no research backing for such a suggestion, but the possibility must be kept open.

Despite the shortage of research, Bernstein's theory, in conjunction with the findings of social anthropologists on the one hand, and psychometricians on the other, points the way towards future knowledge. It seems certain that our knowledge of social class sub-cultures will play an important part in this process.

Conclusion

This paper has attempted to develop a perspective, according to which the well-known head-counting association between social class and variations in school achievement may be used as a basis for investigation of the social and psychological processes which go to make up the system of education. The crucial distinction to be made is that between social class analysis as an aspect of societal functioning and the influence of cultural experience upon educational adaptiveness of the child.

Once we begin to concentrate upon the latter kind of question, we must place the social class background of the child in its proper context of other aspects of his culture. For example, the local community and its culture, his religion, his family structure, his peer-group and so on are all important aspects of the total cultural experience which 'produces' him before he goes to school and which influences his responses to the demands of school when he starts going to it. There is a large amount of British and American research which can provide data on the extent to which family background can be said to influence ideas about education and the need to achieve in it. But this is only the superficial aspect of the process of adaptation. We have also to consider how cultural experience provides the individual with the cognitive, cathectic and evaluative habits of thought which are important in the process of education. When we have done this, we will be in a better position to decide whether the explicit and implicit demands of the school system, as they are manifested in consequences upon children, are relevant to our aims for education.

References

Argyle, M. (1964) Introjection: a form of social learning. *Brit. J. Psychol.* **55**, 391–402.

Argyle, M. and Robinson, J. (1962) Two origins of achievement motivation. *Brit. J. Soc. Clin. Psychol.* **1**, 107–20.

Banfield, J., Bowyer, C. and Wilkie, E. (1966) Parents and education. *Educ. Research* **9**, 63–6.

Bernstein, B. (1964) Elaborated and restricted codes: their social origins and some consequences. In *American Anthropologist*, special publication: Gumpertz, J. J. and Hymes, D. (eds) The ethnography of communication. **66**, 55–69.

Bernstein, B. (1965) A sociolinguistic approach to social learning. In *Penguin Survey of the Social Sciences*, 144–66.

Bruckman, I. R. (1966) The relationship between achievement motivation and sex, age, social class, school stream and intelligence. *Brit. J. Soc. Clin. Psychol.* **5**, 211–20.

Bruner, J. S., Olver, R. R. and Greenfield, P. M. (1966) *Studies in Cognitive Growth*, New York: Wiley.

Campbell, W. J. (1952) The influence of home environment on the educational progress of selective secondary school children. *Brit. J. Educ. Psychol.* **22**, 89–100.

Child, D. (1966) Personality and social status. *Brit. J. Soc. Clin. Psychol.* **5**, 196–9.

Clausen, J. A. and Williams, J. (1963) Sociological correlates of child behaviour. In Stevenson, H. W., Kagan, J. and Spiker, C. (eds) *Yearbook of National Society for Studies in Education*, **62**, 62–107.

Cohen, E. (1965) Parental factors in educational mobility. *Sociology of Education*, **38**, 404–25.

Dale, R. R. and Griffith, S. (1966) Selected findings from a five-year study of academic deteriorators in a grammar school. *Educ. Research* 8, 146–54.

Davis, A. (1948) *Social Class Influences upon Learning.* Cambridge, Mass.: Harvard University Press.

Douglas, J. W. B. (1964) *The Home and the School; a Study of Ability and Attainment in the Primary School.* London: MacGibbon & Kee.

Elder, G. H. (1965) Life opportunity and personality: some consequences of stratified secondary education in Britain. *Sociology of Education* 38, 173–202.

Farber, B. (1965) Social class and intelligence. *Social Forces* 44, 215–25.

Fraser, E. (1959) *Home Environment and the School.* SCRE publication no. 43. University of London Press.

Himmelweit, H. T. (1955) The psychological aspects of social differentiation. *International Social Science Bulletin* 7, 29–35.

Hyman, H. H. (1953) The value systems of different classes. In Bendix, R. and Lipset, S. (eds) *Class, Status and Power,* 426–42. Glencoe, Illinois: Free Press.

Jackson, B. and Marsden, D. (1961) *Education and the Working Class.* London: Routledge & Kegan Paul.

Kahan, M., Butler, D. and Stokes, D. (1966) On the analytical division of social class. *Brit. J. Sociol.* 17, 122–32.

Kahl, J. A. (1953) Educational and occupational aspirations of 'common man' boys. *Harvard Educ. Review* 23, 186–203.

Katz, F. M. (1964) The meaning of success: some differences in value systems of social classes. *J. Soc. Psychol.* 62, 141–8.

Kohn, M. L. (1963) Social class and parent-child relationships: an interpretation. *Amer. J. Sociol.* 69, 471–80.

Lambert, W. E. and Klineberg, O. (1964) Cultural comparisons of boys' occupational status aspirations. *Brit. J. Soc. Clin. Psychol.* 3, pt 1, 56–65.

Roach, J. L. and Gursslin, O. R. (1967) An evaluation of the concept 'culture of poverty'. *Social Forces* 45, 383–92.

Robinson, W. P. (1964) The achievement motive, academic success and intelligence test scores. *Brit. J. Soc. Clin. Psychol.* 4, 98–103.

Rosen, B. C. (1956) The achievement syndrome: a psychocultural dimension of social stratification. *Amer. Sociol. Review* 21, 203–11.

Rosen, B. C. and D'Andrade, R. (1959) The psycho-social origins of achievement motivation. *Sociometry* 22, 185–218.

Sewell, W. H., Haller, A. O. and Strauss, M. A. (1957) Social status and educational and occupational aspiration. *Amer. Sociol. Review* 22, 67–73.

Stacey, B. G. (1965) Some psychological aspects of intergeneration occupational mobility. *Brit. J. Soc. Clin. Psychol.* 4, 275–86.

Strauss, M. A. (1962) Deferred gratification, social class, and the achievement syndrome. *Amer. Sociol. Review* 27, 326–35.

Sugarman, B. N. (1966) Social class and values as related to achievement and conduct in school. *Sociol. Review* 14, 287–301.

Swift, D. F. (1966) Social class and achievement motivation. *Educ. Research* 8, 83–95.

Swift, D. F. (1967) Social class mobility ideology and 11-plus success. *Brit. J. Sociol.* 18 (2), 165–86.

Triandis, H. C. (1964) The influence of culture on cognitive processes. In Berkowitz, L. (ed.) *Advances in Experimental Social Psychology.* New York: Academic Press.

Turner, R. H. (1966) Acceptance of irregular mobility in Britain and the United States. *Sociometry* 29, 334–52.

Wall, W. D., Schonell, F. J. and Olson, W. C. (1962) *Failure in School.* Hamburg: Unesco Institute for Education. Reviewed by Chazan, M. (1963) in *Brit. J. Educ. Psychol.* 33, pt 3, 338.

Warren, N. (1966) Social class and construct systems: examination of the cognitive structure of two social class groups. *Brit. J. Soc. Clin. Psychol.* 5, 254–63.

30 The class and the élite

T. S. Eliot

It would appear, according to the account of levels of culture put forward . . . that among the more primitive societies, the higher types exhibit more marked differentiations of function amongst their members than the lower types.* At a higher stage still, we find that some functions are more honoured than others, and this division promotes the development of *classes*, in which higher honour and higher privilege are accorded, not merely to the person as functionary but as member of the class. And the class itself possesses a function, that of maintaining that part of the total culture of the society which pertains to that class. We have to try to keep in mind, that in a healthy society this maintenance of a particular level of culture is to the benefit, not merely of the class which maintains it, but of the society as a whole. Awareness of this fact will prevent us from supposing that the culture of a 'higher' class is something superfluous to society as a whole, or to the majority, and from supposing that it is something which ought to be shared equally by all other classes. It should also remind the 'higher' class, in so far as any such exists, that the survival of the culture in which it is particularly interested is dependent upon the health of the culture of the people.

It has now become a commonplace of contemporary thinking, that a society thus articulated is not the highest type to which we may aspire; but that it is indeed in the nature of things for a progressive society eventually to overcome these divisions, and that it is also within the power of our conscious direction, and therefore a duty incumbent upon us, to bring about a classless society. But while it is generally supposed that

Source: T. S. Eliot, *Notes Towards the Definition of Culture*, Faber (1948), 35–49.

* I am anxious to avoid speaking as if the evolution of primitive culture to higher forms was a process which we knew by observation. We *observe* the differences, we *infer* that some have developed from a stage similar to that of the lower stages which we observe: but however legitimate our inference, I am here not concerned with that development.

class, in any sense which maintains associations of the past, will disappear, it is now the opinion of some of the most advanced minds that some qualitative differences between individuals must still be recognized, and that the superior individuals must be formed into suitable groups, endowed with appropriate powers, and perhaps with varied emoluments and honours. Those groups, formed of individuals apt for powers of government and administration, will direct the public life of the nation; the individuals composing them will be spoken of as 'leaders'. There will be groups concerned with art, and groups concerned with science, and groups concerned with philosophy, as well as groups consisting of men of action: and these groups are what we call élites.

It is obvious, that while in the present state of society there is found the voluntary association of like-minded individuals, and association based upon common material interest, or common occupation or profession, the élites of the future will differ in one important respect from any that we know: they will replace the classes of the past, whose positive functions they will assume. This transformation is not always explicitly stated. There are some philosophers who regard class divisions as intolerable, and others who regard them merely as moribund. The latter may simply ignore class, in their design for an élite-governed society, and say that the élites will 'be drawn from all sections of society'. But it would seem that as we perfect the means for identifying at an early age, educating for their future role, and settling into positions of authority, the individuals who will form the élites, all former class distinctions will become a mere shadow or vestige, and the only social distinction of rank will be between the élites and the rest of the community, unless, as may happen, there is to be an order of precedence and prestige amongst the several élites themselves.

However moderately and unobtrusively the doctrine of élites is put, it implies a radical transformation of society. Superficially, it appears to aim at no more than what we must all desire—that all positions in society should be occupied by those who are best fitted to exercise the functions of the positions. We have all observed individuals occupying situations in life for which neither their character nor their intellect qualified them, and so placed only through nominal education, or birth or consanguinity. No honest man but is vexed by such a spectacle. But the doctrine of élites implies a good deal more than the rectification of such injustice. It posits an *atomic* view of society.

The philosopher whose views on the subject of élites deserve the closest attention, both for their own value and because of the influence they exert, is the late Dr Karl Mannheim. It is, for that matter, Dr Mannheim who has founded the fortunes, in this country, of the term élite. I must remark that Dr Mannheim's description of culture is different from that given in the previous chapter of this essay. He says (*Man and Society*, 81):

A sociological investigation of culture in liberal society must begin with the life of those who create culture, i.e. the intelligentsia and their position within society as a whole.

According to the account which I have given, a 'culture' is conceived as the creation of the society as a whole: being, from another aspect, that which makes it a society. It is not the creation of any one part of that society. The function of what Dr Mannheim would call the culture-creating groups, according to my account, would be rather to bring about a further development of the culture in organic complexity: culture at a more conscious level, but still the same culture. This higher level of culture must be thought of both as valuable in itself, and as enriching of the lower levels: thus the movement of culture would proceed in a kind of cycle, each class nourishing the others.

This is, already, a difference of some importance. My next observation is that Dr Mannheim is concerned rather with élites than with an élite.

We may distinguish [he says, in *Man and Society*, 82] the following types of élites: the political, the organizing, the intellectual, the artistic, the moral and the religious. Whereas the political and organising élites aim at integrating a great number of individual wills, it is the function of the intellectual, aesthetic, and moral-religious élites to sublimate those psychic energies which society, in the daily struggle for existence, does not fully exhaust.

This departmentalization of élites already exists, to some extent; and to some extent it is a necessary and a good thing. But, so far as it can be observed to exist, it is not *altogether* a good thing. I have suggested elsewhere that a growing weakness of our culture has been

the increasing isolation of élites from each other, so that the political, the philosophical, the artistic, the scientific, are separated to the great loss of each of them, not merely through the arrest of any general circulation of ideas, but through the lack of those contacts and mutual influences at a less conscious level, which are perhaps even more important than ideas. The problem of the formation, preservation and development of the élites is therefore also the problem of the formation, preservation and development of *the* élite, a problem upon which Dr Mannheim does not touch.

As an introduction to this problem, I must draw attention to another difference between my view and that of Dr Mannheim. He observes, in a statement with which I agree (p. 85):

The crisis of culture in liberal-democratic society is due, in the first place, to the fact that the fundamental social processes, which previously favoured the development of the culturally creative élites, now have the opposite effect, i.e. have become obstacles to the forming of élites because wider sections of the population take an active part in cultural activities.

I cannot, of course, admit the last clause of this sentence as it stands. According to my view of culture, the whole of the population *should* 'take an active part in cultural activities'—not all in the same activities or on the same level. What this clause means, in my terms, is that an increasing proportion of the population is concerned with group culture. This comes about, I think Dr Mannheim would agree, through the gradual alteration of the class-structure. But at this point it seems to me that Dr Mannheim begins to confuse élite with *class*. For he says (p. 89):

If one calls to mind the essential forms of selecting élites which up to the present have appeared on the historical scene, three principles can be distinguished: selection on the basis of *blood*, *property* and *achievement*. Aristocratic society, especially after it had entrenched itself, chose its élites primarily on the blood principle. Bourgeois society gradually introduced, as a supplement, the principle of wealth, a principle which also obtained for the intellectual élite inasmuch as education was more or less available only to the offspring of the well-to-do. It is, of course, true that the principle of achievement was combined with the two other principles in earlier periods, but it is the important contribution of modern democracy as long as it is rigorous, that the achievement principle increasingly tends to become the criterion of social success.

I am ready to accept, in a rough and ready way, this account of three historical periods. But I would remark that we are here not concerned with élites but with *classes* or, more precisely, with the evolution from a class to a classless society. It seems to me that at the stage of the sharpest division into classes we can distinguish an élite also. Are we to believe that the artists of the middle ages were all men of noble rank, or that the hierarchy and the statesmen were all selected according to their pedigrees?

I do not think that this is what Dr Mannheim wishes us to believe; but I think that he is confusing the élites with the dominant section of society which the élites served, from which they took their colour, and into which some of their individual members were recruited. The general scheme of the transition of society, in the last five hundred years or so, is usually accepted, and I have no interest in questioning it. I would only propose one qualification. At the stage of dominance of *bourgeois* society (I think it would be better to say, for this country, 'upper-middle-class society') there is a difference applying particularly to England. However powerful it was—for its power is now commonly said to be passing—it would not have been what it was, without the existence of a class above it, from which it drew some of its ideals and some of its criteria, and to the condition of which its more ambitious members aspired. This gives it a difference in kind from the aristocratic society which preceded it, and from the mass-society which is expected to follow it.

I now come to another statement in Dr Mannheim's discussion, which seems to me wholly true. His intellectual integrity prevents him from dissimulating the gloom of our present position; but he succeeds, so far as I can judge, in communicating to most of his readers a feeling of active hopefulness, by infecting them with his own passionate faith in the possibilities of 'planning'. Yet he says quite clearly:

We have no clear idea how the selection of élites would work in an open mass society in which only the principle of achievement mattered. It is possible that in such a society, the succession of the élites would take place much too rapidly and social continuity which is essentially due to the slow and gradual broadening of the influence of the dominant groups would be lacking in it.*

This raises a problem of the first importance to my present discussion, with which I do not think Dr Mannheim has dealt in any detail: that of the *transmission of culture*.

When we are concerned with the history of certain parts of culture, such as the history of art, or of literature, or of philosophy, we naturally isolate a particular class of phenomena; though there has been a movement, which has produced books of interest and value, to relate these subjects more closely to a general social history. But even such accounts are usually only the

history of one class of phenomena interpreted in the light of the history of another class of phenomena and, like that of Dr Mannheim, tend to take a more limited view of culture than that adopted here. What we have to consider is the parts played by the élite and by the class in the transmission of culture from one generation to the next.

We must remind ourselves of the danger, mentioned in the previous chapter, of identifying culture with the *sum* of distinct cultural activities; and if we avoid this identification we shall also decline to identify our group culture with the sum of the activities of Dr Mannheim's élites. The anthropologist may study the social system, the economics, the arts, and the religion of a particular tribe, he may even study their psychological peculiarities: but it is not merely by observing in detail all of these manifestations, and grasping them together, that he will approach to an understanding of the culture. For to understand the culture is to understand the people, and this means an imaginative understanding. Such understanding can never be complete: either it is abstract—and the essence escapes—or else it is *lived*; and in so far as it is *lived*, the student will tend to identify himself so completely with the people whom he studies, that he will lose the point of view from which it was worth while and possible to study it. Understanding involves an area more extensive than that of which one can be conscious; one cannot be outside and inside at the same time. What we ordinarily mean by understanding of another people, of course, is an approximation towards understanding which stops short at the point at which the student would begin to lose some essential of his own culture. The man who, in order to understand the inner world of a cannibal tribe, has partaken of the practice of cannibalism, has probably gone too far: he can never quite be one of his own folk again.*

I have raised this question, however, solely in support of my contention that culture is not merely the sum of several activities, but a *way of life*. Now the specialist of genius, who may be fully qualified on the ground of his vocational attainment for membership of one of Dr Mannheim's élites, may very well not be one of the 'cultured persons' representative of group culture. As I have said before, he may be only a highly valued contributor to it. Yet group culture, as observable in the past, has never been co-extensive with class, whether an aristocracy or an upper middle class. A very large number of members of these classes always have been conspicuously deficient in 'culture'. I think that in the past the repository of this culture has been *the* élite, the major part of which was drawn from the dominant class of the time, constituting the primary consumers of the work of thought and art produced by the minority members, who will have originated from various classes, including that class itself. The units of this majority will, some of them, be individuals; others will be families. But the individuals from the dominant

---

* Dr Mannheim proceeds to call attention to a tendency in mass-society to renounce even the achievement principle. This passage is important; but as I agree with him that the dangers from this are still more alarming, it is unnecessary to quote it here.

** Joseph Conrad's *Heart of Darkness* gives a hint of something similar.*

class who compose the nucleus of the cultural élite must not thereby be cut off from the class to which they belong, for without their membership of that class they would not have their part to play. It is their function, in relation to the producers, to transmit the culture which they have inherited; just as it is their function, in relation to the rest of their class, to keep it from ossification. It is the function of the class as a whole to preserve and communicate standards of *manners*—which are a vital element in group culture.* It is the function of the superior members and superior families to preserve the group culture, as it is the function of the producers to alter it.

In an élite composed of individuals who find their way into it solely for their individual pre-eminence, the differences of background will be so great, that they will be united only by their common interests, and separated by everything else. An élite must therefore be attached to *some* class, whether higher or lower: but so long as there are classes at all it is likely to be the dominant class that attracts this élite to itself. What would happen in a classless society—which is much more difficult to envisage than people think—brings us into the area of conjecture. There are, however, some guesses which seem to me worth venturing.

The primary channel of transmission of culture is the family: no man wholly escapes from the kind, or wholly surpasses the degree, of culture which he acquired from his early environment. It would not do to suggest that this can be the *only* channel of transmission: in a society of any complexity it is supplemented and continued by other conduits of tradition. Even in relatively primitive societies this is so. In more civilized communities of specialized activities, in which not all the sons would follow the occupation of their father, the apprentice (ideally, at least) did not merely serve his master, and did not merely learn from him as one would learn at a technical school—he became assimilated into a way of life which went with that particular trade or craft; and perhaps the lost secret of the craft is this, that not merely a skill but an entire way of life was transmitted. Culture—distinguishable from knowledge about culture—was transmitted by the older universities: young men have profited there who have been profitless students, and who have acquired no taste for learning, or for Gothic architecture, or for college ritual and form. I suppose that something of the same sort is transmitted also by societies of the masonic type: for initiation is an introduction into a way of life, of however restricted viability, received from the past and to be perpetuated in the future. But by far the most important channel of transmission of culture remains the family: and when family life fails to play its part, we must expect our

* To avoid misunderstanding at this point, it should be observed that I do not assume that 'good manners' should be peculiar to any one stratum of society. In a healthy society, good manners should be found throughout. But as we distinguish between the meanings of 'culture' at the several levels, so we distinguish also between the meanings of more and less conscious 'good manners'.

culture to deteriorate. Now the family is an institution of which nearly everybody speaks well: but it is advisable to remember that this is a term that may vary in extension. In the present age it means little more than the living members. Even of living members, it is a rare exception when an advertisement depicts a large family of three generations: the usual family on the hoardings consists of two parents and one or two young children. What is held up for admiration is not devotion to a family, but personal affection between the members of it: and the smaller the family, the more easily can this personal affection be sentimentalized. But when I speak of the family, I have in mind a bond which embraces a longer period of time than this: a piety towards the dead, however obscure, and a solicitude for the unborn, however remote. Unless this reverence for past and future is cultivated in the home, it can never be more than a verbal convention in the community. Such an interest in the past is different from the vanities and pretensions of genealogy; such a responsibility for the future is different from that of the builder of social programmes.

I should say then that in a vigorous society there will be present both class and élite, with some overlapping and constant interaction between them. An élite, if it is a governing élite, and so far as the natural impulse to pass on to one's offspring both power and prestige is not artificially checked, will tend to establish itself as a class—it is this metamorphosis, I think, which leads to what appears to me an oversight on the part of Dr Mannheim. But an élite which thus transforms itself tends to lose its function as élite, for the qualities by which the original members won their position, will not all be transmitted equally to their descendants. On the other hand, we have to consider what would be the consequence when the converse took place, and we had a society in which the functions of class were assumed by élites. Dr Mannheim seems to have believed that this will happen; he showed himself, as a passage which I have quoted shows, aware of the dangers; and he does not appear to have been ready to propose definite safeguards against them.

The situation of a society without classes, and dominated exclusively by élites, is, I submit, one about which we have no reliable evidence. By such a society, I suppose we must mean one in which every individual starts without advantage or handicap; and in which, by some mechanism set up by the best designers of such machinery, everybody will find his way, or be directed, to that station of life which he is best fitted to fill, and every position will be occupied by the man or woman best fitted for it. Of course, not even the most sanguine would expect the system to work as well as that: if, by and large, it seemed to come nearer to putting the right people in the right places than any previous system, we should all be satisfied. When I say 'dominated', rather than 'governed' by élites, I mean that such a society must not be content to be *governed* by the right people: it must see that the ablest artists and architects rise to the top, influence taste, and execute the important public commissions; it must do the same by the other arts and by science; and above all, perhaps, it must be such that the ablest minds will find expression in speculative thought. The system must not only do all this for society in a particular situation—it must *go on* doing it, generation after generation. It would be folly to deny that in a particular phase of a country's development, and *for a limited purpose*, an élite can do a very good job. It may, by expelling a previous governing group, which in contrast to itself may be a *class*, save or reform or revitalize the national life. Such things have happened. But we have very little evidence about the perpetuation of government by élite, and such as we have is unsatisfactory. A considerable time must elapse before we can draw any illustration from Russia. Russia is a rude and vigorous country; it is also a very big country; and it will need a long period of peace and internal development. Three things may happen. Russia may show us how a stable government and a flourishing culture can be transmitted only through élites; it may lapse into oriental lethargy; or the governing élite may follow the course of other governing élites and become a governing class. Nor can we rely upon any evidence from the United States of America. The real revolution in that country was not what is called the Revolution in the history books, but is a consequence of the Civil War; after which arose a plutocratic élite; after which the expansion and material development of the country was accelerated; after which was swollen that stream of mixed immigration, bringing (or rather multiplying) the danger of development into a *caste* system* which has not yet been quite dispelled. For the sociologist, the evidence from America is not yet ripe. Our other evidence for government by élite comes chiefly from France. A governing class, which, during a long period in which the Throne was all-powerful, had ceased to govern, was reduced to the ordinary level of citizenship. Modern France has had no governing class: her political life in the Third Republic, whatever else we may say of it, was *unsettled*. And here we may remark that when a dominant class, however badly it has performed its function, is forcibly removed, its function is not wholly taken over by any other. The 'flight of the wild geese' is perhaps a symbol of the harm that England has done to Ireland—more serious, from this point of view, than the massacres of Cromwell, or any of the grievances which the Irish most gladly recall. It may be, too, that England has done more harm to Wales and Scotland by gently attracting their upper classes to certain public schools, than by the wrongs (some real, some imaginary, some misunderstood) voiced by their respective nationalists. But here again, I wish to reserve judgment about Russia. That country, at the time of its revolution, may still have been at so early a stage of its development, that the removal of its

upper class may prove not only not to have arrested that development but to have stimulated it. There are, however, some grounds for believing that the elimination of an upper class at a more developed stage can be a disaster for a country: and most certainly when that removal is due to the intervention of another nation.

I have, in the preceding paragraphs, been speaking mainly of the 'governing class' and the 'governing élite'. But I must remind the reader again that in concerning ourselves with class *versus* élite, we are concerned with the total culture of a country, and that involves a good deal more than government. We can yield ourselves with some confidence to a governing élite, as the republican Romans surrendered power to dictators, so long as we have in view a *defined purpose* in a crisis – and a crisis may last a long time. This limited purpose also makes it possible to choose the élite, for we know what we are choosing it for. But, if we are looking for a way to select the right people to constitute every élite, for an indefinite future, by what mechanism are we to do this? If our 'purpose' is only to get the best people, in every walk of life, to the top, we lack a criterion of who are the best people; or, if we impose a criterion, it will have an oppressive effect upon novelty. The new work of genius, whether in art, science or philosophy, frequently meets with opposition.

All that concerns me at the moment is the question whether, by education alone, we can ensure the transmission of culture in a society in which some educationists appear indifferent to class distinctions, and from which some other educationists appear to want to remove class distinctions altogether. There is, in any case, a danger of interpreting 'education' to cover both too much and too little: too little, when it implies that education is limited to what can be taught; too much, when it implies that everything worth preserving can be transmitted by teaching. In the society desired by some reformers, what the family can transmit will be limited to the minimum, especially if the child is to be, as Mr H. C. Dent hopes, manipulated by a unified educational system 'from the cradle to the grave'. And unless the child is classified, by the officials who will have the task of sorting him out, as being just like his father, he will be brought up in a different —not necessarily a better, because all will be equally good, but a different—school environment, and trained on what the official opinion of the moment considers to be 'the genuinely democratic lines'. The élites, in consequence, will consist solely of individuals whose only common bond will be their professional interest: with no social cohesion, with no social continuity. They will be united only by a part, and that the most conscious part, of their personalities; they will meet like committees. The greater part of their 'culture' will be only what they share with all the other individuals composing their nation.

The case for a society with a class structure, the affirmation that it is, in some sense, the 'natural'

---

* I believe that the essential difference between a caste and a class system is that the basis of the former is a difference such that the dominant class comes to consider itself a superior *race*.

society, is prejudiced if we allow ourselves to be hypnotized by the two contrasted terms *aristocracy* and *democracy*. The whole problem is falsified if we use these terms antithetically. What I have advanced is not a 'defence of aristocracy' – an emphasis upon the importance of one organ of society. Rather it is a plea on behalf of a form of society in which an aristocracy should have a peculiar and essential function, as peculiar and essential as the function of any other part of society. What is important is a structure of society in which there will be, from 'top' to 'bottom', a continuous gradation of cultural levels: it is important to remember that we should not consider the upper levels as possessing *more* culture than the lower, but as representing a more conscious culture and a greater specialization of culture. I incline to believe that no true democracy can maintain itself unless it contains these different levels of culture. The levels of culture may also be seen as levels of power, to the extent that a smaller group at a higher level will have equal power with a larger group at a lower level; for it may be argued that complete equality means universal irresponsibility; and in such a society as I envisage,

each individual would inherit greater or less responsibility towards the commonwealth, according to the position in society which he inherited—each class would have somewhat different responsibilities. A democracy in which everybody had an equal responsibility in everything would be oppressive for the conscientious and licentious for the rest.

There are other grounds upon which a graded society can be defended; and I hope, in general, that this essay will suggest lines of thought that I shall not myself explore; but I must constantly remind the reader of the limits of my subject. If we agree that the primary vehicle for the transmission of culture is the family, and if we agree that in a more highly civilized society there must be different levels of culture, then it follows that to ensure the transmission of the culture of these different levels there must be groups of families persisting, from generation to generation, each in the same way of life.

And once again I must repeat, that the 'conditions of culture' which I set forth do not necessarily produce the higher civilization: I assert only that when they are absent, the higher civilization is unlikely to be found.

31 Mass civilization and minority culture

F. R. Leavis

And this function is particularly important in our modern world, of which the whole civilization is, to a much greater degree than the civilization of Greece and Rome, mechanical and external, and tends constantly to become more so.

Culture and Anarchy, 1869

For Matthew Arnold it was in some ways less difficult. I am not thinking of the so much more desperate plight of culture today,* but (it is not, at bottom, an unrelated consideration) of the freedom with which he could use such phrases as 'the will of God' and 'our true selves'. Today one must face problems of definition and formulation where Arnold could pass lightly on. When, for example, having started by saying that culture has always been in minority keeping, I am asked what I mean by 'culture,' I might (and do) refer the reader to *Culture and Anarchy*; but I know that something more is required.

In any period it is upon a very small minority that the discerning appreciation of art and literature depends: it is (apart from cases of the simple and familiar) only a few who are capable of unprompted, first-hand judgment. They are still a small minority, though a larger one, who are capable of endorsing such first-hand judgment by genuine personal response. The accepted valuations are a kind of paper currency based upon a very small proportion of gold. To the state of such a currency the possibilities of fine living at any time bear a close relation. There is no need to elaborate the metaphor: the nature of the relation is suggested well enough by this passage from Mr I. A. Richards, which should by now be a *locus classicus*:†

But it is not true that criticism is a luxury trade. The rearguard of Society cannot be extricated until the vanguard has gone further. Goodwill and intelligence are still too little available. The critic, we have said, is as much concerned with the health of the mind as any doctor with the health of the body. To set up as a critic is to set up as a judge of values. . . . For the arts are inevitably and quite apart from any intentions of the artist an appraisal of existence. Matthew Arnold, when he said that poetry is a criticism of life, was saying something so obvious that it is constantly overlooked. The artist is concerned with the record and perpetuation of the experiences which seem to him most worth having. For reasons which we shall consider . . . he is also the man who is most likely to have experiences of value to record. He is the point at which the growth of the mind shows itself.

This last sentence gives the hint for another metaphor. The minority capable not only of appreciating Dante, Shakespeare, Donne, Baudelaire, Conrad (to take major instances) but of recognizing their latest successors constitute the consciousness of the race (or of a branch of it) at a given time. For such capacity does not belong merely to an isolated aesthetic realm: it implies responsiveness to theory as well as to art, to science and philosophy in so far as these may affect the sense of the human situation and of the nature of life. Upon this minority depends our power of profiting by the finest human experience of the past; they keep alive the subtlest and most perishable parts of tradition. Upon them depend the implicit standards that order the finer living of an age, the sense that this is worth more than that, this rather than that is the

Source: F. R. Leavis, *Education and the University*, Chatto & Windus (1943), 143–5.

*'The word, again, which we children of God speak, the voice which most hits our collective thought, the newspaper with the largest circulation in England, nay with the largest circulation in the whole world, is the *Daily Telegraph*!'— *Culture and Anarchy*.

It is the *News of the World* that has the largest circulation today.

† *The Principles of Literary Criticism*, 61.

direction in which to go, that the centre* is here rather than there. In their keeping, to use a metaphor that is metonymy also and will bear a good deal of pondering,

* . . . The mass of the people is without any suspicion that the value of these organs is relative to their being nearer a certain ideal centre of correct information, taste and intelligence, or farther away from it.

is the language, the changing idiom, upon which fine living depends, and without which distinction of spirit is thwarted and incoherent. By 'culture' I mean the use of such a language. I do not suppose myself to have produced a tight definition, but the account, I think, will be recognized as adequate by anyone who is likely to read this pamphlet.

32 Education and economic development

John Vaizey

What is known of the established relationships between education and economic development? This is a question that I have studied for several years, and I wish to summarize my views here. It would perhaps be as well to enter here my caveat that the inter-relationships between education, productivity, the economy and society are enormously complex and that we know little about them. I will leave on one side for the moment, too, accusations of philistinism—I love the arts—need I say more? I write as an economist who has worked in many fields of economics, but I also write as one who has taught for seventeen years, and who has been involved in the administration of public school systems for almost as long. I reject the distinction between 'economist' and 'educator'—though, in economics (as elsewhere) to assume the mantle of educator is, I have discovered, to lose caste in some circles. Perhaps the wisest place to begin would be the widely repeated statements about the part of economic growth which has been measured and attributed to education in a number of—especially—American publications. In particular, this part of my paper draws upon the analyses published by Mr Edward Denison: before I describe it I should emphasize that the statistical work he has done has been extremely laborious, and I have the highest admiration for it. This work is an attempt to evaluate the benefits of education. Many benefits are non-commensurate without an assumption that a common numerical value can be assigned to them (and these numbers—indeed the very process of assigning numbers—are, of course, in dispute). My own original work lay in the back-breaking task of trying to evaluate the costs of education.

In principle, the work rests upon a series of hypotheses, and a series of calculations derived from these hypotheses. It is argued, first, that after standardizing for ability, race, social class, sex and other socio-cultural factors, a relationship has been established

Source: *Journal of Educational Thought* (1968), **2** (3), 1959–66.

between educational attainment and lifetime earnings. These relationships are investigated by many methods, but the primary source is census data which relate years of education to occupation and income. The life-time earnings have to be standardized, of course, for price changes and life-expectancy. They incorporate, therefore, both data from the past, and assumptions—or extrapolations—about the future. These lifetime earnings, properly discounted, can be expressed as a rate of return on the cost of education. The cost of education may be measured in a variety of ways, but usually in this work it is calculated as what is called the opportunity cost, that is to say total educational costs plus loss of earnings which would have been made had the students been in employment when they were at college or at high school.

Using an orthodox production function of the Cobb-Douglas type, other inputs are similarly evaluated, and in the large area which is left as a residual after such identifiable inputs as the contributions of the growth in the size of the labour force, changes in its age structure, and changes in the capital stock and in its structure, and other certain measurable inputs have been abstracted from the growth rate, it is calculated that the residual is mainly due to education and to the growth of knowledge.

If I may, I would like to quote Professor Harry Johnson on this:[1]

The essence of it is to regard 'capital' as including anything that yields a stream of income over time, and income as the product of capital. From this point of view, as Fisher pointed out, all categories of income describe yields on various forms of capital, and can be expressed as rates of interest or return on the corresponding items of capital. Alternatively, all forms of income-yielding assets can be given an equivalent capital value by capitalizing the income they yield at an appropriate rate of interest. By extension, the growth of income that defines economic development is necessarily the result of the accumulation of capital, or of 'investment'; but 'investment' in this context must be defined to include such diverse activities as adding to material capital, increasing the health, discipline, skill and education of the human population, moving labour into more productive occupations and locations, and applying existing knowledge or discovering and applying new knowledge to increase the efficiency of productive processes. All such activities involve incurring costs, in the form of use of current resources, and investment in them is socially worth while if the rate of return over cost exceeds the general rate of interest, or the capital value of the additional income they yield exceeds the cost of obtaining it. From the somewhat different perspective of planning economic development, efficient development involves allocation of investment resources according to priorities set by the relative rates of return on alternative investments.

Thus underlying this work is a formidable battery of neo-classical capital theory, and complex and thorough statistical work. Before I say what I understand the work to have shown I had better mention the objections.

Now the opposition to this chain of reasoning is twofold. It concentrates first upon the relationship between subsequent earnings and educational careers. It argues that the returns to labour are what economists call conventional or institutional returns, which bear little relationship to the orthodox reasoning of market economics. In other words the labour market is not appropriately described by the perfect competition model. And secondly and more notably, following the attack by Professor Kaldor and others, they refute the assumption upon which the work ultimately rests, namely the existence of a production function of this type. Professor Kaldor said at the same meeting as that from which I quoted Professor Johnson: 'All such estimates are derived from hypotheses concerning the so-called "production function" and the price system (it is a mild description to call them "strong assumptions") which have no theoretical or empirical basis whatever.' As Mr Robert Neild said (again at the same place—it was a lively affair): 'It was evident from the discussion that the division between those who believe in the marginal productivity theory of distribution and those who do not was a matter of faith; it was not something that could be resolved by discussion (or conversion).'[2]

This is not the place to discuss the validity of the arguments to and fro. It is sufficient to say that the very basis of the matter is in dispute. I would merely say that in principle this work of Denison's, and other studies, if its assumptions are accepted, does seem to show the rates of return on education are certainly no lower than those from physical capital; and secondly,

that of all the factors that contribute to growth, the biggest is that which is attributable to education, and these results have been found to be the case not only in the United States, but in a number of other countries where similar calculations have been made. The policy conclusions are obvious; broadly speaking too little has been devoted to human capital in the United States, and a reallocation of resources away from physical capital to human capital would have accelerated growth. (Harberger and others claim to have found the opposite in India, and elsewhere.) But even more important than the general results is the general claim of reasoning that policy for growth ought to be couched in terms that explicitly include education in the equations. This is an extremely important point— and it is one now accepted in long-term looks at the economy. It is not accepted, I think, in short-term macro-economic work; one sees no sign of it in Treasury or NIESR forecasts of the short-term growth rates. I write this in parenthesis as a note of caution to those who believe that all economists accept in their hearts, and in their heads, the economic importance of education. They don't. I will not dwell here on the issue that this work has raised for the organization of education. Broadly they concern the question whether education ought to be bought or sold on the market or not. Milton Friedman has argued strongly on moral grounds that it ought to be sold on the market. I would merely point out that this is not self-evidently so—and further, that 'market economics', as a moral doctrine, rests on solipsism which appears to be a logical contradiction in this context. Further, I see no reason to assume that pure competition would prevail in the supply or demand for education. (I have expounded these views at length elsewhere and my arguments have never been answered.)

The second point I would wish to make is that calculations have been made differentiating the different roles of education throughout the world, and the results tend to lead one to suppose that no less important than the quantity of education is its quality. It would be interesting to see a completely different mode of approval, through what people had learned what thing, or what ways of behaviour, rather than just the crude years of schooling. But in the absence of such studies we must deal with the quantity of material that is available at present. The evidence of the Coleman Report, and English evidence, suggest of course that the school, as such, is less important in social conditioning than other conditioning agencies (mostly the family).

The evidence, so far as I can interpret it, tends to suggest that the more education you have the lower the increment of output which comes from additions to education. That is to say, if you start with somebody who has zero education and give him a small amount of education, the returns are very large; but it tends to fall the more education you have. On the other hand, there is little evidence to suggest that in very rich societies the returns to education are lower than the returns to education in poor societies. In other words, it does not look as yet as though we have reached the stage where education gives diminishing returns because of the very affluence of the society. The answer to this paradox must lie in the complementarities in the situation, rather than in anything else.

As I have said, argument will rage back and forth as to the validity of these types of calculation. I am myself more agnostic about them than many people, particularly in the United States, would tend to be, and I have grave doubts about many of the figures presented, and much of the reasoning that lies behind them. But I think they tend to confirm what intuitively is not entirely unobvious, namely that technologically progressive societies, which also tend to have fairly high and sustained growth rates, tend to spend substantial sums of their Gross National Product on education, and that since the proportion of the Gross National Product spent on education is rising throughout the world, the potential growth rate is also rising. The evidence for these two very general propositions, drawn both from economic history and from recent economic analysis, is most striking. There are the examples of the German technical education system, the American high school and land grant college system, the Japanese education system, both after the Meiji era and at present, the Soviet education system, and (I would add) particular parts of the English education system. Here, again, there is a real problem, I think, in interpreting the story as to which is cause and which is effect. There seems to me to be little doubt that, viewed historically, German experience of widespread technical education and widespread literacy, does suggest that technical education played a key role in their economic development. On the other hand, there is little sign that the quality or volume of education played any crucial part in the British industrial revolution, and we could equally draw attention to examples from throughout the world of places where the education system has hindered development. Examples of this may well be classical China, some of the colonialist education systems. (Alfred Marshall would have held the English upper-class education system of the nineteenth century was a similar case.) Some people would argue the contemporary arts-biased education system of sixth form and university in England now was anti-economic growth. One has to be very careful to separate out arguments about volume and about quality: arguments about education for all from arguments about education for key groups.

Some detailed research has been done on this question in the United States and points to the importance both of widespread general education and of the very skilled immigrant groups who started America on the path to world supremacy. Professor Cremin and Mr Habakkuk have done signal service in unravelling parts, at least, of that story. As we are lacking any serious historical studies of education, with a few

honourable exceptions, we are not in a position yet to assent to, or to deny, the general propositions which have been advanced by economists and historians about the relative importance of education in economic development. One sees the general outline, but the truth lies in the detail.

Certainly when we turn to the developing world a sustained controversy has raged between what one may call those who assign a key role to 'the big leap forward' in education, and their opponents. If I may, I will caricature them as on the one hand, the manpower planners, typified in the Ashby Report on Nigeria, and on the other hand those who have criticized the colonialist and neo-colonialist education system for creating a semi-educated urban unemployed population.

Now if we look at this in context, I think we see the outlines of a debate which, at the moment, rages back and forth, about the nature of education's contribution to economic growth, and the reciprocal relationship between education and economic growth. On the one hand, you have those who argue as follows: that as economic growth takes place, skilled manpower plays a critical role in the development of the socio-economic structure; that rough forecasts can be made for the requirements of manpower over the next twenty or thirty years; that these can be re-interpreted into educational categories and that this will give you an outline of the bias which ought to be put into the education system. At the same time, they would acknowledge that the education is expanding greatly, largely because of social pressures for more education. Now these social pressures are not merely a desire for education in itself; they are of course also the quite ordinary economic calculations of ordinary families, that education leads to higher incomes. In other words, I doubt whether the dichotomy between social and economic demands for education can be justified, and whether broadly this type of demand for education may be categorized as more social than economic. It is the mixture—the nature of the educational provision—which is derived from manpower forecast targets. These manpower forecast targets, interpreted into educational categories, therefore give you what might be called an 'ideal' or model educational structure towards which you have to move your existing educational provision.

I say all this without regard to the validity of attempts to forecast manpower requirements, for long periods ahead, and to deduce educational categories and totals from it. There is many a slip 'twixt cup and lip, and I think detailed manpower forecasts for long periods ahead have little validity, either conceptually or in practice. The only satisfactory ones, it seems to me, are those for specific types of skill in the short period. Manpower forecasts seem to me to multiply almost all known forecasting errors, and are usually only correct by accident.

Further, the main uses to which the (derived) educational totals are put seem to me to be to put the screws on educational conservatives. The totals are so big, that people are told that the very size of the expansion entails a qualitative change in the provisions.

Now, of course, what is lacking here is to some extent a critical discussion of the content of education. In its most explicit formulation, the discussion is about whether the skills as set out by the manpower planners are actually the kind of skills that society needs. Implicit in the manpower programmes may well be a view of the nature of the future economy and the society which would not be acceptable. And secondly, the discussion is about the implicit values and outlook which is associated with a particular structure of education. In the developing nations the educational system derived from manpower targets characteristically has a larger higher education system, and above all a larger secondary education system, than that which would be derived from the pressure of parents and politicians, which tends to be a more orthodox pyramid in shape. The opponents of this mode of reasoning underlying present manpower plans, and education policies drawn from them, call attention not only to the whole range of extremely dubious assumptions, which are made in devising these manpower targets, but also to the fact that unless the manpower is most carefully fed into jobs in the developing economy, the leads and lags which develop may well be worse than the maladjustments which would arise in an almost uncoordinated development of the education system. Thus, for example, in the Nigerian case, the substantial problems associated with the great growth of primary education (which, to be fair, are contrary to the findings of the Ashby Report), would be taken as an instance of the over-emphasis on education, which has ultimately resulted from unrealistic manpower targets.

Furthermore, some thinkers would argue that the education system in developing countries ought specifically to be biased in a rural direction, and that the whole emphasis of the manpower planners' approach has been to over-emphasize formal education as against informal education, and to over-emphasize education for urban environments as against education which is truly nation-building. Now if we took this reasoning, which underlies the debate which has been specifically about African education in the last ten years or so, and applied it to Europe, I think we see much the same kind of argument taking place. A similar dichotomy about content and structure is implicit in much of the discussion now going on in Europe.

I must say that it seems to me that there is dangerous over-simplification in the contemporary search for one cause of economic growth, and coming down on education and research as the major element. I have read a great many—certainly not all but a great many—of the books and articles which have appeared on economic growth in the last fifteen years, and the general impression which is left in my mind is that the causes of growth are generally unknown and are extraordinarily complicated. I do not believe for a moment that it is simply expenditure on education or simply expenditure on research and development which causes economic growth, any more than I believe that it is simply investment in physical capital, though I think that view comes nearer the truth than most. This is one of my general reasons for being extremely dubious about the apparent precision and carefulness of all figures in this field.

What, in summary, is the mainline argument that seems to command widespread assent? Education affects social relationships, and it affects people's outlook on life. It gives people general and particular skills. It is the combination of these social relationships, skills and outlooks, with the managerial structure, the government and above all physical capital, which together affects the rate of growth. In other words, my examination of the problem, far from beginning to tease out the individual contributions of individual factors or sub-factors to economic growth, lays emphasis upon the complementarities. I think here, too, I would lay great emphasis upon the fact that one of the major causes of economic growth is the international migration of skills, abilities and technologies. I think that Professor Bruce Williams has made a profound contribution to the discussion of the brain drain and the alleged technological gap between Western Europe and North America, when he emphasizes this point. 'R and D is important for growth but the idea that a country's growth depends on its own R and D overlooks the great importance of the international movement of ideas, of machines which embody the results of R and D, and of capital transfers to make possible the use in various countries of technological and managerial inventions made elsewhere.'[3] One of the things that he is saying is that, in so far as our education broadens and opens the mind to new ideas from other parts of the world, the more likely it is that people in this country will be able to adopt consciously growth-oriented policies (on the assumption that those policies are inherently desirable in themselves, which is an issue I prefer to leave open).

Finally, all the discussion points to the fact that in Britain especially, we have tended to neglect middle-level manpower, and we have tended to neglect the technical orientation of management. There has scarcely been a report in the last twenty years that has not, in one way or another, made precisely that point. Now this is a general argument that I think summarizes practically all that the pundits have to say on this point. It is the middle-level person—the average man—who appears too often to have been the clue to economic development. And it is precisely this kind of person that most European systems of education have chosen to exclude in the past, and leave to informal on-the-job training. It follows, therefore, that what America has to teach us has less to do with high-level manpower—where, as the brain drain shows, we do relatively well—but with the ordinary person. I think that a careful reading of Mr Denison's work confirms that he would share this view, so that at the last, all is reconciled.

Notes

1 John Vaizey, ed., *The Residual Factor and Economic Growth* (Paris: OECD 1964), 221.

2 Ibid., 138, 273.

3 B. R. Williams, *Technology, Investment and Growth* (Chapman & Hall, 1967), 4.

33 Guiding instincts

Maria Montessori

In nature too, we find two forms of life, adult life and infant life, different and often contrary. Adult life is characterized by struggle, the struggle of adaptation to the environment as described by Lamarck, or the struggle of competition and natural selection described by Darwin—a struggle not only for the survival of the species but also for selection in sexual competition.

What happens among fully grown animals might be compared with the happenings in the social life of men. Here, too, we find the effort of self-preservation and defence against enemies; here, too, struggles and labours to achieve adaptation to the environment; and here, too, love and sexual conquest. In such struggle and competition Darwin saw the workings of evolution, and the explanation of the survival of physical forms, just as materialistic historians have attributed the historical evolution of mankind to struggle and competition among men.

But whereas in explaining human history we have no other data than the doings of the adult, it is not so in nature. On the contrary, the real key to the life that persists and establishes itself in nature, revealing the innumerable and marvellous variety of creatures, lies in the chapter set apart for infancy. All creatures are weak before they grow strong enough to struggle, and all begin at a stage where there can be no question of adaptation of their organs for these organs do not yet exist. No living creature begins as an adult.

There is thus a hidden part of life with other forms, other resources, other motive impulses, than those apparent in the interplay between the strong individual and his environment. This chapter, the chapter of *childhood in nature*, holds the real key to life, for what happens to the adult can explain only the hazards of survival.

Biological investigations of the infant life of creatures have thrown light on the most marvellous and complex aspect of nature, revealing staggering realities, sublime possibilities, which fill all living nature with poetry and almost with religion. In this field biology has followed and brought to light the creative and conservative aspects of the species, showing the existence of instincts that act as inner guides to living creatures, and which, to distinguish them from the mass of impulsive instincts connected with immediate reactions between a creature and its environment, may be termed 'guiding instincts'.

In biology all existing instincts have always been grouped into two fundamental classes, according to their ends, viz. instincts for the preservation of the individual and instincts for the preservation of the species. Both cases offer aspects of struggle, connected with transient episodes, and as it were, with encounters between the individual and its environment; and at the same time in both cases there are instincts that show themselves as constant vital guides, with an eminently conservative function. For instance, among the instincts for the preservation of the individual, the aspect of episodic struggle is represented by the instinct of defence against unfavourable or threatening causes. Among the instincts for the preservation of the species there is the episodic instinct aroused by encounters with other creatures in the form either of sexual union or sexual conflict. These episodic details, as the more noticeable and violent, were the first to be recognized and studied by biologists. But later on more study was devoted to the instincts for the preservation of the individual and the species in their conservative and constant aspect. These are the guiding instincts, with which is bound up the very existence of life in its great cosmic function. Such instincts are not so much reactions to the environment as delicate inner sensibilities, *intrinsic to life*, just as pure thought is an entirely intrinsic quality of the mind. We might continue the comparison and look on them as divine thoughts working in the inmost centres of living creatures, leading them subsequently to action

Source: Maria Montessori, *The Secret of Childhood*, Longmans (1936), 250–61.

on the outer world in realization of the divine plan. The guiding instincts therefore have not the impulsive character of episodic struggles, but those of an intelligence, a wisdom leading creatures on their journey through time (the individuals), and through eternity (the species).

The guiding instincts are especially wonderful when they are directed to guiding and protecting infant life at its beginnings; when a creature is still hardly in existence or immature, but is none the less on the road towards full development. At such a stage it has not acquired its racial characteristics, it has neither strength nor resistance nor the biological weapons of struggle, nor hope of a final victory as the sure prize of survival. Here the guiding instinct acts as at once a form of maternity and a form of education, and both are deep hid, like the secret of creation from nothing. Such guidance carries a helpless creature to safety when it has in itself neither material nor strength to save itself.

One of these guiding instincts concerns motherhood, the wonderful instinct described by Fabre and by modern biologists as the key to the survival of creatures. The other concerns the development of the individual, and has been dealt with by the Dutch biologist, De Vries, in his study of the sensitive periods.

The maternal instinct is not confined to the mother, though she, as direct procreatrix of the species, has the larger share in this task of protection. It is to be found in both parents, and sometimes pervades a whole social group of creatures. A profounder study of what is known as the maternal instinct leads us to recognize it as a mysterious energy, which is not necessarily associated with living creatures, but which exists as a protection to the species even without material vehicle, as in the words of the Book of Ecclesiasticus, 'From the beginning, and before the world, was I created.'

The term *maternal instinct* is thus a generic term for the guiding instinct of preservation of the species. There are certain characteristics which dominate this domain in all species; the maternal instinct means a sacrifice of all other instincts existing in the adult for ensuring its survival. The fiercest animal will show a gentleness and tenderness at variance with its nature; the bird, which flies so far in search of food or to flee from danger, will remain still to watch over its nest, finding other means of defending itself from danger, but never that of flight. Instincts inherent in the species suddenly change in character. Besides this, in many species, a tendency to construction and work appears such as is never found in the same creatures at other times, for once arrived at adult state they adapt themselves to nature as they find it. The new instinct of protection of the species leads to a constructive labour so as to prepare a dwelling and shelter for the new-born young. In this every species and variety of creature obeys a special guidance. None takes the first material it finds within its reach, or adapts its manner of building to locality. No, its instructions are definite and unvarying. The manner of building the nest, for instance, is one of the differential characteristics of the different varieties of birds. Among insects we find stupendous examples of constructive work; the hives of bees are palaces of a perfectly geometrical architecture, which a whole society has combined to build to house the new generation. There are other less striking cases which are none the less extremely interesting, like spiders, which are exceptional in that they build also for themselves, and know how to stretch such wide and slender nets for their enemies. All at once the spider radically changes her work and, forgetting her own necessities, begins to make a tiny sack of new, very fine, densely woven tissues, which are quite waterproof. Often the sack has double walls, making it an excellent shelter in the damp, cold places in which certain varieties of spiders live. There is thus real wisdom in regard to the exigencies of the climate. Inside, in safety, the spider lays her eggs. But what is strange is that she has a passionate affection for her sack. In certain laboratory observations it has been noticed that such spiders, with their grey, slimy bodies in which no amount of searching will ever find a heart, can die of grief if their sack is torn and destroyed. In fact, it has been discovered that the spider, where she can, remains as attached to her work as if the sack were an extension of her body. She loves the sack, but she has no feeling for the eggs, nor for the tiny live spiders that will come forth from them. She seems indeed quite unaware of their existence. Instinct has led this mother to work for the species, without having the living creature of the species as direct object. There can thus be an *instinct without object*, acting irresistibly, representing an obedience to an inner command to do what is necessary, and bringing a love for what has been commanded.

There are butterflies which, their whole lives through, suck the nectar of flowers without being aware of any other enticements or any other food. But when the time comes for them to lay their eggs, they never lay them on flowers. They are then otherwise guided; the food-seeking instinct proper to the individual changes, and they are led to seek another environment, one that is suited to a new species needing other food. And yet these butterflies are unaware of such food, just as they will never know the species that is to come. They bear in themselves a command of nature, foreign to their own being. The cochineal insect and others similar never lay their eggs on the upper side of the leaves that will serve as food to the tiny grubs, but on their under surfaces, so that the grubs may be sheltered and hidden. We find a like 'intelligent reflection' among a large number of insects, which also never eat the plants they choose for their offspring. They have therefore a theoretical knowledge of how their children will feed, and they even foresee the dangers of rain and sun.

The adult creature with the mission of protecting the new creatures, thus changes its characteristics and transforms its own nature, as though a time had come in which the usual law governing its life stood still in expectation of a great event in nature—the miracle of creation. Then it does something that is not living but, one might say, a rite to be performed in the presence of this miracle.

One of nature's most resplendent miracles is indeed the power of the newly born, with no experience at all, to find their way about and protect themselves in the outer world, guided by partial and transitory instincts which show themselves as *Sensitive Periods*. Here the instinct is truly and literally a guide leading them gradually through successive difficulties and animating the new creatures with irresistible power. It is plain that nature has not surrendered the protection of the newly born to the adult; she holds the reins tight and keeps a vigilant watch on the observance of her precepts. The adult must collaborate within the limits set by the guiding instincts for the protection of the species. Often, as we see in fishes and insects, the two forms of guiding instinct, that in the adult and that in the new creature, act separately and independently, so that parents and children never meet. In high animals, on the other hand, the two instincts gradually converge in the meeting of parent and offspring, and harmonious collaboration ensues. It is in the encounter of the maternal guiding instincts with the sensitive periods of the newly born that conscious love develops between parent and child. Or else maternal relations may extend to the whole of an organized society, which treats the new offspring as a whole, the living, impersonal products of a race. This we find among social insects like bees, ants, and so forth.

Love and sacrifice are not the causes of the protection of the species, but the effects of an animating guiding instinct of which the roots stretch down to the vast creative laboratory of life, from which every species draws its forces of survival. Affectionate feeling only renders the task imposed an easier one, giving to effort that especial delight that is found in perfect obedience to the order of nature.

If we wished to embrace the whole adult world in a single glance, we might say that from time to time there is a breach of the laws proper to it, the laws that are most apparent in nature and which therefore are believed to be absolute and unchangeable. And, lo! these invincible laws are broken; they stay their working, as though to leave place for something higher, and they bow before factors in contradiction to themselves. That is to say, they remain suspended to further new laws which appear in the infant life of the species. It is thus that life is maintained; it is renewed by such suspension, which allows it to reach inward towards eternity.

Now we may ask, what is the part of man in these laws of nature? Man, it is said, contains in himself as in a supreme synthesis all the natural phenomena of the beings beneath him; he epitomizes and transcends them. And what is more, by the privilege of mind, he enhances them with the sparkling splendour of the mind, which is made up of imagination, feeling and art.

How then are the two forms of life presented in mankind and under what sublime aspects do they reveal themselves? The fact is, the two lives are not apparent. Seek as we will through the world of men, we must say that it embraces only a world of adults of which the prevailing features are struggle, efforts at adaptation, and labour for outward conquests. The events of the world of men all converge on conquest and production, as though there were nothing else to be considered. Human effort clashes and is broken in competition, like a tempered blade against a breastplate. If the adult considers the child, he does so with the logic he brings to bear on his own life. He sees in the child a different and useless creature and he keeps him at a distance; or else, through what is called education, he endeavours to draw him prematurely and directly into the forms of his own life. He acts as one might imagine a butterfly acting were it to break the chrysalis of its larva to bid it fly, or a frog were it to drag its tadpoles out of the water, doing its best to make them breathe through lungs and change their ugly black colour for green.

That is more or less what man does to his children. The adult exhibits before them his own perfection, his own maturity, his own historical example, calling upon the child to imitate him. He is far from realizing that the different characteristics of the child need a different environment and means of life suited to this other form of existence.[1]

How can we explain such a mistaken conception in the loftiest, furthest evolved being, gifted with mind of his own? Is the dominator of his environment, the creature full of power, able to work with an immeasurable superiority over all other living things?

Yet he, the architect, the builder, the producer, the transformer of his environment, does less for his child than the bees, than the insects, than any other creature.

Can the highest and most essential guiding instinct of life be totally absent in mankind? Can mankind be truly helpless and blind before the most staggering phenomenon of universal life, upon which the existence of the species depends?

Man should feel something of what other creatures feel, for in nature everything is transformed but nothing is lost, and the energies that govern the universe are especially indestructible. They persist even when deviated from their proper object.

Where does man the builder build especially for his child? The child should live in a state of beauty, in which man expresses his loftiest forms of art, an art that is not contaminated or determined by any outward need. In which an impulse of generous love stores up riches that cannot be utilized in the world of production. Are there places where man feels the need to suspend and forget his usual characteristics, where he perceives that the essential thing that maintains life is something other than struggle? Where he perceives as a truth rising from the deep that to oppress others is not the secret of survival or the important thing in life, but of purely individual concern? Where therefore a surrender of self seems truly life-giving? Is there no place where the soul aspires to break through the iron laws that hold it bound to the world of outward things? Is there no anxious quest for a miracle, a need for a miracle to continue life? And at the same time an aspiration towards something beyond the furthest span of individual life, stretching into eternity? It is by this road that salvation lies. In such places man feels the need to renounce his laborious reasoning and is ready to believe the incredible. For all these are the feelings that should be aroused in man by facts analogous to those that lead all living creatures to a suspension of the laws of their nature, to a holocaust of themselves, so that life may be carried forward towards eternity. Yes, there are places where man no longer feels the need for conquest, but the need of purification and innocence, so that he yearns for simplicity and peace. In that innocent peace, man seeks a renewal of life, as it were a resurrection from the weight of the world.

Yes, there must be grandiose feelings in man, diverse from those of everyday life and opposed to them.

This is the divine voice that no one can still, and which calls men with a loud voice, calling them together to gather round the Child.

Note

1 Alice Meynell in more than one of her essays brings historical confirmation of the insensibility of past ages to childhood. In *The Seventeenth Century* she writes of Lucy Hutchinson as 'a child such as those serious times desired that a child should be; that is, she was as slightly a child, and for as brief a time, as might be. Childhood, as an age of progress, was not to be delayed, as an age of imperfection was to be improved, as an age of inability was not to be exposed except when precocity distinguished it. It must at any rate be shortened.' Again, in *That Pretty Person*, she notes how: 'As the primitive lullaby is nothing but a patient prophecy (the mother's), so was education, some two hundred years ago, nothing but an impatient prophecy (the father's) of the full stature of body and mind.' Thus John Evelyn's child '—"that pretty person" in Jeremy Taylor's letter of condolence—was chiefly precious to him inasmuch as he was, too soon, a likeness of the man he never lived to be. . . .

'Evelyn and his contemporaries dropped the very word child as soon as might be, if not sooner. When a poor little boy came to be eight years old they called him a youth. . . . It is difficult to imagine what childhood must have been when nobody, looking on, saw any fun in it; when everything that was proper to five years old was a defect. . . .

'They took their children seriously, without relief. Evelyn has nothing to say about his little ones that has a sign of a smile in it. Twice are children not his own mentioned in his diary. Once he goes to the wedding of a maid of five years old—a curious thing, but not, evidently, an occasion of sensibility. Another time he stands by, in a French hospital, while a youth of less than nine years of age undergoes a frightful surgical operation "with extraordinary patience". "The use I made of it was to give Almighty God hearty thanks that I had not been subject to this deplorable infirmitie." This is what he says.' TRANSLATOR

34 English for maturity

David Holbrook

I wish to avoid discussion of 'educating against the environment'. It may be part of our work: but to contemplate teaching in such terms seems to me dangerously negative. We must first know why we educate at all—and it is not by any means simply to make our pupils dissatisfied with their environment. Of such dissatisfaction rock 'n' roll, 'teenage' hooliganism and motor-suicide, are in any case expressive enough. What is missing from the music of our young people, from their entertainment, and from their social life together is the germ of positive vitality. They have few cultural sources of succour, to develop positive attitudes to life, and develop human sympathy. The home is afflicted by the influence of the mass-media, by the pressure of advertising and by the new illiteracy. As Richard Hoggart points out, such traditions as standing by one another, or of passing on traditional wisdom, have declined in working people's lives under these influences. Thus it remains to the school—and mainly the secondary modern school—to supply these positives.

By what human activities can such positives be supplied? By those which, in any society of the future I can imagine, would occupy our major effort in living: activities devoted to the 'something' outside the individual. Not, that is, to the 'fulfilment of the individual', or the 'individual's fullest self-expression'—filling the personal sack—which is how our greedy society spends its time, but to the development of that richness of the individual being which releases sympathy and creative energy in community.

This is achieved by the arts: and it was to them civilized and leisured communities of the past gave their effort—to coming together in submission to embodiments of the human spirit. It is by these that men come to possess their traditions and values—possess them in their thought and feeling, rather than as acquired fragments of knowledge about them. And we possess our traditions largely through and in *the*

Source: *English for Maturity*, Cambridge University Press (1965), 17–19, 30–1.

word. What D. H. Lawrence called 'spontaneous creative fullness of being' is, paradoxically, achieved only by what Mr T. S. Eliot has called the obtaining of tradition: 'it cannot be inherited, and if you want it you must obtain it by great labour.' The obtaining of tradition is largely a matter of possessing our native language, using it responsibly, and maintaining its vitality. The Englishman develops a fullness of being only in so far as he possesses the English language more deeply and extends his responsiveness to it. Keeping the English word alive, therefore, is crucial to any future flowering of English civilization: and crucial to our own need for positive attitudes to life. As Keats said, 'English ought to be kept up.'

The implications for English in the secondary modern school would seem to be plain. But they are often not plain when one begins to ask, among a group of other teachers, why we teach English. What do we reply to D. H. Lawrence's cry, 'The great mass of the population should never be taught to read and write. Never.'?

The answer lies, I think, in the insistence, such as that of George Sampson in his very fine book *English for the English*, on education which is a 'civilizing and humanizing practice', 'part of the act of living' rather than a preparation for life or, worse still, for 'earning a living'.

The best of the primary schools, certainly at the infant stage, have made their work accord to these requirements: where the selection examination casts the shadow of the world of greed over the school perhaps the primary schools are less successful. But in the earlier years they have converted school into the embryonic experience of civilized life which it should be. The public is often angry (or guilty) about the degree to which infant pupils enjoy themselves, 'playing about'. But the primary schools have demonstrated that at the centre of education there needs to be that pleasure which propagates sympathy and is the basis of civilization: the pleasure of organizing experience in art. The primary school concentrates on the development of beings: the secondary schools have to turn their attention to pupils as workers, intellectuals and technologists. A minority are groomed for the best places and academic achievements: the rest follow as best they can, and every pupil's sensibility, his civilization, is left to take care of itself. Our education begins by being one thing and ends by being another: the result is too often the inarticulate scientist, the illiterate workman, the immature being.

Let me try to put together, as simply and positively as I can, the aims of education in the secondary modern school, as I feel they should be, and the aims of English as the central and dominating subject, as it must needs be. My argument derives a good deal from that book which I cannot hope to emulate, *English for the English*, and I hope the reader who is irritated with my inadequate statement will turn to George Sampson's distinguished essay.

Most of the skills and capacities our pupils will require when they leave school will be learnt after they leave, in the factory, shop, or office. A few special skills, such as the ability to type, they can learn quickly, if they need them, at evening classes after they are fifteen: or they may go on to a technical college after they complete their secondary education. We have no need, therefore, to concern ourselves, even if it were correct to do so, with education for 'earning a living': we educate for living. . . .

No doubt much waste and anxiety would be removed from our life if communications were improved. Yet it is not the wires that are crossed, but complexities in human nature. No two people are alike, to the despair of the commercial mind. Each human being has infinite capacities and infinite variations of spirit—and each life in time is a unique mystery. The communications experts really seem to act as if human beings are a form of rather inefficient thinking machine: the fundamental assumptions of communications experts and 'cybernetics' specialists often seem to deny the mystery of the flesh that can think and be aware of its existence. For our purposes the main objection to the 'communications' preoccupation is that it is related to the concern to make education serve practical ends— to be for 'earning a living'. Short-sightedly, too, for the more effective organizer or workman, the more effective 'communicator', will be the man who is trained in his whole sensibility, trained not only to use language but to live wholly. The quality of feeling, of perception, of conceptual thought in each of us, and our sense of order in experience—all these depend upon our language habits in a much more complex way than is covered by the term 'communications'. And much of the communications experts' expertise, their smart terms, their analogies with calculating machines, and their mechanical talk about brain cells and impulses, merely hides their intolerance of the infinite intractability of language and of life. And it is with language and life, in all their intractability, that we must first learn to deal, before we set out to organize industry, to administer society, or help solve world problems.

35 English for the rejected

David Holbrook

If you want to have a bright discussion on the merits of the latest process of automation you will not be able to have it with James or Rose of 4C. But suppose you want a second-hand door, or to find someone who will sit in a copse and wait patiently to destroy every pigeon that comes there in a day—then James is your boy. Or if you were hurt on a mountain in the snow, and one of the party had to be left with you, to keep you comfortable and awake, and fed with hot fluids, wouldn't you find that Rose would take to you, like, say, a mother animal? Unbright, limited, dumb—all these, but yet these children sometimes manage a home from 4 p.m. until the widowed father comes home at 8 p.m. Or can be and are trusted all day mucking out pigs with a tractor; or as a lorry-driver's mate on Saturday handling animals. They suffer as keenly as 'bright' children: they love, certainly, as fully. Some are obviously going to be more successful as lovers, husbands and parents than some dons. For affection, loyalty, kindness, warmth of feeling, these children may sometimes be found to be unequalled. Are they 'lesser beings'? This question I hope will be in the reader's mind throughout this book—*because our society and its system of education at the moment imply inevitably and often mercilessly that children who do badly in intelligence tests are inferior creatures.* Such mere organizational changes as the comprehensive school do not amend this fundamental wrong. Below I reveal the capacities for fineness and vivid perception of an average class of such children. They are not capable of certain intellectual uses of the intelligence. But they *have* intelligence and they are human.

We need to be reminded of other qualities in human beings which are by no means dim, even in those we call the dim. We need to bring ourselves to value these creatures as creatures, as equal in terms of their wider needs, to develop what potentialities they have. Once we stop despising them because they cannot perform

Source: *English for the Rejected,* Cambridge University Press (1964), 6–8, 10–11.

'brainy' tasks, we can then see how monstrous it is to give them worse equipment, worse accommodation, overcrowded classes, and a lesser education than their fellows. We can see that it is inhuman that the teachers who choose to work with 'Cs and Ds' are exploited, discouraged, not given real responsibilities, refused sufficient free time for preparation and thought about their work, refused money for books—and even driven out of the work they love. Yet this is what is happening, here and there. Touches of such blight pervade all 'low stream' education, because our society implies that to be a 'dreg' is to be a failure, against a scale of mere acquisitive 'success'. Our brightly painted 'teenage secondary modern' girls with bouffant hair styles, frilly petticoats, and a libidinous flair to their manner are *quite justifiably* flaunting their vitality against these implications given them by the school. The sad fact is that their demonstration is so empty of true culture, and is only acquisitive itself.

Perhaps we can begin to develop an education based on *a real acceptance of the nature of these children and their needs,* and do away with the present hidden frustration in the 'low streams' of many of our schools. If we can, we can begin a positive revolution against under-privilege in secondary education, towards a truly democratic recognition of the needs of each creature in our community to become civilized and to realize his potentialities. From this revolution in attitudes and content, changes in prestige, then in organization, then perhaps in social life may come—even perhaps demands for sound popular culture established in the school experience. Three-eighths of our population is a large proportion—some 20,000,000 by the time they all grow up, the 'dregs'. Their lives could be enriched by their school experience much more than they are at the moment—if we study their needs and try to meet them.

This book is about ways of helping to make these children literate. It is based on some limited experience, of a poet and writer who chose for a time to become part-time teacher with a few less able children. If I learnt nothing else, I did learn that for these children there is no point in thinking in terms of 'subjects'— apart from games, art, crafts, dancing and music, everything else virtually became English. Their most successful mathematics was related to stories about hire purchase or car rallies. The only sense of history they could gain was that given by imaginative accounts of, say, a medieval peasant's life. In geography they responded to what was really anthropology, much mixed with imaginative fantasy about modes of life in other lands. And all these subjects by the time they were interpreted to 3C became, virtually, English, and *mostly imaginative English, in the context of a close personal relationship with the teacher*—closer than that in other kinds of teaching except perhaps in the infant classes of the primary school.

This central subject is for them the main means towards self-expression, self-knowledge, imaginative order, understanding of the world, the possession of values, and a guide to conduct. One must, with these children, stop thinking in terms of 'teaching a subject', and think rather of educating the child, giving each creature what he may be given of civilized powers and refinement, and effective release of his potentialities. This is even more evident in the less able child than it is in the brighter child whom I was considering in *English for Maturity*. This is why in this book I discuss the work of nineteen children in detail: I try to show why at the centre of English as a central subject there must be imaginative work, serving each child's inward needs. And I try to show that this can best be done in the context of a sympathetic relationship with the teacher that can only be called a form of love, so deep do these children's emotional needs enter one's soul. . . .

In this book I shall use the term 'the poetic function'. By this I mean the capacity to explore and perceive, to come to terms with, speak of, and deal with experience *by the exercise of the whole mind and all kinds of apprehensions, not only intellectual ones*. This poetic function, I consider, is neglected too much in all education and not least in the education of children deficient in intellect. I want to try to establish in this book that nourishing what I call the poetic function is certainly the most important work with less able children, and that the most efficient work a teacher of backward children *can* do *is* the free, informal, imaginative and often pleasurable and rewarding work of creative English, towards literacy and insight into personal and external reality. This is the best way even if one conceives of the work as merely 'training operatives for the lower echelons of industry' as some depressing person once expressed the function of the secondary modern school in the *Guardian*. (To conceive of one's work in such terms seems to me not only inhuman but inefficient, as will appear.)

I also wanted to imply that what I say here about 'backward' teaching is true of all education. . . .

36 Elementary forms of religious life

Émile Durkheim

Our study is not of interest merely for the science of religion. In fact, every religion has one side by which it overlaps the circle of properly religious ideas, and there, the study of religious phenomena gives a means of renewing the problems which, up to the present, have only been discussed among philosophers.

For a long time it has been known that the first systems of representations with which men have pictured to themselves the world and themselves were of religious origin. There is no religion that is not a cosmology at the same time that it is a speculation upon divine things. If philosophy and the sciences were born of religion, it is because religion began by taking the place of the sciences and philosophy. But it has been less frequently noticed that religion has not confined itself to enriching the human intellect, formed beforehand, with a certain number of ideas; it has contributed to forming the intellect itself. Men owe to it not only a good part of the substance of their knowledge, but also the form in which this knowledge has been elaborated.

At the roots of all our judgments there are a certain number of essential ideas which dominate all our intellectual life; they are what philosophers since Aristotle have called the categories of the understanding: ideas of time, space,* class, number, cause, substance, personality, etc. They correspond to the most universal properties of things. They are like the solid frame which encloses all thought; this does not seem to be able to liberate itself from them without destroying itself, for it seems that we cannot think of objects that are not in time and space, which have no number, etc. Other ideas are contingent and unsteady; we can con-

Source: Émile Durkheim, *Elementary Forms of Religious Life*, New York: Collier (1961), 21–33.

* We say that time and space are categories because there is no difference between the role played by these ideas in the intellectual life and that which falls to the ideas of class or cause (on this point see Hemelin, *Essai sur les éléments principaux de la représentation*, 63, 76).

ceive of their being unknown to a man, a society or an epoch; but these others appear to be nearly inseparable from the normal working of the intellect. They are like the framework of the intelligence. Now when primitive religious beliefs are systematically analyzed, the principal categories are naturally found. They are born in religion and of religion; they are a product of religious thought. This is a statement that we are going to have occasion to make many times in the course of this work.

This remark has some interest of itself already; but here is what gives it its real importance.

The general conclusion of the book which the reader has before him is that religion is something eminently social. Religious representations are collective representations which express collective realities; the rites are a manner of acting which take rise in the midst of the assembled groups and which are destined to excite, maintain or recreate certain mental states in these groups. So if the categories are of religious origin, they ought to participate in this nature common to all religious facts; they too should be social affairs and the product of collective thought. At least—for in the actual condition of our knowledge of these matters, one should be careful to avoid all radical and exclusive statements—it is allowable to suppose that they are rich in social elements.

Even at present, these can be imperfectly seen in some of them. For example, try to represent what the notion of time would be without the processes by which we divide it, measure it or express it with objective signs, a time which is not a succession of years, months, weeks, days and hours! This is something nearly unthinkable. We cannot conceive of time, except on condition of distinguishing its different moments. Now what is the origin of this differentiation? Undoubtedly, the states of consciousness which we have already experienced can be reproduced in us in the same order in which they passed in the first place; thus portions of our past become present again, though being clearly distinguished from the present. But howsoever important this distinction may be for our private experience, it is far from being enough to constitute the notion or category of time. This does not consist merely in a commemoration, either partial or integral, of our past life. It is an abstract and impersonal frame which surrounds, not only our individual existence, but that of all humanity. It is like an endless chart, where all duration is spread out before the mind, and upon which all possible events can be located in relation to fixed and determined guide lines. It is not *my time* that is thus arranged; it is time in general, such as it is objectively thought of by everybody in a single civilization. That alone is enough to give us a hint that such an arrangement ought to be collective. And in reality, observation proves that these indispensable guide lines, in relation to which all things are temporally located, are taken from social life. The divisions into days, weeks, months, years, etc., correspond to the periodical recurrence of rites, feasts, and public ceremonies.* A calendar expresses the rhythm of the collective activities, while at the same time its function is to assure their regularity.†

It is the same thing with space. As Hamelin has shown, space is not the vague and indetermined medium which Kant imagined; if purely and absolutely homogeneous, it would be of no use, and could not be grasped by the mind. Spatial representation consists essentially in a primary co-ordination of the data of sensuous experience. But this co-ordination would be impossible if the parts of space were qualitatively equivalent and if they were really interchangeable. To dispose things spatially there must be a possibility of placing them differently, of putting some at the right, others at the left, these above, those below, at the north of or at the south of, east or west of, etc., etc., just as to dispose states of consciousness temporally there must be a possibility of localizing them at determined dates. That is to say that space could not be what it is if it were not, like time, divided and differentiated. But whence come these divisions which are so essential? By themselves, there are neither right nor left, up nor down, north nor south, etc. All these distinctions evidently come from the fact that different sympathetic values have been attributed to various

regions. Since all the men of a single civilization represent space in the same way, it is clearly necessary that these sympathetic values, and the distinctions which depend upon them, should be equally universal, and that almost necessarily implies that they be of social origin.*

Besides that, there are cases where this social character is made manifest. There are societies in Australia and North America where space is conceived in the form of an immense circle, because the camp has a circular form;† and this spatial circle is divided up exactly like the tribal circle, and is in its image. There are as many regions distinguished as there are clans in the tribe, and it is the place occupied by the clans inside the encampment which has determined the orientation of these regions. Each region is defined by the totem of the clan to which it is assigned. Among the Zuñi, for example, the pueblo contains seven quarters; each of these is a group of clans which has had a unity: in all probability it was originally a single clan which was later subdivided. Now their space also contains seven quarters, and each of these seven quarters of the world is in intimate connection with a quarter of the pueblo, that is to say with a group of clans.‡ 'Thus,' says Cushing, 'one division is thought to be in relation with the north, another represents the west, another the south,' etc.§ Each quarter of the pueblo has its characteristic colour, which symbolizes it; each region has its colour, which is exactly the same as that of the corresponding quarter. In the course of history the number of fundamental clans has varied; the number of the fundamental regions of space has varied with them. Thus the social organization has been the model for the spatial organization and a reproduction of it. It is thus even up to the distinction between right and left which, far from being inherent in the nature of man in general, is very probably the product of representations which are religious and therefore collective.‖

Analogous proofs will be found presently in regard to the ideas of class, force, personality and efficacy. It is even possible to ask if the idea of contradiction does not also depend upon social conditions. What makes one tend to believe this is that the empire which

* See the support given this assertion in Hubert and Mauss, *Mélanges d'histoire des religions* (*Travaux de l'année sociologique*), chapter on *La Représentation du temps dans la religion*.
† Thus we see all the difference which exists between the group of sensations and images which serve to locate us in time, and the category of time. The first are the summary of individual experiences, which are of value only for the person who experienced them. But what the category of time expresses is a time common to the group, a social time, so to speak. In itself it is a veritable social institution. Also, it is peculiar to man; animals have no representations of this sort.

This distinction between the category of time and the corresponding sensations could be made equally well in regard to space or cause. Perhaps this would aid in clearing up certain confusions which are maintained by the controversies of which these questions are the subject. We shall return to this point in the conclusion of the present work.

* Or else it would be necessary to admit that all individuals, in virtue of their organo-physical constitution, are spontaneously affected in the same manner by the different parts of space: which is more improbable, especially as in themselves the different regions are sympathetically indifferent. Also, the divisions of space vary with different societies, which is a proof that they are not founded exclusively upon the congenital nature of man.
† See Durkheim and Mauss, 'De quelques formes primitives de classification', in *Année Sociologique*, vi, 47 ff.
‡ See Ibid., 34.
§ 'Zuñi Creation Myths', in *13th Report of the Bureau of American Ethnology*, 367 ff.
‖ See Hertz, 'La prééminence de la main droite. Étude de polarité religieuse', in the *Revue Philosophique*, Dec. 1909. On this same question of the relations between the representation of space and the form of the group, see the chapter in Ratzel, *Politische Geographie*, entitled 'Der Raum in Geist de Völker'.

the idea has exercised over human thought has varied with times and societies. Today the principle of identity dominates scientific thought; but there are vast systems of representations which have played a considerable role in the history of ideas where it has frequently been set aside: these are the mythologies, from the grossest up to the most reasonable.* There, we are continually coming upon beings which have the most contradictory attributes simultaneously, who are at the same time one and many, material and spiritual, who can divide themselves up indefinitely without losing anything of their constitution; in mythology it is an axiom that the part is worth the whole. These variations through which the rules which seem to govern our present logic have passed prove that, far from being engraven through all eternity upon the mental constitution of men, they depend, at least in part, upon factors that are historical and consequently social. We do not know exactly what they are, but we may presume that they exist.†

This hypothesis once admitted, the problem of knowledge is posed in new terms.

Up to the present there have been only two doctrines in the field. For some, the categories cannot be derived from experience: they are logically prior to it and condition it. They are represented as so many simple and irreducible data, imminent in the human mind by virtue of its inborn constitution. For this reason they are said to be *a priori*. Others, however, hold that they are constructed and made up of pieces and bits, and that the individual is the artisan of this construction.‡

But each solution raises grave difficulties.

Is the empirical thesis the one adopted? Then it is necessary to deprive the categories of all their characteristic properties. As a matter of fact they are distinguished from all other knowledge by their universality and necessity. They are the most general concepts which exist, because they are applicable to

all that is real, and since they are not attached to any particular object they are independent of every particular subject; they constitute the common field where all minds meet. Further, they must meet there, for reason, which is nothing more than all the fundamental categories taken together, is invested with an authority which we could not set aside if we would. When we attempt to revolt against it, and to free ourselves from some of these essential ideas, we meet with great resistances. They do not merely depend upon us, but they impose themselves upon us. Now empirical data present characteristics which are diametrically opposed to these. A sensation or an image always relies upon a determined object, or upon a collection of objects of the same sort, and expresses the momentary condition of a particular consciousness; it is essentially individual and subjective. We therefore have considerable liberty in dealing with the representations of such an origin. It is true that when our sensations are actual, they impose themselves upon us *in fact*. But *by right* we are free to conceive them otherwise than they really are, or to represent them to ourselves as occurring in a different order from that where they are really produced. In regard to them nothing is forced upon us except as considerations of another sort intervene. Thus we find that we have here two sorts of knowledge, which are like the two opposite poles of the intelligence. Under these conditions forcing reason back upon experience causes it to disappear, for it is equivalent to reducing the universality and necessity which characterize it to pure appearance, to an illusion which may be useful practically, but which corresponds to nothing in reality; consequently it is denying all objective reality to the logical life, whose regulation and organization is the function of the categories. Classical empiricism results in irrationalism; perhaps it would even be fitting to designate it by this latter name.

In spite of the sense ordinarily attached to the name, the apriorists have more respect for the facts. Since they do not admit it as a truth established by evidence that the categories are made up of the same elements as our sensual representations, they are not obliged to impoverish them systematically, to draw from them all their real content, and to reduce them to nothing more than verbal artifices. On the contrary, they leave them all their specific characteristics. The apriorists are the rationalists; they believe that the world has a logical aspect which the reason expresses excellently. But for all that, it is necessary for them to give the mind a certain power of transcending experience and of adding to that which is given to it directly; and of this singular power they give neither explanation nor justification. For it is no explanation to say that it is inherent in the nature of the human intellect. It is necessary to show whence we hold this surprising prerogative and how it comes that we can see certain relations in things which the examination of these things cannot reveal to us. Saying that only on this condition is experience itself possible changes the

* We do not mean to say that mythological thought ignores it, but that it contradicts it more frequently and openly than scientific thought does. Inversely, we shall show that science cannot escape violating it, though it holds to it far more scrupulously than religion does. On this subject, as on many others, there are only differences of degree between science and religion; but if these differences should not be exaggerated, they must be noted, for they are significant.

† This hypothesis has already been set forth by the founders of the *Völkerpsychologie*. It is especially remarked in a short article by Windelbrand entitled 'Die Erkenntnisslehre unter dem Völkerpsychologischen Gesichtspunke', in the *Zeitsch. f. Völkerpsychologie*, vii, 166 ff. Cf. a note of Steinthal on the same subject, ibid., 178 ff.

‡ Even in the theory of Spencer, it is by individual experience that the categories are made. The only difference which there is in this regard between ordinary empiricism and evolutionary empiricism is that according to this latter, the results of individual experience are accumulated by heredity. But this accumulation adds nothing essential to them; no element enters into their composition which does not have its origin in the experience of the individual. According to this theory, also, the necessity with which the categories actually impose themselves upon us is the product of an illusion and a superstitious prejudice, strongly rooted in the organism, to be sure, but without foundation in the nature of things.

problem perhaps, but does not answer it. For the real question is to know how it comes that experience is not sufficient unto itself, but presupposes certain conditions which are exterior and prior to it, and how it happens that these conditions are realized at the moment and in the manner that is desirable. To answer these questions it has sometimes been assumed that above the reason of individuals there is a superior and perfect reason from which the others emanate and from which they get this marvellous power of theirs, by a sort of mystic participation: this is the divine reason. But this hypothesis has at least the one grave disadvantage of being deprived of all experimental control; thus it does not satisfy the conditions demanded of a scientific hypothesis. More than that, the categories of human thought are never fixed in any one definite form; they are made, unmade and remade incessantly; they change with places and times. On the other hand, the divine reason is immutable. How can this immutability give rise to this incessant variability?

Such are the two conceptions that have been pitted against each other for centuries; and if this debate seems to be eternal, it is because the arguments given are really about equivalent. If reason is only a form of individual experience, it no longer exists. On the other hand, if the powers which it has are recognized but not accounted for, it seems to be set outside the confines of nature and science. In the face of these two opposed objections the mind remains uncertain. But if the social origin of the categories is admitted, a new attitude becomes possible, which we believe will enable us to escape both of the opposed difficulties.

The fundamental proposition of the apriorist theory is that knowledge is made up of two sorts of elements, which cannot be reduced into one another, and which are like two distinct layers superimposed one upon the other.* Our hypothesis keeps this principle intact. In fact, that knowledge which is called empirical, the only knowledge of which the theorists of empiricism have made use in constructing the reason, is that which is brought into our minds by the direct action of objects. It is composed of individual states which are completely explained† by the psychical nature of the individual. If, on the other hand, the categories are, as we believe they are, essentially collective representations, before all else, they should show the mental states of the group; they should depend upon the way in which this is founded and organized, upon its morphology, upon its religious, moral and economic institutions, etc. So between these two sorts of

representations there is all the difference which exists between the individual and the social, and one can no more derive the second from the first than he can deduce society from the individual, the whole from the part, the complex from the simple.* Society is a reality *sui generis*; it has its own peculiar characteristics, which are not found elsewhere and which are not met with again in the same form in all the rest of the universe. The representations which express it have a wholly different content from purely individual ones and we may rest assured in advance that the first add something to the second.

Even the manner in which the two are formed results in differentiating them. Collective representations are the result of an immense co-operation, which stretches out not only into space but into time as well; to make them, a multitude of minds have associated, united and combined their ideas and sentiments; for them, long generations have accumulated their experience and their knowledge. A special intellectual activity is therefore concentrated in them which is infinitely richer and complexer than that of the individual. From that one can understand how the reason has been able to go beyond the limits of empirical knowledge. It does not owe this to any vague mysterious virtue but simply to the fact that according to the well-known formula, man is double. There are two beings in him: an individual being which has its foundation in the organism and the circle of whose activities is therefore strictly limited, and a social being which represents the highest reality in the intellectual and moral order that we can know by observation—I mean society. This duality of our nature has as its consequence in the practical order, the irreducibility of a moral ideal to a utilitarian motive, and in the order of thought, the irreducibility of reason to individual experience. In so far as he belongs to society, the individual transcends himself, both when he thinks and when he acts.

This same social character leads to an understanding of the origin of the necessity of the categories. It is said that an idea is necessary when it imposes itself upon the mind by some sort of virtue of its own, without being accompanied by any proof. It contains within it something which constrains the intelligence and which leads to its acceptance without preliminary examination. The apriorist postulates this singular quality, but does not account for it; for saying that the

---

* Perhaps some will be surprised that we do not define the apriorist theory by the hypothesis of innateness. But this conception really plays a secondary part in the doctrine. It is a simple way of stating the impossibility of reducing rational knowledge to empirical data. Saying that the former is innate is only a positive way of saying that it is not the product of experience, such as it is ordinarily conceived.

† At least, in so far as there are any representations which are individual and hence wholly empirical. But there are in fact probably none where the two elements are not found closely united.

* This irreducibility must not be taken in any absolute sense. We do not wish to say that there is nothing in the empirical representations which shows rational ones, nor that there is nothing in the individual which could be taken as a sign of social life. If experience were completely separated from all that is rational, reason could not operate upon it; in the same way, if the psychic nature of the individual were absolutely opposed to the social life, society would be impossible. A complete analysis of the categories should seek these germs of rationality even in the individual consciousness. We shall have occasion to come back to this point in our conclusion. All that we wish to establish here is that between these indistinct germs of reason and the reason properly so called, there is a difference comparable to that which separates the properties of the mineral elements out of which a living being is composed from the characteristic attributes of life after this has once been constituted.

categories are necessary because they are indispensable to the functioning of the intellect is simply repeating that they are necessary. But if they really have the origin which we attribute to them, their ascendancy no longer has anything surprising in it. They represent the most general relations which exist between things; surpassing all our other ideas in extension, they dominate all the details of our intellectual life. If men did not agree upon these essential ideas at every moment, if they did not have the same conception of time, space, cause, number, etc., all contact between their minds would be impossible, and with that, all life together. Thus society could not abandon the categories to the free choice of the individual without abandoning itself. If it is to live there is not merely need of a satisfactory moral conformity, but also there is a minimum of logical conformity beyond which it cannot safely go. For this reason it uses all its authority upon its members to forestall such dissidences. Does a mind ostensibly free itself from these forms of thought? It is no longer considered a human mind in the full sense of the word, and is treated accordingly. That is why we feel that we are no longer completely free and that something resists, both within and outside ourselves, when we attempt to rid ourselves of these fundamental notions, even in our own conscience. Outside of us there is public opinion which judges us; but more than that, since society is also represented inside of us, it sets itself against these revolutionary fancies, even inside of ourselves; we have the feeling that we cannot abandon them if our whole thought is not to cease being really human. This seems to be the origin of the exceptional authority which is inherent in the reason and which makes us accept its suggestions with confidence. It is the very authority of society,* transferring itself to a certain manner of thought which is the indispensable condition of all common action. The necessity with which the categories are imposed upon us is not the effect of simple habits whose yoke we could easily throw off with a little effort; nor is it a physical or metaphysical necessity, since the categories change in different places and times; it is a special sort of moral necessity which is to the intellectual life what moral obligation is to the will.†

---

* It has frequently been remarked that social disturbances result in multiplying mental disturbances. This is one more proof that logical discipline is a special aspect of social discipline. The first gives way as the second is weakened.

† There is an analogy between this logical necessity and moral obligation, but there is not an actual identity. Today society treats criminals in a different fashion than subjects whose intelligence only is abnormal; that is a proof that the authority attached to logical rules and that inherent in moral rules are not of the same nature, in spite of certain similarities. They are two species of the same class. It would be interesting to make a study on the nature and origin of this difference, which is probably distinguished between the deranged and the delinquent. We confine ourselves to signalizing this question. By this example, one may see the number of problems which are raised by the analysis of these notions which generally pass as being elementary and simple, but which are really of an extreme complexity.

But if the categories originally only translate social states, does it not follow that they can be applied to the rest of nature only as metaphors? If they were made merely to express social conditions, it seems as though they could not be extended to other realms except in this sense. Thus in so far as they aid us in thinking of the physical or biological world, they have only the value of artificial symbols, useful practically perhaps, but having no connection with reality. Thus we come back, by a different road, to nominalism and empiricism.

But when we interpret a sociological theory of knowledge in this way, we forget that even if society is a specific reality it is not an empire within an empire; it is a part of nature, and indeed its highest representation. The social realm is a natural realm which differs from the others only by a great complexity. Now it is impossible that nature should differ radically from itself in the one case and the other in regard to that which is most essential. The fundamental relations that exist between things—just that which it is the function of the categories to express—cannot be essentially dissimilar in the different realms. If, for reasons which we shall discuss later, they are more clearly disengaged in the social world, it is nevertheless impossible that they should not be found elsewhere, though in less pronounced forms. Society makes them more manifest but it does not have a monopoly upon them. That is why ideas which have been elaborated on the model of social things can aid us in thinking of another department of nature. It is at least true that if these ideas play the role of symbols when they are thus turned aside from their original signification, they are well-founded symbols. If a sort of artificiality enters into them from the mere fact that they are constructed concepts, it is an artificiality which follows nature very closely and which is constantly approaching it still more closely.* From the fact that the ideas of time, space, class, cause or personality are constructed out of social elements, it is not necessary to conclude that they are devoid of all objective value. On the contrary, their social origin rather leads to the belief that they are not without foundation in the nature of things.†

---

* The rationalism which is imminent in the sociological theory of knowledge is thus midway between the classical empiricism and apriorism. For the first, the categories are purely artificial constructions; for the second, on the contrary, they are given by nature; for us, they are in a sense a work of art, but of an art which imitates nature with a perfection capable of increasing unlimitedly.

† For example, that which is at the foundation of the category of time is the rhythm of social life; but if there is a rhythm in collective life, one may rest assured that there is another in the life of the individual, and more generally, in that of the universe. The first is merely more marked and apparent than the others. In the same way, we shall see that the notion of class is founded on that of the human group. But if men form natural groups, it can be assumed that among things there exist groups which are at once analogous and different. Classes and species are natural groups of things.

If it seems to many minds that a social origin cannot be attributed to the categories without depriving them of all speculative value, it is because society is still too frequently regarded as something that is not natural; hence it is concluded that the

Thus renovated, the theory of knowledge seems destined to unite the opposing advantages of the two rival theories, without incurring their inconveniences. It keeps all the essential principles of the apriorists; but at the same time it is inspired by that positive spirit which the empiricists have striven to satisfy. It leaves the reason its specific power, but it accounts for it and does so without leaving the world of observable phenomena. It affirms the duality of our intellectual life, but it explains it, and with natural causes. The categories are no longer considered as primary and unanalyzable facts, yet they keep a complexity which falsifies any analysis as ready as that with which the empiricists content themselves. They no longer appear as very simple notions which the first comer can very easily arrange from his own personal observations and which the popular imagination has unluckily complicated, but rather they appear as priceless instruments of thought which the human groups have laboriously forged through the centuries and where they have accumulated

representations which express it express nothing in nature. But the conclusion is not worth more than the premise.

the best of their intellectual capital.* A complete section of the history of humanity is resumed therein. This is equivalent to saying that to succeed in understanding them and judging them, it is necessary to resort to other means than those which have been in use up to the present. To know what these conceptions which we have not made ourselves are really made of, it does not suffice to interrogate our own consciousnesses; we must look outside of ourselves, it is history that we must observe, there is a whole science which must be formed, a complex science which can advance but slowly and by collective labour, and to which the present work brings some fragmentary contributions in the nature of an attempt. Without making these questions the direct object of our study, we shall profit by all the occasions which present themselves to us of catching at their very birth some at least of these ideas which, while being of religious origin, still remain at the foundation of the human intelligence.

* This is how it is legitimate to compare the categories to tools; for on its side, a tool is material accumulated capital. There is a close relationship between the three ideas of tool, category and institution.

37 Radical conceptual change and the design of honours degrees

Leonard Jackson

The case for conservatism: limits of existing knowledge

I want to argue in this article that most serious discussion of educational issues, whether in this journal or any other, is effectively vacuous since it ignores the question of content. I would of course accept that most discussion of the content of education is vacuous in its own right. There are very few teachers, of any subject whatsoever, who can discuss the general educational justification *for* their own subject, applying anything like the same standards of rigour and adequacy that they and their peers apply to discussions *within* their own subject; so that one is almost forced, if one wishes to undertake serious discussion at all, back to the statistical enquiries, and the input-output models, of sociologists and economists. But two wrongs do not make a right. It is my thesis that educational policies, possible and actual, have two determinants, an external and an internal one. The external one is the state of society. The internal one is the state of available knowledge. The two are connected; but for analytical purposes they have to be distinguished; and any serious discussion of education at any level must be adequate in terms of both.

It is the state of society which determines the demand for degrees—from potential undergraduates on the one hand and from employers on the other. And in a broad sense it is the state of society which determines the types of degree that are needed, or at least in demand. But it is the state of available knowledge which determines whether these demands can in truth be met, or whether they will have to be fudged. Not every degree one might like to have can at present be constructed. Sometimes this is because there are not enough teachers, books and so on of the right kind. Sometimes it is because human knowledge simply does not extend so far. To give a neutral example, one can have a subject of mathematical physics, which studies the mathematical properties of

Source: *Higher Education Review* (1969), **1** (3), 70–85.

physical processes, because enough is known about these processes. One could not have a corresponding subject, mathematical literature, though no doubt literature has many interesting mathematical properties —for example properties invariant under translation from one language to another—since nobody knows what these are.

Let me now give two slightly less neutral examples. It would be very valuable if we could have degree courses in the study of human thought—or cognitive behaviour, to use a more precise, but no more explanatory term. But it is quite impossible, since nothing serious is known about the way human beings think; though we have a few marginal insights, which may well be grossly misleading, into phenomena like learning. Similarly it would be very valuable if we could have degree courses in the study of human communication— if indeed that is significantly different from the study of human thought. But again, nothing of any great importance is known about human communication, at least at a theoretical level. A great deal of descriptive material is available, about the press, and advertising, and the arts, and literature, and languages. And it all fits, in a loose way, under the rubric 'communication', along with telegraphy, information theory, cybernetics, some bits of philosophy and anthropology and a few other oddments. But no organizing concepts exist to draw this heterogeneous mass together.[1] We are limited by the current state of human knowledge not, in this instance, at the level of fact, but of theoretical interpretation.

It is interesting to consider what usually takes place, when a subject unfortunately does not happen to exist, but would be important if it did. What happens as a rule is that the subject is treated rather like God: if it does not exist, it is invented, and it is then given a gaseous body and a very high status, and declared to be immanent in everything. This is always happening in the field of communication. One thinks of that odd subject General Semantics—a peculiar kind of therapy, aimed at curing diseases of the nervous system by semantic analysis, and hence abolishing war—created by Alfred Korzybski in the thirties;[2] or the more recent development by which Marshall McLuhan[3] stopped being a literary critic and became a minor prophet. One is tempted to think of Bernstein[4] in this way too—the sweeping, exciting generalizations about language which float so far above any empirical data exhibited; and are being widely used now as an all-purpose kit to explain differences in educability. The pattern is always the same—an important insight into the communication process is blown up into a magnificent global half-truth.

It seems to me that the respectable reason for the notorious conservatism of academics is the shadow of McLuhanism which hangs over most attempts at academic innovation that involve going outside existing subject boundaries. There are, of course, several unrespectable reasons as well—such as laziness and fear, of which dons have a fair share. But I would not respect a scholar who did not have somewhere the feeling that the body of human knowledge represents a small area of intellectual order, hacked, by generations of pioneering effort, out of sheer chaos; and the corollary is, that to go outside the boundaries of the existing order may be to attempt to teach chaos. Most of this article will be devoted to discussing situations in which it is necessary to make quite radical changes, on academic grounds. Yet, basically, I share this cautious feeling. Part of my objection to discussing education in purely economic and social terms is that it leads one to advocate the teaching of subjects which would be extremely useful but do not yet exist—economics, for example, which directly enables businessmen to calculate what decisions they ought to make, or the sort of sociology that will produce social engineers, who can solve 'social problems' without making any inconvenient political demands.

The case for innovation: recent discovery and conceptual change

The case I have put so far is a purely conservative one: that whatever the social demands may be, you cannot without absurdity attempt to teach a subject which is not there to be taught. One must be careful not to press this argument too far. It is the boundaries of human knowledge which set absolute limits on our power to create new courses, not the boundaries of existing subjects. It is perfectly possible to construct a new degree course by combining elements of a number of old ones; the new universities and the colleges of technology, in their different ways, have had considerable success in doing this. The view that all such combinations are in the nature of the case inferior to the old single honours degree, and the variant of it, implied in the last UGC report,[5] that all the interesting new combinations have been used up, I take to be not conservative but insane.

It is of course true that some combinations of subject are better than others; and it is possible by applying quite commonsense principles to distinguish between a good joint honours or general degree and a bad one. Thus the London University BA General degree is a very badly designed one; it consists of three subjects more or less arbitrarily selected from London University's enormous platter, with no necessary relationship between them. The individual syllabuses are more or less those of the corresponding single subject degrees, shortened by leaving out arbitrary chunks rather than by replanning from the beginning. There is no cross-fertilization between the separate subjects; it is possible for a student to do subjects potentially as closely connected as English, psychology, and philosophy and find no overlap between them at all. He is worked harder than a corresponding single honours candidate, and gets a less good education.

One could in fact produce quite a good specification of the ideal multi-subject degree by formulating the principles on which the London BA General is constructed, and taking the contrary of each. Thus the subjects an ideal degree might contain (one would say) should be related to one another; the syllabuses should be rethought from the beginning so that this could be done; in the final combination, ideally, the same topic should be treated several times from different points of view, so that the overall treatment is deepened; and the degree ought to be progressive, demanding rather more intellectual sophistication from the student at the end than it does at the beginning. There are multi-subject courses which go some way towards meeting this requirement, and not all of them are new; one of the better ones is Oxford's Literae Humaniores. Another, in principle though not in practice, is PPE.

I am not here primarily concerned with the type of innovation which merely involves recombining existing subjects. The criteria needed—economic viability, in terms of demand for the combination and availability of staff, and academic viability in the terms already indicated—are obvious enough, and require no analysis from me. But the case of PPE is a point to much deeper questions. Here we have a course which was unquestionably viable academically—at least in principle—which could have formed a closely integrated study of centrally important issues. But under pressure of the internal development of its constituent subjects—or at least, of their development in Oxford in the forties and fifties—it simply fell apart. (I am not, of course, saying that this development was independent of the social system. Clearly, in a Marxist country, PPE would have been a closely integrated degree—whatever one may think of the doctrines it would have been integrated around.) Anyway it is clear that a change in the state of knowledge or opinion may make a previously viable course into an academic nonsense.

Are there also cases where the internal development of separate subjects makes possible new and very close combinations of subject? Are there, to put it more generally, cases where recent changes in the state of knowledge render it desirable to construct what are, in essential ways, completely new subjects? It is my intention in this article to give an example of just such a change, and to suggest two types of degree which ought to be radically reformed to accommodate this change. I shall have to limit myself to these specific examples (though always with a general reference in mind) merely to keep the discussion within bounds. But I think it important to begin by stating what I believe to be the general case for radical innovation upon academic grounds, and the criterion upon which we can judge such innovation to be justified.

It seems to me, then, that one can apply to all forms of serious intellectual activity the theory that Kuhn[6] applies to science. One must make a fundamental distinction between normal discovery, or development, in a subject, and basic conceptual change. Let us go back some distance in time and consider the subject that was once called natural history—the study and classification of various species of plants and animals. Then, normal discovery and development would include both the discovery of new species, and the development of new classificatory schemes. Both types of change would of course have a considerable impact on degree syllabuses.

But now consider the impact of Darwin's *Origin of Species*. This is a book which in a sense is about natural history; certainly, after it, it is impossible to look either at newly discovered species or new classificatory schemes in quite the old way. But it does not fall within natural history. It provides an answer to a question which the old science never asked. The old science said: 'What different species are there, and how do they resemble each other?' The new science—let us call it evolutionary biology—says: 'How did the differentiation of species occur?' The old science had its classificatory schemes, which were convenient descriptive tools. For the new science, a classificatory scheme is an evolutionary hypothesis. You can argue about its truth or falsehood. It is no accident that the new science called into question the whole world picture of ordinary men.

A new subject exists, in my terms, when there has been a Darwinian change in an old one; when the experts themselves are largely fumbling with the wrong questions, and the layman, reacting in a puzzled way with his whole world picture questioned, is often nearer the heart of the matter than they are. Looking back at PPE, one can see that what really killed it as a meaningful exercise was the minor Darwinian revolution of the rise of 'ordinary-language' philosophy in the forties and fifties. One has to be careful with Darwinian revolutions; they have a destructive effect on one's nice degree courses.

A case of radical conceptual change: modern linguistics and psychology[7]

One case of radical conceptual change, which has taken place in our own time and ought now to be influencing the planning of new degrees, has occurred within the subject of linguistics. Linguistics is the scientific study of human language, and one of the curiosities of our university system is that it is usually studied, for a first degree, as an ancillary subject in modern language degrees, if it is studied at all. The branch of linguistics which is chosen is, generally, historical philology; and something of this enters into English degrees as well. Given its defined scope as the scientific study of human language one would expect it to form a central part of degrees in psychology – the scientific study of behaviour —and sociology—the scientific study of society and social interaction. But as a matter of fact it does not.

This is mainly because the sort of questions usually asked in linguistics have little relevance to the study of behaviour in general. The original subject—called then simply Grammar—was a descriptive study of Latin and Greek. It was the central subject of medieval and renaissance education, and continued to much later times; but the eighteenth and nineteenth centuries, in what can fairly be called a minor Darwinian revolution, shifted the focus of serious intellectual interest to the question: 'how did different languages develop from one another?' They also went a great way towards answering that question: historical philology, or the study of language change—which is in great part historical phonology, or the study of sound change—is one of the great scientific achievements of the human mind. It has left a permanent impress on our universities: to this day, if you say you are doing linguistic research, most educated men will assume it must be historical in character. The subject is also deadly dull.

Modern linguistics began as a reaction against this. Languages were studied synchronically—that is, as they existed, at a single point in time, usually the present day—and treated as self-existent systems, like the social systems of sociology. De Saussure,[8] who has some claim to be called the founder of linguistics, has been said to be influenced by the sociologist Durkheim. Later American linguistics, from Bloomfield[9] on, was influenced by behaviourist psychology; which led to attempts to describe language without reference to 'mentalistic' concepts like 'meaning'. By the fifties it would not have been unreasonable to describe linguistics as a set of technical methods, or procedures, of classification, segmentation, and contrast, for providing objective descriptions of the languages in texts; it didn't matter what kind of text; it might be anything from a literary work to a transcription of a conversation.

There are two key words here. One is *methods*. The other is *objective*. Linguistics defined itself as a science in terms of the objective methods it claimed to use; and indeed the elaboration and detail of these methods, as presented in some of the standard texts (e.g. Zellig S. Harris, *Methods in Structural Linguistics*[10]—later republished as *Structural Linguistics*), beggar all description. One got the distinct impression that, armed with his methods, the linguist did not need actually to understand the language he described; indeed, to understand it might lessen his objectivity. Not every linguist was convinced: Abercrombie, for example, dubbed some of these methods 'pseudo-procedures'.[11] What results did these methods produce? A set of 'objective' linguistic descriptions; a natural history of language. (The subject has been called, though for different reasons, 'taxonomic' linguistics.) An evolutionary theory already existed, of course, in historical philology. The new linguistics was relevant to this. Its relevance to any other of the sciences or the humanities was quite marginal, and there would certainly have been little point in introducing it into first degrees in these subjects.

The essence of a Darwinian revolution is that a new question is asked about the old facts. The Darwin of twentieth century linguistics is Noam Chomsky,[12] and the question he asked was this: 'what does the native speaker of a language need to know in order to speak that language?' The importance of this question is that it makes linguistics into a branch of psychological theory. As a result it becomes possible to use psychological arguments to decide linguistic questions—for example, questions about what are called linguistic universals, which bear some teasing resemblances to what used to be known as innate ideas; and to use arguments from linguistics to refute theories within psychology—for example, most forms of learning theory. This is an astonishing unification of very diverse fields; particularly when one adds that certain familiar positions in the philosophy of mind and of language also come under question.

I do not propose to give even a summary of the full transformationalist argument here. It is a very complicated one, and it requires some acquaintance with formal logic,[13] automata theory,[14] linguistic theory,[15] and psychological theory[16] to be properly understood. I will merely indicate how a small part of it goes. We start with the basic question: what does a native speaker need to know in order to speak his language? That implies a simpler question, of the type psychologists have tended to dismiss as 'philosophical': what *counts* as 'speaking a language'? It cannot be merely producing expressions already heard: a parrot can do that. You can speak a language only if you can use whichever of the expressions of that language you happen to need, when you need it; but there are infinitely many such expressions. (There is a simple proof of this.) It follows immediately that you cannot have learnt them individually, since you have only had a finite lifetime to learn them in. As a matter of fact, nearly all the expressions you produce, of more than a few words in length, are new coinages. What you have learnt, therefore, is not any particular set of expressions, but how to make up new expressions which nevertheless belong to your language. (Some of the simpler types of possible learning theory in psychology collapse at this point.)

To say that a man has learnt how to make up the expressions of a language is to say that he has learnt a grammar—though he may not be conscious of the fact, or know any grammatical terminology. (He has learnt a dictionary as well, in the same unconscious sense, and a set of phonetic contrasts called usually distinctive features, and a few other things.) The question is *what*

grammar he has learned—for on the basis of current psychological theories some grammars are a lot easier to learn than others, and some are impossible. What Chomsky did was to make a mathematical model of the various possible types of grammar.[17] It turned out that the only type complex enough to fit human language reasonably well was a type which could not be learnt on the basis of current psychological theory. *Nor, as a matter of fact, could it be discovered on the basis of the discovery procedures of which the old linguistics was so proud.*

This juxtaposition is not an accident. It is easy to see—once one becomes interested enough to look—that modern psychology too is a subject which defines itself as a science in terms of the objective nature of its discovery procedures—in this case, experiments—rather than in terms of the refutability of its general theories. And into these methods are built certain reductive hypotheses—empiricist hypotheses—about the nature of man, which are fairly clearly false—and can in this one case actually be shown to be false. The stream of linguistic work which is transformational is now very broad, and it has many implications. But Chomsky himself has developed his position into an attack on the whole empiricist framework of modern psychology.

This, incidentally, is by no means an anti-scientific attitude. Linguistics is almost the only behavioural science whose theories are strictly refutable in the Popperian sense,[18] like the theories of chemistry or physics; and it is the only one which makes detailed non-statistical predictions about behaviour. (They are not very interesting predictions—linguistics can tell you what the structure of a man's sentences will be, but not what he is going to say.) The point is, that to be experimental is not the same thing as to be scientific. But the new linguistics is strongly mentalistic. A psychology influenced by transformational grammar would not cease to use behaviour as evidence, but its subject matter would be not merely items of behaviour but whole behavioural repertoires and the systematic abilities—mental faculties, to use an older term—which lie behind them. In this sense psychology would become the science of mental life.

Radical conceptual change in a practical first degree: psychology

If I am right about the impact of modern linguistics on psychology as a science, it seems fairly clear that it ought to have a considerable impact on psychology as an honours degree course. It is true that there is a great deal of controversy over the results I have mentioned, but a close inspection shows that most of the controversy is entirely beside the point, and corresponds mainly to ignorance of the relevant fields of study. Linguists, ignorant of the necessary mathematics, go to great trouble to produce systems of linguistic description which are terminologically different from existing ones, but have an identical mathematical model;[19] psychologists, ignorant of the relevant aspects of philosophy of science, demand experimental evidence for *empirical* results which neither admit nor require *experimental* confirmation; and so on. All this is merely good evidence that new undergraduate courses are required, which will provide the necessary elementary information when the psychologist, linguist, etc. is young; so that even if the new insights are finally rejected, they are rejected on relevant grounds.

But, as I have already indicated, constructing a new course is a practical problem as well as a theoretical one. A degree course is not only a theoretical construction; it is a social institution. A psychology degree is a course designed and taught by professional psychologists and intended to produce professional psychologists. However firmly one might believe that psychology should be reformed on a rationalist basis, the subject which actually exists is an empiricist one, and that is what the student has to be trained in—but one can open his eyes to alternative conceptions and possibilities. For this purpose the multi-subject honours degree is an ideal construction. In the major part of the degree course one can aim at, and reach, the ordinary standards of single honours psychology. In suitable ancillary subjects—in this case, linguistics and certain aspects of philosophy—one can open up the deeper questions I have indicated. The problem is of course to keep the separate sections of such a degree from falling apart.

We are attempting to produce a degree of this kind in my own college, which is Enfield College of Technology. Enfield is a moderately large technical college, doing almost exclusively university level work, and due to combine fairly soon with Hendon College of Technology and whatever is left of Hornsey College of Art to form one of the new polytechnics. Its problems—staff, finance, and so on—are much those of a university, only rather more severe. The degree I am describing is at an advanced planning stage; the plans may yet be changed, for external reasons. But they will serve for my present purpose, which is merely to illustrate how it is possible to solve the general problem, of incorporating radical conceptual change into a practical honours degree. (This, incidentally, is the *only* problem I am concerned with in this article. Designing a new degree is at least as complicated as designing, say, a new airliner; there are hundreds of intellectual problems to solve. In this article I have completely ignored many of the most important—for example, the vocational aspects of the degree, to which we devoted a great deal of attention.)

We propose to put a general introduction to psychology into the first two terms of the degree, and combine it with a very different subject—an introduction to literature. At the end of this time the student will get a chance—which we regard as quite important—to opt out of psychology and specialize either in English (in the option which is discussed in the next section) or modern languages (which I do not here discuss). In this way we hope to deal with the radical disillusionment with psychology felt, understandably enough, by many students as soon as they have found out what the subject is really like.

In the next four terms five subjects will be studied in parallel. Three of these are straight psychology, of an orthodox enough kind, though each has a different emphasis: *biological approaches to behaviour*, *basic psychological processes*, and *social psychology*. Two are in ancillary subjects, or in our terms 'core subjects', designed to be closely related to the problems of psychology, but show it up in a completely new light. One is linguistics and the psychology of language: not a complete treatment, of course, but a very selective one, concentrating on the aspects indicated earlier. The other is philosophy—again a selective treatment, consisting of four relevant aspects: logic, and philosophy of language, science (more especially social and behavioural science) and mind. These two syllabuses, linguistics and philosophy, have been very closely integrated, with term by term and almost week by week correspondence; thus formal logic and the grammar of a natural language, English, are developed in parallel.

The final year is devoted entirely to psychology; it has several interesting technical features, which I omit here, as not germane to the argument.

Now only about a tenth of the student's time, on the degree as a whole, will be spent on linguistics or philosophy, and then only on carefully selected aspects. The usual criticism that is levelled against this approach to degree planning is that there can be no time to develop the minor subjects as disciplines in their own right. This criticism of course is true; but it largely misses the point of an ancillary subject. What is important is not that the student should gain a general picture of philosophy, but that he should be able to understand a philosophical discussion of the nature of psychological explanation. What is important is not that he should gain a general picture of linguistics, but that he should grasp the nature of the challenge which one branch of linguistics poses to accepted models of psychological theory.

I am sure that this approach is the only practical way to incorporate radical conceptual change into a first degree course. The important point is that it is not necessary for the teachers of the main subjects to agree with all the implications of the minor one. I am sure few of my psychologist colleagues would take my extreme view of the significance of modern work on language for psychology. I believe they find it interesting and well worth studying; and that is enough. The total redefinition of the subject which I believe to be necessary is a job for the next generation; it is part of our business to make sure they are properly equipped for their job.

Radical conceptual change in a practical first degree: English

On present plans, those students on the course I have described who do not begin to specialize in psychology at the beginning of their third term, will read either English or modern languages. (I ought to say here that we have had the opportunity of discussing these options with our future partners at Hendon College of Technology, and profited greatly by these discussions, particularly when we disagreed—which was a fair amount of the time!) I will confine myself here to the English option; and, as before, omit many important aspects of the degree to concentrate on the problem of accommodating radical conceptual change. One must say straight away that linguistics offers much less of a radical challenge to the central discipline of an English degree—which is literary criticism and analysis—than it does to psychology. The reason that linguistics offers a challenge to psychology is that it deals in a scientific way with a behavioural phenomenon too complicated to fit into psychological theory. But the phenomena considered by linguistics are too *simple* to interest the literary critic; he takes as his primary data perceived properties of language for which no school of linguistics can yet supply an adequate theoretical treatment.

The real challenge to the traditional English degree is from the social and behavioural sciences as a whole. The reason is that these sciences offer a radically different conception of man from that offered by literature—or, for that matter, from that offered by ordinary social living. It is a theoretical and objective conception; and with conceptions of this kind the English graduate is not at home. The major weakness of the English degree, considered as an educational device, is its lack of theoretical content. By that I mean that no theoretical questions are ever raised, even about such central matters as the status of works of literature, and the reasons for choosing some works for study rather than others. There may in fact be very good reasons why one should study, say, the particular works that appear in the London or the Oxford degree syllabuses—but the undergraduate is never asked to consider what these reasons might be. The Cambridge Leavisite tradition, on the other hand, devotes considerable attention to the question of just what works should be admitted to the canon, and makes very extensive claims about the social significance of that canon. But again the argument is conducted exclusively in terms of particular cases, and general questions are not raised. Leavis himself published a paper which could stand as a defence of this piecemeal approach.[20]

But either of these approaches has a rather worrying educational effect. Broadly speaking, the English graduate has no capacity for general theories. He is very good at making delicate judgements on particular cases of great complexity. He is imaginative, if a trifle woolly, when making generalizations about schools, periods, influences, and genres. He is very bad indeed at handling theories more general than this—theories about the place of literature itself within society, or as a source of understanding of human behaviour. No doubt one reason for this is that the understanding provided by literature is of a different logical kind from the understanding provided by any

form of science. But the average English graduate would not be well equipped to understand even this proposition.

He would indeed be likely to reject the polysyllabic vacuity of some sociological theory, or the cruder inadequacies of behaviourist psychology, on grounds of taste alone; and in an ideal world where everybody read English before being permitted to embark on these marginal subjects, that would, perhaps, be enough. In the real world the effect is that the view of the English graduate becomes one specialist point of view among others, distinguished from the others only by the fact that its exponents sometimes have the arrogant habit of arguing for the centrality of their own discipline, without being able to back their claim by a single general argument. It is probably true that a good tradition of literary criticism implies human insights and a rich common culture among the critics. But if they cannot explain to the outside world what those insights are, then the common culture is little more than a cult.

This general weakness in English degrees goes along with a more specific one, which generations of undergraduates have noticed. The founding fathers of the subject were misled by a false analogy with Literae Humaniores, to put historical philology into the English degree. What they failed to notice was that while most of the interesting books in English literature were written in its last six centuries, most of the interesting linguistic changes took place in the first six. Accordingly there is a permanent tension in English degrees between linguistic studies and literary ones. Some books are texts; some, works of literature; very few authors, like Chaucer and the Gawain poet, achieve status as both. In Greats, one studies Homer and reads Homer; studies Virgil and reads Virgil. In English degrees, one studies the Anchoress's Guide and reads *Measure for Measure*.

Naturally, the vast majority of students, who are interested in literature, find philology a nuisance and a bore. More to the point, it is of no use to them. When they come to do literary criticism, which is their main business, philology has no help to give. Yet they need insight into language, and ways of expressing this insight; so they resort to the linguistic folklore which is all the average English speaker has available. Fortunately we can go some way towards solving this problem, and the more general theoretical one, at the same time. Suppose we replace historical philology by the relevant synchronic behavioural science—*linguistics and the psychology of language*, with English as the major language of illustration for the linguistics—and add certain aspects of *philosophy*, in particular, philosophy of science, language, and mind. We then have a limited paradigm of the methods of science applied to human behaviour, along with a general discussion of the applicability of these methods. That is a partial solution to half the problem; it tells the student something of what one means by a 'scientific' understanding of behaviour.

It does not show him what the status of literary understanding is: and I know no simple way to do this. Perhaps a complete course in sociology, with adequate philosophical criticism, running alongside a literature course, would do it by contrast; but that would take several extra years, and is not very practical. One partial solution is to make a comparative study of various critical approaches to literature, in the light of the illumination they bring to particular texts, and (in some cases) in the light of the various social science models which they employ; and to combine this with some study of the appropriate branch of philosophy, aesthetics. This is in fact what we are proposing to do, calling the new subject thus constructed 'theory of literature' (without any implication that we have, or could construct, any complete theory). In the degree I have been discussing, the student who specializes in literature will also carry, in the first two terms, *psychology*, in the next four, *linguistics* and *philosophy*, and in the last three, *theory of literature*. Of these, the introduction to psychology and the linguistics and philosophy will be shared with students who are specializing in psychology; and we hope to run common seminars.

Conclusion: the broader implications

I don't want to make exaggerated claims for the particular proposals we are making in this group of degrees, whether in the English option, the psychology option, or the modern languages option that I have not here discussed. Our own proposals, like all practical ones, seem to me inadequate. In an ideal world I will see my ideal degree course. But I still think there are certain general lessons that can be drawn.

First: the design of degree courses is a very difficult business if it is to be done properly. I have just taken six thousand words to discuss one intellectual problem that arises in the course of it; and I have only been able to give a few superficial indications of all the issues we had to consider. I think the design and redesign of honours degree courses—and the fundamental analysis of the current state of knowledge, on which it would have to be based—should be taken far more seriously in higher education, and occupy a great deal more of our time. There is far more to be done in reorganizing our knowledge than in the fiddling about around the edges of it that constitutes most research.

Second: there is one thing only that terrifies me. It is the thought of meeting, and trying to justify our proposals to, the sort of don who just doesn't see the problem. The man who can't see anything in particular that is wrong with existing degree courses; supposes that 'different' must mean 'worse'; and can't see the point of any extensive analysis which might prove otherwise; the sort of idiot who inspired that passage in the last UGC report about the new universities probably having used up all the good new ideas about arts degrees. I don't suppose I shall meet him. Presumably no one concerns himself seriously with the affairs of colleges like mine unless he is interested in new ideas. But the thought is enough to wake one up sweating in the middle of the night.

Notes

1 Colin Cherry, *On Human Communication* (London, 1966). (A good general survey, recently brought up to date.)

2 A. Korzybski, *Science and Sanity* (Lancaster, Science Press 1933); S. I. Hayakawa, *Language in Thought and Action* (Allen & Unwin 1965). (Of these two, the first is quite insane; the second is a sensible school textbook.)

3 M. McLuhan, *The Medium is the Massage* (Penguin 1968). (This is the final reductio ad absurdum. But the process was well under way with *The Gutenberg Galaxy* (Routledge & Kegan Paul 1962) much earlier.)

4 Basil Bernstein, A Sociolinguistic Approach to Social Learning, in *Penguin Survey of the Social Sciences*, 1965. (Bernstein is a more serious figure than the others; but try taking a tape recording of an academic at a cocktail party, transcribing it, and comparing it with the examples of working-class speech Bernstein quotes. It is revealing.)

5 University Development 1962–7 (HMSO 1968).

6 T. S. Kuhn, *The Structure of Scientific Revolutions* (Chicago University Press 1962).

7 (See, for the whole of this section): J. Thorne, Review of P. Postal, *Constituent Structure*, Journal of Linguistics, **1**(1), 73.

8 F. de Saussure, *Cours de Linguistique Générale* 1916. Translation: *Course in General Linguistics* (London 1966).

9 L. Bloomfield, *Language* (Allen & Unwin 1933).

10 Z. S. Harris, *Structural Linguistics* (London 1960).

11 David Abercrombie, Pseudo-Procedures in Linguistics, in *Studies in Phonetics and Linguistics* (OUP 1965).

12 N. Chomsky, *Syntactic Structures* (Mouton 1957); *Language and Mind* (Harcourt & Brace 1968). (These are two slim paperbacks from the vast Chomsky bibliography which I despair of summarizing. After them, try *Aspects of the Theory of Syntax* (MIT 1965); *Topics in the Theory of Generative Grammar* (Mouton 1966) and works in the bibliographies of these.)

13 E.g. as in H. B. Curry, *Foundations of Mathematical Logic* (McGraw-Hill 1963); R. M. Smullyan, *Theory of Formal Systems* (Princeton 1961).

14 B. A. Trakhtenbrot, *Algorithms and Automatic Computing Machines* (Heath 1963).

15 J. Lyons, *Introduction to Theoretical Linguistics* (CUP 1968).

16 T. R. Dixon and D. L. Horton, *Verbal Behavior and General Behavior Theory* (Prentice-Hall 1968).

17 N. Chomsky, *Three Models for the Description of Language* (IRE Trans. Inform. Theor. 1956) reprinted in Luce, Bush and Galanter (eds); *Readings in Mathematical Psychology*, **2** (Wiley 1965); *Handbook of Mathematical Psychology* (Luce *et al.* ed.) **2**, ch. 11. (These are the fundamental references in the field.)

18 K. R. Popper, *The Logic of Scientific Discovery* (Hutchinson 1968).

19 Paul Postal, *Constituent Structure* (Mouton 1964).

20 F. R. Leavis, *Literary Criticism and Philosophy*. *The Common Pursuit* (Chatto & Windus 1952; also in Penguin Books).

38 The content of science courses

F. R. Jevons

What goes into a first degree course? My interest in this question has been sharpened recently by having to face it in a particularly acute form. In the Science Greats course,[1] which we started in the faculty of science at Manchester in October 1966 (the official name is Honours School of Liberal Studies in Science), we are aiming to produce some sort of scientific equivalent to a kind of graduate who has traditionally come mostly from the arts sides of our universities: the well-educated 'generalist' who plays his role in society (and earns his salary) more by virtue of a well-developed mind than of any highly specialized knowledge. We want graduates who bring a scientific background to jobs which go beyond science in any strict sense; for instance, as administrators, or as politicians, framing and executing policies which optimize the use of science for national goals, or as managers in a science-based industry, fitting a company's research and development policy to its overall aims and relating technical possibilities to commercial opportunities.

It might seem that to be adequately equipped for such tasks nothing less than several honours degrees would suffice. One might want two or three degrees in pure and applied physical, life and earth sciences to start with, quite apart from a good deal of history, politics, economics, industrial sociology and so on. But in practice, this just won't do. Formal education can be overdone. Human ageing and patterns of careers mean that for many people, and especially those aiming at the top in management or administration, lengthening the stay in the relatively cloistered atmosphere of our universities soon becomes a mixed blessing. Even those who aspire to academic research must beware of becoming perpetual students.

First degree standards

Yet the amount of knowledge available is already vast and is increasing at an unprecedented rate. As

Source: *Higher Education Review* (1969), **1** (2), 45–54.

Professor de Solla Price of Yale has shown,[2] the overall growth of science has been roughly exponential, with a doubling period of ten to twenty years. Thus most of the scientists who have ever lived are alive today, and most of the scientific papers that have ever been published have been published in the lifetime of most of the people now teaching science.

How is this reflected in the standard of our existing first degrees? Senior physicists and engineers seem agreed that the sorts of problems they had in their finals would be considered not much above 'A' level standard now. On the other hand, Medawar[3] has argued that, in the life sciences, the factual content of our examinations is *lower* now that it was some generations ago. The contradiction is, I think, only apparent. It is largely resolved by the increasing scope of theory, its greater capacity for organizing and unifying facts. Physics has had a strong theoretical framework for centuries now, and the sophistication of that theory continues to increase. Chemistry has reached maturity rather more recently. At the teaching level, it has been considerably transformed even within the last few decades by theories of chemical binding and reaction mechanisms. Biology is in the process of undergoing an analogous change, with the rise of molecular and cell biology. Here, as in chemistry, there has been considerable scope for replacing the descriptive, 'natural history' approach and dealing less with particular examples and more with general principles.

Even though theory can do something to make the stockpile of facts manageable, it offers no easy way out of the educational dilemma. For one thing, mastering more sophisticated theory does tend to make more strenuous intellectual demands on students. For another, particular facts remain the stuff of life and all-embracing theory can never replace them. I feel a certain sympathy with those who have grim forebodings of students who know a great deal about theories of covalent bond formation, but not the formula of methane. Stocking up with facts is not in itself the main purpose of undergraduate education, but developing skill at coping with facts is of the very essence.

All-or-none attitude to science education

A good deal of soul-searching about the contents of our first degree courses is thus called for. We should not shirk it by adopting an all-or-none attitude to the teaching of science—either going the whole hog to the intense specialization demanded by modern scientific research, or resting content with the all but nothing that many of our ablest arts students now get before they give up maths and science when barely in their teens. It is the products of the latter course who tend to become mandarins of Whitehall or captains of industry. They may well have the qualities required – the facility with words and with people, the mental agility to take synoptic views and so on. But how far has lack of scientific background handicapped them in an increasingly science-permeated environment? Bagrit, for instance, has called for 'science-orientated humanists' to be at the head of affairs,[4] and Price for a kind of 'intellectual broker' to act as middleman between the realms of science and of politics.[5]

The all-or-none attitude to science education is a by-product of the reliance that is placed in England— to an extent unparalleled in other comparable countries —on the value of early specialization leading to study in depth. It does not matter greatly what subject area has been studied, so the argument goes, because anybody who has been well trained by studying *something* in depth will be able to apply his mind later to anything that he happens to find he needs. This view has considerable merit. Unfortunately, however, science is a serious limitation to its applicability. It is exceedingly difficult in practice just to pick up science, and especially physical science, starting virtually from scratch. Anyone can pick up a bit of history (I am not suggesting that anyone can become a *good* historian, but only that anyone can become a historian of sorts). With physics or chemistry, on the other hand, the problem is of a different order of magnitude.

The meaning of 'depth'

What really is 'depth'? Everyone seems agreed that depth is something one should find in an honours degree course, but there is less agreement on what it consists of and how it can be achieved. Some say that it is a function of the intense concentration and focusing of attention that it takes to master some necessarily small subject area. Others say that it means coming to see the subject in its setting and with its implications—developing an 'overview' rather than 'tunnel vision'—and that it is this wider grasp which makes the difference between an honours degree and a high-level certificate of proficiency for a laboratory technician. In other words, according to this second view, depth really implies breadth.

It is clear, I think, that depth and breadth are not mutually exclusive but complementary. A simple geometrical model of knowledge is inadequate and misleading, because depth is not synonymous with narrowness. I can conceive all too easily of a three-year course that deals with nothing but chemistry, say, or botany, and yet fails to achieve any real measure of intellectual depth. This would be the case if it concentrated on multiple exemplification—more compounds and their reactions, or more plants and their life-cycles. Depth is not a presence-absence phenomenon but a matter of degree. It can vary between the negligibly small and the unattainably great. No practicable teaching can go more than a fraction of the way up the scale. A claim to have dealt with a topic exhaustively in a course betrays the half-baked scholar, with no conception of what serious scholarship really is.

The Science Greats course

Some of the factors leading to depth in teaching have to do with the possibilities of doing things like relating different parts of the subject-matter, seeing situations or problems from more than one point of view and assessing conflicting evidence. It is important here to be aware that it is the *students* who have to be put in a position to do these things; it is not enough for the lecturer to do them.

To construct our Science Greats course at Manchester, we have deliberately set out to exploit certain opportunities of an 'arts' approach. We have not been content with merely juxtaposing half a traditional science subject and half a traditional arts subject, as seems to happen in some joint honours courses. The aim is to achieve more coherence—both in content and in style—between physical science and liberal studies in science, which are the two main subjects running through all three years of the course.

One virtue of arts topics is the scope they give for reading extensively (as distinct from the intensive study of a few textbooks), for dealing with the material in a critical or at least selective way, and for using it to develop coherent arguments in extended prose. These are also features of the topics which make up liberal studies in science, defined in our regulations as science considered from the economic, social, historical and philosophical standpoints. They offer that kind of intellectual depth which comes from relating different parts of the subject-matter, and they are relevant to careers which have to do, in broad terms, with the economic and social roles of science.

In the first year, the approach is largely historical: it covers the economic history of Britain during the last two centuries, illustrating the role of science and technology in economic development; and the history of science, designed largely to illuminate its social relations. In the second and third years, serious discussion of more recent science becomes possible because of the students' greater scientific background. This includes the interaction of economics and science in such developments as radio and synthetic rubber and the problems of combining technical and other factors in planning large technological projects. There are also courses in the relations between science and politics and in the sociology of science.

Details of the teaching style naturally vary between these courses, but a common feature is that there is less emphasis on taking and learning lecture notes than on reading and writing essays. Possibly this is one thing that has made students take to this part of their studies, and we have accordingly thought about the extent to which a similar teaching style can be used in the physical science courses. Contrary to standard practice in science courses, considerable responsibility is thrown on the students to tackle carefully selected reading matter, and teaching time is used less to 'cover the syllabus' than to discuss points of interest or difficulty from it. The approach becomes a sort of 'investigational' one, though the emphasis is on reading rather than on laboratory work. Essay-writing can still be used to some extent to stimulate reading, check its effectiveness and impose intellectual discipline, but because of the nature of the subject-matter it has to be replaced partly by solving of problems.

It is in the choice of teaching material for the physical science courses that the most overwhelming embarrassment of riches presents itself. Self-discipline on the part of teachers is all the more necessary to keep down the amount of material covered; attempts to 'get more in' are liable to defeat our educational purpose. As it is impossible anyway to include all the specific material that a graduate might require (this applies to all courses, but to ours especially), attention is focused less on what is taught than how.

Some people have urged us to be really modern and base the teaching on some new approach such as materials science or information theory or cybernetics, but we have resisted the temptation to put our eggs in some such bright new basket. Instead, we are being relatively traditional and are dealing with what are recognized to be basic areas in physics and chemistry, together with some attention to engineering applications. There are two reasons for this. First, it seems the best way to improve communication with specialists, since the assumptions a specialist makes about what a scientifically literate person already knows are bound to be conditioned by prevalent views on what constitutes basic material. Second, we shall be pleased if at least a substantial minority of our graduates opt for school-teaching, and for that purpose it is necessary to put a layer or two on top of school science. Naturally, our graduates will know less physics or chemistry than the products of traditional courses in those subjects, but they will know quite a lot, and they might even be at an advantage with some new developments, such as physical science as an 'A' level subject or some of the more drastic transformations of the sixth form scene that are now in the air.

Degree of expertise

An objection that some people see to our plan of studies is that there is no subject in which our graduates will be really expert. But the more closely the meanings of the words 'subject' and 'expert' are examined, the more fluid the concepts become. To take first the matter of expertise, it is clearly a matter of degree, just as is depth. There are precious few things that any newly-hatched science graduate is properly qualified to do, and this applies even to the budding research worker, where the match between course content and job content is about as close as one can get. It is sometimes supposed that a first degree marks some definite watershed at which formal instruction can end and independent investigation can begin. This view is considerably oversimplified. An apprenticeship in research is a normal part of the training of a research worker, and the PhD, not the BSc, is the nearest thing we have to a licence to be a research scientist.

Further, the relation between first degree standard and the research front varies widely. In many of the more highly developed subjects, course work at postgraduate level is already common, and it is both desirable and inevitable that it should increase. Less highly developed subjects often afford easier opportunities for research-type project work even at undergraduate level. The prospect of an early start on research is in itself an attraction for some students. Perhaps it is as well, all the same, not to go too far in this direction. It may not be in the students' best long-term interest if it leads to undue neglect of fundamental training on an adequately wide base.

Arbitrariness of subject boundaries

This raises the issue of the second uncertainty: what is a 'subject'? How big is it? The way we carve up the realm of knowledge depends on arbitrary decisions. As Locke said, 'the boundaries of species, whereby men sort them, are made by men'. Is chemistry a subject? Or heterocyclic organic chemistry? Or molecular science, or physical science, or just science? It is an illusion to suppose that we get any help from names here. A subject is as big or as small as we choose to make it.

Quite apart from size, the traditional subjects are arbitrary also in the patterns of intellectual coherence on which they are based. However much we may be disposed by early upbringing to regard some patterns as 'natural', there are often alternatives which are equally valid. History, for instance, may be studied in periods, or it may follow certain ideas or activities or institutions through the centuries: it may, in short, have either horizontal or vertical integration. In a somewhat analogous way, the study of living organisms may be divided into botany and zoology, or it may adopt the molecular biology or cell biology approach, cutting across the distinction between plants and animals.

One type of intellectual coherence can be roughly described as looking at many things in one way. A number of traditional single-discipline subjects follow this type. But there is another type, which consists of looking at one thing in several ways. The classical example—it is literally 'classical'—is Greats at Oxford, which is largely a multi-disciplinary study of the ancient civilizations. The precise, 'hard' core is linguistic, and to it are added other aspects including the literary, historical and philosophical. Some of the courses of regional studies now available at a number of universities appear to be analogous in that there is a basis in the language of the region, supplemented by a study of its literature, thought, institutions and so on.

The Science Greats course at Manchester is constructed on a formally similar pattern: this is the reason for the name. The precise core is provided by physical science, and it is supplemented by the more open-ended treatment of science considered from the economic, social, historical and philosophical points of view.

Qualities of administrators

I pass now from considering the contents of courses in themselves to the relation they bear to the ingredients of some types of career. An item of outstanding importance is administration. Most graduates have to shoulder administrative responsibilities sooner or later, and this includes even those who remain primarily professional scientists as they attain seniority. It may be useful, however, in order to isolate the qualities required for good administration, to consider here in particular an archetypical case, namely, the administrative grade of the British Civil Service—an administrative élite if ever there was one.

Administration is a 'generalist' activity. Specialists are distrusted because they are considered less likely to take the broad, unbiased view. This is one reason why most of our high-level administrators are arts-trained. (Not that arts courses are unspecialized, of course, but they do tend to specialize on 'irrelevant' areas.) Administration, it is said, is 'done with the seat of the pants' and is a skill largely independent of the nature of the activity being administered.

The selection procedure used for recruitment claims to be independent of the subject studied at university and to assess only general intellectual calibre. Yet arts graduates, and in particular historians and classicists, predominate among the entrants. The low proportion of science graduates can be partly explained by motivation: most good science students want to continue with science beyond graduation. But that is not all there is to be said. An interesting point emerges from a recent analysis by Dodd[6] of success ratios among those who do apply for entry. Success in the competition—I refer to the Method II open competition—correlates well with class of degree for historians and classicists, but badly for scientists. Among historians, there was one success for every 1·4

candidates with a first class, for every 4·8 with an upper second and for every 18 with a lower second; among classicists, the corresponding figures were 2·6, 5·0 and 31 but among scientists 3·4, 2·4 and 6·5. I take this to mean that the skills that administration calls for—at least in so far as they are identified by the selection procedure—are not absent among science students but are less closely related to those which make for success in science courses than to those which lead to good performance in history or classics.

One may readily accept as a fact that the skills typically called for by science and by administration do not fully coincide, but that does not excuse what many consider one of the scandals of our educational system. If students from traditional science courses have been able to develop the verbal dexterity and other skills basic to administration and related 'generalist' activities, it is as much despite as because of anything provided by their education beyond O level. This need not be so, at least not to the extent that it is at present.

Employment in industry

One virtue of a degree in some standard subject such as physics or chemistry is that, when a graduate comes to look for a first job, recruiting officers from firms know—or at least think they know—what they are getting and so have some idea where in the firm to place him initially. But even when employment is specifically as a physicist or chemist in the first instance, it often does not remain so for long.

Some figures on actual employment are available from the 1965 manpower survey.[7] Of the 127,000 qualified scientists and engineers identified as employed in industry, more than two-thirds are shown as engaged on work other than research and development (nearly half the scientists, and about three-quarters of the engineers and technologists). These proportions are almost certainly under-estimates. Only about two-thirds of the total estimated manpower stock was accounted for, and firms like to emphasize their research activity, for reasons of prestige among others, and therefore tend to class as research some activities about which others might have doubts. (There is a story of a large science-based firm which conducted a use of time survey among its employees: one instruction for filling up the forms was, if in doubt, call it R and D.)

Some people might interpret these figures as a sign of under-employment of scientists, a waste of their knowledge and talents; but this is not necessarily so. People trained in science can be very useful outside research and development. Indeed, some diagnoses of our national ills point to weakness here as one of the crucial ones. Our relative failure to make the best use of the very healthy state of fundamental science in Britain, to squeeze maximum wealth and welfare out of knowledge, may well be due to managerial rather than scientific deficiencies. The Central Advisory

Council for Science and Technology has argued that more qualified manpower should be used in production, marketing and other management functions rather than in research and development,[8] and the Swann Report echoed this sentiment.[9]

Obviously the types of training desirable for graduate recruits to industry are very varied, and no simple generalization can cover all cases. For many jobs, specialized knowledge is undoubtedly required, and for some nothing less than a PhD will do. However, McCarthy's study estimated industrial demand for specialists to do research as 'a maximum of 30 per cent of all science- and technology-based graduates'.[10] For the other jobs, too much specialist education may even be a handicap. One vociferous member of the anti-PhD lobby is Dr Duncan Davies,[11] now Deputy Chairman of ICI Mond Division. It does seem to be the case that, in terms of the particular choices of research topics, of attitudes to problem-solving and of the motivation engendered, PhD work in universities is often at cross-purposes with some major requirements of industry.

The conclusion from all this is that, over large sectors of employment, highly specialized scientific knowledge at entry is less important than a sound basic training coupled with at least a receptiveness to a wide variety of disciplines. Our experience with the Science Greats course at Manchester has already confirmed that lack of a great mass of highly specialized knowledge does not make science students unattractive to industrial employers. Our first graduates will not emerge until June 1969, but we took steps to provide our students in the summer of 1968 with vacation jobs of a kind likely to give them useful experience and help their subsequent career development. There were 171 offers of jobs for thirty-one first and second year students. Twenty-seven of them took jobs with employers ranging from International Computers, ICI, Mullards and Thomas de la Rue to the BBC, and most of the employers have said that they would be prepared to offer permanent jobs, circumstances permitting.

A student-orientated approach

Where does all this leave us as regards defining first degree standards? None of the criteria seems satisfactory. Attempts to define in absolute terms either the level of competence that a degree should indicate, or the area over which it should spread, lose themselves in uncertainties or founder on inconsistencies. It cannot be done in terms of prospective job content; nor are there adequate academic criteria of depth, or field of knowledge, or relation to the research front.

I have not been critical of criteria merely out of wilful iconoclasm, however. There is a positive aspect as well, and it is this. If, in our thinking on these matters, we weight the interests of subjects less, we can weight those of students more. The only criterion of honours standard that I can still regard as generally applicable and acceptable is one that is based on students and not on subjects—namely, that an honours degree is given for three years' hard, mind-stretching work by students of honours calibre.

Universities are, it is true, guardians of scholarship, and one of their duties is to promote the interests of subjects. But they also have responsibilities to their students, and the teaching function is likely to be best served by an explicitly student-orientated approach. Attempts to apply subject-orientated criteria can do harm. From an uncritical acquiescence to the pressures of 'so little time' and 'so much to do', they lead to overcrowded syllabuses, lectures that hurry through facts and examinations that call for mere regurgitation of them. Moreover, the repercussions extend beyond universities to the earlier stages of education. Suggestions for reducing specialization in sixth forms, now widely regarded as a desirable objective, are countered by cries of horror about lowering first degree standards and dark threats of four-year courses.

If only it were more widely recognized that levels of attainment in subjects at the first degree stage are based on arbitrary and relative criteria, not fixed and absolute ones, many educational mistakes could be avoided.[12]

Notes

1 F. R. Jevons, Science Greats, *Listener*, 11 May 1967; A Science Greats course, *Physics Education* (1967), 2, 196.

2 D. J. de Solla Price, *Little Science, Big Science* (Columbia University Press 1965), 6.

3 P. B. Medawar, *The Art of the Soluble*, Methuen, London, 1967, 114 (also in Penguin Books).

4 L. Bagrit, *The Age of Automation*, Penguin Books 1966, 45.

5 D. K. Price, *Government and Science* (New York University Press 1954), 187; F. R. Jevons, Politicians and scientists, *Physics Bulletin* (1968), **19**, 42.

6 C. H. Dodd, Recruitment to the administrative class, 1960–64, *Public Administration*, Spring 1967, 55.

7 Department of Education and Science, Ministry of Technology, *Statistics of Science and Technology* (HMSO 1967).

8 *Technological Innovation in Britain* (HMSO 1968), paras 27 to 29.

9 Cmnd 3760 (HMSO 1968), para. 99.

10 M. C. McCarthy, *The Employment of Highly Specialized Graduates* (Department of Education and Science, HMSO 1968), v.

11 D. S. Davies, The chemistry of the PhD—industrial dissatisfactions, *Times Educational Supplement*, 7 October 1966; Pragmatism in the scientific man-power field, *Chemistry and Industry*, 28 September 1968.

12 The issues raised in this article are more fully discussed in Jevons, *The Teaching of Science* (Allen & Unwin 1969).

39   Social movements and political action: a preliminary view of a student initiated course

Stephen Yeo

In the University of Sussex *B.A. Syllabus* for 1969–70 there appeared a new entry. Under the 'Contextual' courses (courses which all students in a 'school' of studies have to take, regardless of their 'major' subject, some voluntary, some compulsory) in the School of Social Studies was listed a course called 'Social movements and political action'. The course will be taught for the first time in October 1970. Its rubric reads as follows:

> The course has been developed as a result of student initiative and is designed to relate closely to student experience of, and alternative modes of action available within, the contemporary political scene. It will make use of material from history, sociology, political science and other disciplines to examine forms of political action mainly as expressed through social movements. Such areas as political parties, cadre politics, pressure groups, civil disobedience, utopian movements, workers' control, experts and intellectuals, apathy and commitment, individualism and self-help will be examined. Two principal methods of teaching will be used: flexible seminar groups, and lectures given by invited lecturers from within and from outside the University, some of them being individuals who are directly engaged in particular forms of political action.

How the course came into being as an idea, how it became accepted as an option, and what it will contain are of wider interest, and more problematical, than the normal run of university curriculum changes.[1]

Two members of the RSSF (Revolutionary Socialist Student Federation) produced the first document proposing the course, one a student of economics, the other of history. There are many well-tried responses to revolutionary students. They can be, and are, used at will when direct argument would be inconvenient or embarrassing. It is said that they are

in a minority. It is said that the connections they try to make between universities and the capitalism in which they are located are false connections. It is no longer said that there are *no* connections:[2] just that the revolutionaries have got them wrong. It is said that most of them are middle class, reacting in some way to family pressure—looking for a father, on 'ego trips', neurotic in some way.[3] It is said that they are destructive, that they do not come forward with positive and worked out proposals, that when issues crucial to university intellectual and organizational life are decided they are there (when allowed) with their emotions, but not with their brains. This last is the most used response. So that when socialist students proposed a new course, and put ideas on paper, at least one weapon in the armoury of indirect confrontation was not available to faculty members.

Argument in fact had to begin. It began on the basis of a division of 'political and social action' into a number of 'modes'. The political party, cadre politics, pressure groups, trade unions, individualism and self-help, civil disobedience, apathy and withdrawal, experts and intellectuals, communitarianism and syndicalism were the initial units from which a course to be called at that time 'Power and influence in society' was to be constructed. A working party was set up to form more definite proposals. It consisted of a professor of sociology, a professor of politics, a lecturer in politics, a lecturer in sociology, a lecturer in history and the two students, who were later joined by a postgraduate sociology student. One of the provisos which the School of Social Studies insisted on when it set up the working party was 'that the subject matter of such a course would have to be the direct responsibility of academically qualified members of Faculty'. What academic qualification meant in the context of this course, which might differentiate it from other courses sufficiently to be specially mentioned, was never made clear.

The working party began to meet in June 1968.

Source: *Universities Quarterly* (Autumn 1970), 24 (4), 402–21.

Some of its early meetings generated fascinating discussions which themselves should have been part of the proposed course rather than preparatory to it. At one point the professor of politics felt impelled to draw a model of the functioning of the British political system on the blackboard, only to have it attacked as pre-Bagehotian, as the 'dignified' rather than the 'efficient' view. An argument developed, reflecting wide differences in approaches to social science and to politics. There was sharp division between those who wanted the course to start as a 'systematic' examination of the 'structure' of British politics and *all* the movements 'within' that structure, right as well as left, and those who wanted to start from within the perspectives of the various 'modes' suggested.[4]

Ideological and practical conflicts within the working party were set in an urgent political context, local and international. The 'French Revolution' of May and De Gaulle's counterattack against it which started on May 29th had an effect on university moods.[5] The LSE 'troubles' had begun in Autumn 1967, had been experienced directly by some Sussex students, and had led them and others to initiate a student 'critique' of the university.[6] It was stated in this critique that 'for the moment our concern is analysis, not mobilization'. The analysis was ambitious—under three heads: 'Why are we *taught*?, Why are *we* taught?, *Why* are we taught?' One of the sub-questions which was to lead into the demand for this particular course was 'But why are the faculty liberal, why do they wish us to become products of an education which is designed not to produce narrow academic experts but "good citizens"?' There had been a cogent twenty-nine-page critique of the university as a community by a third year social psychologist and an American history graduate student which preceded the *Wine Press Supplement*, but which was never printed in full.[7] It was completed in mid-1967, and could say at that date that 'Sussex shows none of the usual symptoms which indicate a troubled University such as militancy and activist disaffection.' They identified serious problems but they related not to 'the usual slogans of student militancy' but to 'the students' role within the Sussex community'. There were some signs of increasing militancy within Sussex, including meetings to try to relate LSE to the local situation. Maximum 'mobilization', however, did not take place until autumn-spring 1968–9 with the demand for government of Schools by General Assembly. So concrete pressure for a particular course *preceded* more general agitation, and 'success' in that concrete pressure could be quoted during the wider movements as an example of what intelligent militancy could deliver.

The course went twice from the working party to the governing meeting of the School of Social Studies. Once it was insufficiently documented and explicated to be acceptable: the second time in February 1969 it was 'passed' as 'Social movements and political action' with the rubric already quoted. Book lists and glosses on the subject divisions suggested in the rubric—political parties, cadre politics *et al.*—had by then been produced. The speed with which the course went from idea to syllabus was, considering its origins, remarkable for any university. It owed something to the flexibility of Sussex procedures and the substitution of 'Schools of Studies' for departments, and something to the wider political context of that year.[8]

Three elements of the course and its context are worth dissecting. First the nature and ideology of the 'push' behind it; secondly, the nature and ideology of a significant area of the university into which the course was 'pushed'; thirdly, the content of the course itself. On the relationship between these three elements the success or otherwise of the course will depend when it is first taught in October 1970.

A number of different components of the push behind this particular course, and indeed of post-1968 student socialism, are worth singling out for evaluation. There was, first, a pointing to the connections between western capitalism or, if neutral language is preferred, 'advanced industrialism', and universities. 'Universities *are* involved in the political process', was the assertion often made. Few would deny this; the case was made by politicians, economists, and educators after Robbins in the argument for university expansion before it was made by students.[9] Capitalism needs universities as it has never needed them before. In Britain full-time university students have increased from 77,000 in 1947 to 94,000 in 1957, to 169,486 in 1965–6. It should be pointed out that these connections were sometimes asserted in a macro or slogan form.[10] At this level they could be answered (and were by the Vice-Chancellor) in specific terms, demonstrating the 'independence' of research at Sussex. But they were also argued for in more thought-out forms, less easily dismissed.[11]

With this element in the student demand for the course, 'Social movements and political action' cannot be directly concerned. Until recently there was a course available to history majors at the university called 'Universities and society'. Such a theme needs comparative and chronological analysis as well as contemporary study: it needs a course by itself. Some of the connections between 'academic' work and institutions and social systems may become clearer as a result of the course. But that cannot be its central preoccupation.

Nor can the course, except tangentially, confront other important impulses behind recent student socialism. It cannot, for instance, answer the demand for an expression of the position of *the university* as such on urgent contemporary issues. 'Why does this institution appear to hide where it stands?' was asked by the 'February 21st committee' in *An open letter to Sussex Faculty*. 'The February 21st committee demands to know what your institution means.' It was a good question—not to be shrugged off by saying that the university in this sense does not exist as the kind of body which *can* define its collective position, when quite clearly for other purposes it *does* exist in that sense. It cannot take up the criticisms continually made of other courses. These have been made both at the particular level of individual courses, through efforts to organize written evaluations of courses by students, and at the general level of the tendency of the whole education offered:[12]

> We in England lack any coherent understanding of the necessity and theoretical basis of our institutions. There is an almost total lack of conscious reflection on our educational practice as a whole, as a system rigorously examined by philosophical, historical and sociological methods. A general and well apprehended crisis in our educational system, exemplified by the recent spate of government reports and attempts at reform, has failed to generate a critical perspective. Reformism, Liberalism and Empiricism, the defining characteristics of the English ideology and the life's blood of the pedagogues who inculcate it, lead us to assume that the system *as such* is viable and that its evolution through a gradual process of reform is sure and settled. Every 'problem' is picked over until it is a clean little skeleton, but why it is a problem in other words *everything* is taken for granted.

These ideas surround this course but cannot be its centre: the first is a subject for agitation, the second is at too high a level of abstraction to form a coherent course of this type.[13]

Daniel Cohn-Bendit:
> . . . the defence of the students' interests is something very problematic. What are their 'interests'? They do not constitute a class. Workers and Peasants form social classes and have objective interests. Their demands are clear and they are addressed to the management and to the government of the bourgeoisie. But the students? Who are their 'oppressors', if not the system as a whole?

Jean-Paul Sartre:
> Indeed, students are not a class. They are defined by age and a relation to knowledge. By definition, a student is someone who must one day cease to be a student in any society even the society of our dreams.

Daniel Cohn-Bendit:
> That is precisely what we must change. In the present system, they say: there are those who work and those who study. And we are stuck with a social division of labour, however intelligent. But we can imagine another system where everyone will work at the tasks of production—reduced to a minimum thanks to technical progress—and everyone will still be able to pursue his studies at the same time: the system of simultaneous productive work and study.

With the dialogue on the role of students as a 'class' in relation to other classes in the achievement of social change, often acrimonious within the revolutionary movement itself and always central in its debates, we move into an area of great importance in the 'push' behind this new course and of more importance to it than the other elements singled out so far. There has been much recent discussion of the nature of the student movement in relation to the working class movement. In what consists the difference between students and other social groups? How can students relate to outside social movements—as participants, as leaders, as followers? Extreme positions were struck up, although rarely held exclusively or consistently by any individual. There was the 'studentist' extreme and the 'ouvrierist' extreme: in practice during the peak of recent agitation at Sussex and in the thought and writing which that agitation generated the two positions moved closer together.

In the face of large increases in student numbers ('Higher Education has in our generation become a mass commodity for the first time'), in the face of inadequacies or 'contradiction' in the government, social life, teaching and learning experience within expanding universities, and in the face of international example, especially French—students rejected old roles ('the spoiled youth of the upper classes') and looked for new:[14]

> Students do not constitute a class, but a social situation with particular location in class relations. The student is defined traditionally as not of the society but in a separate transitional category. Modes of class behaviour and class expectation are therefore not rigidly applied— deviance, relative freedom and rebellion are allowed for, even expected as a 'phase'. Criticism and deviance are thereby located not as a social force, but as a biographical stage. It is expected that the student will be re-socialized, will redefine himself, in his later accommodation to the system of production.

It was in reaction against that, that alternative views were put; either of students as having an autonomous revolutionary role parallel to that of the working class or, more usually, of students as 'detonators' of more widespread social struggle.[15] To this argument the substance of 'Social movements and political action' must clearly be made directly relevant, whatever position students take up within the debate, or whatever reasons are put forward for rejecting the terms of the debate altogether.

Closely related to this component of student socialism is its pre-occupation with self-conscious thought and discussion about the position of intellectuals in modern societies. Interest in this was more striking at the 'studentist' rather than the 'ouvrierist' end of the spectrum, but everywhere in the student movement it is apparent. The close attention paid to the thought of Gramsci derives partly from this. **A** source of ideas has been the writing of Perry Anderson and others in the *New Left Review*. At one level the most important feature of student thought in this area is its utter lack of deference (which sometimes turns into an unattractive contempt) for previous thinkers, and its huge ambition (which sometimes turns into superficial schematization) for a total re-ordering of the British intellectual scene. Ideas are held to be extremely important, and worth discussing seriously, although always in the context of the social position and actions of their possessors. Any labels of anti-intellectualism which have been fixed on to the student movement by its detractors are false: they derive either from the insistence by students on the context just mentioned or from the reluctance of some students to follow their ideas into the books in order to test and refine them. 'Anti-empiricism' does coincide sometimes with absence of factual knowledge, although it need not.[16] The ambition which follows the diagnosis is daunting—as in a document drawn up by a post-graduate sociology student which formed part of the working party's deliberations:

> Cold War knowledge is therefore an engaged knowledge—a form of understanding which puts its own social order beyond conceptual or empirical question as the superior term of the Democratic/Communist opposition. This engagement has virtually deformed the major institutionalized modes of social understanding in East and West Marxism and Sociology. *The reconstruction of these sciences is, in part, what this course should be about* [my italics].

The task was big enough, without the devastating parenthesis, 'in part'! But the tone is serious and challenging, and such as to suggest that out of it could come work and discussions of an unusually central kind:

> The notions of emancipation and of autonomous knowledge are hopes—hopes which our scientific tradition has presented and yet clearly not realized. It is this gap between the possibilities our intellectual tradition has shown us, and an adequate conceptual accommodation of those possibilities to the modern world, which is at the heart of the student problematic.
>
> That problematic exists for the intelligentsia as a whole—it is a question which has been forced upon these generations of students by their particular experiential situation. Because this question has a particular social carrier it does not cease to be a general question. To negate the students' disquiet, to silence by repression a group which raises an as yet unanswered question of the whole intelligentsia, is to deny that problem posed against one's own existence.

The role of experts and intellectuals as technicians, advisers, critics, and the effect of their increasing numbers was, from early on in the discussions, seen as a key element of 'Social movements and political action'.

But what was in students' minds was more than a sociological analysis of the role of students as a group or intellectuals as a group. What was being asserted, and aimed at, was an ideal combination of theory *and* practice. Personal and corporate moral responsibility for ideas and social functions was a fruitful source of accusation and agitation against those in positions of power, but also a self-accusation levelled at students by students.[17]

> The student has . . . no coherent theory of practice, nor can he easily acquire it. The student just does not encounter many traditions and theories, and he has few means of discovering them by independent intellectual struggle. Faculty members should therefore not be surprised at the more aberrant forms of student political action. That these actions are sometimes counter-productive cannot but please the enemies of the students. But if the problems they raise are real problems, if their struggles have a real point, they should not be left in ignorance.

Separation of study from politics, of university change from social change, was seen as 'the false bourgeois dichotomy of theory and practice'. Some kind of a Marxist *praxis* was being aimed at. A recent social work and community work news-sheet at the university has been given the title *Praxis*. The inherent difficulty of that aim, the felt lack of bearing of much of their study on it, and the necessarily constantly changing political environment at the local level, which alters any temporary balance achieved from day to day during a period of social struggle, were great causes of personal frustration amongst serious socialist students, causes of what appears to the university authorities to be 'under achievement' in 'academic' work. The quest for the single, demonstrably correct practice, of the single demonstrably correct theory, the wish, in this sense, to be 'scientific' socialists while also intervening actively in the social process in a morally repugnant but complex world situation is a tough one. So tough that those unsympathetic with the whole terms in which the aspirations are felt can and do laugh at the inadequacy of attempts to make them real. The context in which these attempts have to be made has changed enormously since most older university teachers had anything to do with politics, if they ever did. There is a strain, felt by students, in accommodating old (First International and beyond) political language and controversy to drastically altered situations. Arguably much of what goes under the label 'Maoism' is only in a formal and theoretical, highly attenuated way connected with 'Marxism-Leninism'. With these aspirations and with these strains part of 'Social movements and political action' should certainly be concerned.[18] Clarification, not solution, of the difficulty can be sought.

With the course *as* practice, which was an idea in the minds of some who pushed for it, it would be difficult to accommodate any valuable term's work. Some saw agitation as valuable in and for itself, separate from any goods which agitation might deliver—such as a new academic course. The strategy was to 'escalate' (the title of the RSSF magazine at Sussex) demands just as soon as previous demands looked to be imminently fulfilled. 'Success', in these terms, meant 'failure'. Reforms achieved meant revolution denied or delayed. Once achieved, once on the syllabus such a course as 'Social movements and political action', in these terms, lost interest. Commitment to make it work, commitment to define its content, to discuss particular units of work was, at best, irrelevant. Demands which could be met were false demands; this one had been met; there must be something wrong with it.

This view of 'Social movements and political action' was undoubtedly an element in the push behind it, and in the subsequent history of that push, even though never exclusively dominating the thinking of any single group. To the extent that participants in the course regard it *as* agitation, regard it as a directly politicizing agency, to that extent it will fail as a serious course—to that extent also it will fail to achieve the goals set for it by those who struggled for it. Students should realize, apart from anything else, that some tactics (particularly the view of tactic *as* strategy) while capable of being defended in theoretical terms to their own satisfaction are counter-productive in their effect upon other students, and in their blocking of valuable social and academic reforms.[19]

The University of Sussex in its idea of itself (to the extent that any such thing exists) or at least in its ideas of itself, necessarily expressed mostly by leading faculty members, has from the start been concerned with the question 'What is taught?'[20] Much and important intellectual effort went into the structuring of the syllabus and into its particular courses. The *B.A. Syllabus* is arguably the University's most important achievement to date. It can best be appreciated not by students, but by faculty who have been students elsewhere or who have taught elsewhere. At least where the study of history is concerned it would be difficult to improve the range and type of course available to undergraduates—from any ideological position anywhere on the left. Courses do not always live up to their labels, but the labels are excellent.

It will be worth briefly examining relevant elements of the self-perception of the university into which 'Social movements and political action' was pushed, as expressed by people who have written or spoken about courses, students and other matters. The relationship between that self-perception and the push already dissected will, as already suggested, be a factor in the experience of the course when first taught. We shall proceed by asking a series of questions, looking for answers where they already exist in print, and considering the relationship of those answers to this course and its context.

Question 1. What, at the most 'philosophical' level, is the education of this university all about?

A relevant question, too often avoided.[21] This university is to be part of 'a company which recognizes in its dealing with the world of scholarship no frontiers of race or religion or politics.'[22] 'A forum where the resources of trained intelligence are applied as keenly to men's ultimate convictions as to the atom or the cell' or 'a cloister where people take refuge from such contentious issues'? 'Perhaps the deepest implication of our rearrangement of the curriculum is that we have opted, even if more by instinct than by deliberation, for the former course.'[23] 'I think the students are pressing for a participation in an institution that gives them a greater purpose in living and purpose in being here. I think Universities have sinned in that respect.'[24]

Nothing here which argues against 'Social movements and political action'; on the contrary, some identification with current student concerns.

Question 2. What idea is there as to the relationship between the student, his education at Sussex and outside society?

Again, conceded to be an important question for evaluating curriculum and other university products.[25] One distinctly Arnoldian (in the sense of Matthew Arnold's idea of 'culture') answer from Sir John Fulton: 'to raise the powers of the individuals committed to his [the teacher's] charge to their highest capacity, in the confidence that, if they have been so prepared, the future which they shape will be the best attainable' —but with more dominative overtones reluctantly expressed.[26] Another answer which adds an explicit element of social criticism:[27]

> it is not really possible for an institution of higher education to provide so directly for 'the sort of society in which its graduates will be living or working' without being compelled to examine critically the assumptions and dynamic of that society of industrial technology.

A persistent answer from Asa Briggs that 'judgment' is as important as expertise—'national survival, human survival cannot be guaranteed by experts alone: separated teams of experts, indeed, could lead us to disaster'—that the relationship between subjects is as important a perception to acquire as a single specialism, for people who leave university after three years.[28]

Question 3. What is thought to be happening in relation to students and politics?

Answers suggest that the view is of something deep, something which has to be referred to 'society' or world politics for understanding rather than to psychological explanations (although there are elements of these around), above all something about which there is a curious uncertainty, hesitancy—in places one might say even evasiveness. There is something of all these in the interestingly elusive coda to

Asa Briggs's paper to the Quail Roost Seminar of December 1968.[29] As there is in the Director of the University Health Service's recent book on *Student Casualties* (1969).[30]

Professor Marie Jahoda, asked to explain student unrest to the select committee last year, dismissed conspiracy theories and the contagion-via-the-mass-media theory. She preferred to say

> that there is something in the modern situation of young people which does indeed create very deep frustrations which are taken out at the best object you have available. The question 'why now and not previously?' may have something to do with the notion that these frustrations have been building up gradually in a more and more complicated world where many of us do not see a clear way out, and the lack of clarity about the modern problem has finally hit the student population that has, after all, tried over the last 10–15 years various other ways—dress, Rock, Rockers and Mods, and drugs, and all sorts of ways of escaping. Now these other ways do not seem quite so interesting any more to the young, and now they have settled on trying to do something about their own institutions.

Questions 2 and 3 produce answers, immediately controversial and questionable answers, which directly lead into and justify, precisely because of their assumptions, a course like 'Social movements and political action'.

Question 4. What specific ideas as to the nature of learning and the forces it generates have there been at the university which might have an echo, even if unintended and foresworn, in the student 'push' already anatomized?

One interesting answer comes from Boris Ford's article, 'What is a University?', already quoted. Two assertions made there stand out. One that 'the *first* place for participation is at the heart of the learning process'. This was used to justify the teaching in 'small collaborative groups' rather than in the 'mass lecture'. It is commonly used to justify the tutorial system at Sussex. In that system there is not the teaching of a set body of knowledge broken up into eight units, but the learning by active cooperation between tutor and student and a body of knowledge which is recognized to have rough edges and to be a matter for enquiry and research rather than simple transmission. At some points the student is subordinate to the tutor, some would say at most points: but most would admit the legitimacy, even desirability, of allowing the units of work to arise out of the student's need, temperament and interest rather than out of a tutor's idea of a rigidly programmed course.

The other is more elusive. Professor Ford wishes to emphasize 'words like *passion, creativity, emotional*' in university studies as opposed to 'the noble if chilling ideal of the established academic mind'. He quotes Dr F. R. Leavis to this effect (the Greynog address on 'English Unrest and Continuity', *Times Literary Supplement*, 29.5.1968): the 'saving spirit' is the 'living principle', 'the creative and unifying principle of life, made strongly active', 'perhaps one might add that creativity creates significance and reality'. It is unfair to refer to, rather than to expound, the ideas of Dr Leavis like this, let alone Boris Ford. Both of them may be hostile to most manifestations of recent student social movements but none the less, in so far as it is clear what Professor Ford *is* in favour of in the *New Statesman* article, it seems to be not unlike recent student ideas as to the meaning, in political terms, of *consciousness* realized in action, and closely linked, in its very definition, to action.

Question 5. What is the university idea of itself as a social organization?

Direct quotation is less useful in our answer to this question, than the experience of the writer as a member of the faculty. The predominant idea here should be the word *community*.[31] It is wrong, so the idea runs, to think of students *versus* faculty, or even students as a group as opposed to faculty as a group. We are a community. A pluralist community, with many different tastes, friends, opinions, temperaments, all of which cross student/faculty lines. Anyone with good ideas as to what should be done at the university, how it should be done, by whom it should be done, has 'the proper channels' to go through to get his ideas expressed, and if supported, implemented. Our basic job is intellectual and rational, the exploration of new knowledge, the testing and teaching of old. That job is done together, with 'no frontiers'. Lines of research are pursued via faculty, postgraduates, even undergraduates, and via many 'institutes' and 'centres'. They are pursued freely and in relation primarily to intellectual interest, in a context of 'usefulness' but not with that context as the primary imperative. Any conflict which may exist is argumentative and rational, not interest based and social. As Asa Briggs wrote recently on the question of personal files,[32]

> it is necessary in the light of recent events for universities to explore all the relevant issues and to be willing, once the arguments have been sorted out, to change their procedures if it is decided that change will lead to improvement. By the very nature of a university, it is essential that all arguments and their implications must be fully examined and not taken for granted. Unless universities operate in this kind of way—and not through direct action on the part of individuals or groups—they will be untrue to their own character . . .

From the answers to our questions, necessarily selective and without doubt unacceptable to many members of the university faculty who have not been quoted, arise further important questions. Both the components of the push behind the course and of the self-perception of the university into which it was pushed suggest that there is a definite job to be done by a course like 'Social movements and political action'. That job should, initially, be stated ambitiously via questions arising out of the material in the order presented in this article.

In what sense, and how, do societies (capitalist and others) get the social movements they need in order to survive? Is there a simple one-to-one relation between social systems and social movements and institutions? If so, how does any movement alter that relation, become an instrument of change rather than an agent of stability? What is the relationship between economic and political power in specific societies and the relationship between each of them and social movements? Is the nature of institutions and their surrounding social systems best revealed and transmitted to wide numbers of people within them by social movements employing a strategy of 'demands' and 'confrontation'? How do class-based, and/or interest-expressing movements come into being and operate? What is the relation of student movements to them—in theory and practice? What is the position and role of intellectuals and experts in specific societies? What have been the ideas as to the relation between, and ideal combination of, theory and practice held by individual thinkers and activists, and how have these ideas worked out in social movements? How have 'men's ultimate convictions', in Professor Corbett's phrase, found expression in political action and social movements? What are the implications of the belief that there is a single correct theory of a single correct practice at any one moment in time in any one society? How does it relate to a view of a university which claims not to be dominative in its mode of operation and choice of subjects for study and research and which recognizes 'no frontiers of race or religion or politics'? How can we more directly, in Professor Ford's phrase, 'examine critically the assumptions and dynamic of (a) society of industrial technology'? Do existing courses do that, for the most part? Can this one do so more explicitly? What are the difficulties and possibilities of real inter-disciplinary work related to specific problems? What are the assumptions behind ideas that problems are best located within and only scientifically soluble within individual academic specialisms? How far do explanations of social movements in terms of the function which they serve for their members really work? What types of social movements are acceptable to and generated by institutions and societies which regard themselves as 'communities' where conflict should be subordinate to rational presentation and evaluation of arguments—arguments, which are 'sifted' and then accepted or rejected because of their consensus-approved rationality rather than because of any interest or power considerations? Is it just universities which see themselves in this light, or do states (e.g. the United States of America)? How do social movements and intellectuals respond to such ideology?

Such questions are easier to ask than to answer in forms amenable to treatment in an eight-unit seminar and lecture course. Reading lists and individual seminar outlines will not be pursued here. An approach will be suggested which can only be effectively tested via specific topics when 'Social movements and political action' is first taught.

The rubric quoted at the start of this article mentioned six forms of social movement—political parties, cadre politics, pressure groups, civil disobedience, utopian movements, workers' control. In any one student's or seminar group's experience of the course not all those areas could in anything more than a superficial sense be treated. The plan for a series of lectures 'some of them [from] individuals who are directly engaged in particular forms of political action' will supplement necessary omissions if a selected number of these areas are to be effectively studied in an individual seminar. Four areas in eight seminars might be the maximum coverage possible.

The perspective of the course, if it is to remain true to the impulses originally behind it, must be the making of social movements and modes of political action more intelligible, and the implications of choices not to be involved in social movements and choices of modes of political inaction more fully understandable, to students. Overall surveys of types of social movement precisely defined, preoccupation with classification, argument about what is or what is not, for example, a pressure group, and the manifold subdivisions into which any one mode might be divided by social scientists, will not be the main themes of the course. Clarity will, naturally, be sought and definitions will be used where appropriate, but not at the expense of the historical specificity of the material studied. The historical dimensions will indeed, at least by one faculty member involved, be stressed.

With each mode chosen three main lines of inquiry should be pursued. Reading lists and seminar discussions can be arranged around these divisions.

First an historical inquiry. How did a particular mode—for example the political party—come, for us in this society, to be an option? How did it come into being and in what circumstances? How has it developed over time? This line of inquiry will clearly be vital for the understanding of the nature of the modes chosen for study. Not all modes listed are or were available in all societies, for definite and important reasons. Some modes are peculiarly characteristic of some societies. Some modes take very different forms in different societies. Why?

Second, an inquiry, from two points of view, into theory. From the point of view of practitioners in the mode, what theory or theories are held implicitly or explicitly about society and social action as part of their practice within the mode? What do specific social movements look like and imply to those inside them? From the point of view of us, temporarily, in the course, as students of society outside any single mode, what theory or theories are implied by commitment to a particular mode?

Third, an inquiry into the functioning and effectiveness of the selected modes. What can social scientists tell us as to the working out in practice in specific societies of different types of social movements and political action? How effective are they, and have they been, and in what circumstances, and effective for what? Detailed empirical study of the functioning and consequences of, for example, pressure groups.

Some such division of labour over a limited territory should, within the inevitable limitation of faculty and students' knowledge, work, and experience, give coherence to a course which, within the context earlier described, will at the very least be a worth-while experiment.

Notes

1 In at least one recent writer's opinion, student-initiated courses will proliferate over the next few years: 'I expect the single greatest change in American universities and colleges in the next decade to be in the disruption of the courses of studies . . . and an unbelievably greater emphasis upon student-initiated and in many cases student-conducted courses'. James Jarrett, Response to Northrop Frye, in W. R. Niblett, ed., *Higher Education: Demand and Response* (1969), 52. Even in the U.K. things have probably altered since Maurice Hutt, the then Senior Proctor of the University of Sussex, could write 'few of them [the students] would seriously object to the university's laying down what they should study', in David Daiches, ed., *The Idea of a New University: an experiment in Sussex* (1964), 51.

2 . . . 'Universities are not independent communities of altruistic scholars, they are national institutions whose actions are limited by external pressures and constraints, and whose policies are determined by internal balances of powerful forces.' Geoffrey Lockwood, Planning Officer, Sussex in the seventies, in *Focus, the news magazine of the University of Sussex*, October 1969. Political students could not have put it better.

3 This line has been warned against by the Director of the University Health Centre at the University of Sussex: 'The temptation to explain away student revolt by reference to psychiatric or pseudo-psychiatric factors needs to be resisted. The argument that students are in revolt, adolescents revolt, and therefore the student revolt is an adolescent revolt, is a specious one. The adolescent revolt is a constant, always with us. At any given period of history the incidence and distribution of pathological manifestations of adolescent revolt may be explained in terms of family structure and family stresses, but these factors do not account for short-term historical swings. The homes of the politically apathetic students of the 1950's did not differ radically from the homes of the militant students of the 1960's and the differences in mood and behaviour must be explained in social and political terms.' Anthony Ryle, *Student Casualties* (1969), 127–8.

4 The former position was worked out in a paper for the working party called 'Doctrines and structures of contemporary politics', E. A. Brett and B. D. Graham (July 1968).

5 Patrick Seale and Maureen McConville, *French Revolution 1968* (1968), 57: 'Every country in the world with troublesome students now asks itself the question: Could it happen here? None can feel complacent . . . no one should under-estimate the intelligence, audacity and sheer strategic skill of the student leaders who, in cafés and on university campuses around the world, are planning to give the adults hell.'

6 Published as a *Wine Press Supplement*, 1 February 1968.

Wine Press was the student newspaper.

7 A copy of this critique and of the other ephemeral documents referred to in this article are in the author's possession.

8 The historical background, chapter in vol. 1 of the *Report from the Select Committee on Education and Science*, session 1968–9, *Student Relations*, calls 1966 'Increasing belligerency and the growth of political consciousness'; 1967 'New issues in the U.K.'; 1968 'The year of crisis'.

9 It has been well expounded by Gareth Stedman Jones, The meaning of the student revolt, in *Student Power*, ed. Alexander Cockburn and Robin Blackburn (1969), 30–6.

10 See 'A fact sheet on the connections between the University of Sussex and the U.S. and British Military-Industrial complex' issued by the February 21st committee.

11 See a paper by David Griffiths, 'Innovation and change in the University of Sussex with particular reference to the examination system' (October 1968) and also a paper by seven revolutionary students, 'Perspectives on the role of students in revolutionary action' where although it was asserted that 'Universities serve as "capital goods industries" for the system of production —they provide a factor of production which is at once Labour and Capital'; the relative autonomy of the University from the social order (especially in England) was also interestingly recognized.

12 From a paper 'Why do we not learn the theory of our education?' submitted to the School of Social Studies during student agitation for changes in the constitution of the School. A February 21st committee document was more forthright: '. . . you are educated to avoid political commitment, to look at the world "objectively", never to take sides in any issue but always to search for complexity and qualifications. You are being trained to take a job with a corporation or serve in some section of the government bureaucracy: that is to take a place in the hierarchy, lower than some but higher than most. Communist education however seeks to create a new sort of man; one who neither exploits nor is exploited, who serves not the corporations but the people.' See 'Education for what?', February 21st committee.

13 Interview published in *Le Nouvel Observateur*, 20 May 1968, reprinted in Herve Bourges, ed., *The Student Revolt* (1968).

14 'Perspectives on the role of students in revolutionary action' by seven Sussex students.

15 See, for this discussion, *Students for Socialism*, a twenty-six page pamphlet published in July 1968 by The Socialist Club of the University of Sussex and signed by students from thirteen other university socialist societies; also Ernest Mandel, *From Revolt against the*

Bourgeois University to Revolt Against Capitalist Society, pamphlet (June 1968); also *Red Letter* no. 9, 10 June 1968, 'A Report written by Alan Woods after his visit to France, 24–27 May.'

16 'Clearly we cannot conjure a theory from nothing. We cannot close the gap without *work*'; see 'Why do we not learn the theory of our education?', already quoted.

17 Both last two quotes from the same document as quoted immediately above.

18 There is an interesting article by Northrop Frye: The university and personal life: student anarchism and the educational contract', in W. R. Niblett, ed., *Higher Education, Demand and Response* (1969), 35–51. He describes contemporary student radicalism as operating in a context of 'the decline of the sense of continuity and teleology' compared to 1930s politics. He asks, 'What is it then, that the more restless and impatient students of our time are trying to break through their university training to get?' And answers, 'they are seeking guidance to the existential questions which have largely overwhelmed what confidence they ever had in the discipline of thought. In other words their quest is a religious one, and they are looking for answers to religious questions that the university, *qua* university, cannot answer. ... The scholar can only deal with these questions as a person, not as a scholar, but no one who would turn away a serious student on the ground that these questions were out of his field deserves the title of teacher. The professor in our own day is in the same position as the modern doctor who has to try to cure Weltschmertz as well as bellyaches. The doctor may long for the simple old days when hysteria and hypochondria were specific disturbances of the womb or the abdomen, but he is not living in those days, and must struggle as best he can with the intangible.'

19 For one document which comes close to the view being attacked here see Leicester RSSF, *University and Revolution* (1968), 24–8. One paragraph asserts (p. 26), 'Next we come to the vital issue of curricula and teaching methods: and as our strategy itself is informed by an ideology we must make demands for counter-curricula and student lectureships on the grounds that *students have participated in their shaping* rather than on their own merits. The point of this is that we do not allow ourselves to be compromised pragmatically: our struggle must be ideological'.

20 Its first Vice-Chancellor, in his essay: 'New universities in perspective', in David Daiches, ed., *The Idea of a New University; an experiment in Sussex* (1964) 13, asked the question 'What should they teach?' quite baldly. Its present Vice-Chancellor outlined an answer in his 'Drawing a New Map of Learning', ibid., 60–81.

21 Boris Ford, 'What is a university?', *New Statesman*, 24 October 1969: 'the *quidditas* of universities, to make use of Stephen Daedaus's terminology, is a topic which most of us who work in them seem content to avoid'.

22 Sir John Fulton, 'New universities in perspective', in David Daiches, ed., op. cit., 18.

23 J. P. Corbett, 'Opening the mind', in David Daiches, ed., op. cit., 36.

24 Professor Marie Jahoda, Report from the Select Committee on Education and Science, Session 1968–9,

Student Relations, vol. II, *Full Committee Evidence and Appendices*, para. 665.

25 Professor Asa Briggs, University challenge: universities and the community, in *Only Connect: Four Studies in Modern Communication* (1968), 77: 'the changes that have taken place and are taking place in the university curriculum will be judged, whether the universities like it or not, by the calibre of university graduates in realizing in action—some call it "real life"—not necessarily what they have learned directly at universities—much of that is quickly forgotten—but what they have learned indirectly and generally through a university education'.

26 'It will not be possible completely to avoid seeking to discover the shape of the future which has to build upon the foundations of today's education. If our present society could look forward with assurance to a long period of stability ... the character of the education appropriate to it would be one thing: but for a world of rapid change—technological, social and political—it must be another. Thus whether we hold to our traditional educational practices or whether we change them, we are, in either case, saying our say about the future. Within the limits of human foresight we must see that what we choose is relevant to the needs of the long-term as well as to those of the short-term future.' Sir John Fulton 'New universities in perspective', in David Daiches, ed., op. cit., 17.

27 Boris Ford, What is a university?

28 'I think universities are very much concerned with, or should be concerned with, the common element in education which cuts across the subject dividing lines. One hopes that within this common work it will be possible to develop methods which carry students beyond expert knowledge.' Report from the Select Committee on Education and Science, Session 1968–9, *Student Relations*, vol. V, *Sub-Committee B. Evidence and Appendices*, para. 1,064.

29 Development in higher education in the United Kingdom: nineteenth and twentieth centuries, in W. R. Niblett, ed., *Higher Education: Demand and Response* (1969), 115–16.

30 See pp. 15–16: 'a movement expressed in new attitudes to politics and to personal relationships, to new forms of sexual behaviour and, less hopefully, to the cults of drug-taking and dropping out. The apparent certainties of science and the control over nature that these give are seen as less satisfying than the attempt to understand human problems and to explore experience and feeling: an attitude summarized in 1968 by the French students with slogans such as "l'imagination au pouvoir". The instability of the modern world, a felt revulsion against its violence and injustices, makes it difficult for many contemporary students to identify with any stable system of belief; at a time when the demands made by society are more and more complicated, the relation of the individual to society is becoming more cautious and less committed ... it is a backcloth above all of uncertainty'.

31 For a hostile view of this, see Leicester RSSF, *University and Revolution* (1968), 13–15, Community as a liberal ideology.

32 University of Sussex, *Files relating to individual members of the University. A Statement by the Vice-Chancellor* (March 1970).

40 The concept of equality of educational opportunity[1]

James Coleman

The concept of 'equality of educational opportunity' as held by members of society has had a varied past. It has changed radically in recent years, and is likely to undergo further change in the future. This lack of stability in the concept leads to several questions. What has it meant in the past, what does it mean now, and what will it mean in the future? Whose obligation is it to provide such equality? Is the concept a fundamentally sound one, or does it have inherent contradictions or conflicts with social organization? But first of all, and above all, what is and has been meant in society by the idea of equality of education opportunity?

To answer this question, it is necessary to consider how the child's position in society has been conceived in different historical periods. In pre-industrial Europe, the child's horizons were largely limited by his family. His station in life was likely to be the same as his father's. If his father was a serf, he would likely live his own life as a serf; if his father was a shoemaker, he would likely become a shoemaker. But even this immobility was not the crux of the matter; he was a part of the family production enterprise and would likely remain within this enterprise throughout his life. The extended family, as the basic unit of social organization, had complete authority over the child, and complete responsibility for him. This responsibility ordinarily did not end when the child became an adult because he remained a part of the same economic unit and carried on this tradition of responsibility into the next generation. Despite some mobility out of the family, the general pattern was family continuity through a patriarchal kinship system.

There are two elements of critical importance here. First, the family carried responsibility for its members' welfare from cradle to grave. It was a 'welfare society', with each extended family serving as a welfare organization for its own members. Thus it was to the family's

Source: *Harvard Educational Review*, special issue (Winter 1968), 38 (1), 7–22.

interest to see that its members became productive. Conversely, a family took relatively small interest in whether someone in *another* family became productive or not—merely because the mobility of productive labor between family economic units was relatively low. If the son of a neighbor was allowed to become a ne'er-do-well, it had little real effect on families other than his own.

The second important element is that the family, as a unit of economic production, provided an appropriate context in which the child could learn the things he needed to know. The craftsman's shop or the farmer's fields were appropriate training grounds for sons, and the household was an appropriate training ground for daughters.

In this kind of society, the concept of equality of educational opportunity had no relevance at all. The child and adult were embedded within the extended family, and the child's education or training was merely whatever seemed necessary to maintain the family's productivity. The fixed stations in life which most families occupied precluded any idea of 'opportunity' and, even less, equality of opportunity.

With the industrial revolution, changes occurred in both the family's function as a self-perpetuating economic unit and as a training ground. As economic organizations developed outside the household, children began to be occupationally mobile outside their families. As families lost their economic production activities, they also began to lose their welfare functions, and the poor or ill or incapacitated became more nearly a community responsibility. Thus the training which a child received came to be of interest to all in the community, either as his potential employers or as his potential economic supports if he became dependent. During this stage of development in eighteenth-century England, for instance, communities had laws preventing immigration from another community because of the potential economic burden of immigrants.

Further, as men came to employ their own labor outside the family in the new factories, their families became less useful as economic training grounds for their children. These changes paved the way for public education. Families needed a context within which their children could learn some general skills which would be useful for gaining work outside the family; and men of influence in the community began to be interested in the potential productivity of other men's children.

It was in the early nineteenth century that public education began to appear in Europe and America. Before that time, private education had grown with the expansion of the mercantile class. This class had both the need and resources to have its children educated outside the home, either for professional occupations or for occupations in the developing world of commerce. But the idea of general educational opportunity for all children arose only in the nineteenth century.

The emergence of public, tax-supported education was not solely a function of the stage of industrial development. It was also a function of the class structure in the society. In the United States, without a strong traditional class structure, universal education in publicly-supported free schools became widespread in the early nineteenth century; in England, the 'voluntary schools', run and organized by churches with some instances of state support, were not supplemented by a state-supported system until the Education Act of 1870. Even more, the character of educational opportunity reflected the class structure. In the United States, the public schools quickly became the common school, attended by representatives of all classes; these schools provided a common educational experience for most American children—excluding only those upper-class children in private schools, those poor who went to no schools, and Indians and Southern Negroes who were without schools. In England, however, the class system directly manifested itself through the schools. The state-supported, or 'board schools' as they were called, became the schools of the laboring lower classes with a sharply different curriculum from those voluntary schools which served the middle and upper classes. The division was so sharp that two government departments, the Education Department and the Science and Art Department, administered external examinations, the first for the products of the board schools, and the second for the products of the voluntary schools as they progressed into secondary education. It was only the latter curricula and examinations that provided admission to higher education.

What is most striking is the duration of influence of such a dual structure. Even today in England, a century later (and in different forms in most European countries), there exists a dual structure of public secondary education with only one of the branches providing the curriculum for college admission. In England, this branch includes the remaining voluntary schools which, though retaining their individual identities, have become part of the state-supported system.

This comparison of England and the United States shows clearly the impact of the class structure in society upon the concept of educational opportunity in that society. In nineteenth-century England, the idea of *equality* of educational opportunity was hardly considered; the system was designed to provide *differentiated* educational opportunity appropriate to one's station in life. In the United States as well, the absence of educational opportunity for Negroes in the South arose from the caste and feudal structure of the largely rural society. The idea of differentiated educational opportunity, implicit in the Education Act of 1870 in England, seems to derive from dual needs: the needs arising from industrialization for a basic education for the labor force, and the interests of parents in having one's own child receive a good education. The middle classes could meet both these needs by providing a free system for the children of laboring classes, and a tuition system (which soon came to be supplemented by state grants) for their own. The long survival of this differentiated system depended not only on the historical fact that the voluntary schools existed before a public system came into existence but on the fact that it allows both of these needs to be met: the community's collective need for a trained labor force, and the middle-class individual's interest in a better education for his own child. It served a third need as well: that of maintaining the existing social order—a system of stratification that was a step removed from a feudal system of fixed estates, but designed to prevent a wholesale challenge by the children of the working class to the positions held for children of the middle classes.

The similarity of this system to that which existed in the South to provide differential opportunity to Negroes and whites is striking, just as is the similarity of class structures in the second half of nineteenth-century England to the white–Negro caste structure of the southern United States in the first half of the twentieth century.

In the United States, nearly from the beginning, the concept of educational opportunity had a special meaning which focused on equality. This meaning included the following elements:

(1) Providing a *free* education up to a given level which constituted the principal entry point to the labor force.

(2) Providing a *common curriculum* for all children, regardless of background.

(3) Partly by design and partly because of low population density, providing that children from diverse backgrounds attend the *same school*.

(4) Providing equality within a given *locality*, since local taxes provided the source of support for schools.

This conception of equality of opportunity is still

held by many persons; but there are some assumptions in it which are not obvious. First, it implicitly assumes that the existence of free schools eliminates economic sources of inequality of opportunity. Free schools, however, do not mean that the costs of a child's education become reduced to zero for families at all economic levels. When free education was introduced, many families could not afford to allow the child to attend school beyond an early age. His labor was necessary to the family—whether in rural or urban areas. Even after the passage of child labor laws, this remained true on the farm. These economic sources of inequality of opportunity have become small indeed (up through secondary education); but at one time they were a major source of inequality. In some countries they remain so; and certainly for higher education they remain so.

Apart from the economic needs of the family, problems inherent in the social structure raised even more fundamental questions about equality of educational opportunity. Continued school attendance prevented a boy from being trained in his father's trade. Thus, in taking advantage of 'equal educational opportunity', the son of a craftsman or small tradesman would lose the opportunity to enter those occupations he would most likely fill. The family inheritance of occupation at all social levels was still strong enough, and the age of entry into the labor force was still early enough, that secondary education interfered with opportunity for working-class children; while it opened up opportunities at higher social levels, it closed them at lower ones.

Since residue of this social structure remains in present American society, the dilemma cannot be totally ignored. The idea of a common educational experience implies that this experience has only the effect of widening the range of opportunity, never the effect of excluding opportunities. But clearly this is never precisely true so long as this experience prevents a child from pursuing certain occupational paths. This question still arises with the differentiated secondary curriculum: an academic program in high school has the effect not only of keeping open the opportunities which arise through continued education, but also of closing off opportunities which a vocational program keeps open.

A second assumption implied by this concept of equality of opportunity is that opportunity lies in *exposure* to a given curriculum. The amount of opportunity is then measured in terms of the level of curriculum to which the child is exposed. The higher the curriculum made available to a given set of children, the greater their opportunity.

The most interesting point about this assumption is the relatively passive role of the school and community, relative to the child's role. The school's obligation is to 'provide an opportunity' by being available, within easy geographic access of the child, free of cost (beyond the value of the child's time), and with a curriculum that would not exclude him from higher education. The obligation to 'use the opportunity' is on the child or the family, so that his role is defined as the active one: the responsibility for achievement rests with him. Despite the fact that the school's role was the relatively passive one and the child's or family's role the active one, the use of this social service soon came to be no longer a choice of the parent or child, but that of the state. Since compulsory attendance laws appeared in the nineteenth century, the age of required attendance has been periodically moved upward.

This concept of equality of educational opportunity is one that has been implicit in most educational practice throughout most of the period of public education in the nineteenth and twentieth centuries. However, there have been several challenges to it; serious questions have been raised by new conditions in public education. The first of these in the United States was a challenge to assumption two, the common curriculum. This challenge first occurred in the early years of the twentieth century with the expansion of secondary education. Until the report of the committee of the National Education Association, issued in 1918, the standard curriculum in secondary schools was primarily a classical one appropriate for college entrance. The greater influx of noncollege-bound adolescents into the high school made it necessary that this curriculum be changed into one more appropriate to the new majority. This is not to say that the curriculum changed immediately in the schools, nor that all schools changed equally, but rather that the seven 'cardinal principles' of the NEA report became a powerful influence in the movement towards a less academically rigid curriculum. The introduction of the new nonclassical curriculum was seldom if ever couched in terms of a conflict between those for whom high school was college preparation, and those for whom it was terminal education; nevertheless, that was the case. 'The inequality' was seen as the use of a curriculum that served a minority and was not designed to fit the needs of the majority; and the shift of curriculum was intended to fit the curriculum to the needs of the new majority in the schools.

In many schools, this shift took the form of *diversifying* the curriculum, rather than supplanting one by another; the college-preparatory curriculum remained though watered down. Thus the kind of equality of opportunity that emerged from the newly-designed secondary school curriculum was radically different from the elementary-school concept that had emerged earlier. The idea inherent in the new secondary school curriculum appears to have been to take as given the diverse occupational paths into which adolescents will go after secondary school, and to say (implicitly): there is greater equality of educational opportunity for a boy who is not going to attend college if he has a specially-designed curriculum than if he must take a curriculum designed for college entrance.

There is only one difficulty with this definition: it takes as *given* what should be problematic—that a given boy is going into a given post-secondary occupational or educational path. It is one thing to take as given that approximately 70 per cent of an entering high school freshman class will not attend college; but to assign a *particular child* to a curriculum designed for that 70 per cent closes off for that child the opportunity to attend college. Yet to assign all children to a curriculum designed for the 30 per cent who will attend college creates inequality for those who, at the end of high school, fall among the 70 per cent who do not attend college. This is a true dilemma, and one which no educational system has fully solved. It is more general than the college/noncollege dichotomy, for there is a wide variety of different paths that adolescents take on the completion of secondary school. In England, for example, a student planning to attend a university must specialize in the arts or the sciences in the later years of secondary school. Similar specialization occurs in the German gymnasium; and this is wholly within the group planning to attend university. Even greater specialization can be found among noncollege curricula, especially in the vocational, technical, and commercial high schools.

The distinguishing characteristic of this concept of equality of educational opportunity is that it accepts as given the child's expected future. While the concept discussed earlier left the child's future wholly open, this concept of differentiated curricula uses the expected future to match child and curriculum. It should be noted that the first and simpler concept is easier to apply in elementary schools where fundamental tools of reading and arithmetic are being learned by all children; it is only in secondary school that the problem of diverse futures arises. It should also be noted that the dilemma is directly due to the social structure itself: if there were a virtual absence of social mobility with everyone occupying a fixed estate in life, then such curricula that take the future as given would provide equality of opportunity relative to that structure. It is only because of the high degree of occupational mobility between generations—that is, the greater degree of equality of *occupational* opportunity —that the dilemma arises.

The first stage in the evolution of the concept of equality of educational opportunity was the notion that all children must be exposed to the same curriculum in the same school. A second stage in the evolution of the concept assumed that different children would have different occupational futures and that equality of opportunity required providing different curricula for each type of student. The third and fourth stages in this evolution came as a result of challenges to the basic idea of equality of educational opportunity from opposing directions. The third stage can be seen at least as far back as 1896 when the Supreme Court upheld the southern states' notion of 'separate but equal' facilities. This stage ended in 1954 when the Supreme Court ruled that legal separation by race inherently constitutes inequality of opportunity. By adopting the 'separate but equal' doctrine, the southern states

rejected assumption three of the original concept, the assumption that equality depended on the opportunity to attend the same school. This rejection was, however, consistent with the overall logic of the original concept, since attendance at the same school was an inherent part of that logic. The underlying idea was that opportunity resided in exposure to a curriculum; the community's responsibility was to provide that exposure, the child's to take advantage of it.

It was the pervasiveness of this underlying idea which created the difficulty for the Supreme Court. For it was evident that even when identical facilities and identical teacher salaries existed for racially separate schools, 'equality of educational opportunity' in some sense did not exist. This had also long been evident to Englishmen as well, in a different context, for with the simultaneous existence of the 'common school' and the 'voluntary school', no one was under the illusion that full equality of education opportunity existed. But the source of this inequality remained an unarticulated feeling. In the decision of the Supreme Court, this unarticulated feeling began to take more precise form. The essence of it was that the *effects* of such separate schools were, or were likely to be, different. Thus a concept of equality of opportunity which focused on *effects* of schooling began to take form. The actual decision of the Court was in fact a confusion of two unrelated premises: this new concept, which looked at results of schooling, and the legal premise that the use of race as a basis for school assignment violates fundamental freedoms. But what is important for the evolution of the concept of equality of opportunity is that a new and different assumption was introduced, the assumption that equality of opportunity depends in some fashion upon effects of schooling. I believe the decision would have been more soundly based had it not depended on the effects of schooling, but only on the violation of freedom; but by introducing the question of effects of schooling, the Court brought into the open the implicit goals of equality of educational opportunity—that is, goals having to do with the *results* of school—to which the original concept was somewhat awkwardly directed.

That these goals were in fact behind the concept can be verified by a simple mental experiment. Suppose the early schools had operated for only one hour a week and had been attended by children of all social classes. This would have met the explicit assumptions of the early concept of equality of opportunity since the school is free, with a common curriculum, and attended by all children in the locality. But it obviously would not have been accepted, even at that time, as providing equality of opportunity, because its effects would have been so minimal. The additional educational resources provided by middle- and upper-class families, whether in the home, by tutoring, or in private supplementary schools, would have created severe inequalities in results.

Thus the dependence of the concept upon results or effects of schooling, which had remained hidden until

1954, came partially into the open with the Supreme Court decision. Yet this was not the end, for it created more problems than it solved. It might allow one to assess gross inequalities, such as that created by dual school systems in the South, or by a system like that in the mental experiment I just described. But it allows nothing beyond that. Even more confounding, because the decision did not use effects of schooling as a criterion of inequality but only as justification for a criterion of racial integration, integration itself emerged as the basis for still a new concept of equality of educational opportunity. Thus the idea of effects of schooling as an element in the concept was introduced but immediately overshadowed by another, the criterion of racial integration.

The next stage in the evolution of this concept was, in my judgment, the Office of Education Survey of Equality of Educational Opportunity. This survey was carried out under a mandate in the Civil Rights Act of 1964 to the Commissioner of Education to assess the 'lack of equality of educational opportunity' among racial and other groups in the United States. The evolution of this concept, and the conceptual disarray which this evolution had created, made the very definition of the task exceedingly difficult. The original concept could be examined by determining the degree to which all children in a locality had access to the same schools and the same curriculum, free of charge. The existence of diverse secondary curricula appropriate to different futures could be assessed relatively easily. But the very assignment of a child to a specific curriculum implies acceptance of the concept of equality which takes futures as given. And the introduction of the new interpretations, equality as measured by results of schooling and equality defined by racial integration, confounded the issue even further.

As a consequence, in planning the survey it was obvious that no single concept of equality of educational opportunity existed and that the survey must give information relevant to a variety of concepts. The basis on which this was done can be seen by reproducing a portion of an internal memorandum that determined the design of the survey:

The point of second importance in design [second to the point of discovering the intent of Congress, which was taken to be that the survey was not for the purpose of locating willful discrimination, but to determine educational inequality without regard to intention of those in authority] follows from the first and concerns the definition of inequality. One type of inequality may be defined in terms of differences of the community's input to the school, such as per-pupil expenditure, school plants, libraries, quality of teachers, and other similar quantities.

A second type of inequality may be defined in terms of the racial composition of the school, following the Supreme Court's decision that segregated schooling is inherently unequal. By the former definition, the question of inequality through segregation is excluded, while by the latter, there is inequality of education within a school system so long as the schools within the system have different racial composition.

A third type of inequality would include various intangible characteristics of the school as well as the factors directly traceable to the community inputs to the school. These intangibles are such things as teacher morale, teachers' expectations of students, level of interest of the student body in learning, or others. Any of these factors may affect the impact of the school upon a given student within it. Yet such a definition gives no suggestion of where to stop, or just how relevant these factors might be for school quality.

Consequently, a fourth type of inequality may be defined in terms of consequences of the school for individuals with equal backgrounds and abilities. In this definition, equality of educational opportunity is equality of results, given the same individual input. With such a definition, inequality might come about from differences in the school inputs and/or racial composition and/or from more intangible things as described above.

Such a definition obviously would require that two steps be taken in the determination of inequality. First, it is necessary to determine the effect of these various factors upon educational results (conceiving of results quite broadly, including not only achievement but attitudes towards learning, self-image, and perhaps other variables). This provides various measures of the school's quality in terms of its effect upon its students. Second, it is necessary to take these measures of quality, once determined, and determine the differential exposure of Negroes (or other groups) and whites to schools of high and low quality.

A fifth type of inequality may be defined in terms of consequences of the school for individuals of unequal backgrounds and abilities. In this definition, equality of educational opportunity is equality of results given *different* individual inputs. The most striking examples of inequality here would be children from households in which a language other than English, such as Spanish or Navaho, is spoken. Other examples would be low-achieving children from homes in which there is a poverty of verbal expression or an absence of experiences which lead to conceptual facility.

Such a definition taken in the extreme would imply that educational equality is reached only when the results of schooling (achievement and attitudes) are the same for racial and religious minorities as for the dominant group.

The basis for the design of the survey is indicated by another segment of this memorandum:

Thus, the study will focus its principal effort on the fourth definition, but will also provide information relevant to all five possible definitions. This insures the pluralism which is obviously necessary with respect to a definition of inequality. The major justification for this focus is that the results of this approach can best be translated into policy which will improve education's effects. The results of the first two approaches (tangible inputs to the school, and segregation) can certainly be translated into policy, but there is no good evidence that these policies will improve education's effects; and while policies to implement the fifth would certainly improve education's effects, it seems hardly possible that the study could provide information that would direct such policies.

Altogether, it has become evident that it is not our role to define what constitutes equality for policy-making purposes. Such a definition will be an outcome of the interplay of a variety of interests, and will certainly differ from time to time as these interests differ. It should be our role to cast light on the state of inequality defined in the variety of ways which appear reasonable at this time.

The survey, then, was conceived as a pluralistic instrument, given the variety of concepts of equality of opportunity in education. Yet I suggest that despite the avowed intention of not adjudicating between these different ideas, the survey has brought a new stage in the evolution of the concept. For the definitions of equality which the survey was designed to serve split sharply into two groups. The first three definitions concerned input resources: first, those brought to the school by the actions of the school administration (facilities, curriculum, teachers); second, those brought to the school by the other students, in the educational backgrounds which their presence contributed to the school; and third, the intangible characteristics such as 'morale' that result from the interaction of all these factors. The fourth and fifth definitions were concerned with the effects of schooling. Thus the five definitions were divided into three concerned with inputs to school and two concerned with effects of schooling. When the Report emerged, it did not give five different measures of equality, one for each of these definitions; but it did focus sharply on this dichotomy, giving in chapter 2 information on inequalities of input relevant to definitions one and two, and in chapter 3 information on inequalities of results relevant to definitions four and five, and also in chapter 3 information on the relation of input to results again relevant to definitions four and five.

Although not central to our discussion here, it is interesting to note that this examination of the relation of school inputs to effects on achievement showed that those input characteristics of schools that are most alike for Negroes and whites have least effect on their achievement. The magnitudes of differences between schools attended by Negroes and those attended by whites were as follows: least, facilities and curriculum; next, teacher quality; and greatest, educational backgrounds of fellow students. The order of importance of these inputs on the achievement of Negro students is precisely the same: facilities and curriculum least, teacher quality next, and backgrounds of fellow students, most.

By making the dichotomy between inputs and results explicit, and by focusing attention not only on inputs but on results, the Report brought into the open what had been underlying all the concepts of equality of educational opportunity but had remained largely hidden: that the concept implied *effective* equality of opportunity, that is, equality in those elements that are effective for learning. The reason this had remained half-hidden, obscured by definitions that involve inputs, is, I suspect, because educational research has been until recently unprepared to demonstrate what elements are effective. The controversy that has surrounded the Report indicates that measurement of effects is still subject to sharp disagreement; but the crucial point is that *effects* of inputs have come to constitute the basis for assessment of school quality (and thus equality of opportunity) in place of using certain inputs by definition as measures of quality (e.g. small classes are better than large, higher-paid teachers are better than lower-paid ones, by definition).

It would be fortunate indeed if the matter could be left to rest there—if merely by using effects of school rather than inputs as the basis for the concept, the problem were solved. But that is not the case at all. The conflict between definitions four and five given above shows this. The conflict can be illustrated by resorting again to the mental experiment discussed earlier—providing a standard education of one hour per week, under identical conditions, for all children. By definition four, controlling all background difference of the children, results for Negroes and whites would be equal, and thus by this definition equality of opportunity would exist. But because such minimal schooling would have minimal effect, those children from educationally strong families would enjoy educational opportunity far surpassing that of others. And because such educationally strong backgrounds are found more often among whites than among Negroes, there would be very large overall Negro-white achievement differences—and thus inequality of opportunity by definition five.

It is clear from this hypothetical experiment that the problem of what constitutes equality of opportunity is not solved. The problem will become even clearer by showing graphs with some of the results of the Office of Education Survey. The highest line in Figure 1 shows the achievement in verbal skills by whites in the urban Northeast at grades 1, 3, 6, 9 and 12. The second line shows the achievement at each of these grades by whites in the rural Southeast. The third shows the achievement of Negroes in the urban Northeast. The fourth shows the achievement of Negroes in the rural Southeast.

When compared to the whites in the urban Northeast, each of the other three groups shows a different pattern. The comparison with whites in the rural South shows the two groups beginning near the same point in the first grade, and diverging over the years of school. The comparison with Negroes in the urban Northeast shows the two groups beginning farther apart at the first grade and remaining about the same distance apart. The comparison with Negroes in the rural South shows the two groups beginning far apart and moving much farther apart over the years of school.

Which of these, if any, shows equality of educational opportunity between regional and racial groups? Which shows greatest inequality of opportunity? I think the second question is easier to answer than the first. The last comparison showing both initial difference and the greatest increase in difference

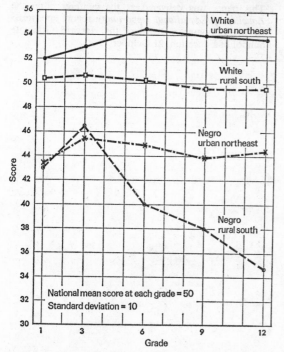

Figure 1. Patterns of achievement in verbal skills at various grade levels by race and region.

over grades 1 through 12 appears to be the best candidate for the greatest inequality. The first comparison, with whites in the rural South, also seems to show inequality of opportunity, because of the increasing difference over the twelve years. But what about the second comparison, with an approximately constant difference between Negroes and whites in the urban Northeast? Is this equality of opportunity? I suggest not. It means, in effect, only that the period of school has left the average Negro at about the same level of

achievement relative to whites as he began—in this case, achieving higher than about 15 per cent of the whites, lower than about 85 per cent of the whites. It may well be that in the absence of school those lines of achievement would have diverged due to differences in home environments; or perhaps they would have remained an equal distance apart, as they are in this graph (though at lower levels of achievement for both groups, in the absence of school). If it were the former, we could say that school, by keeping the lines parallel, has been a force towards the equalization of opportunity. But in the absence of such knowledge, we cannot say even that.

What would full equality of educational opportunity look like in such graphs? One might persuasively argue that it should show a convergence, so that even though two population groups begin school with different levels of skills on the average, the average of the group that begins lower moves up to coincide with that of the group that begins higher. Parenthetically, I should note that this does *not* imply that all students' achievement comes to be identical, but only that the *averages* for two population groups that begin at different levels come to be identical. The diversity of individual scores could be as great as, or greater than, the diversity at grade 1.

Yet there are serious questions about this definition of equality of opportunity. It implies that over the period of school there are no other influences, such as the family environment, which affect achievement over the twelve years of school, even though these influences may differ greatly for the two population groups. Concretely, it implies that white family environments, predominantly middle class, and Negro family environments, predominantly lower class, will produce no effects on achievement that would keep these averages apart. Such an assumption seems highly unrealistic, especially in view of the general importance of family background for achievement.

However, if such possibilities are acknowledged, then how far can they go before there is inequality of educational opportunity? Constant difference over school? Increasing differences? The unanswerability of such questions begins to give a sense of a new stage in the evolution of the concept of equality of educational opportunity. These questions concern the *relative intensity* of two sets of influences: those which are alike for the two groups, principally in school, and those which are different, principally in the home or neighborhood. If the school's influences are not only alike for the two groups, but very strong relative to the divergent influences, then the two groups will move together. If school influences are very weak, then the two groups will move apart. Or more generally, the relative intensity of the convergent school influences and the divergent out-of-school influences determines the effectiveness of the educational system in providing equality of educational opportunity. In this perspective complete equality of opportunity can be reached only if all the divergent out-of-school influences vanish, a condition that would arise only in the advent of boarding schools; given the existing divergent influences, equality of opportunity can only be approached and never fully reached. The concept becomes one of degree of proximity to equality of opportunity. This proximity is determined, then, not merely by the *equality* of education inputs, but by the *intensity* of the school's influences relative to the external divergent influences. That is, equality of output is not so much determined by equality of the resource inputs, but by the power of these resources in bringing about achievement.

Here, then, is where the concept of equality of educational opportunity presently stands. We have observed an evolution which might have been anticipated a century and a half ago when the first such concepts arose, yet one which is very different from the concept as it first developed. This difference is sharpened if we examine a further implication of the current concept as I have described it. In describing the original concept, I indicated that the role of the community and the educational institution was relatively passive; they were expected to provide a set of free public resources. The responsibility for profitable use of those resources lay with the child and his family. But the evolution of the concept has reversed these roles. The implication of the most recent concept, as I have described it, is that the responsibility to create achievement lies with the educational institution, not the child. The difference in achievement at grade 12 between the average Negro and the average white is, in effect, the degree of inequality of opportunity, and the reduction of that inequality is a responsibility of the school. This shift in responsibility follows logically from the change in the concept of equality of educational opportunity from school resource inputs to effects of schooling. When that change occurred, as it has in the past few years, the school's responsibility shifted from increasing and distributing equally its 'quality' to increasing the quality of its *students*' achievements. This is a notable shift, and one which should have strong consequences for the practice of education in future years.

Note

1 This paper was delivered at the conference on the *Equality of Educational Opportunity* report sponsored by the Colloquium Board of the Harvard Graduate School of Education, 21 October 1967.

Set books

Title	Author	Date	Publisher
School and Society (Course Reader)	Cosin, B. R., Dale, I. R., Esland, G. M. and Swift, D. F. (eds)	1971	Routledge & Kegan Paul/ The Open University Press
Letter to a Teacher	School of Barbiana	1971	Penguin
Language, the Learner and the School	Barnes, D. *et al.*	1969	Penguin
The Social Construction of Reality	Berger, P. L. and Luckmann, T.	1962	Allen Lane The Penguin Press
Asylums: Essays on the Social Situation of Mental Patients	Goffman, E.	1968	Penguin
Implementing Organizational Innovations	Gross, N.	1971	Harper and Row
The Underachieving School	Holt, J.	1971	Penguin
How Children Fail	Holt, J.	1969	Penguin
Hightown Grammar: The School as a Social System	Lacey, C.	1970	Manchester University Press
The Long Revolution	Williams, R.	1965	Penguin
Knowledge and Control	Young, M. F. D.	1971	Collier-Macmillan